THE BELIEVER'S GUIDE TO BIBLE CHRONOLOGY

Charles Ozanne

authorHOUSE®

AuthorHouse™ UK Ltd.
500 Avebury Boulevard
Central Milton Keynes, MK9 2BE
www.authorhouse.co.uk
Phone: 08001974150

First published by AuthorHouse 1/07/2011

ISBN: 978-1-4389-4323-7

Printed in the United States of America
Bloomington, Indiana

This book is printed on acid-free paper.

TABLE OF CONTENTS

The Believer's Guide to Bible Chronology

Introduction

Why another book on Bible Chronology? Are there not enough already - all claiming to have reached finality! A perfect scheme is indeed the ultimate aim but as long as that goal has not been achieved, there is room for another attempt. Chronology may seem a tedious subject to the uninitiated. But God is not of that opinion at all! He has set in the heavens a gigantic clock "for signs, and for seasons, and for days and years" (Gen. 1:14). He has also filled the Scriptures with chronological details, which arguably provide a concatenated scheme of dating from the creation of Adam and Eve to the Crucifixion of Christ and beyond.

These time notes are not difficult to understand if taken at their face value. I took up the study of chronology when still young in the faith because I wanted a straightforward, uncomplicated subject, something within my capability at that stage in my life. Half a century on, my estimate has not radically changed. I remain of the opinion that Bible chronology is basically a straightforward, uncomplicated subject. The difficulties for the most part can be resolved by noting carefully what is written and by comparing scripture with scripture. There remains however an unresolved chasm between the dates suggested by the Bible and those confidently asserted on the basis of ancient texts and archaeology.

The importance of Bible chronology consists in the fact that our faith is rooted in history. From Abraham onwards Israel's history rubs shoulders with those of other nations, Egypt and Assyria in particular. Jesus Christ Himself is a real person whose life and death are historical events. Dates are readily available for almost every important person and event on the world stage, yet the dates of the Lord Jesus Christ are still in dispute, as also those of many of the pivotal people and events of the Old Testament including Abraham, the Exodus, the Conquest of Canaan, and the Kings of Israel and Judah. It is the aim of every Bible chronology to put to rights this unfortunate state of affairs. There is however still no consensus, no agreement in spite of the many books on the subject. Hopefully the present work will make a contribution and will prove convincing to some who share my convictions. I cannot hope for more.

In particular the period of the Kings has attracted the attention of scholars. Ever since the discovery of the Assyrian Eponym Canon in the 1860s and '70s there has been a problem in reconciling the dates revealed in the Bible with those demanded by the Eponym Canon. The course increasingly followed by recent researchers, evangelical as much as liberal, has been to accept the Assyrian dates as correct and then to make adjustments to the Bible by assuming co-regencies between various kings. The harmonisation which has received the most acclaim is that of Edwin R. Thiele which is still widely accepted more than fifty years after its initial publication in 1951. Thiele came up with an explanation of the data in the Books of Kings which agrees perfectly with the dates assumed for the Assyrian Eponym Canon. Since that was exactly what scholars wanted to hear, they naturally welcomed it with open arms and have done so ever since.

An increasing number however in recent years have remarked on its arbitrary and subjective nature. The details of Thiele's scheme have proved less important than the underlying purpose, that of harmonising the Bible with the dates already accepted for the period in question.

There have always been a few who have regarded this consensus with profound suspicion. Many have worked on the principle that both systems should be given equal value and status and have worked manfully to bring them together without doing violence to either side. Of this sort was George Smith who first published the Assyrian Eponym Canon in 1875, and more recently Oswald T. Allis in 1972. This approach, however, has proved inadequate to explain the widening gap between the Eponym Canon and the Bible. A more fruitful approach includes the recognition that the Eponym Canon is *incomplete*, concealing some undisclosed chasms in its earlier phases.

In this study the Bible is treated as the primary and normative source and the Assyrian evidence as secondary. My method has been to work out my chronology solely from the Bible, and then to look for ways to harmonise the resultant scheme with those of other nations, Assyria in particular. I have made a careful study of the Assyrian evidence, and would like to think that I have succeeded to some extent in explaining how the discrepancies arose. I admit however that a complete explanation has yet to be formulated.

Bible chronology continues to fascinate the Christian public as shown by the many works on the subject in recent years. The most biblical of all is that by Floyd Nolan Jones (New Leaf Press Edition, 2005). Here we have a magnificent volume by someone who is not ashamed to declare his total belief in the Bible as preserved in the King's James Version. While agreeing with the spirit of this work and benefiting from some of his insights, I have to admit that I am not really in agreement with him at any stage of the inquiry. Dr Jones has written a fine book, but all too often he follows a wrong course and arrives at the wrong conclusions. This only goes to show that there is still room for another attempt at solving the riddle of Bible chronology.

It may seem strange to some that those who accept the Bible as their final authority cannot agree among themselves on a subject like chronology. But this should not really be considered so very strange. A true appraisal of any subject involves a combination of knowledge and under-standing – a knowledge of the relevant facts both biblical and nonbiblical, and an understanding of their significance. Those with the most thorough knowledge of the facts often lack understanding, whereas those with the potential for understanding are usually deficient in knowledge. It is the responsibility of the reader to use the understanding that God has given him to choose between the various schemes on offer or, better still, devise a more accurate scheme for himself on the basis of his accumulated knowledge. There is always room for improvement since no-one yet knows as he ought to know (1 Cor. 8:2). No one scheme is totally correct and most of them are seriously wrong!

Dr Jones berates those who do not share his "Biblicist" faith. His definition of a Biblicist is "that the person so designated has chosen to believe God's many promises that, despite all textual criticism objections to the contrary, He would forever preserve His infallible Word. Moreover, the meaning intended to be conveyed by this Word carries with it the concept that such a person trusts that the Authorized Bible (Hebrew Masoretic and Greek Textus Receptus) in his hand is a fulfilment of these promises" (pp.3-4).

But what if the manuscripts disagree, as they frequently do? In such cases some sort of textual choice cannot be avoided. To choose one group of manuscripts (the majority) and pronounce them infallible is no less a critical decision than to choose a smaller group of manuscripts (the oldest) and assume that they are nearer the Divine Original. Personally I find the latter course a lot more credible. Even the Masoretic Text of the Old Testament exhibits many solecisms and discrepancies which are more reverently explained as copyist errors than eccentricities of the Holy Spirit.

I believe with all my heart that the Word of the Lord is firmly fixed in the heavens (Psalm 119:89), and that one day soon it will be restored to us in all its pristine perfection. I look forward to that day while rejoicing in the fact that the Bible in our hands is as near correct as makes no practical or doctrinal difference. Few indeed are the errors, most of them trivial and none that seriously impinges on any important matter.

In the present work the whole panorama of Bible chronology is subjected to close examination from the creation of Adam and Eve to the end of Acts. My aim has been to open up that system of dating which commends itself as most probably correct from a biblical perspective. To what extent I have succeeded I leave others to decide.

Finally I would like to express my thanks to my wife Rozelle for her patience and encouragement; to the Librarian and staff of Tyndale House, Cambridge, for supplying me with numerous articles; and to Roger Barnett, Brian Sherring, and Michael Penny for their useful suggestions and practical help.

Charles Ozanne
Guernsey

O LORD, my heart is not lifted up;
My eyes are not raised too high;
I do not occupy myself with things
     too great for me and too marvellous for me.
But I have calmed and quietened my soul,
     like a weaned child with its mother;
     like a weaned child is my soul within me.

O Israel, hope in the Lord
     from this time forth and for evermore.   Psalm 131

Chapter One

From Adam to the Exodus

The chronology of the Bible is a source of endless wonder and fascination to myself and many others. The Bible is so full of dates and numbers it would seem at first sight an easy task to add them up and to arrive without undue labour at an exact chronology of dated events from the first Adam to the Second. There is indeed a broad agreement among believing students, but an exact chronology has proved exceedingly elusive. It is especially in the period of the Kings that the majority have become unstuck, and their failure at this point has had a knock-on effect right back to Adam. I am however firmly of the opinion that a close attention to detail, and to the Divine revelation as a whole, must inevitably lead to the truth. It is with that conviction and in that spirit that I embark on the present work.

Genesis 1:1

The Divine fiat which brought the cosmos into existence is mentioned in the first verse of Genesis: "In the beginning God created the heavens and the earth." This statement reminds us of John 1:1-2, "In the beginning was the Word, and the Word was with God, and the Word was God. He was in the beginning with God." There is however a profound difference between these two beginnings. In the case of the Word it is a beginning without beginning since there was no time when the Word was not with God and when the Word was not God. There was no actual beginning to that unique union and unity. But in the case of the world there certainly was a beginning. There must have been a point in time when the hand of the Lord laid the foundations of the earth and His right hand spread out the heavens (Isaiah 48:13), whether or not we can know when that beginning actually was. This is where Genesis 1, verses 1 and 2 come in.

Genesis 1:1-2

The precise grammatical relationship between the first two verses has provoked a considerable literature. In fact whole books have been written on these verses alone, how they are related and what exactly they imply. My treatment of Bible chronology is *Anno Hominis* rather than *Anno Mundi*: it traces the years of mankind, not necessarily those of the world. The detailed exposition of Genesis 1 is not therefore my immediate concern. I will therefore restrict myself to a brief word.

Traditionally the first verse of Genesis has been regarded as the record of a cosmic creation which preceded the six days. It laid the foundation on which, in the days or periods which followed, was built the magnificent superstructure with which we are all familiar. This however has been questioned by a number of recent commentators. By them the first verse is regarded as a title or summary of the opening chapter as a whole.

Opinion is divided, but to me it makes more sense if the first verse is a summary of the creative work and definitive product, which is sketched so deftly in the rest of the chapter. This may be inferred from the verb "create" itself, which implies something beautiful and finished, unlike the dark and watery waste described in the second verse. It may be inferred also from the words "heaven and earth" which for later writers meant the universe as a masterpiece of created order and beauty, as when the psalmist declares, "Blessed is he … who made heaven and earth, the sea, and all that is in them"(Psalm 146:5-6). It is implied further in Genesis 2:4 which contains the heading to the next section: "These are the generations of the heavens and the earth when they were created." It is the generation (or "begettings") of the finished work as described in the previous chapter, not what sprang from the formless waste of Genesis 1:2. Finally, it may be inferred from Psalm 33:6, "By the word of the Lord the heavens were made, and by the breath of his mouth all their host." The word of the Lord ("And God said") occurs eight times in Genesis one, the first of which is in verse 3.

The earth in its condition of waste and void is no part of the subsequent creation. It is simply the groundwork, the raw material, out of and around which the creation developed. It is true of course that the planet itself was created by God and this fact is included in the first verse. This however was just the starting-point, the waste-land awaiting creative development. We of course would like to go behind all this and inquire how long the world had been in this formless state before the Spirit of God hovered over the face of the waters. But the writer does not stoop to satisfy our curiosity. He has a nobler theme to expound: the marvellous work of creation itself described in the rest of the chapter.

In six days

Whether the "days" of Genesis 1 are literal days or simply *literary* days is difficult to decide. On the side of literalness are the plain statements in Exodus 20:11 and 31:17 that "in six days the Lord made heaven and earth …" On the side of literariness there are reasons for thinking the days may be a schematic arrangement for the successive stages of God's creation. There is the fact that the seventh day appears to have no end. It has no "evening and morning" like the previous days, and in Hebrews 4 the prospect of entering God's Sabbath-rest presupposes that God has never ceased to rest and that His Sabbath-rest is still in progress. That being the case, there is the possibility that the days of Genesis 1 represent stages of creative activity rather than literal days of 24 hours, and that Exodus 20:11 and 31:17 draw an analogy rather than a strict correspondence between the days of creation and the days of the week.

If it be asked how the plants and fruit trees (created on the third day) could have survived without the benefit of sunlight (created on the fourth day), it only needs to be pointed out that light was created on the first day. Moreover, the time is coming when the sun and moon will no longer be needed, for the glory of the Lord will provide the necessary light and the Lamb Himself will be the focal point of that light (Rev. 21:23-24). That is how it was in the beginning: the glory of the Lord gave light to the world. The earth in its diurnal passage would have crossed this source of light as it now crosses the sun.

If the days were possibly long periods of time, does that give scope and credence to the theory of evolution? Many would say that it does. But Genesis 1 emphasizes that the plants, trees, sea-creatures, fish, and birds were each and all created "according to its kind". These words occur ten times in Genesis 1. There is potential for considerable variation within the limits of the "kind" (species or genus), but no scope at all for the transformation of one kind into another. If this formula is not used in the case of man, it is only because there is only one kind of man. "After his kind" does not apply to mankind.

At the same time the position of some creationists that the entire universe is extremely young deserves our respect and attention. It is highly significant that competent scientists feel able to take this stance in the face of so much seemingly contrary evidence and the full force of scientific opinion. Henry M. Morris for example, in his commentary on Genesis, states his conviction: "As far as the creation of the universe is concerned, this took place five days earlier than the creation of man" (1976: 45). Such dogmatism on the part of a scientist is remarkable, and Henry Morris does not stand alone. I have before me a book entitled *In six Days*, edited by John F. Ashton (2001), in which no less than fifty scientists express their view that everything had its origin not so very long ago, in six days.

An argument for literal days could be the mutual dependence of different orders of creation, such as plants on insects, flowers on bees. Could flowers have pollinated without the assistance of bees? Without bees a different mechanism must have operated, but of that there is no hint in

Genesis. Arguably the whole ecosystem is so interconnected that no part of it could function in isolation without the support of all the rest. The statement in Romans 5:12 that sin entered the world through one man, and death through sin, would seem to preclude the presence of death in the world prior to the fall of Adam, unless only the death of mankind is meant. Of the first day it is said, "God called the light 'Day', and the darkness he called 'Night'. And there was evening and there was morning, the first day." Statements of this nature have led many to conclude that the days of Genesis 1 point to literal days consisting of evening and morning, darkness and light. Personally I incline to this point of view.

When did the day begin?

It is disputed by scholars whether the day in the Bible began in the evening or the morning. Many would say it began in the evening, but here in Genesis 1 there can be little doubt that it begins in the morning with the creation of light. Genesis 1:3 goes on to mention the day before the night ("God called the light Day and the darkness he called Night"), and concludes with the statement, "And there was evening (terminating the daylight) and there was morning (terminating the darkness), day one." The word translated "and there was" is the same as "came to pass" or "happened". First the evening happened as the day came to an end, and then the morning happened as the night came to an end. It is the same in verses 14 and 16: the day precedes the night and the creation of the sun precedes the creation of the moon and stars.

This appears to be the regular practice throughout the Bible, but with regard to festivals and special occasions it is stipulated that they should commence the previous evening. In Exodus 12:18 for example it says, "In the first month, on the fourteenth day of the month at evening, you shall eat unleavened bread." The feast was to begin in the evening preceding the fifteenth, but the day is still called the fourteenth day of the month. It is the same with regard to the Day of Atonement: "On the ninth day of the month beginning at evening, from evening to evening shall you keep your Sabbath" (Lev. 23:32). Here also the evening before the tenth, when the Sabbath began, is still called the ninth. There may be exceptions but this appears to be the general rule.

The eleven *Toledoth*

The body of the book of Genesis, Genesis 2:4 to the end, consists of eleven sections each beginning with the words (*we*)*'elleh toledoth*,"(Now) these are the generations of", or (in the case of Genesis 5:1) *zeh sepher toledoth*, "This is the book of the generations of..." It is depressing to find responsible writers still maintaining that these captions are subscripts to sections rather than headings. One would have thought that the examples outside of Genesis (supposing that Genesis is not itself decisive) would have been sufficient to settle this matter once and for all. In Numbers 3:1, "Now these are the generations of Aaron and Moses", and Ruth 4:18, "Now these are the generations of Perez", these words are clearly the headings to the following sections. This is also the case in Matthew 1:1 where the Gospel begins, "(The) book of the generation of Jesus Christ, son of David, son of Abraham."

The word *toledoth*, generations, is from the root *yalad*, to beget. It denotes that which is generated, begotten or produced by the person or object whose generations are described. Thus the generations of Perez are his descendants down to David, and the section headed "The generations of Terah" is not about Terah himself, but about his son Abraham whose life is described in some detail. The following gives the interrelation of the eleven *toledoth* sections of Genesis, Genesis 2:4 to 50:26:-

A. 2:4 "The heavens and the earth" - The rejected son Cain and his descendants
  B. 5:1 "Adam" - The two seeds, Noah and the Nephilim
    C. 6:9 "Noah" - Judgment on mankind, the earth left to Noah
      D. 10:1 "The sons of Noah" - The nations descended from Noah's sons
              "according to their families"
        E. 11:10 "Shem" - Shem's descendants in Mesopotamia
          F. 11:27 "Terah" - The story of Abraham
A. 25:12 "Ishmael" - The rejected son and his descendants
  B. 25:19 "Isaac" - The two seeds, Jacob and Esau
    C. 36:1 "Esau" - Esau's departure, the land left to Jacob
      D. 36:9 "Esau father of Edom" - The chiefs descended from Esau
              "according to their families"
        E. 37:2 "Jacob" - Jacob's descendants in Egypt.

Adam's and Abraham's descendants follow the same general pattern as shown in the two series above. In each case the rejected son comes first and is subsequently banished. We then find two more seeds, one true and one false. In the third sections the rejected seed is dealt with, leaving the true seed in control. The fourth sections explain the subsequent history of the rejected seed, before reverting, in the fifth sections, to the later history of the true seed. Standing on its own in the middle, on centre stage so to speak, is the all-important history of Abraham, the father of the faithful.

In the following tables *Anno Hominis* years are given in terms of completed years after the creation of man. The figures given in the Samaritan Text and the Greek Septuagint are here compared with those of the Hebrew Masoretic Text. The Samaritan Pentateuch was that used by the mixed population of Samaria after the Jews returned from exile under Ezra and Nehemiah. In its present form it dates at least from the second century BC, but is based on much older texts. The Greek Septuagint (LXX for short) was translated for the most part in the third and second centuries BC. The Pentateuch was made in Alexandria in the first half of the third century. The original translation is designated Old Greek (OG), but there are a number of revisions and recensions. One of these is the Lucianic recension made by Lucian the martyr towards the end of the third century AD.

Remarks

The three tables below represent three different chronological traditions for the patriarchal age, as preserved respectively in the Hebrew Masoretic Text (the MT), the Greek Septuagint (the LXX), and the Samaritan Text of Genesis 5 and 11. It is widely reconised that the Masoretic Text, the one translated in our Bibles, is alone worthy to be regarded as the original and authoritative text, and that the Septuagint and Samaritan versions betray their secondary character by their greater regularity and schematizing tendencies.

1) The Samaritan figures are far more uniform than the Hebrew original. Uniformity in the antediluvian period is achieved by radically reducing the ages at begetting of Methuselah and Lamech; and in the postdiluvian period by increasing the ages at begetting of all the patriarchs except for Shem and Terah whose ages were considered high enough already. Likewise the ages at death display in general a steady decrease from Adam at 930 to Terah at 145 – with the exception of Enoch and Noah. In particular, the ages at death of Jared, Methuselah and Lamech had to be reduced considerably or they would not have died before the Flood. They are each reduced by exactly the required amount: they all die in the very year of the Flood! We cannot but agree with Gerhard Larsson that "an alteration from the almost perfect Samaritan system to the irregular Hebrew system seems quite incredible" (1973: 57). The reverse must be the case: the irregularities of the Hebrew have been smoothed out in the Samaritan Text.

The Samaritan Text

```
0        500      1000     1500     2000     2500     3000
| | | | | | | | | | | | | | | | | | | | | | | | | | | | |
Adam
0-----------------------|930
   Seth
   130--------------------|1042
     Enosh
     235---------------------|1140
       Kenan
       325----------------------|1235
         Mahaleel
         395----------------------|1290
           Jared
           460--------------------|1307
             Enoch
             522------|887
               Methuselah
               587------------------|1307
                 Lamech
                 654----------------|1307
                   Noah
                   707----------------------|1657
                         Shem
                         1207--------|1707
                         Arpachshad
                         1307-------|1745
                           Shelah
                           1442-------|1875
                             Eber
                             1572---|1842
                               Peleg
                               1706-|1945
                                 Reu
                                 1836-|1943
                                   Serug
                                   1968-|2068
                                     Nahor
                                     2098-|2167
                                       Terah
                                       2177-|2252
```

The Septuagint Text

```
0         500        1000       1500       2000       2500       3000
| | | | | | | | | | | | | | | | | | | | | | | | | | | | | | | | | |
Adam
0------------------------|930
        Seth
        230----------------------|1142
            Enosh
            435----------------------|1340
                Kenan
                625---------------------|1535
                    Mahalalel
                    795--------------------|1690
                        Jared
                        960----------------------|1922
                            Enoch
                            1122-----|1487
                                Methuselah
                                1287---------------------|2256
                                    Lamech
                                    1454----------------|2207
                                        Noah
                                        1642---------------------|2592
                                            Shem
                                            2144-----------|2744
                                                Arpachshad
                                                2244-----------|2809
                                                    Cainan
                                                    2379---------|2839
                                                        Shelah
                                                        2509--------|2969
                                                            Eber
                                                            2639---------|3143
                                                                Peleg
                                                                2773----|3112
                                                                    Serug
                                                                    3035---|3365
                                                                        Nahor
                                                                        3165|3373
                                                                            Terah
                                                                            3264-
```

The Masoretic Text

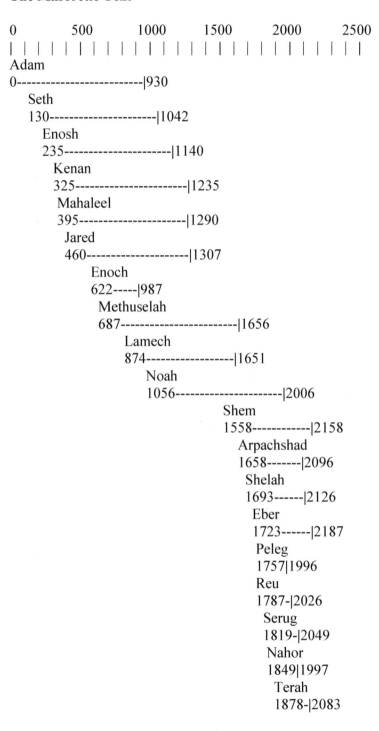

```
0          500       1000      1500      2000      2500
| | | | | | | | | | | | | | | | | | | | | | | | | | | |
Adam
0-----------------------|930
   Seth
   130---------------------|1042
      Enosh
      235---------------------|1140
         Kenan
         325----------------------|1235
         Mahaleel
         395---------------------|1290
            Jared
            460--------------------|1307
               Enoch
               622-----|987
               Methuselah
               687-----------------------|1656
                  Lamech
                  874------------------|1651
                     Noah
                     1056---------------------|2006
                        Shem
                        1558------------|2158
                           Arpachshad
                           1658-------|2096
                           Shelah
                           1693------|2126
                              Eber
                              1723------|2187
                              Peleg
                              1757|1996
                              Reu
                              1787-|2026
                                Serug
                                1819-|2049
                                Nahor
                                1849|1997
                                  Terah
                                  1878-|2083
```

2) The Septuagint is also far more uniform in character than the Hebrew. As a general rule 100 years are added to the Hebrew figures at the ages of begetting. But where these figures seemed high enough already - as with Jared, Methuselah, Lamech, Noah, Shem and Terah - little or no alteration is made. The ages at death for the patriarchs before Shem are the same as in the Hebrew, with the exception of Lamech. For the postdiluvian patriarchs, whose ages at death are not recorded, the remaining years stay the same from Peleg to Terah, with the exception of

Nahor. The net result is that 1,386 years are added to the chronology down to Terah at the age of 70 (586 years before the Flood and 800 years after),without increasing the longevity of the early patriarchs. Moreover, Methuselah appears to outlive the Flood by 14 years!

The motive may have been in part, as Larsson suggests, to bring the chronology of the Bible into line with Manetho's official Egyptian chronology compiled a short while before. The interpolation of *Cainan*, who is given exactly the same numbers as his successor Shelah, had the effect of adding another 130 years to the chronology. It also gives complete regularity to the genealogical table: ten generations before the Flood and ten generations after, the tenth in each case being the father of three sons.

The "second Cainan" is included in the Septuagint version of Genesis 10:24 and 11:12f. He is completely unknown to the Hebrew text and is omitted also in the Septuagint of 1 Chronicles 1:17. In Luke 3:36 alone does he appear in our Bibles. Only a Biblicist of the stamp of Floyd Nolan Jones finds it necessary to defend the presence of this Cainan in Luke. According to him Cainan was not the son of Arphaxad but the *brother* of Arphaxad. But it does not seem possible to extract this meaning from the words "of Arphaxad". Most probably he has been interpolated in Luke under the influence of the Septuagint in order to make up an artificial total of 77 names.

Another intruder in the text of Luke is *Admin* given in many versions as the father of Amminadab in verse 33. This name which looks like a shortened form of Amminadab is nowhere found in the Old Testament (see 1 Chron. 2:10; Ruth 4:18-20), or the New (Matt. 1:4). This genealogy already offers a significant array of 'sevens' without the additions of Admin or a second Cainan. Counting forward from Abraham, we have 14 generations to David and 56 to Christ; and counting backwards from Abraham, 14 generations to Enoch and 21 to God. Likewise in Matthew 1 there are only 41 names, but taking David as the pivotal figure, there are 14 generations back to Abraham, 14 to Josiah and 28 to Christ. In Matthew David is the key figure whose kingly role defines the character of Matthew's Gospel. In Luke however it is Abraham whose role as father of the faithful defines the character of Luke-Acts.

Noah was a postdiluvian patriarch as well as an antediluvian patriarch. If his name is included in both lists of patriarchs the same pattern (of ten generations both before and after the Flood with the tenth in each case having three sons) is achieved in a more subtle and interesting way.

3) Such apparent anomalies as Shem outliving all his descendants (except for Eber) down to and including Terah, and Eber outliving (it would seem) even Abraham, his descendant in the sixth generation, are ironed out in the Septuagint and Samaritan versions. In fact all Abraham's progenitors are made to die before Abraham's departure for Canaan, so underlining this event as a new beginning in sacred history. In the Samaritan Text Abraham leaves for Canaan in the very year of his father's death, on the (erroneous) assumption that he was the eldest of Terah's three sons.

4) Looking further afield, many examples could be cited of the ironing out of apparent problems in the Septuagint and Samaritan versions. For example, their alteration of Genesis 2:2 from "seventh day" to "sixth day" ("And on the sixth day God finished his work"); their addition of the words "and in the land of Canaan" to Exodus 12:40 (removing all doubt as to how this verse should be interpreted), and the alteration in the Septuagint of Amram's age from 137 to 132 in Exodus 6:20, thereby achieving a regular decline in age: Jacob 147, Levi 137, Kohath 133, Amram 132, Aaron 123, Moses 120. In the same version the day the Flood began, the 17th day of the second month, is changed to the 27th day of the second month. A Flood duration of exactly a year is thus obtained (Gen. 7:11; 8:4). Other "problem" passages such as 1 Samuel 13:1 and Jeremiah 52:28-30 are simply removed from the text.

5) There has been considerable discussion on the relative value of the chronologies provided by the Greek manuscripts for the kings of Israel and Judah. E.R. Thiele found in this version the same harmonizing tendencies as he had previously found in the Septuagint itself. It was his considered opinion that "the evidence points definitely to the Hebrews as possessing the earliest and most accurate figures for the kings of Israel and Judah", and that "the numbers found in the Greek manuscripts give evidence of effort to produce a chronological pattern clearer and more consistent than that found in the Hebrew figures" (1974: 190).

Gershon Galil is substantially of the same opinion (1996: 127-144). He concludes that C_2 (one of the Lucianic manuscripts) is "an artificial adaptation of the MT chronology, indicating that attempts had already been made at a relatively early time to resolve the many discrepancies between the chronological data in MT ... The chronology of C_2 is undoubtedly lacking any historical value." As for BL representing the other Lucianic manuscripts: "the system of chronological data in MT is historically conceivable, which is not the case in the BL manuscripts. The data in the latter may be assumed to be a mere emendation of the original data preserved in MT."

Floyd Nolan Jones, who besides his work on Chronology is author of a book entitled *The Septuagint: A Critical Analysis* (2000), concludes that "the LXX as it is today is highly inaccurate and deficient as a translation" (2005:13). Speaking of the period of the Kings he notes that Josephus, in the few places where he differs from the Hebrew Masoretic Text, is not in agreement with the Septuagint. This would seem to indicate, either that Josephus did not consider the LXX reliable, or that the LXX did not exist in his day!

Others however have defended the Greek tradition with equal conviction, notably J.D. Shenkel (1968) and Christine Tetley (2005). In view of Tetley's meticulous research into the Old Greek and Lucianic texts it would be cavalier of me to say they do not contain the occasional good reading. But personally I am not happy with a situation in which the Hebrew is presumed to be wrong on numerous occasions just because the Greek seems to give a more acceptable text. I remain of the opinion that the Hebrew Masoretic Text is decidedly superior to any others on offer. In the words of Gerhard Larsson, "all chronological differences between the MT and LXX can be explained as rational alterations from MT to LXX *while alterations in the other direction make no sense*" (1983: 402, italics his).

Genesis 5 and 11

It used to be argued, and still is by some, that the genealogies of Genesis 5 and 11 contain numerous gaps and cannot therefore be utilised for chronological purposes. It is implied that the construction of a biblical chronology is impossible: the necessary material for such a chronology is lacking, and the Bible was never intended for that purpose anyway. If this is the case our enterprise is frustrated at the outset, nipped in the bud so to speak, and there is nothing more to be said.

A leading advocate of this theory was J.C. Whitcomb in Appendix 2 of the evangelical classic *The Genesis Flood* by Henry M. Morris and J.C. Whitcomb (1961). I find it significant however that the scientist of these two, Henry Morris in his commentary on Genesis, takes the opposite view. He there says, "The record is perfectly natural and straightforward and is obviously intended to give ... the only reliable chronological framework we have for the antediluvian period of history" (1976: 154).

In the view of K.A. Kitchen, a leading Egyptologist of conservative persuasion, "we can neither date the flood before Abraham nor the creation before Noah merely by counting the Genesis figures continuously as did the worthy Archbishop Ussher in the carefree days when no evidence from outside the Bible was even imagined, still less thought about or seen. And in the context of that external data, any such literalism fails" (2003: 441). That is what decides the issue for scholars today, the argument from science that the evidence outside the Bible, be it archaeological or geological, does not fit easily into the biblical framework. Hence, it is claimed, the Bible cannot be taken literally, though the meaning that springs from the page is undeniably clear.

There is no valid reason for assuming gaps in the record, nor does this occur in the history of interpretation until the last quarter of the nineteenth century. It is just another argument for prolonging the history of the world. The ancients did it by emending the revealed data, moderns by imposing on the Bible an alien and ungrammatical sense. On the whole the Bible's own chronology is transparent and straightforward, but a great deal of damage has been done, not only here but in many other places, by the revealed data being chopped and changed to bring it into line with preconceived ideas. We cannot go far wrong if we stick closely to what is revealed in its plain grammatical sense.

The years of the antediluvian patriarchs are recorded in Genesis 5. This record presents no problems unless one be found in the concluding verse: "And Noah was 500 years old; and Noah begat Shem, Ham, and Japheth." This does not mean that Noah had three sons in one year, nor even that Shem was the eldest. Noah was 600 years old at the time of the Flood's arrival (Gen. 7:6), and Shem was 100 years old "two years after the Flood" (Gen. 11:10). The two years are to be reckoned from the beginning of the Flood as in Genesis 9:28, not from its end a year later as some have supposed. Noah therefore must have been 502 when Shem was born. The order of birth can be learned from two other scriptures: Genesis 9:24, which should be translated "his youngest son" (that is Ham), and Genesis 10:21 where Shem is described as "brother of Japheth the eldest". The order of birth therefore was Japheth, Shem, Ham.

The same literary device occurs again in Genesis 11:26: "And Terah lived 70 years, and begat Abram, Nahor, and Haran." We are not to understand by this that Abram was the eldest: possibly Haran was since he "died before his father Terah in the land of his birth" (11:28). Abram in fact, as we shall see, was not born until his father was 137 years old. Hence in Genesis 5:32 and 11:26 the most important son is put first and in neither case was he the eldest.

His days shall be 120 years

In Genesis 6:3 there is reference to a period of 120 years. "And the Lord said, My spirit shall not always strive with man, for that he also is flesh: yet his days shall be an hundred and twenty years." This is a verse which is difficult to translate for reasons both grammatical and lexicographical, but the *KJV* translation is probably close to the truth. The last clause has been taken to mean that the life-span of the human race is here limited to 120 years. But that cannot be right since men continued to live in excess of 120 years for many centuries after this.

The obvious sense is that the human race is granted a respite of 120 years before the judgment of the Flood. Man's downward spiral in sexual depravity had reached an all-time low in their intermarriage with "the sons of God", the fallen angels who lusted after the daughters of men (Gen. 6:1-2). As a result of this hybrid union the human race had become corrupted both morally and physically, and their offspring were the giant race of the *Nephilim* who roamed the earth in those days "and also after that". The life-span of this hybrid race was accordingly limited to 120 years, but their nemesis would be no natural death, but the judgment of the Flood as is afterwards explained.

In spite of what womankind had done through co-habiting with the "sons of God", their offspring were still flesh. As such they would be given 120 years in which to mend their ways. It was at the Flood that "all flesh" perished (6:13,17), including the Nephilim, addressed in verse 3.

In the year 600 years

Genesis 7:11 and 8:13 present a perplexing little problem which is very rarely discussed. The majority of commentators seem to be unaware that any problem exists. In Genesis 7:11 we are told the precise date in which "all the fountains of the great deep were broken up". It happened in the 600th year of Noah's life, in the second month and the seventeenth day of the month. The date is obviously an important one since the day and month are included. Yet it apparently contradicts Genesis 7:6 where we are told that "Noah was 600 years old when the flood of waters came upon the earth." The question is: was Noah a full 600 years old as the idiom "a son of 600 years" would seem to indicate, or was he only 599 as the expression "in the year 600 years" would normally imply?

The two texts are obviously intended to complement, not contradict, one another, yet on their face value they differ by one year. There are two possibilities: either Genesis 7:6 is to be understood as inclusive reckoning, meaning in effect that Noah was 599 years old, or Genesis 7:11 is to be understood as exclusive reckoning, indicating that Noah was a full 600 years old. For the first possibility there is no warrant whatsoever. The idiom "a son of so many years" is invariably used of completed years, just as we do ourselves when we say that someone is so many "years old". Hence we have no alternative but to fall back on the second possibility.

It says literally, "In the year 600 years to the life of Noah". We might compare Numbers 33:38-39 where we read that Aaron died "in the year the 40 to the coming out of the sons of Israel from the land of Egypt," or 1 Chronicles 26:31, "In the year the 40 to the reign of David ..." The construction is the same or similar in all three places, but in the latter two the numeral is reckoned inclusively, in the sense of "fortieth". In Genesis 7:11 however the meaning has got to be "In the year when Noah was 600 years old", which is how *The New English Bible* translates it.

There is however another possibility which comes to mind. Noah was still 599 when the Flood began, but in course of the Flood he turned 600 and was still 600 when the flood-waters dried up (Gen. 8:13). Arguably this is what Genesis 7:6 says, "And Noah was 600 years old when (actually *and*) the Flood was, waters upon the earth"? At first blush it would seem to solve the problem. But what about the death of Methuselah? Methuselah died at the age of 969 in the very year of the Flood, 1656 years from the creation of man. But if Noah was only 599, the year would have been 1655 and Methuselah would have been still alive! There is no escaping the fact that Noah was a full 600 years old when the Flood of waters arrived.

In Genesis 8:13 the construction is slightly different, "In (the year) 601 years, in the first (month), in (day) one to the month, the waters were dried up from the earth." The word for "year" is omitted, but the meaning is the same. By this time (on this very day in fact) Noah would have been reckoned "a son of 601 years", that is 601 years old. It is the same in 1 Kings 6:1 which says literally, "In 80 years and 400 years to the coming out of the sons of Israel from the land of Egypt, in the fourth year, in the month Ziv (that is the second month) to the reigning of Solomon over Israel, he built the house of the Lord." Should we therefore reckon these years as a full 480 years as in Genesis 8:13? I am inclined to think that we should. It is a question of interpretation rather than translation. These passages are examples of exclusive reckoning whereas in other places the reckoning is inclusive.

It seems to have been the Israelite custom to reckon their years from the nearest important event. This might be the accession of the reigning monarch (1 Kings 14:25 etc.), the going into exile (2 Kings 25:27; Ezekiel 1:2), King Josiah's Passover (Ezekiel 1:1), or the Exodus (Num. 1:1; Deut. 1:3). These are all of short duration, the longest being 52 years (2 Kings 15:27), and are reckoned inclusively. However, Genesis 7:11; 8:13 and 1 Kings 6:1 are in a different category. They span much longer periods and represent (I believe) completed years, a full 600 and 601 in the case of Noah, and a full 480 in the case of Solomon.

The days of the Flood-year

On this Umberto Cassuto's *Commentary on the Book of Genesis* (Part Two: 43-45) may be compared. The sequence of day periods covering the year of the Flood is given in Genesis 7 and 8. Not all the day periods are mentioned, but assuming the months are all the same length (namely, thirty days as presupposed in 8:3-4) the complete year can be filled out as follows. The dates stated in the text are underlined.

> Gen. 6:22: 1/1: Ark completed: beginning of Flood year
>   40 days (inclusive)
> 7:4,10: 10/2: Flood to begin in seven days
>   7 days
> 7:11,12: 17/2: Noah 600: Rained 40 days and 40 nights
>   40 days
> 7:17: 27/3: End of 40 days
>   110 days
> 8:3-4: 17/7: Ark came to rest after 5 months (150 days)
>   74 days
> 8:5: 1/10: Tops of the mountains seen
>   40 days (inclusive)
> 8:6: 10/11: The raven sent
>   7 days
> 8:8-9: 17/11: The dove sent and returned
>   "another 7 days"
> 8:10-11: 24/11: The dove sent again and returned
>   "another 7 days"
> 8:12: 1/12: The dove sent again but did not return
>   30 days
> 8:13: 1/1 Noah 601: The water dried from the earth
>   56 days
> 8:14: 27/2: The earth had dried out.

It was 40 days inclusively reckoned from 1/1 to 10/2 (that is the tenth day of the second month on this side of the Atlantic!) and I have assumed that the same applies to the forty days of 8:6. In 8:12 however, where it says "forty days and forty nights", I understand it to mean a full 40 days. In this way a consistent picture emerges totalling 360 days from 1/1 to 1/1. The specific mention of 150 days, or five 30-day months, between 17/2 and 17/7, encourages us to look for more 30-day months in this narrative, and we are not disappointed. There are in fact seven more:

From 1/1 to 1/10: nine months
From 1/1 to 1/1: twelve months
From 10/2 to 10/11: nine months
From 17/2 to 17/11: nine months
From 27/3 to 27/2: eleven months
From 1/10 to 1/1: three months
From 1/12 to 1/1: one month

A schematic calendar of 360 days was in use in ancient Egypt from as far back as the Old Kingdom (third millennium BC), and in Babylonia from at least the beginning of the first millennium. These were brought into line with the solar year by the addition of five or six so-called *epagomenal* days (from *epact*, defined as "the number of days by which the solar year exceeds the lunar year") at the year's end. It may have been the same at the time of the Flood though the recurring 30-day months in various multiples would rather suggest the addition of an embolismic or leap month (a second Elul, a repeat of the twelfth month, bearing in mind that the year began at Tishri prior to the Exodus) every fifth or sixth year. At any rate the reference to 150 days between 17/2 and 17/7 presupposes a luni-solar year of 360 days. The attempt by many, including Cassuto, to impose a lunar calendar on this narrative is shown to be wrong by this information.

Another possibility, advanced by Creationists, is that "the spin rate" of the earth on its axis was altered at the time of the Flood. Prior to that epoch the year was exactly 360 days in length, consisting of twelve months of 30 days. This is an interesting theory, possibly correct, though difficult to prove, I imagine.

Where was Abraham born?

As everyone knows Abraham was born in Ur of the Chaldees (Gen.11:28,31), but where exactly was this city? Consult any Bible Dictionary or Atlas and you will find Ur of the Chaldees located in Southern Mesopotamia not far from the Persian Gulf (modern Tell el-Muqayyar in S. Iraq). But this identification has never been universally accepted and should probably be rejected. According to Roger Henry, "This Ur must be in the land of the Urartians of Armenia. They were the people of the god 'Chaldae' and their homeland included Ararat" (2003: 43).

An ancient identification is with Urfa (=Edessa), 32 km NW of Harran. Muslim legend associates the place with Abraham; a cave beneath Urfa's citadel is said to be Abraham's birthplace. D.J. Wiseman (*The Illustrated Bible Dictionary*, in loc.) considers this unlikely on philological grounds. But the likelihood remains that Abraham haled from this part of the world if not from Urfa itself. There are several places in the region with names such as Saruc (=Serug), Till-Turahi (=Terah) and Nahor. See Lennart Moller (2002: 25f.).

In what year was Abraham born?

The date of Abraham's birth must be one of the most important events in the history of the Old Testament, and to mark this event we have discovered a chronological peculiarity such as occurs nowhere else. This is the only place in the entire Bible where the relevant data indicate a gap in the chronology. The existence of a gap at this point has been assumed by at least two other writers (R.G. Fausset and Sir Robert Anderson), but neither did so for the right reason and neither discerned the correct length of it. It is the only genuine chasm in the entire dating and has the effect of separating the history of the chosen race from the preceding history.

Abraham on leaving Haran was 75 years old (Gen. 12:4), and this took place after his father's death in Haran at the age of 205. This may be inferred from Genesis 11:32-12:1, but if any doubt should still exist we have it from the mouth of Stephen that Abraham was sent from Haran "after the death of his father" (Acts 7:4). It is usually assumed that Abraham departed from Haran immediately after his father's death, and this indeed would be a natural assumption were there not other considerations which strongly point to a different conclusion.

When considering any passage of Scripture we must never lose sight of the Bible as a whole, for the Bible is a complete universe in which every part agrees perfectly with every other part. In Peter's second epistle there is a curious expression which provides indirectly the clue we are looking for. This expression is "Noah the eighth" (2 Peter 2:5). Exegetes have been puzzled by this phrase and have translated it "Noah with seven others". Whatever justification there may be for this in Greek idiom it is certainly not what it says, and our first concern is to explain what the

Bible actually says supposing a literal interpretation is forthcoming. Of what Noah was the eighth we are not told. He was not the eighth generation from Adam, but the tenth. In Jude 14 there is a reference to "Enoch the seventh from Adam". Enoch was indeed the seventh generation from Adam, but his son was Methuselah, not Noah.

If we think of these patriarchs as kings, as they probably were, then it is their *succession*, rather than their generations, which is all-important. A king whose son dies before he does is succeeded by his grandson. Thus Louis XVI of France was grandson of Louis XV, and Louis XV great-grandson of Louis XIV. The intervening generations have no place in the succession. Though not the eighth in order of generation, Noah was in fact the eighth in order of succession. Two of his predecessors died, or departed, before the deaths of their fathers. Enoch was translated before the death of his father Jared, and Lamech died before the death of his father Methuselah, so forfeiting their place in the succession. Noah, therefore, was the eighth inheritor of the dominion entrusted by God to Adam. What is more, Noah's predecessor, the long-lived Methuselah, died in the very year of the Flood. It follows from this that Noah did not enter into his inheritance until after the Flood. There were therefore *seven* antediluvian inheritors concluding with Methuselah.

Another character called "eighth" in the New Testament is the Beast in Revelation 17:11. Like Noah he is represented as eighth in a series of kings. He will be eighth in succession, but he also "belongs to the seven". In his human embodiment he will be one of the first seven kings, and as such he will die of a sword wound, doubtless in heroic circumstances (Rev. 13:3,12,14). Then after an interval he will come to life again, ascending from the abyss in a mock resurrection (17:8). He will then rule as "eighth", the number of resurrection. The parallel with Noah is obvious. Noah died a symbolic death in the waters of the great Flood, and rose therefrom as if by resurrection to rule over a world cleansed of its sin and guilt. Noah is a true type of Christ, but the Beast will be His counterfeit and impersonator.

In the fact that Noah is the eighth and the first to rule after the Flood lies the key to Abraham's dates, for it is a remarkable fact that the rulers of God's people in the Old Testament appear in multiples of seven. There were 14 judges, 21 kings of Judah, and 21 kings of Israel. It would seem therefore that there ought as well to be seven (or a multiple of seven) postdiluvian patriarchs (in succession). Yet if no interval is allowed between the death of Terah and the call of Abraham, there were only six. Noah was succeeded by Shem, Shem by Eber, Eber who outlived Abraham by four years by Isaac, Isaac by Jacob, and Jacob by Joseph. Abraham's inclusion is demanded not only by his importance, but also by the numerical requirement that there should be seven postdiluvian inheritors. This calls for an interval of at least five years between Terah's death and Abraham's call (Gen. 12:1). If this is correct the following result is achieved:-

> 7 Antediluvian Inheritors
> 7 Postdiluvian Inheritors
>   14 in all
> 7 Major Judges
> 7 Minor Judges
>   14 in all
> 21 Kings of Judah
> 21 Kings of Israel
>   14 recognised kings (Matthew 1:17)

The seven major judges were Othniel, Ehud, Barak, Jephthah, Gideon, Samson, and Samuel; the seven minor judges, Shamgar, Tola, Jair, Ibzan, Eli, Elon, and Abdon. This division is explained in the next chapter. The 21 kings of Israel include Saul and his son Ishbosheth, who is said in 2 Samuel 2:10 to have reigned over Israel for two years. Altogether there were 42 kings, 21 of the house of David and 21 others.

So far we have argued for an interval of at least five years between Terah's death and Abram's call to leave Haran for the land that God would show him, but the exact length of the interval still remains to be determined. This may be established from the total number of years from Adam to the Exodus. But before this can be determined we need to examine the reference to 430 years in Exodus 12:40.

The 430 years of sojourning

Exodus 12:40, taken in isolation, may be translated in two different ways. In the *Kings James Version* we find, "Now the sojourning of the children of Israel, who dwelt in Egypt, was 430 years." But in the *Revised Version* it says, "Now the sojourning of the children of Israel, which they sojourned in Egypt, was 430 years." According to this translation the Israelites spent a full 430 years in Egypt, but if the *KJV* is correct their sojourn in Egypt may have covered only part of the total 430 years of sojourning.

The Greek Septuagint and Samaritan versions remove all possibility of doubt by adding the words "and in the land of Canaan" after (or before) the word "Egypt". Josephus also leaves no room for doubt how Exodus 12:40 should be understood. He says, "They left Egypt in the month of Xanthicus, on the 15th day of the lunar month; 430 years after our forefather Abraham came into Canaan, but 215 years only after Jacob removed into Egypt" (*Antiquities of the Jews*, II.15.2). Xanthicus is the name he uses for Abib or Nisan, the first month of the ecclesiastical year. This is the usual Jewish interpretation, even without the aid of Galatians 3:17 which for us clinches the matter.

Already in 1844 Henry Browne complained, "Modern critics, however, have abandoned the old interpretation". It is no different today: modern critics both liberal and orthodox have continued to abandon the old interpretation. That the Septuagint and Josephus are correct, however, is proved by Galatians 3:17. We there read that "A covenant confirmed beforehand by God, the law, which came 430 years after, doth not disannul, so as to make the promise of none effect" (*RV*). Here we have an authoritative commentary on Exodus 12:40 which tells us that the covenant (with Abraham), or its ratification, preceded the giving of the law by 430 years. Hence Exodus 12:40 is best translated, "Now the sojourning of the sons of Israel (who sojourned in Egypt) was 430 years."

The only occasion which answers to a formal ratification of the covenant made with Abraham is that described in Genesis 15, when the Lord passed between the pieces of the sacrificial animals which Abraham had divided. This event is undated, but seems to have taken place some nine or ten years after the original promise in Genesis 12 (cp. Gen. 16:3). It is this original promise which Paul refers to in Galatians 3 (see verses 8 and 18). So the covenant referred to is that of Genesis 12 as ratified in Genesis 15. Since the ratification is not dated it is from the original promise that the 430 years are measured. These 430 years are exactly bisected by the descent into Egypt, as Josephus observed.

However, those who follow Paul in reckoning the 430 years from the "covenant afore-validated" are by no means agreed on the exact starting-point of the period. Some have opted for Genesis 15:18 where the word "covenant" is first used with reference to Abraham. Others have preferred Genesis 17 where the covenant of circumcision was instituted, Abraham being 99 years old. Those who believe the 400 years of Genesis 15:13 and Acts 7:6 are the years of bondage in Egypt have thought the 430 years should begin from an event thirty years before the descent into Egypt - from Genesis 35:9-11 perhaps, where Jacob's name is changed to Israel and the terms of the covenant are repeated.

In theory Genesis 15 and 17 are both possible starting-points. Paul however emphasises the promises made to Abraham (Gal. 3:16,17,18,19,21,22,29). In Galatians 3:8 he refers specifically to the promise of Genesis 12:3. "In thee shall all the families of the earth be blessed." For "families of the earth" however he substitutes "nations", from Genesis 18:18. In verse 16 he draws attention to the words "and to thy seed" in the promises made to Abraham. These words first occur in Genesis 12:7 ("to thy seed") and 13:15 ("and to thy seed"). It is evidently these initial promises which Paul has in mind. Hence there is good reason for reckoning the 430 years from Genesis 12 rather than Genesis 15 (undated) or Genesis 17 (twenty-four years later).

Furthermore, if the *sojourning* or *dwelling* of Exodus 12:40 includes their sojourning in Canaan, it must surely cover their entire sojourning and not just part of it. The verb is first used of Abraham in Genesis 13:12, "Abram *dwelt* in the land of Canaan."

Objections

This resolution of the 430 years has been attacked on many fronts. By some it has been declared untenable on the grounds that the words "children of Israel" in Exodus 12:40 indicate Israel's descendants, and therefore cannot include Abraham, Isaac, and Israel himself. But it needs to be borne in mind that *Bene Yisra'el* simply means "Israelites", just as *Bene 'Ammon* means "Ammonites". It is perfectly understandable that Abraham, Isaac and Jacob should be referred to as "Israelites" in their capacity as founding fathers, and therefore members, of the Israelite nation.

Another example of the same logic is Genesis 46:8, "Now these are the names of the children of Israel which came into Egypt: *Jacob* ..." Jacob is himself numbered with his 33 sons and daughters born to him by Leah! Even more remarkable is Exodus 1:5 where Jacob is himself included among the 70 persons "issuing from the loins of Jacob"! (see Gen.46:26-27). In these verses Jacob is counted among his own offspring, just as in Exodus 12:40 Abraham, Isaac and Jacob are all included in "the children of Israel". These statements are not wrong; they are simply *quaint*. They may not comply with Western-type logic, but their meaning is perfectly clear.

The 400 years of stranger-dom

Genesis 15:13 may be translated, "And he (the Lord) said unto Abraham, Know of a surety that thy seed shall be a stranger in a land that is not theirs, and they shall serve them, and they (in turn) shall afflict them - four hundred years." The only significant alteration I have made to the *King James Version* is the insertion of a dash before "four hundred years". The question is, what are the boundaries of this reference to 400 years?

Abraham's seed were strangers in both Canaan and Egypt. Their plight as strangers in the land of Canaan is stated in Genesis 17:8; 37:1 and Hebrews 11:9. They were also strangers in the land of Egypt as the people of Israel are constantly reminded (Exod. 22:21; 23:9 etc.). It was in fact in Egypt that they became bondservants (Exodus 1:14), and there that they were afflicted (Exodus 1:11). This may also be inferred from Genesis 15:14, "And also that nation whom they serve, will I judge: and afterwards shall they come out with great substance."

The period of 400 years looks at first sight as if it defines the time of their affliction, and is in fact explained by most commentators as the length of their stay in Egypt. This however cannot be right for at least two reasons. In the first place, they were not afflicted all the time they dwelt in Egypt, but only after the death of the Pharaoh who had known Joseph (Exodus 1:8). And secondly, their entire stay in Egypt was only 215 years as explained above. The conclusion is unavoidable that the 400 years includes the whole period of stranger-dom of Abraham's seed in both Canaan and Egypt.

Unless this period is to be understood as a round number (which is unlikely in my view), it has to begin thirty years later than the 430 years. The whole sojourning of Abraham and his seed amounted to 430 years, but that of *his seed* only 400 years. The most appropriate beginning for this period is Genesis 21 where we learn that Abraham made a great feast in celebration of Isaac's weaning. It was on this occasion that Ishmael was cast out and Isaac was recognised as Abraham's seed and heir (cp. Genesis 21:12. "In Isaac shall thy seed be called").

This chapter does not tell us how old Isaac was at his weaning, but if we are right in reckoning the 400 years from this event, he must have been five years old. At a later period in Israel's history it was apparently quite usual to wean children at the age of three, as shown in 2 Maccabees 7:27, "My son, have pity upon me that carried thee nine months in my womb, and gave thee suck three years" - the words of the noble mother whose sons were tortured to death by Antiochus. In patriarchal times the period may well have been extended to five years. Ages three and five were both significant as 2 Chronicles 31:16 and Leviticus 27:5-6 bear witness.

It is intrinsically unlikely (don't you think?) that God would have left this young nation, this tender plant, in Egypt for 400 years. After all, they had done nothing wrong to deserve such punishment. Even 215 years may seem a long time, but for at least half that time they were well looked after. We do not know when the Pharaoh who knew not Joseph appeared on the scene, but it was probably shortly before the birth of Moses, eighty years before the Exodus.

In the fourth generation

It says in Genesis 15:16, "But in the fourth generation they shall come hither again; for the iniquity of the Amorites is not yet full." But from when are these four generations to be reckoned, from Isaac or from the descent into Egypt? If the former is the case, they are equivalent to the 400 years previously mentioned, a hundred years to a generation. This is the view of many scholars. Assyrian parallels are adduced to prove that the Hebrew word for generation (*dor*) can sometimes mean lifetime or century. This is comparable to saying that an English word must have a certain meaning because that is the meaning of its equivalent in French or German. On this basis it could be argued that poison is synonymous with fish, to bless the same as to wound, and that the week has eight days! Such reasoning, however, has no validity at all unless the meaning of the word in question cannot be figured out from its usage in the mother tongue. In the case of *dor* there are plenty of examples in the Old Testament to establish its meaning without recourse to other Semitic languages. Consider the following:

Deut. 23:2-3: "even to the third generation"
Deut. 23:8: "the children that are born to you (in the) third generation"
Deut. 29:22: "the generation to come, your children ..."
Judges 2:10: "that generation ... another generation"
Job 42:16: "After this Job lived 140 years, and saw his son and his son's
　　　　sons, four generations"
2 Kings 10:30 (15:12): "your (that is *Jehu's*) children of the fourth
　　　　(generation) shall sit on the throne of Israel"

The word "generation" is not expressed in the last reference but is clearly implied. Jehu was succeeded by his son (Jehoahaz), his grandson (Jehoash), his great-grandson (Jeroboam), and his great-great-grandson (Zechariah), four generations excluding himself. But by far the most significant of the passages just quoted is Job 42:16, referring as it does to patriarchal times. We are here told that Job lived "after this" 140 years and saw his children to the fourth generation.

One commentator, fellow Guernseyman Carteret Priaulx Carey (1858), has this to say on Job 42:16: "As we do not know how old he (Job) was when his affliction came upon him, we cannot precisely determine the age at which he died; but as he had, previously to his affliction, a family of ten children, all grown-up, he could not have been less than sixty or seventy years. And as in other respects God gave him twice as much as he had before, so perhaps also in this. The half, then, of one hundred and forty gives us seventy, and the two periods united make two hundred and ten - an age which unquestionably places Job in patriarchal times."

If this reasoning is sound, we have Job living about the same number of years as the Israelites stayed in Egypt. Reckoning 45 years to a generation Job's great-great-grandchildren would have been around thirty years old when their forebear died at the age of 210.

```
Job at 45 -  a father
       90 -  a grandfather
      135 -  a great-grandfather
      180 -  a great-great-grandfather
      210 -  his great-great-grandchildren now 30 years old
```

If the same arithmetic is applied to the descendants of Abraham, we have the Israelites coming out of Egypt in the fourth generation from their going down to Egypt. In Genesis 15:14 it is said of Egypt, "And also that nation, whom they shall serve, will I judge: and afterwards shall they come out with great substance." And then in verse 15, "in the fourth generation they shall come hither again". It is the fourth generation of those who went down to Egypt, not the fourth generation of those who lived as strangers in Canaan and Egypt, which is meant.

The generations in Egypt

The evidence is inescapable that the Israelites sojourned in Egypt for only half the 430-year period. This conclusion is strongly confirmed by the genealogies of specific families recorded in Genesis and Exodus. Thus the combined ages at death of Moses' father and grandfather, Amram and Kohath (the latter being numbered among those who went down to Egypt in Genesis 46:11), together with Moses' age in the year of the Exodus, comes to only 350 years (137+133+80, Exodus 6:18-20; 7:7). There is no reason for supposing that Moses' ancestry is abridged as is frequently asserted. It is here stated (6:16) that Levi had three sons, Gershon, Kohath and Merari; and we know from Genesis 46:11 that these were his sons in the first generation. We are then told that Kohath had four sons, Amram, Izhar, Hebron and Uzziel, and it is natural to assume that these also were his sons in the first generation. Finally we read that "Amram took to wife Jochebed his father's sister and she bore him Aaron and Moses."

Here we are informed not only that Amram was Moses' father but also that his mother was Levi's daughter. That Jochebed was a true daughter of Levi, and not merely a descendant of his, is confirmed by Numbers 26:59: "The name of Amram's wife was Jochebed the daughter of Levi, *who was born to Levi in Egypt.*" The concluding words are clearly intended to distinguish Jochebed from Levi's other children, who were born to him not in Egypt but in Canaan (Gen. 46:11). Even with the shorter chronology this is only just possible. If Levi was 120 at the birth of Jochebed, she would still have been 59 at the birth of Moses!

H.H. Rowley has this to say on the significance of Numbers 26:59. "To suppose that this means that she (Jochebed) was a long-range descendant of Levi's born centuries after his migration to Egypt is to reduce it to nonsense. The clear meaning of the passage is that whereas Levi took with him three sons when he went to Egypt, Jochebed was born to him later, and the genealogy of Moses and Aaron, which linked them to Levi through their mother by a single link, and through their father by two links, is clearly intended to be a firm one" (1950: 73).

Other families show considerable variation though the same sort of time-scale is implied. Nahshon for example, chosen from the tribe of Judah to assist Moses with the census, was in the fifth generation from Judah (Gen. 46:12; Num. 1:7; 1 Chron. 2:9,10). Bezalel the craftsman was in the sixth generation from Judah (Exod. 31:2; 1 Chron. 2:18-20). Elishama, chosen from the tribe of Ephraim to help with the census, was in the eighth generation from Joseph (Num. 1:10; 1 Chron. 7:22-26). Zelophehad's daughters were in the sixth generation from Joseph (Num. 26:33; 27:1). Achan, who belonged to the generation which entered the promised land, was in the fourth generation from Judah if there are no omissions (Joshua 7:1). Joshua at the other extreme was in the ninth generation from Ephraim and the tenth from Joseph (1 Chron. 7:23-27).

According to Genesis 15:16 Abraham's descendants would return to the land of Canaan in the fourth generation. If this refers to the generation that went down to Egypt, it is exactly what we would expect over a period of 215 years. The fact that particular families do not work out at four generations is only to be expected. The norm was to be four generations.

Israel's population explosion

The proportion of over-twenties to under-twenties varies hugely across the world today. In some developing countries, such as Mexico, as much as 60 percent of the population are under twenty, but only half that amount in more developed countries. The situation in pre-Exodus Israel was rather exceptional. On the one hand the great ages reached in those days (between 120 and 130) would indicate an excess of over-twenties. On the other hand, the large number of babies being born might suggest a disproportionate amount of under-twenties.

Again, we do not know the age-limit of those enumerated in the census of Numbers 1. The words "from twenty years and upwards"(1:3) would seem to imply that there was no upper limit. But the verse goes on to say "all in Israel who are able to go to war." We are thinking therefore of those eligible for military service. The upper limit might be 60, or it might be 80 or even 100. But the lack of definition suggests there was no upper limit: all those able to fight are included irrespective of age. Caleb at 85 was as strong as he had been forty years previously. "I am", he says, "still as strong today as I was in the day that Moses sent me; my strength now is as my strength was then, for war and for going and coming" (Joshua 14:11). Joshua himself can hardly have been less; he was probably around 90 at the time of the conquest.

Assuming for the sake of argument that there were roughly the same number of males in each 20-year age bracket, we can calculate the average number of males to a family. If those enumerated in the census were those from 20 to 60 years of age, there would have been about 300,000 in each 20-year bracket. If those under twenty were also 300,000, we have only to divide this number by the number of firstborn (namely 22,273, Numbers 3:43) to establish the number of males in the average family. This is supposing, as will be explained in a minute, that the firstborn were those of the rising generation only, and for practical purposes were limited therefore to those under twenty. This works out as about 13.5 males to a family.

If however the upper limit in the census was 80 years, there were 200,000 under twenty and only nine boys to a family. If the upper limit was 100, there would be 120,000 under twenty and only 5.4 boys to the average family. A family averaging about ten boys to a family is not incredible considering the circumstances of the time.

It is expressly stated that in the land of Goshen, where they lived in Egypt, they were fruitful and increased greatly in number (Gen. 47:27). After Joseph's death "the Israelites were fruitful and multiplied greatly and became exceedingly numerous, so that the land was filled with them" (Exodus 1:7). The situation is stated succinctly by Moses: "Your forefathers who went down into Egypt were seventy in all, and now the Lord your God has made you as numerous as the stars in the sky" (Deut. 10:22). The greatly extended lifespan (compared with today) would have enabled a fertile male to father a large number of children, especially if more than one partner was involved. Some of them must have had a second wife or concubine, though it is not known how widespread this practice was. When, for example, the baby boys were being drowned in the Nile, there would have been an excess of young girls. Then the surviving males would have taken more than one wife resulting in no overall lowering of the population.

How many were there altogether?

As for the total number involved it is only possible to generalise. Assuming the upper limit in Numbers 1 to be (on average) 80 years, we may extrapolate the numbers as follows:-

600,000 men from 20 to 80 years
600,000 women from 20 to 80
200,000 boys under 20
200,000 girls under 20
150,000 (say) men over 80
150,000 women over 80
22,000 male Levites (Numbers 3:39)
22,000 female Levites.

If these figures are even approximately correct we have a total not far short of two million (1,944,000). In addition there was the "mixed multitude" who went up with them and of course "very much livestock, both flocks and herds" (Exodus 12:38). In sum, the total number must have been in the region of two million, even without the indefinite mixed multitude.

According to James K. Hoffmeier an even larger number is implied. He says, "A total of 3-4 million is likely. Three million alone results from adding a wife and three children per family" (2005:153). This is assuming there were 600,000 families. But Hoffmeier's arithmetic is flawed, since all the male children of the 600,000, except for those under twenty, would themselves be included in the 600,000. The evidence points to two million, not three or four. Even so the number is still very large, far in excess of anything scholars such as Hoffmeier would consider logistically or demographically possible.

What was the rate of increase?

Another problem which many have found unnerving is the phenomenal rate of growth presupposed by these figures. On our chronology it is required that the 68 or 70 males who went down to Egypt with Jacob had become nearly two million only 215 years later. To achieve this amazing increase they would have had to double their numbers every fourteen years over fifteen generations.

This amounts to an annual increase of nearly five percent (4.8 or 4.9). According to the *New Encyclopaedia Britannica* (2002), "the highest known rate for a national population" was experienced in Kenya in the 1980s when the increase approximated 4.1 percent. This would suggest that the rate of increase of the Israelites in Egypt has no parallel on record. These figures should not be used to cast doubt on the census figures in Numbers 1, but they may of course prompt a re-examination of the chronology advocated in this treatise.

It would certainly ease the situation if the 430 years of Exodus 12:40 could be measured from a later point than Genesis 12. An alternative might be Genesis 33:18, when Jacob returned to Shechem with his eleven sons at the end of his twenty-year exile in Paddan-aram. That would satisfy the criterion, "the sojourning of *the sons of Israel* … was 430 years". But it does not sit so easily with Galatians 3:16-18 which speaks only of the promises made to Abraham. All in all Genesis 12 remains the least objectionable starting-point.

The tribes of Judah and Levi

The tribe of Judah presents the population explosion at its most acute. Judah's three sons, Shelah, Perez and Zerah grew to 74,600 in only 215 years (Numbers 1:27). This tribe must have doubled its numbers every 14.8 years. At its least acute is the tribe of Levi. Kohath, second son of Levi, was born in Egypt (Gen. 46:11). The total number of Kohath's male descendants "from a month old and upward" is given as 8,600 (Numbers 3:28), these being divided between his four sons, Amram, Izhar, Hebron, and Uzziel. This family would have had to double just over twelve times in order to reach 8,600, that is once every eighteen years. The Bible draws attention to the astonishing fertility of the Hebrew women (Exodus 1:7,12,19; Deut. 10:22; 26:5). They had moreover the invigorating and sustaining power of God who had said to them, "Do not be afraid to go down to Egypt; for I will there make you a great nation" (Gen. 46:3).

More examples of rapid growth

To illustrate our meaning here are two examples of rapid growth from the record of these times.

1) Jacob himself had eleven sons in only seven years (Gen. 29:31 to 30:24). It was after the birth of Joseph, his eleventh son, that Jacob asked Laban to allow him to go home (30:25). So Joseph was born at the end of the 14 years of service, that is seven years after Jacob had married his two wives (29:16-30). This was followed by another six years while Jacob served Laban for his flocks (Gen. 31:41).

Leah's first four sons were born in the first four years of marriage (29:31-35). In the meantime Rachel, having discovered her own barrenness, had offered her maid Bilhah to Jacob. Bilhah's first son, Dan, may have been born before Judah, Leah's fourth, and her second, Naphtali, not long after (30:1-8). Leah would have quickly discovered that she had stopped conceiving and have followed her sister's example in offering her maid to Jacob (30:9-13). Leah herself may have conceived again before the birth of Zilpah's second son, and have given birth to her last two sons in the sixth and seventh years of her marriage. Rachel gave birth to Joseph also in the seventh year.

Year	Leah	Bilhah	Zilpah	Rachel
1	Reuben			
2	Simeon			
3	Levi	Dan		
4	Judah	Naphtali		
5			Gad	
6	Issachar		Asher	
7	Zebulun			Joseph

Floyd Nolan Jones disagrees with this scenario. He thinks that Jacob married both his wives before either of the seven-year periods began. Otherwise, he says, there is insufficient time for Judah to be born, grow up, have children *and grandchildren* before going down to Egypt only 40 years after Joseph's birth. In this he is right if (but only if) Hezron and Hamul, Judah's grandsons (Gen.46:12), were already born before the descent into Egypt as Genesis 46 would seem to require. I shall come to this in a moment.

According to Genesis 29:21 Jacob said to Laban, "Give me my wife, for my days are fulfilled, that I may go in unto her" (*KJV*). But to what days was he referring when he said "my days are fulfilled"? These were not the seven years of service just mentioned, says Dr Floyd Jones. What is implied is "a certain number of days from the time the contract was made until he could actually take Rachel to wife. The number itself was always left to the determination of the contracting party" (2005:64).

It was therefore the short period of preparation, a month or two at the most, set by the bride's father, which had then expired. This however is not a natural reading of the text and I know of no commentator who accepts it. Dr Jones says that Ussher took this stance before his chronology was corrected by Bishop Lloyd. If that was the case Ussher was mistaken. Jacob would not have had to ask Laban for his wife if the exact number of days had previously been arranged.

The expression "the days are fulfilled" is of frequent occurrence, and the days (or time) referred to has to be determined from the context. In 1 Samuel 18:26 it refers to the time set aside for David before marrying Michal, Saul's daughter. The exact period is not specified but it must have been long enough for him to kill at least one hundred Philistines. In 1 Chronicles 17:11 the expression means "When your life is completed". In Exodus 23:26 the Israelites are told, "None shall miscarry or be barren in your land; I will fulfil the number of your days", and so on. In Genesis 29:25 Jacob protests, "What is this you have done to me? Did I not serve with you for Rachel?" Yes, he had served seven years for Rachel and those days were now fulfilled.

In Genesis 29:21 the reference can only be to the seven years previously mentioned. Jacob had been counting the days, but Laban had to be reminded.

2) Joshua was descended in the ninth generation from Joseph's son Ephraim (1 Chron. 7:20-27). Ezer and Elead, Ephraim's second and third sons, were killed by men of Gath as a result of a cattle raid in which they were involved. After this Ephraim had another son, Beriah, from whom Joshua was descended in the eighth generation. If Joseph (born A.H.2265) was 32 years old at the birth of Ephraim (cp. Gen. 41:45-52), and Ephraim say 35 at the birth of Beriah, we are left with only 140 years in which to fit eight generations before the birth of Joshua about fifty years before the Exodus. This represents an average of 17.5 years to a generation. Many versions try to rationalise the text of Chronicles here but at the expense of truth. The *KJV* gives the most accurate translation.

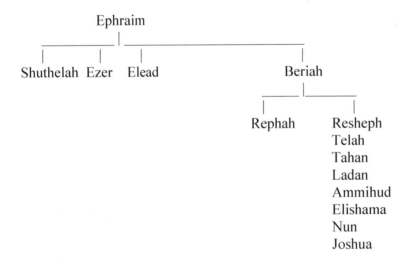

Genesis 46 in the dock

Even more surprising results are reached if Genesis 46 is understood to record, without exception, only those who went down to Egypt. This indeed accords with the prima facie sense of the passage, but in the case of Judah it leads to results which are impossible to accept. Judah was born in the year 2263, forty-two years before the descent into Egypt. He did not marry his Canaanite wife until after Joseph had been sold into Egypt at the age of seventeen, A.H.2283 (Gen. 37:2; 38:1). So he cannot have been less than twenty when he left his brothers and married the daughter of Shua. His sons Perez and Zerah were born after the marriage and death of his sons Er and Onan and after his third son Shelah had grown to maturity (38:6-30), yet Perez himself had children before the descent into Egypt (in 2305) according to the prima facie sense of Genesis 46:12. It is however clearly impossible to squeeze three generations into only 22 years.

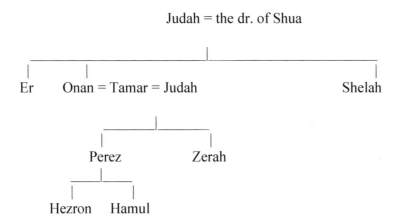

Judah = the dr. of Shua

| | | | |
| Er | Onan = Tamar = Judah | | Shelah |

Perez   Zerah

Hezron   Hamul

This leads to the unexpected conclusion that Genesis 46 includes two descendants of Jacob, Hezron and Hamul, who were not born until after the descent into Egypt. There may be a pointer to this in verse 27: "all the persons of the house of Jacob, that came into Egypt, were seventy." Yet, on its own showing, two of these, Ephraim and Manasseh, were really born in Egypt. If these two were born in Egypt there could have been others. The same liberty is taken in Genesis 35:23-26, where Jacob's sons are enumerated. "These", it says, "were the sons of Jacob who were born to him in Paddan-aram", yet one of them was not born in Paddan-aram at all. Benjamin was born some distance from Bethlehem, as the writer has just recorded.

But why should Hezron and Hamul be added to the list when they were not born until about 17 years after the descent into Egypt? They were added surely because of Hezron's importance as the ancestor of David and Christ. Here we see God's elective purpose in operation in the choice of Hezron rather than Hamul, just as it had already operated in the choice of Perez rather than Zerah, though Zerah is also given a tantalizing promise in the form of the scarlet thread that was tied to his hand by the midwife (38:27-30). It is because of Hezron's subsequent importance that this addition is made to the list. Though not present in person, Hezron and Hamul were nevertheless present in the loins of their father (Heb.7:10).

Two anomalies avoided

Not content with this scenario, Dr Jones is forced into a merciless compression of the chronology in order to bring Hezron and Hamul into the picture. There are in particular two anomalies which he is forced to accept. The first is that Jacob's marriage to Leah and Rachel took place before the first seven-year period began and consequently that Judah was born only four years after Jacob's arrival in Paddan-aram. This however involves a most unnatural reading of Genesis 29, as we have already seen.

The second anomaly is that Judah "went down from his brothers" (Gen.38:1) immediately after Jacob's return to the land of Canaan (33:18) instead of after the sale of Joseph to Midianite merchantmen where it is placed in the book of Genesis ("at that time", 38:1). While admitting that it is grammatically possible to place this episode some years earlier, Keil significantly remarks, "this assumption is rendered extremely improbable, if not impossible, by the fact that Judah was not merely accidentally present when Joseph was sold, but was evidently living with his brethren, and had not yet set up an establishment of his own."

Without making these assumptions it is impossible to squeeze three generations into the time allowed between Judah's birth and his going to Egypt. Even with these assumptions it is only just possible. When however it is recognised that Hezron and Hamul were not born until later, the chronology falls into place without any forcing at all. The salient dates cannot be fixed with absolute certainty, but the following cannot be far from the truth:

2252	Jacob goes to Paddan-aram at 77 years of age
2259	End of the first 7 years. Jacob marries Leah and Rachel
2260	Birth of Reuben
2261	Birth of Simeon
2262	Birth of Levi
2263	Birth of Judah
2266	Joseph is born (at the end of the 14 years of service)
2272	Jacob returns to Canaan after 20 years (Gen.31:41)
2283	Joseph at 17 is sold to Egypt
2283	Judah at 20 leaves his brothers and home
2284	Er is born to Judah
2285	Onan is born
2287	Shelah is born
2303	Shelah at 16 is grown up
2304	Perez and Zerah are born to Judah and Tamar
2305	They go down to Egypt.

How many went down?

The totals mentioned in Genesis 46 (33+16+14+7, vv.15,18,22,25) come to exactly 70 as noted in verse 27. These included Jacob himself and all his descendants, mostly male it seems, though a couple of daughters are mentioned, Jacob's daughter Dinah and Serah daughter of Asher. There must in fact have been a comparable number of girls (Gen.37:35; 46:7), but these were the only two to set up households of their own. All the rest would have married their cousins within the tribal family. The fact that only one Canaanite mother is mentioned (46:10) proves that marriages to Canaanite girls were strongly discouraged, frowned upon by the people as much as by the Lord. The Lord had His own way of dealing with Judah's unacceptable marriage to the daughter of Shua which threatened to pollute the ancestry of Christ (38:1-12). Not counting Joseph, his two sons and Jacob, there were 66 persons "not including Jacob's sons' wives", who came with Jacob into Egypt, as again noted in verse 26.

Acts 7:14 gives yet another total. According to Stephen, Jacob *and all his kindred* were 75 persons in all. This number evidently includes Jacob's sons' wives who were omitted in the Genesis numbering. Excluding Hezron and Hamul there were 64 persons who went down to Egypt with Jacob. Add to that number the eleven wives of the patriarchs and we have the number

75. Joseph's wife is not counted because she was already in Egypt. Judah's first wife had died (Gen.38:12), but he was also married to Tamar, the mother of Perez and Zerah. If Jacob himself is included in the 75, as may well be the case, there were only ten wives, not eleven.

Commentators continue to inform us that the number 75 is derived from the Septuagint. It is true that the LXX has 75 in Genesis 46:27 and Exodus 1:5, but it is not so clear how that number is arrived at. The sum of the four totals in the LXX version of Genesis 46 (33,16,18 and 7) comes to 74, not 75, but the compiler may not have realised that Jacob is included in the first group. If he is added again the total is 75. Some additional names are given in verse 20, namely three grandsons and two great-grandsons of Joseph. If these five are added to the Hebrew 70, the total of 75 is obtained. But in verse 27 he contradicts himself by saying that *nine* souls were born to Joseph in Egypt. It is left unresolved whether the 75 is to be explained as 70+5 (Joseph's grandsons and great-grandsons) or 66+9 (all Joseph's descendants). It is hard to believe that such a confused text is the source of Stephen's inspired statement.

It looks very much as if the LXX compiler was familiar with the same tradition as Stephen respecting the number of Israelites who went down to Egypt. He has tried to give a rational explanation of this number, but lacking the key he has got it all wrong. Ephraim and Manasseh were far too young to have children, let alone grandchildren, and there is no reason one can think of why they should be included. Dr Jones' comment is to the point. "The painfully obvious conclusion before us is that – by not grasping the true explanation of the 66, 70, and 75 – the translator of the Septuagint tried to 'correct' what he perceived as a 'scribal error' in the Hebrew text. In so doing he *created* one!" (p.69).

Are the numbers exaggerated?

The truly mind-numbing size of the numbers in Numbers has raised doubts in people's minds whether in fact the numbers are correct. Could the Hebrew have been misunderstood or has the text been tampered with in later times?

One can sympathise with those who find such large numbers, such a huge migration, impossible to accept. But it is less easy to sympathise with those who maintain that the Hebrew text has been mistranslated or misunderstood. For Hoffmeier "the problem does not lie with the text but in how one translates the word '*eleph*", the word translated "thousand". This word could mean "clan", he says, rather than thousand, as when Gideon says "My *clan* is the weakest in Manasseh" (Judges 6:15); or alternatively "military unit", as when David is told by his father to take ten cheeses to "the commander of their *thousand*" (1 Sam. 17:18).

No one doubts that '*eleph* can mean "clan" on occasions (e.g. Isaiah 60:22; Zech. 9:7; 12:5,6) or even "district" as in the phrase "the thousands of Judah" (1 Sam. 23:23; Micah 5:2), but these meanings are a natural development from the original "thousand". We find a similar development in our word "hundred" which, from being a large number, came to mean "a subdivision of a county or shire, having its own court" (OED). But the literal sense of hundred was never lost, and that applies to '*eleph* as well.

Others have suggested that '*eleph* might be repointed '*alluph* in the sense of commander or captain (literally *chiliarch*). One place cited by Kenneth Kitchen where this meaning would fit is 1 Kings 20:30 (2003: 264). We read there that when the wall at Aphek collapsed 27,000 Syrians were killed. Would not 27 *officers* make better sense? It might appear so, but what right have we to change the meaning of words to suit our private reservations? The number 27,000 may be justified on the assumption that many thousands of Syrians were scaling the wall, and many more underneath it, when the wall miraculously collapsed. The resultant death-toll could well have been as stated if the Lord willed it so. There are other places in the Old Testament where the numbers appear to be exaggerated (e.g. 1 Samuel 6:19). All these call for careful examination, but it is doubtful if the solution is ever to be found in changing the meaning of *'eleph.*

Many writers have felt these numbers to be impossibly high, giving rise to several ingenious attempts to cut them down to size on the grounds that they have been misunderstood or corrupted in process of transmission. One of the most recent of these is by Colin J. Humphreys in his (otherwise) ground-breaking work *The Miracles of Exodus* (2003: 104-9) and in his article of 1998. Humphreys revives the idea of G.E. Mendenhall (1958) that the Hebrew word translated "thousand" *('eleph)* meant originally a military unit or troop consisting of just a few soldiers. According to Mendenhall, "The old Federation system broke down early in the Monarchy if not before. The royal army included units of approximately a thousand men under the command of an officer appointed by the king. This system was naturally read back into the census lists of the federation period, yielding impossibly high figures."

When, for example, the number of fighting Reubenites in the census of Numbers 1 is given as 46 thousand 500 men, the original meaning was 46 troops consisting of 500 men. In this case a troop would have consisted of ten or eleven men. Adding up the entire list, Humphreys arrives at 598 troops consisting of 5 thousand 550 men. According to Humphreys the 5 thousand was later added to the 598 to make 603,550, the total given in Numbers 1:46. He does the same for the enumeration of Numbers 26 where another census records the fighting population at the end of the wilderness period. Overall the number of men to a troop ranges from five to fourteen.

Working on this principle the total number of those who left Egypt was in the region of 20 thousand (as opposed to 20 hundred thousand!), a far more reasonable and manageable figure. But it is difficult to see how an *'eleph* could have come to signify a troop of only five or six men, nor is there any support for this meaning in the rest of the Old Testament.

Besides, the number 603,550 cannot be so easily disposed of. It is mentioned again in Numbers 2:32 and Exodus 38:26, and the less precise 600,000 in Exodus 12:37 and Numbers 11:21. Moreover, the number of talents and shekels paid into the sanctuary fund corresponds exactly to 603,550 at the rate of half a shekel per head (Exodus 38:25-26). The total given is 100 talents and 1,775 shekels. A talent was worth 3,000 shekels, so 100 talents correspond to 300,000 shekels. Add to that 1,775 shekels and we have 301,775 shekels which is exactly half the required amount in half shekels.

The text as it stands in the book of Numbers is internally sound and consistent. A list of twelve numbers, correct to the nearest hundred (or fifty in the case of Gad), is accurately totalled at 603,550. The correctness of the total confirms the accuracy of the component parts, in the same way as the component parts confirm the accuracy of the total. The numbers are certainly large, but the text itself gives no cause for suspicion. It is the same in Numbers 26. The numbers are correct to the nearest hundred, except in the case of Reuben where a more precise number is given (43,730), and the total (601,730) is the correct sum of the twelve component parts. If the numbers did not add up or were irreconcilable in some way, there would be a sound reason for suspecting a copyist's error or some corruption of the text. Where however there is internal consistency and mathematical exactitude, what justification is there for assuming a corrupt text?

An actual discrepancy

Interestingly there *is* a genuine discrepancy in Numbers 3. There the total number of Levites from a month old and upward is given as 22,000 (3:39). But the total for the three clans previously mentioned (to Gershon 7,500; to Kohath 8,600; to Merari 6,200) comes to 22,300. The stated figure 22,000 must be correct since the number of the firstborn of all the tribes (22,273, v.43) is said to exceed the number of Levites by 273 (v.46). So how do we explain the fact that the three numbers do not add up to 22,000?

It has been suggested that 300 Levites were themselves firstborn and therefore not eligible to represent the firstborn of the other tribes. That is a possible solution which requires no alteration of the text. But if that were the case, we would expect the fact to be mentioned. Others have suspected a corruption in the text on the grounds that numbers are particularly susceptible to corruption, and there is certainly evidence of this in the rest of the Old Testament. Possibly the clan of Kohath was really 8,300 rather than 8,600 (*sls* for *ss*, the accidental omission of one letter in Numbers 3:28).

Whatever the solution, here we do have a discrepancy real or apparent, and it calls for an explanation. But in Numbers 1 and 26 there is no discrepancy at all. Hence it is totally gratuitous to start altering the text as if a problem existed.

The number of firstborn

According to Numbers 3:43 the total number of firstborn males, of a month old and upwards, was 22,273. Taken at its face value this implies, according to Humphreys, that the average mother had about a hundred children, 50 sons and 50 daughters! Since this is clearly impossible, the numbers as they stand cannot be correct. That at least is what we are told.

Faced with a problem of this nature, the first thing to do is to read carefully what is said, and then use a little commonsense. In nine cases out of ten the problem will disappear. This problem is addressed by James Orr (among others) in his book *The Problem of the Old Testament* (1906: 367f.). It is unlikely, says Orr, that persons who were themselves married and heads of families would be reckoned as firstborn. Only the firstborn of contemporary households are included, not their fathers, grandfathers or great-grandfathers. When the firstborn in Egypt were killed, all were included "from the firstborn of Pharaoh that sat on his throne unto the firstborn of the captive that was in the dungeon" (Exodus 12:29). Pharaoh's eldest son died, but not Pharaoh himself though he too was most probably a firstborn son. Likewise the firstborn of the captive died, but not the captive himself even if he happened to be a firstborn. There was someone dead in every household, but in no household more than one (Exodus 12:30).

This consideration practically limits the firstborn to those under twenty. If there were 200,000 of these, the number of males to a family would not have exceeded an average of nine. If this is correct, the problem is solved without driving a coach and four through the pages of Scripture.

A more pressing problem: logistics

A more pressing problem, one which has caused so many people to doubt the current text, is that of logistics: how this vast multitude could be supplied, maintained and deployed in the wilderness. I have it on good authority that to supply such a large number of people a daily ration of 900 tons of food would be needed, 2400 tons of firewood, and about two and a half million gallons of water! And that does not include water for washing, or fodder and water for their flocks and herds. Furthermore, to provide camping space for two million people would require about 500 square miles, or an area 60 miles long by eight miles wide!

For these statistics I am indebted to *Operation Exodus* (1957), a small book by Major-General D.J. Wilson-Haffendon whose experience in the army must have given him a unique insight into the problems involved. It is little wonder that so many thoughtful people have baulked at the high numbers in Exodus and Numbers. Impossible, you may think! But Wilson-Haffendon, with firsthand knowledge of the logistics involved, had no hesitation in accepting the numbers as they stand. Should not we do the same?

The problem should not be exaggerated. The Egyptians, anxious to get rid of the Israelites who had caused them so much suffering, "gave them whatever they asked for, so they plundered the Egyptians" (Exodus 12:36). The prediction that they would "come out with great possessions" was certainly fulfilled (Gen. 15:14). They would have taken with them everything they needed for the first week or so. Furthermore, it was springtime. In the spring the desert blossoms for a few weeks providing fodder for the cattle. There would also have been *rain*, water both for themselves and for their flocks.

Colin Humphreys quotes from the great Czech explorer Alois Musil. "If the Israelites migrated from Egypt in the month of March and if there had been an abundance of rain on the peninsula of Sinai that year they would have found rain pools of various sizes in all the cavities and in all the hollows of the various riverbeds, and they would comfortably have replenished their water bags and watered their flocks" (Humphreys: 233).

Later on, of course, they were amply provided for by the manna, quails, and the miraculous supply of water. But even at this stage of their journey their needs were supplied.

Humphreys is not alone in thinking that the Red Sea crossing was at the Gulf of Aqaba. This is considered impossible by Hoffmeier and others of his kind, but there is a lot of supporting evidence for this point of view as will be sketched in the next chapter. The Israelites crossed into the land of *Midian* where Moses had already spent forty years of his life. It is in that region that Mount Sinai (also called Horeb where Moses saw the burning bush, Exodus 3:1) is to be sought, not in the so-called Sinai Peninsula, its traditional location. Following ancient records and modern explorers, Humphreys has mapped out in detail their journey from Egypt to the Red Sea.

From Succoth to the head of the Gulf of Aqaba is more than 180 miles. Travelling (say) fourteen hours a day (both day and night, Exodus 13:21) at two miles per hour, they would have covered 28 miles a day. At that rate they would have reached Aqaba in 6.5 days. The complete journey from Rameses in the land of Goshen would have taken seven or eight days. With the best will in the world (and they certainly had every incentive) they cannot have travelled much faster for two reasons: first the huge numbers involved including old people and children, and secondly the "large droves of livestock, both flocks and herds" (Exodus 12:38). Flocks and herds have their own chosen pace, and it is not fast! Wilson-Haffendon says they would have travelled at *one* mile per hour! That is probably more realistic.

Objections

Hoffmeier of course will have none of this. In his view, "Not only would there be serious logistical problems for millions of people camping and moving about in Sinai, but such a horde would have created a demographic disaster departing Egypt and arriving in Canaan" (p.153).

He finds many reasons for rejecting so large a number. (1) They could not have lived within the restricted area of the northeastern Delta; (2) They would have simply overwhelmed their taskmasters! (3) Pharaoh's 600 chariots could never have succeeded against 600,000 fighting men; (4) Armies in the ancient Near East were miniscule compared with this. At Qarqar for example there were only 53,000 troops amassed against Shalmaneser III; (5) If millions had arrived in Canaan the archaeological record would attest to such an influx; (6) Several million Israelites would simply have overwhelmed the peoples of Canaan in the Late Bronze Age; (7) Jericho at its maximal size measured only the size of seven football fields. Hazor, the largest in all Canaan, occupied only 210 acres. Fortified cities such as these should not have been a serious challenge to an army of 600,000.

Hoffmeier is an acknowledged authority in the field of Egyptology and archaeology. His objections call for an informed reply by someone of equal standing and expertise. It is obvious however that the Israelites had no training in warfare. They had on the contrary the resigned slave-mentality of those who had been long maltreated and abused. They would have been no match against Pharaoh's trained cavalry and would have had little or no idea of their own potential as a fighting force.

The midwives

Another problem which is often raised in this connection is that of the midwives: according to Exodus 1:15, only two midwives sufficed for the entire people of Israel. This mention of two midwives comes at a point 135 years after their arrival in Egypt, when the population may have been in the region of 50,000. It is often averred that the presence of only two midwives presupposes a relatively small number of prospective mothers. But Keil is doubtless correct in saying that these midwives "were no doubt the heads of the whole profession, and were expected to communicate their instructions to their associates." In Egypt today, according to R.E.D. Clark, one midwife is needed for a population of 2000, and this might suggest there were 25 midwives under the overall direction of Shiphrah and Puah. But the Hebrew women were not as the Egyptian women (Exodus 2:19): it was quite usual for them to give birth before the midwife arrived. In practice they probably helped one another and only called for the midwife in difficult cases.

This selfsame day

Another indication that the Israelites spent a full 430 years in Egypt has been found in the words "this selfsame day" in Exodus 12:41. We there read: "And at the end of the 430 years, *on this selfsame day*, all the host of the Lord went out from the land of Egypt." According to R.K. Harrison, Exodus 12:41 "clearly indicates that the 'selfsame day' constituted the 430th anniversary of the time when Jacob and his family first entered Egypt, thus assuring a lengthy stay in that land." (1970: 168) If this is the meaning of the phrase it could as well indicate the 430th anniversary of the covenant made with Abraham. But in fact no such meaning is intended, for the words simply look back to verse 17 where by the same expression emphasis is laid on the first day of the feast of Unleavened Bread as being the selfsame day as the Exodus from Egypt. It is the same in verse 51 as well.

By the same reasoning one would have to conclude that the Flood began on Noah's 600th birthday. For it says in Genesis 7:11-13, "In the year 600 of Noah's life, in the second month, on the seventeenth day of the month ... *on this selfsame day* Noah and his sons ... entered the ark." But this is an unwarranted conclusion, not least because Noah's years seem to be reckoned in Genesis from the beginning of the year, as may be inferred from Genesis 8:13 where, on the new year's day, his age has gone up to 601. Similarly in Ezekiel 40:1 ("In the 25th year of our exile, at the beginning of the year, on the tenth day of the month ... on this selfsame day the hand of the Lord was upon me"), it is very doubtful whether the intended meaning is that 25 years to the day had elapsed since the beginning of the Exile. This however is the meaning imposed on it by E.R. Thiele and others. In all these places the words "on this selfsame day"(which are the same in each case) are only for emphasis, resuming and focusing attention on the day already mentioned.

The conclusion of the matter

So far we have learnt that Abraham's father, Terah, died in the year 2083, and that his death was followed by an interval of not less than five years prior to Abraham's call and departure for Canaan. This in turn preceded the Exodus by 430 years, so constituting a minimum of 2518 years from Adam to the Exodus. That is the minimum: is there any way of determining how long it really was?

I believe there is. There is a cryptic time period in the Bible known as the Times of the Gentiles, and it has long been surmised that the length of this period is 2,520 years. This much is known for certain, that the last week of years of Daniel's famous prophecy, that of the Seventy

Weeks, will consist of two half-weeks of 1,260 days, making 2,520 in all. A fulfilment in days is well established, but could there also be an application, or applications, in years? Long before the Jehovah Witnesses latched on to this idea and misapplied it in the interests of their own theory, it had been noticed by certain prophetic students that the period of Israel's servitude and exile, beginning with Nebuchadnezzar, had lasted about 2,520 years. There were in fact exactly 2,520 years from the first year of Nebuchadnezzar (604 BC) to the beginning of Israel's restoration (in 1917): 604+1917-1, there being no year zero between 1 BC and AD 1. Could there also be another application at the beginning of Bible history?

The characteristic feature of these 'times of the Gentiles' is that during them Israel is either 'off the stage' (so to speak) so far as their Divine mission is concerned, or subservient to foreign powers. They are times when the Gentiles are in control. Such a time was the period from Adam to the Exodus. For the greater part of it there was no Israel at all, and even when there was they were not an independent people. Not even Abraham had any inheritance in the land of Canaan, not even a square foot (Acts 7:5). He and his descendants were strangers and pilgrims sojourning in a land owned and occupied by Gentiles, and ultimately became slaves to a foreign power. Most definitely these were Gentile times. It is surely appropriate that they should be 2,520 years in duration.

By this the interval between the death of Terah and the call of Abraham can be confidently fixed at *seven* years. Abraham was the contemporary of Eber, his great-great-great-great-grandfather, and even Shem was still alive when Abraham was 143 years old. The epithet Hebrew (*'Ivri*) was applied to Abram (Gen. 14:13) and his descendants on account of the importance of Eber (*'Ever*), the successor of Noah and Shem, who outlived his children to the fifth generation and almost outlived Abraham himself. The following are the more important dates of the patriarchal period from the birth of Abraham onwards.

Birth of Abraham	AH 2015	
Call of Abraham	2090	(Gen. 12:4)
Birth of Isaac	2115	(Gen. 21:5)
Death of Shem	2158	
Birth of Jacob	2175	(Gen. 25:26)
Death of Eber	2187	
Death of Abraham	2190	(Gen. 25:7)
Death of Isaac	2295	(Gen. 35:28)
Descent into Egypt	2305	(Gen. 47:9)
Death of Jacob	2322	(Gen. 47:28)

Joseph was thirty years old when he stood before Pharaoh (Gen.41:46). He was 37 therefore after the seven plentiful years, and 39 when he made himself known to his brothers (Gen.45:6). Assuming it was in the same year that Jacob went down to Egypt with his family and flocks, Joseph would still have been 39 years old. Jacob was 130 when he arrived in Egypt (Gen.47:9), and so must have been 91 when Joseph was born. These are Joseph's dates:-

Birth of Joseph	2266
Death of Joseph	2376 (Gen.50:26)

Joseph was sold into Egypt at the age of 17 (Gen.37:21), in the year 2283, and he entered into Pharaoh's service at the age of 30 (41:46) - in 2296. This was one year after his grandfather Isaac had died. The descent into Egypt exactly bisects the 430 years of sojourning. There were

215 years from the call of Abraham to the descent into Egypt, and another 215 years till the Exodus.

In terms of the oral transmission of primeval knowledge, Joseph was only five mouths removed from Adam. Adam would have told Methuselah whom he knew for 243 years; Methuselah Shem whom he knew for 98 years; Shem Isaac whom he knew for 43 years; and Isaac Joseph whom he knew for 30 years. Joseph could have told Jochebed (Levi's daughter born in Egypt) or Amram (Levi's grandson), and they in turn would have told Moses their son, making Moses the seventh in oral succession. Even if one or two of these links is doubtful (Isaac - Joseph for example: perhaps we should include Jacob), it is safe to say that Moses, when writing Genesis, did not have to rely on traditional story-telling or legendary material: he had it direct from Adam himself through the medium of reliable witnesses. The early *toledoth* of Genesis were doubtless already in written form long before the time of Moses.

Summary

The first chapter of Genesis lies outside the scope of this treatise. Nevertheless, by way of introduction a few comments are offered on how it might be interpreted. From 2:4 onwards the book of Genesis consists of eleven sections beginning "These are then generations of" (or, in the case of 5:1, "This is the book of the generations of"). These were found to be headings, rather than subscripts as some have supposed.

The dates of the patriarchs, both before and after the Flood, are laid out in Genesis 5 and 11. No reason was found for preferring the figures in the Samaritan or Septuagint texts to those in the Hebrew Masoretic Text. The secondary nature of the Samaritan and LXX versions is shown up in various ways, not least the regularity of their respective schemes. Nor was there found any reason for departing from the literal, surface meaning of these chapters, in spite of assertions that they are only summaries of a much longer pre-history of mankind.

Noah was found to be a full 600 years old at the time of the Flood, not 599 as Genesis 6:11 appears to state in our versions. The Flood-year itself is reckoned in terms of luni-solar months of 30 days each.

Abraham was born in Ur of the Chaldees, but where should we look for this place? More probably it was situated in Armenia, in the vicinity of Mount Ararat than in southern Babylonia where it is usually located. More important than where Abraham was born is *when* he was born. Rulers of God's people in the Bible appear in multiples of seven. Noah was eighth in a series according to 2 Peter 2:5, but his predecessor, Methuselah, died in the year of the Flood. There were therefore *seven* antediluvian patriarchs in succession. It was noted that the rulers of God's people in the Old Testament occur in multiples of seven: 14 judges, 21 kings of Israel and 21 kings of Judah. There were also seven postdiluvian patriarchs, but only on the assumption that a short interval ensued between the death of Terah and the call of Abraham. For Abraham to outlive Eber this interval must have been at least five years.

The next link in the chain is the 430 years of Exodus 12:40. The traditional understanding, based on Galatians 3:17, that this period is reckoned from the call of Abraham when he was 75 years old, was found to accord best with the evidence. There were 215 from this point to their going down to Egypt and another 215 years to the Exodus. The 400 years of Genesis 15:13 is probably reckoned from Isaac's weaning in Genesis 21, assuming he was five years old at this time.

The shorter chronology, here presupposed, is confirmed by the reference to the fourth generation in Genesis 15:16 ("they shall come back here in the fourth generation"). It is also confirmed by the genealogies of specific families, notably that of Moses. Moses' mother was the daughter of Levi, born to him in his old age in Egypt (Num. 26:59). That would not have been possible if they had stayed more than 215 years in Egypt.

The promise of rapid growth is fully confirmed by the census totals give in Numbers 1. These presuppose a population of about two million by the time of the Exodus. Jacob who had eleven sons in only seven years is himself a good example of rapid growth. Joshua and Judah are other examples. The view that Jacob married both his wives at the beginning of his 14-year service is not supported by Genesis 29:20-21.

There is however a problem with Judah. Judah was Jacob's fourth son born to him after he had been with Laban for eleven years. That being the case, there is no time for his son Perez to have had children of his own before the descent into Egypt as implied in Genesis 46:12. This leads to the unexpected conclusion that Perez' sons, Hezron and Hamul, were actually born some years later in Egypt. They are included in Genesis 46 only because Hezron was the ancestor of David and Christ.

There are three figures given for those who went down to Egypt, 66, 70 and 75 (Acts 7:14). The 66 were those who went down to Egypt not including Jacob himself and his sons' wives (Gen.46:26). The 70 included Jacob, Joseph and his two sons (46:27). The 75 included also his kindred, namely the son's wives, excluding probably Hezron and Hamul who were not even born at this stage. The Septuagint text has 75 as well, but this text is so confused that it cannot seriously be considered the source of Stephen's inspired statement.

Various objections to the large numbers in Numbers 1 and 26 were considered next. The attempt by Colin J. Humphreys and others to cut the numbers down to size was found to be misconceived. Likewise objections arising from the fact there were too few midwives and firstborn to suit such a large population were easily answered. The logistical problem of deploying and supplying such a huge multitude is a more serious consideration. But even this has been exaggerated. They would have taken with them enough provisions for the first week or so, and being March or April, there would have been enough surface water to satisfy their immediate needs and to water their cattle.

The final consideration is the total number of years from Adam to the Exodus. A minimum of 2518 is required to allow Abraham to outlive Eber. The actual number was, we believe, 2520 this being the number of the Times of the Gentiles. This number tends to appear when Israel is out of the land or subservient to foreign powers. Abraham left Haran "after the death of his father" (Acts 7:4). It was not however immediately after the death of his father, but after an interval of seven years. Why did Abraham have to wait so long in Haran? The answer is he was awaiting further instructions from the Lord. In Mesopotamia he had been told to leave his native land but not his final destination (Acts 7:3). After seven years in Haran he was directed to travel on to Canaan (Gen. 12:1-5).

Chapter Two

From the Exodus to the Temple

The total for this period, from the Exodus to the foundation of Solomon's Temple, is given in 1 Kings 6:1. It was 480 years. In our versions it is translated 480th, a total of 479 years. But it seems probable, as I have already had occasion to mention, that in line with Genesis 7:11 and 8:13 a full 480 years is intended. If that is the case, there were exactly three thousand years (2520+480) from the creation of Adam to the foundation of the Temple. Seeing that the total is given, it should not be too difficult to fit together the pieces of the jigsaw which are scattered over the intervening period.

The 480 years: an exact datum

Before embarking on this task, a few remarks may be in order in defence of the plain grammatical meaning of 1 Kings 6:1. This verse is of fundamental importance to the pursuit of a truly biblical chronology, and perhaps for that reason it has been assailed from so many quarters. For many a literal 480 years has seemed to imply too long a period for archaeological convenience. It puts the Exodus and the conquest of Canaan in the fifteenth century BC and this is far too early for conventional archaeology. The view is commonly held that the number 480 is an artificial combination of twelve forties, representing twelve generations of 40 years. Some have derived this from the succession of high priests in 1 Chronicles 6:3-10, others from the succession of Judges in combination with Moses, Saul and David, or in some other way. The basic assumption is that the revealed chronology of the Bible is artificial and worthless.

Kenneth Kitchen has "two equally workable options for the origin of 480 years." "First, it could be an era date made up of twelve 40-year 'full generations,' such as 12 x 40 = 480 ... Or else, second, the 480 years are in fact a selection from the 554 + xyz years aggregate, on some principle not stated" (2003: 307 f.). He seems to prefer the second option, but either way the net result (which is all that concerns him) is that the 480 years are an artificial invention, the true figure being more in the region of 300 years. His method is typical of modern evangelical scholarship: whenever there is a conflict between the Bible and archaeology it is always the Bible which has to be adjusted. But Kitchen is driven by a particular view of Near Eastern chronology of which he himself is the main architect. It is this chronology which is seriously flawed as writers such as David Rohl and Roger Henry have been at pains to point out.

There is nothing in the Bible to suggest that the 480 years are too long for the period in question. The high-priestly succession agrees perfectly with this figure. Only the genealogy of David is too short to cover the allotted time (Ruth 4:18-22). David is here in the fifth generation from Nahshon, who was a man of prestige at the time of the Exodus (Numbers 1:7). Clearly some names have been omitted in David's ancestry. At least one writer, D.A. Courville, has thought it probable that some names are omitted between Salmon and Boaz. But this is unlikely in view of Matthew 1:5, "And Salmon begat Boaz by Rahab". More probably some names are omitted between Obed and Jesse. Obed was remembered as the son of Boaz and Ruth (Ruth 4:17), Jesse as the father of David, but the intervening generations were forgotten.

There is of course nothing unusual about names being omitted from biblical genealogies. The high-priestly succession is itself abbreviated in Ezra 7 where six generations are omitted between Azariah and Meraioth (cp. 1 Chron. 6:7-10). The reason in this case is that only those men of Ezra's forebears who possessed the high priesthood are recorded, the rest being omitted. Again, all three groups of fourteen names in Matthew 1 are incomplete. In the first group (as we have just seen) some four to seven names are omitted between Obed and Jesse. In the second group three kings - Ahaziah, Joash and Amaziah - are omitted between Joram and Uzziah, and also

Jehoiakim between Josiah and Jechoniah. In the third group at least one name is omitted, namely Assir who according to 1 Chronicles 3:17 was the son of Jehoiachin (=Jechoniah) and the father of Shealtiel. His name was omitted in obedience to the Lord's command to Jeremiah, "Write this man childless!" (Jer. 22:30). It is likely that Assir is not the only omission since the parallel genealogy in Luke has 22 names between Shealtiel and Christ as opposed to 13 in Matthew. The fact that David has no genealogy in the short term serves to underline his humble origin which is implied in the Bible (2 Sam.7:8; Psalm 78:70-71).

The date of the Exodus

Happily the shorter chronology is now in retreat as scholars in increasing numbers find that a fifteenth century Exodus accords with the evidence far better than a thirteenth century Exodus. Notable among these is David Rohl in his ground-breaking work on Egyptian chronology *A Test of Time: The Bible - From Myth to History* (1995). His may not be the last word on the subject, but he does point the way toward a solution which confirms the Bible record rather than undermines it. For example on the subject of Jericho he says, "In the late 1950s there was only one conclusion which could be drawn from Kenyon's discovery: the story of Joshua's conquest of Jericho had to be a myth" (p.302). And it was not only Jericho: archaeology simply was not confirming anything from Israel's early history.

On the basis of Rohl's "new chronology" the situation is radically changed. Almost every event in Israel's early (and not so early) history is remarkably confirmed and illustrated by archaeological discovery. The remains of Middle Bronze Age Jericho provides all the evidence we could wish that the walls of Jericho came tumblin' down. Rohl notes that "In the trench at the foot of the mound Kenyon found a thick deposit of red-brown earth which she interpreted as the remains of the great MB city wall which had collapsed outwards and fallen down into the defensive ditch. The walls of MBA Jericho had indeed tumbled down ..." (p.303-4). Further-more, "Within the MBA city itself all the houses and civic buildings had been blackened by a severe conflagration. In some places the ash and debris was a metre in depth." Compare Joshua 6:24. In fact, all the key sites: Jericho, Debir, Lachish, Gezer, Bethel, Gibeon, Shechem, and Hazor all suffered destruction by fire in the Middle Bronze Age.

Rohl's work has been carried further by Roger Henry in *Synchronized Chronology: Rethinking Middle East Antiquity* (2002). By a simple, though radical, correction of Egyptian chronology Henry resolves the major problems in Biblical and Greek archaeology. His position is different from Rohl's and probably nearer the truth. Here at least is the promise of a more fruitful approach to ancient history, one which confirms rather than undermines the truth of the Bible. The opportunity is now present to place Israel and the Bible in the mainstream of Near Eastern history to a degree never before achieved.

The route of the Exodus

The crossing of the Red Sea and the site of Mount Sinai are topics which invite caution rather than positive assertion. They have become highly emotive subjects that have provoked very different reactions. The Red Sea is actually the *Reed* Sea in the Hebrew (*Yam Suph*). Most scholars today believe that the Israelites crossed the Re(e)d Sea in the vicinity of the Bitter Lakes north of the Gulf of Suez. According to Hoffmeier the crossing most probably took place at the el-Ballah lakes some 40 km east of the Rameses region. Here there are plenty of reeds on the banks of the lakes whereas in the Red Sea proper (whether Suez or Aqaba) there are no reeds at all to speak of. As for Mount Sinai, for Hoffmeier this is most suitably identified with Jebel Safsafeh in southern Sinai. The er-Rahah plain on the north-west side of Safsafeh occupies one square mile. This he thinks is where the Israelites camped. Seeing however that an area of 500 square miles would have been needed to accommodate the Israelite horde, the er-Rahah plain is clearly inadequate and Safsafeh can be ruled out.

Most scholars would agree that Mount Sinai is to be looked for somewhere in the Sinai Peninsula. There is however an alternative view which has attracted enthusiastic support. It is that the Israelites crossed the Red Sea at the Gulf of Aqaba. This idea has been attractively argued by Colin Humphreys, a distinguished scientist and mathematician from Cambridge University. His book (2003) makes fascinating reading, but in the view of Hoffmeier he "merely demonstrates that a natural scientist, no matter how brilliant, lacks the tools essential for this type of research" (p.136).

Humphreys thinks the Israelites crossed the Gulf of Aqaba at the top end of the Gulf where in fact reeds can still be found. Others, Bob Cornuke in particular, have opted for the southern end near the Strait of Tiran. But the view which has most to commend it is that they crossed at the plain of Nuweiba, 70 km (44 miles) south of Eilat. This they entered through the Wadi Watir which is the only landward entrance to the plain of Nuweiba. Here there is an underwater bridge across the sea where divers have recovered coral-encrusted artefacts such as chariot-wheels and bones. Mount Sinai is to be identified, they think, with the black-topped Jabel al-Lawz, the Almond Mountain, rather than Mount Bedr further south preferred by Humphreys. This is the view of Jonathan Gray and Lennart Moeller (2002), basing their work on the discoveries made by Ronald E. Wyatt between 1978 and 1984.

There are many arguments which tend to support this point of view, but they are not conclusive. For one thing Mount Sinai was situated at Horeb (Deut. 5:2; 1 Kings 5:19; Psalm 106:19), but it was also at Horeb, the mountain of God, that Moses saw the burning bush when tending the flock of his father-in-law, the priest of Midian (Exod. 3:1). Midian was situated on the far side of the Gulf of Aqaba, but Hoffmeier thinks that the Midianites, being a nomadic people, may well have grazed their flocks in nearby Sinai as well in their endless search for pastures green. For another thing, *Yam Suph*, the Sea of Reeds, refers to Aqaba in 1 Kings 9:26 and Jeremiah 49:21, but in Exodus 10:19 it more probably refers to the Gulf of Suez. Yet again, in Galatians 4:25 Mount Sinai is located in Arabia by Paul. But there is evidence that Arabia in Graeco-Roman times was applied to Sinai as well and even the land of Goshen. This can be seen in the Septuagint rendering of Genesis 46:34 where the land of Goshen is located in Arabia.

There are therefore arguments both for and against. In my view there is a lot to be said for the Humphreys-Gray-Moeller version of events and I would heartily recommend their respective presentations.

Two men who actually made it to the top of Jabal al-Lawz are Larry Williams and Bob Cornuke. Convinced that this is the true Mount Sinai and lured by the prospect of gold, Williams and Cornuke entered Saudi Arabia on forged passports. Jabal al-Lawz they found heavily guarded, but evading the Saudi guards, they crawled under the perimeter fence and climbed to the top. There, however, they found not gold, but a top secret Saudi military base! Two huge radars on the summit were aimed toward Israel. If the orders were given to attack Israel, the operation would be coordinated from Jabal-al-Lawz where, once before, God had vowed destruction on those who broke His commandments! The thrilling story of these two adventurers is told by Howard Blum in *The Gold of Exodus: The Discovery of the True Mount Sinai*, New York 1998.

Moses and Aaron: their ages and death

When Moses and Aaron confronted Pharaoh with their petition they were 80 and 83 years old respectively (Exodus 7:7). Furthermore, both of them died in the fortieth year after the Exodus. Aaron died on the first day of the fifth month at the age of 123 (Num. 33:38-39), and Moses about the end of the eleventh month at the age of 120 (Deut. 1:3; 34:5-8). Their sister Miriam died in the first month of the same year, shortly before Aaron (Num. 20:1,28). She was ten or twelve years older than Moses (Exodus 2:4-8), so 130 or more when she died.

From the fact that Moses was 80 in the year before the Exodus and 120 in the year before the entry into Canaan, it might seem safe to conclude that he was 81 when he led the nation out of Egypt. At this juncture, however, there was a change of calendar. Prior to the Exodus the calendar year had begun at Tishri in the autumn, but it was now changed to Nisan in the spring. Moses is told, "This month shall be unto you the beginning of months: it shall be the first month of the year to you" (Exodus 12:2). Hence the calendar year preceding the Exodus was only six months long, Tishri to Adar, 2519, and Moses would still have been eighty years old for a further six months - until Tishri 2520. I conclude therefore that Moses was still 80 years old at the time of the Exodus and his brother Aaron 83.

Moses was born in 2439. He fled to Midian in 2479 when he was 40 years old (Acts 7:23). He was 80 years old in 2519/20 when he remonstrated with Pharaoh and led the nation out of Egypt. And he died in 2559 a few weeks before the close of the year at the age of 120.

The division of the Land

The duration of the Conquest is usually given as seven years, but in fact it was probably little more than six. The spies were sent out from Kadesh-barnea in the second year after the Exodus (Num. 10:11; 13:17-25), at which time Caleb tell us he was 40 years old (Joshua 14:7). The time of year was the late summer, the time of ripening of pomegranates, figs and grapes which they found in abundance in the Valley of Eshcol. From the time the Israelites left Kadesh-barnea till their crossing the brook Zered was 38 years (Deut. 2:14). They crossed the Zered brook shortly before defeating Sihon king of the Amorites and Og king of Bashan, camping in the Zered Valley before moving on to the Arnon river (Num. 21:12-35). And this took place before the close of the fortieth year after the Exodus (Deut. 1:3).

By this time, the fortieth year, Caleb would have been 78 years old (40+38). He was, he says, 85 when he made his bid for the hill country of Hebron, and that was 45 years since Moses had sent him from Kadesh-barnea (Joshua 14:10). It was therefore in the forty-seventh year after the Exodus that the Land was divided up. Hence the Conquest took six calendar years, not seven, and the Division of the Land was in AH 2566.

	Yrs of Exodus	Caleb's age	References
Spies sent out:	2nd	40	Num. 10:11;13:17-25 Joshua 14:7
Brook Zered crossed:	40th	78	Deut. 1:3; 2:14
The land conquered:	47th	85	Joshua 14:10

The 450 years of Acts 13:20

In the *KJV*, which is still preferred by a minority of scholars, these 450 years are linked to the period of the Judges. "And when he had destroyed seven nations in the land of Chanaan, he divided their land to them by lot. And after that He gave unto them judges about the space of 450 years, until Samuel the prophet."

However, the textual evidence is heavily weighted against this reading, and the chronological evidence is equally opposed to it. If there were 480 years from the Exodus to the Temple, the period of the Judges "until Samuel the prophet" cannot have been much more than 300 years. There were in fact 350 years between the division of the Land and the accession of Saul.

Chronologists of the old school such as Martin Anstey give rein to their ingenuity and fantasy in solving this problem on the basis of the traditional translation. They came up with the idea that in addition to straight *Anno Mundi* reckoning there is also what they were pleased to call *Anno Dei* reckoning, according to which all the *Lo-Ammi*, or "Not-my-people", periods are deducted from the total amount. It is claimed that all the years of servitude in the book of Judges are passed over in the Anno Dei reckoning of 1 Kings 6:1, and that if they are added to it no contradiction with Acts 13:20 remains.

Anstey observed that the sum of all the periods in Judges, servitudes as well as judgeships, together with the 40 years ascribed to Eli in 1 Samuel 4:18, comes to exactly 450 years. This to him was more than a coincidence and must account for the 450 years in Acts. However, in place of Samson's 20 year judgeship (which he recognised as falling within the Philistine oppression) he includes Samuel, to whom he ascribes the same number of years. If to these 450 years are added 40 for the wilderness, 7 for the conquest, a conjectured 13 for the interval between the division of the Land and the first servitude, 40 for Saul, 40 for David, and 4 for Solomon, a total of 594 years is arrived at for the period from the Exodus to the foundation of the Temple. Deduct from this 111 years for the six oppressions and 3 for the usurper Abimelech, and the 480 years of 1 Kings 6:1 is precisely what is left! (Anstey: 159)

In this way, with minor variations, Anstey, Anderson and others solved the problem of the 450 years of Acts 13:20, at the same time adding 114 years to the true *Anno Hominis* dating and pushing back the Exodus by that number of years. It is certainly a coincidence that the sum total of the various time-notes in Judges should come to exactly 450 years, but this coincidence should not be allowed to obscure the undoubted fact that this type of solution is totally unacceptable. At all costs the 480 years of 1 Kings 6:1 must be allowed to stand without addition or diminution. The books of Samuel and Kings are straightforward historical accounts and on them we rely for the continuation of the chronology. We must therefore reject any impairment of 1 Kings 6:1, whether it be the critical theory of twelve generations or the uncritical theory of Anno Dei reckoning.

How then do we understand the 450 years of Acts 13:20? This is how the *NIV* translates verses 17 to 20: "The God of the people of Israel chose our fathers; he made the people prosper during their stay in Egypt, with mighty power he led them out of that country, he endured their conduct for about 40 years in the desert, he overthrew seven nations in Canaan and gave their land to his people as their inheritance. All this took about 450 years. After this, God gave them judges until the time of Samuel the prophet ..."

First let it be noted that the words "450 years" are in the dative case. This is in marked contrast with the two references to 40 years in verses 18 and 21 which are both in the accusative case. "The dative implies point of time, not duration" (F.F. Bruce). It implies that 450 years had already elapsed at the division of the Land, commencing presumably with the choice of the fathers, the first event mentioned in the apostle's address. The 450 years are generally explained as comprising the 400 years of sojourning (cp. Acts 7:6), the 40 years in the wilderness, and the 6 years of conquest. These 446 years are considered near enough to 450 to satisfy the words "about 450 years".

To this it may be objected that it was Luke's habitual practice to qualify exact numbers by *hos* or *hosei*, as for example in verse 18, "And for *about* 40 years he bore with them in the wilderness." It was in fact 40 years almost to the day. In order to make up the deficiency of four years we may be justified in including the indefinite period subsequent to the division of the Land, terminating with the attainment of rest as mentioned in Joshua 23:1. The expression "after many days" in that verse does not necessarily indicate an interval of more than four years. In 1 Kings 2:38f. and 18:1 it is used of periods defined as of only three years' duration. That the interval in reality was not very long is suggested by the fact that Joshua was already "old and advanced in years" at the termination of the war (Joshua 13:1). Precisely the same words are used of him in Joshua 23:1.

The Book of Judges

The time has now come to turn to the book of Judges and to weigh up the internal dating of that book. This from one point of view is a work of supererogation since we already know how many years there were between the Exodus and the foundation of Solomon's Temple. We also know that Saul and David both reigned for forty years (Acts 13:21; 2 Sam. 5:4). It is therefore the interrelation of the Judges themselves which needs to be sorted out.

Between the division of the Land and the accession of Saul there were 350 years, but the time-notes for the same period in Judges and 1 Samuel come to 450, and that is not counting the interval before the first judge. Clearly some of the judges must have been contemporaries. Can we be sure which they were, when and where they judged, and the precise dates of each and every one? I believe we can, simply by noting carefully what is written.

The structure of the book of Judges is a useful guide as to its contents and a pointer to its true chronology. The book consists of ten clearly defined sections, of which the central six commence with the same formula: "And the children of Israel (again) did evil in the sight of the Lord." It is the absence of the word "again" in the first and fourth sections which is the key to the structure. By this we know that these six sections are divided into two groups of three. Unfortunately, this is spoilt in the *NIV* which adds "again" to Judges 6:1 without any justification whatsoever. This mistake is corrected in *Today's NIV*. The structure is as follows:-

> A. 1:1-2:5 Conquest and failure
> > B. 2:6-3:6 Disobedience
> > > C. 3:7-11 Othniel: 40 years
> > > > D. 3:12-31 Ehud: "again"
> > > > > E. 4:1-5:31 Barak: "again"
> > > C. 6:1-10:5 Gideon: 40 years
> > > > D. 10:6-12:15 Jephthah: "again"
> > > > > E. 13:1-16:31 Samson: "again"
> A. 17:1-18:31 Conquest and lawlessness
> > B. 19:1-21:25 Disobedience

The first two sections are united by the references to Joshua's death (1:1; 2:8), and the last two by references to Moses' and Aaron's grandsons, "Jonathan the son of Gershom the son of Moses" (18:30) and "Phinehas the son of Eleazar the son of Aaron" (20:28). These indicate that all four sections belong to the same early days soon after the death of Joshua. The last two sections are also brought together by the statement, twice repeated in each section, that "In those days there was no king in Israel" (17:6; 18:1; 19:1; 21:25).

It is however the central six sections in which we are chiefly interested at the moment. These are also brought together by striking parallels between them. Only Othniel and Gideon judged Israel for 40 years. There were also 40 years of peace following Barak's victory (5:31), but Barak himself is not associated with them. Ehud and Jephthah were both raised up after 18 years of servitude to the brother nations Moab (3:14 f.) and Ammon (10:8; 11:5). Finally Barak and Samson are associated by the part played by women in their careers. Barak was victorious with the aid of two women, Deborah and Jael; Samson was overcome through the guile of two women, the woman of Timnath and Delilah. By these parallels the structure is confirmed.

Major and Minor Judges

There have been more than one opinion expressed on the identity of the Judges and which ones were Major and which ones Minor. I have already expressed my own view that there were 14 judges, seven major and seven minor. Leon Wood agrees with the number 14, but he plumps for Deborah instead of Barak, and Eli he would reckon as a major judge rather than a minor judge (1975: 7-9). He has therefore eight major judges and six minor. His reasons for preferring Deborah to Barak are as follows.

First, the verb *shaphat*, to judge, is used of Deborah (4:4) but not of Barak. Second, Deborah was undoubtedly the dominant figure, far more so than Barak who simply did what he was told. Third, there could be only one judge at a time and Deborah takes the lead.

My own reasons for preferring Barak are as follows. (1) The chief function of the judge was to save the nation from the grip of their oppressors (2:16), and by "save" is meant defeat them in military combat. On this occasion it was Barak whom the Lord used to rout Sisera and his army (4:15). (2) Deborah played no part in this deliverance. Her role was that of a prophetess, to direct Barak in the name of the Lord to go against Sisera with ten thousand men. (3) It was no credit to Barak that he was so reliant on women, Deborah and Jael, as the Bible makes clear (4:9). He was nevertheless the saviour of the nation from oppression on this occasion. (4) According to Judges 2:18, "Whenever the Lord raised up a judge for them, he was with the judge and saved them out of the hands of their enemies as long as the judge lived." There is no word to the effect that the Lord raised up Deborah. So far from delivering Israel, she was simply adjudicating them in a purely civil capacity all the while the Canaanite oppression was going on. (5) Deborah was a woman. There are not a few dominant women in the Bible, but none of them was divinely appointed leader of God's people.

Turning now to Eli, should he be reckoned as a major Judge or a minor one? The Bible does not distinguish between major and minor Judges, not at least in so many words, so possibly the question should not be asked at all. It is nevertheless a fact that some judges are obviously more important than others, so it is legitimate to ask to which category Eli belongs. Leon Wood gives two reasons for including him with the major Judges: his importance in Israel's history and the amount of space devoted to him. Three verses is the maximum devoted to any other minor Judge (12:8-10).

On the other hand, Eli accomplished no deliverance. In virtue of his position as high priest he performed the civil duties of the judge, but he was powerless to throw off the yoke of the Philistines. Their unwelcome interference became even more oppressive during his term of office and ended in disaster. It was Samuel who by his prayers and moral leadership broke the power of the Philistines (1 Samuel 7). The prominence given to Eli was chiefly in connection with Samuel. His importance lay in the upbringing of Samuel, not in his own role as judge. He is rightly numbered with the minor Judges, not least because he did not have the qualification of a major Judge, that of saving the nation from their oppressors.

There were therefore seven major Judges: Othniel, Ehud, Barak, Gideon, Jephthah, Samson, and Samuel. And seven minor Judges: Shamgar, Tola, Jair, Ibzan, Elon, Abdon, and Eli.

First proposition: the time of Samson's birth

The chronology will be considered by means of seven propositions. Having worked out a scheme which met with my own satisfaction, I was interested to discover that Keil and Delitzsch in their historic commentary have anticipated most of my conclusions. I have all the more confidence on this account that our reconstruction of events is indeed the right and scriptural one. The volume on Judges is written by Keil.

The first proposition is that Samson was born after the beginning of the Philistine servitude. This is proved by the words of the angel to his mother before Samson was conceived: "Lo, thou shalt conceive, and bear a son ... and he shall begin to deliver Israel out of the hand of the Philistines" (Judges 13:5 *KJV*). If the servitude had not already begun, these words would have conveyed no meaning to her. He judged Israel for twenty years (15:20; 16:31), and the servitude lasted forty years (13:1). These figures go to show that Samson judged Israel during the second half of the Philistine oppression.

Second proposition: the end of the Philistine oppression

It is proposed secondly that the Philistine oppression did not come to an end until after their defeat at Ebenezer under the inspired leadership of Samuel (1 Samuel 7). That the servitude was still in progress is made abundantly clear in the early chapters of 1 Samuel. It follows from this that Samson must have died before the end of the servitude, as may be deduced from Judges 15:20, "And he judged Israel *in the days of* the Philistines twenty years", and Judges 13:5, "He shall *begin* to deliver Israel out of the hand of the Philistines." With this Keil agrees:

> At the death of Samson, with which the book of Judges closes,the power of the Philistines was not yet broken; and in chap. 4 of the first book of Samuel we find the Philistines still fighting against the Israelites, and that with such success that the Israelites were defeated by them, and even lost the ark of the covenant. This war must certainly be a continuation of the Philistine oppression, to which the acts of Samson belonged, since the termination of that oppression is not mentioned in the book of Judges; and on the other hand, the commencement of oppression referred to in 1 Sam. 4:9 sqq. is not given in the book of Samuel. Consequently even Hitzig supports the view which I have expressed, that the forty years' supremacy of the Philistines, noticed in Judges 13:1, is carried on into the book of Samuel, and extends to 1 Sam. 7:3,7, and that it was through Samuel that it was eventually brought to a termination (Keil: 282).

Third proposition: Samson's judgeship

The battle of Ebenezer was preceded by a period of twenty years during which the ark remained at Kiriath Jearim (1 Sam. 7:2). Our third proposition is that this period corresponds to Samson's judgeship. This is an obvious deduction from the first two propositions, and it is confirmed by Keil who says, "After the death of Eli, Israel continued for more than twenty years utterly prostrate under the yoke of the Philistines. It was during this period that Samson made the Philistines feel the power of the God of Israel, though he could not deliver the Israelites entirely from their oppression" (p.282).

Thus far Leon Wood is in agreement with our findings. Samson's judgeship, he says, "is best placed between the battle of Aphek (1 Sam. 4:1-11) and the battle of Mizpeh, these battles being just twenty years apart (1 Sam. 7:2)" (p.14).

Fourth proposition: the Philistine and Ammonite servitudes

Our fourth proposition is that the Philistine and Ammonite servitudes began in the same year. This is clearly stated in Judges 10:7-8: "And the anger of the Lord was hot against Israel, and he sold them into the hands of the Philistines, and into the hands of the children of Ammon. And *that year* they vexed and oppressed the children of Israel." Clearly it was in the same year that these two nations vexed and oppressed Israel, though consideration of the Philistine oppression is postponed until Judges 13. The intervening material (10:8b-12:15) deals exclusively with the

Ammonite oppression on the east of the Jordan, from which Jephthah was the deliverer. Keil takes the same view:

> The [Philistine] oppression itself, therefore, commenced at the same time as that of the Ammonites, and continued side by side with it; but it lasted much longer, and did not come to an end till a short time before the death of Elon the judge. This is confirmed beyond all doubt by the fact, that although the Ammonites crossed the Jordan to fight against Judah, Benjamin, and Ephraim, it was chiefly the tribes of Israel who dwelt on the other side of the Jordan that were oppressed by them (chap. 10:8,9), and it was only by these tribes that Jephthah was summoned to make war upon them, and was elected as their head and prince (chap. 11:5-11), and also that it was only the Ammonites in the country to the east of the Jordan whom he subdued then before the Israelites (chap. 11:32,33). From this it is very evident that Jephthah, and his successors Ibzan, Elon and Abdon, were not judges over all Israel, and neither fought against the Philistines nor delivered Israel from the oppression of those enemies who invaded the land from the south-west; so that the omission of the expression, "the land had rest" etc., from chap. 11 and 12, is very significant (280 f.).

Fifth proposition: Eli's judgeship

The next proposition (the fifth) completes the interlocking with 1 Samuel. It is that Eli's 40 years (1 Sam. 4:18) were co-extensive with the 22 years of Jair the Gileadite (10:3), followed by the 18 years of the Ammonite oppression (10:8). As we have seen, Eli's judgeship closely preceded Samson's. After Eli's death there was an interval of about seven months (1 Sam. 6:1) before the ark was returned to Kiriath Jearim, where it stayed 20 years (7:2). It was during these 20 years that Samson judged. If Samson judged during the second half of the Philistine oppression, Eli must have judged during the first half, and that was concurrent with the Ammonite oppression. With this also Keil is in agreement:

> Since Eli died in consequence of the account of the capture of the ark by the Philistines (1 Sam. 4:18), and seven months (1 Sam. 6:1) and twenty years elapsed after this catastrophe before the Philistines were defeated and humiliated by Samuel (1 Sam. 7:2), only the last half of the forty years of Eli's judicial life falls within the forty years of the Philistine rule over Israel, whilst the first half coincides with the time of the judge Jair (282).

It is important to notice that Jair was a Gileadite (Judges 10:3), a man who lived on the east of the river Jordan. This shows that on the death of Tola (10:1-2) the judgeship divided, and from that point forward (till its reunification under Samuel) there were two series of judges, one in the east (though later crossing the Jordan and establishing itself among the northern tribes, 12:8-15) and the other in the west. On the one hand there were in the east Jair, Jephthah, Ibzan, Elon and Abdon; on the other hand Eli, Samson and Samuel in the west. The reunification occurred after Samuel had judged nine years. A diagram may help to clarify this period:

```
East:          Jair 22   |Ammon 18 | Jephthah + 31   |

                         |Philistines 40          |

West:  Tola 23| Eli 40              |Samson 20| Samuel                    |
```

The events from Tola to Samuel may be reconstructed as follows. On the death of Tola there was trouble in Transjordan. To meet this threat a Gileadite by the name of Jair was chosen as his successor. In the absence of a judge in the west Eli, in virtue of his position as high priest, assumed as well the civil duties of the judge. This state of affairs continued for 22 years (10:3), but on the death of Jair the Ammonites overran Transjordan, and in the same year the Philistines, taking advantage of the distress caused by the Ammonites, invaded Israel from the west (10:7; 13:1). For the next eighteen years, during the two oppressions, Eli continued to judge, and eventually died after the disastrous battle of Aphek, in which the ark of the Lord was captured by the Philistines (1 Sam. 4). Acting again in concert with the Philistines, the Ammonites took advantage of their suzerainty in Transjordan to make war on Israel (Judges 11:4). The elders of Gilead were reduced to fetching their bastard brother Jephthah from the land of Tob, and it was he who finally subdued the Ammonites (11:5,6).

In the meantime Samson was earning the status of judge in the west by dint of his savage exploits against the Philistines. After the death of Eli 22 years of the Philistine oppression still remained, but only seven months (1 Sam. 6:1) and twenty years (7:2) are actually mentioned. Samuel told them to get rid of all their foreign gods and Ashtoreths and to commit themselves wholly to the Lord. And this they did, but it must have taken them a year to eighteen months (7:3-4). When the people were ready in heart and mind the climate was right for the great victory which followed (7:10-13). This was brought about by Samuel, who continued to judge only part of Israel for the next nine years, until the death of Abdon (Judges 12:15). The word "judge" is first used of Samuel in 1 Samuel 7:6, "And Samuel judged the people of Israel at Mizpah", and he continued to judge Israel "all the days of his life" (v.15).

In this reconstruction we part company with Keil. In his view, Jair's predecessors, Tola, Abimelech and Gideon, were rulers of "only the northern and possibly also the eastern tribes, to the exclusion of Judah, Simeon, and Benjamin, as these southern tribes neither took part in Gideon's war of freedom nor stood under Abimelech's rule" (p.371). But if that was the case, there was no judge at all over the southern tribes in the years preceding Jair, and when it says "The Land had rest" in Judges 8:28 (as in 5:31; 3:11 and 30) only a part of the Land is meant, not the whole promised land as I believe to be its true significance. I would agree however that Gideon through to Jephthah and his successors form an unbroken series and that their support came chiefly from the more northern tribes.

Sixth proposition: Jephthah's 300 years

My sixth proposition is that the overall chronology of the judges is clamped down by the 300 years of Judges 11:26. The reference is part, an important part, of Jephthah's reply to the king of Ammon who was intent on attacking Israelite territory to the east of the Jordan. The reason given by the king of Ammon for attacking Israel was that Israel, when they came out of Egypt, had seized his land from the Arnon to the Jabbok. Jephthah replied that this allegation was untrue. Israel had taken the land from Sihon king of the Amorites when Sihon had attacked them without cause. In any case that was 300 years ago. If their grievance was so pressing, why had they done nothing about it for so long?

It may be justly argued that this is only an approximate figure and that it would be wrong to regard it as the exact number of years from the defeat of Sihon in the fortieth year of the Exodus (Num. 21:25 f.; Deut.1:3 f.). In the view of Professor Kitchen, "it is fatuous to use this as a serious chronological datum" (2003: 308). "What we have is nothing more than the report of a brave but ignorant man's bold bluster in favor of his people" (p.209). This is simply another example of Kitchen's low opinion of the Bible's reliability on matters chronological. His real reason for rejecting these 300 years is that they do not comply with his scheme of chronology. They have therefore to be explained away in the same way as the 480 years of 1 Kings 6:1.

We have however no alternative in this instance. If we do not treat it as an exact number there is no way of anchoring the chronology of this period. It would be left for ever shunting between the two buffers, the division of the Land at one end and the accession of Saul at the other. If however we understand it to be a precise datum, we can at least give exact dates for all the judges and the intervening oppressions. Hence this is what we shall do.

The events described took place in the fortieth year of the Exodus. There were therefore 339 years from the Exodus to the first year of Jephthah. This leaves 141 years from Jephthah to the foundation of the Temple (cf. 1 Kings 6:1), and 57 years from Jephthah to the accession of Saul. This means that Samuel's judgeship had continued for 35 years by the time of Saul's accession and for about 70 years by the time of his death (1 Sam. 7:15; 25:1).

Seventh proposition: two periods of rest concurrent

For the main period of the Judges, from the division of the Land to the rise of Jephthah, there remain 293 years (from 300 deduct one for the wilderness and six for the conquest). But the sum total of judges and servitudes down to this point is 319, and that is allowing for no interval between the division of the Land and the first servitude. Clearly there are still too many years. Can we find a solution to this problem?

A possible solution is to suppose that Jephthah's 300 years is a round number and that in reality it was more in the region of 330 years. On this basis we could add 30 years to our 293, bringing it up to 323. In that case there would have been an interval of four years before the first oppression. That, however, is far too short. We know from Judges 2:10-13 that before the people began to behave wickedly and to worship the Baals, that whole generation had died and a new one had arisen. At least twenty years is implied. At the other end of the scale Samuel would have judged only five years before the accession of Saul. Samuel, however, was already an old man when Saul became king (1 Sam. 8:1). If he was 25 when Eli died, he would not have been much more than 50 by this time - hardly an old man. Moreover Abdon, the last judge in the north, would have been still alive and co-ruled with Saul for four years, a most unlikely scenario. If Eli is any guide, Samuel was probably about 70 when Saul became king and lived to a hundred or more.

It is not good enough simply to assume that some of the judges were contemporaries. We need to read the text carefully to find out the mind of the Spirit. One important pointer is to be found in Judges 2:18: "And when the Lord raised them up judges, then the Lord was with the judge, and delivered them out of the hand of their enemies all the days of the judge." In other words, peace was guaranteed so long as the judge was alive. During his lifetime another oppression is excluded. This is confirmed by the statements (3:11,30; 5.31; 8:28) that "the Land had rest." I am not alone in believing that "The Land" indicates the promised land of Canaan, and that if any part of it was suffering oppression, it could not be said, "The Land had rest." Leon Wood notes that this particular phrase is used in connection with the first four judges only; for the later ones a different form of words is used, "And he judged Israel" for so many years. "This marked change of expression suggests that the word 'rest' carries a significant connotation, and the most probable idea is that this was a 'rest' for the complete land." (Wood: 13)

Wood concludes from this that "none of the first four oppressions could have been contemporaneous." But is he right in making this deduction? It is here, I believe, that the structure of the book of Judges comes into play. This divides the history into two sections, each describing a consecutive order of events. As we have seen, it is the absence of the word "again" in Judges 6:1 which indicates this important division. The overlapping therefore (if such there is) can only occur in the middle. This brings us to our seventh and last proposition, that the forty years' rest which followed Barak's victory over Sisera (5:31) is one and the same as the forty years' rest associated with Gideon (8:28), and that the seven years' servitude to Midian (6:1) was concurrent with the last seven years of the servitude to Jabin (4:2).

This does not contravene any principle we have mentioned. Jabin king of Hazor reigned in Hazor to the north of Israel. His commander raided Israel from the north and oppressed that part of Israel for the next twenty years. Seven years before the end of that oppression the Midianites raided Israel from the east and overran central Israel for the next seven years. *Barak and Gideon both delivered Israel in the same year.* Barak raised a force of ten thousand men from Zebulun and Naphtali and defeated Sisera at Mount Tabor near the Sea of Galilee.Gideon sent messengers throughout Manasseh, but also into Asher, Zebulun and Naphtali. 32,000 men rallied to his support, but only 300 were needed to destroy the Midianites in the Valley of Jezreel. After Barak's victory "the Land had rest for 40 years" (5:31). But Barak himself is not mentioned or heard of again. However, after Gideon's victory in the same year, "the Land had rest 40 years in the days of Gideon" (8:28). These 40 years are the same as in 5:31, but it was Gideon (not Barak) who carried on as Judge.

This explanation throws light on the curious order in which four judges are mentioned in Hebrews 11:32, namely, "Gideon, Barak, Samson, Jephthah." These names form an introversion in which the first corresponds to the last, and the second to the third. In the words of *The Companion Bible*, "Gideon and Jephthae stand out together as higher examples of faith, Barak and Samson as associated with women, the former in his rise, the latter in his fall." But the order is no less chronological, for Gideon and Barak judged Israel in the same year, and so did Samson and Jephthah. Also in 1 Samuel 12:11, if Barak is read for the enigmatic Bedan, Gideon (Jerubbaal) comes before Barak.

The dates of the Judges

Ref.	East	Servitudes and Judges	West	Year
Judges 3:8		Mesopotamia,8		2587
3:11		Othniel,40		2595
3:14		Moab,18		2635
3:30		Ehud,80		2653
3:31		Shamgar		2733
4:1-3		Canaan "when Ehud was dead"		2733
6:1		Midian,7		2746
4:4 ff.		Barak		2753
8:28 (5:31)		Gideon, 40		2753
9:22		"King" Abimelech, 3		2793
10:1,2		Tola, 23		2796
10:3; 1 Sam.4:18	Jair, 22		Eli, 40	2819
10:8;13:1	Ammon, 18		Philistines, 40	2841
12:7;16:31 1 Sam.7:2	Jephthah, 6		Samson, 20	2859
12:8,9	Ibzan, 7			2865
12:11	Elon, 10			2872
1 Sam.7:6,15			Samuel	2881
12:13,14	Abdon, 8			2882
		Samuel		2890

The period of the Judges from the first servitude to the rise of Jephthah covers 272 years. This allows for an interval of twenty-years between the division of the Land and the invasion of Cushan-Rishathaim (3:8).

The accession of Saul

The fact that Samuel was already an old man when Saul was appointed king would suggest that Samuel had been judging Israel for some considerable time. But the Bible does not tell us how long he had been judging nor even how long he judged overall. Even the numbers relating to Saul's reign are no longer extant in the current text of 1 Samuel. True, the relevant details must originally have been recorded in 1 Samuel 13:1, but this verse unfortunately has suffered in transmission, the numbers having been removed from the text.

The form of this verse is exactly the same as in numerous other passages in the books of Samuel and Kings. It opens with a statement of the king's age when he began to reign, and goes on to say how long he reigned (e.g. 2 Sam. 2:10; 5:4; 1 Kings 14:21). In its present state it can only be translated, "Saul was a year old when he began to reign, and he reigned two years over Israel." This is how it has been understood in the Septuagint and Vulgate, as also in the Jewish Targum ("Saul was an innocent child when he began to reign"). Since however this makes no sense, the only reasonable alternative is that the numbers have been removed (by some over-zealous scribe perhaps), and to translate: "Saul was - years old when he began to reign, and he reigned - [two] years over Israel."

The *Revised Version* inserts "thirty" in square brackets in the first part of the verse. This restoration appears in a later recension of the Septuagint, but is simply "a private conjecture". Even if it should turn out to be right, it does not help us with the length of Saul's reign.

Even the "two" in the Hebrew text of the second part excites suspicion. This it does not only because we know that Saul reigned longer than two years, but because the construction as it stands is contrary to Hebrew idiom. There are two ways of stating "two years" in Hebrew, either the dual form of the noun is used (*shenatayim*), or the word "two" in its absolute form followed by "years" (*shetayim shanim*, so 2 Sam. 2:10; 2 Kings 21:19). The construction here, "two" in its construct form followed by "years" (*shete shanim*) is without parallel. There can be little doubt that "two" is an intrusion and can be safely ignored.

Leon Wood (1979: 122) rightly objects to the view that a number has been omitted before "two", making "thirty-two" or forty-two", because "this is out of keeping with Acts 13:21" (exactly 40). He suggests that the two years point to the lapse of time since Saul's inauguration at Gilgal (1 Sam. 12:14-15). It was, he thinks, after two years that Saul sent back the rest of the people to their homes, as recorded in verse 2. It is however unnatural to translate "when he had reigned two years over Israel" and then attach this clause to the second verse, though this is what the *KJV* has done.

A better suggestion is that made by G.R. Driver. He suggested a confusion between *Beth*, the letter standing for 2, and *Kaph*, the letter standing for 20, due to the similarity of the letters. Better still from our point of view is a confusion between *Beth* and *Mem*, the letter standing for 40. These two letters are also similar in some stages of the Hebrew alphabet.

The Old Testament (as we now have it) fails us at this point. But fortunately the New Testament comes to our rescue once again. Paul tells us in Acts 13:21 that Saul son of Kish, of the tribe of Benjamin, reigned for forty years. The reference significantly is not qualified by "about" as are the other periods mentioned in this passage. There can be no doubt, therefore, that exactly forty years is meant. Saul, like his successors David and Solomon, reigned for forty years, corresponding to the three forties in the life of Moses.

We know from what is said about Ishbosheth that Saul must have reigned for at least 40 years. Ishbosheth was the son of Saul who succeeded him for a short while and he, we are told, was 40 years old when he began to reign (2 Samuel 2:10). Ishbosheth is not included among Saul's sons in 1 Samuel 14:49 at the beginning of Saul's reign. Assuming he was born soon afterwards his first 40 years would correspond exactly to Saul's reign. Saul's reign cannot have been less than 40 years and was in fact exactly that length according to Acts 13:21.

Saul was succeeded by Ishbosheth for two years (2 Sam. 2:10). Saul had four sons according to 1 Chronicles 8:33 and 9:39: Jonathan, Malchi-shua, Abinadab, and Eshbaal (=Ishbosheth). All of these except Ishbosheth were struck down by the Philistines on Mount Gilboa (1 Chron.10:2). His short reign of two years, inclusively reckoned, ran concurrently with the beginning of David's reign.

Solomon's year of accession

The Temple was founded in Solomon's fourth year in the month Ziv, the second month, and this was 480 years after the Exodus (1 Kings 6:1). Hence the Temple was founded in the year 3000. The date of Solomon's accession depends entirely on which month of the year his reign began. If it began in Nisan, the first month, his first year of reign would be 2997. If however it began in Tishri his first year would be 2996.

```
Nisan                                                Ziv
|__2996___|___2997___|___2998___|___2999___||__3000___|
             1st         2nd         3rd        4th

      Tishri                                   |
      |___1st___|___2nd___|___3rd___|___4th___|
```

During the period of the Divided Kingdom, as will be shown in the next chapter, the regnal years of the kings of Judah were invariably reckoned from Tishri, the beginning of the civil year. There is however no certainty that this was the mode of reckoning for the reigns of David and Solomon. In the case of these kings the probability is that their reigns were reckoned from the actual month in which they ascended the throne, and their totals given in terms of calendar years. In the case of David we are distinctly informed that he reigned for 40 years and six months (2 Sam. 5:5), but his total is twice given as 40 years (2 Sam. 5:4; 1 Kings 2:11). From this we infer that in terms of calendar years David's reign covered 40 years, but in fact it lasted for 40 years and six months. If this is correct, then David must have died later in the year than the sixth month, and Solomon's reign was reckoned from Tishri or a later month.

For our present purposes it is not important whether Solomon's reign was reckoned from Tishri (as were the reigns of his successors) or from some other month in the second half of the year. In either case he would have ascended the throne four calendar years (not three) before the foundation of the Temple. His year of accession therefore was 2996.

The completion of the Temple

The Temple was founded in Ziv, the second month of Solomon's fourth year and was finished in Bul, the eighth month of his eleventh year, having been seven years in building (1 Kings 6:37,38). At first sight this looks as if Solomon was really seven and a half years in building the Temple, though still seven in terms of calendar years. This however is only true if Solomon's years are reckoned from Nisan. If in fact they are reckoned from Tishri or from another month (that of his actual accession) in the second half of the year, it would have been only six and a half years in building, though again seven years on inclusive reckoning. A diagram similar to the one above will make this clear:

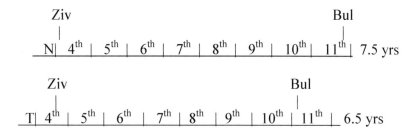

If the second alternative is correct, as seems most probable, Solomon was six and a half years in building the Temple, and the Temple was finished in the year 3006. However, D.J.A. Clines objects to this reasoning on the grounds that the number 7 in 1 Kings 6:38 forms part of a total. Solomon was 7 years in building the house of the Lord and 13 years in building his own house (7:1), making 20 years in all (9:10). Only exclusive 7 + excl. 13 = excl. 20, according to Clines (1974: 31). But this is not necessarily the case. If the actual figures were 6.5 and 12.5 respectively, a total of 19 years would still count as 20 years on inclusive reckoning.

It is difficult to be sure in this case. But we do know that Solomon's successors in the southern kingdom reckoned their regnal years from Tishri. But if Solomon had reckoned his years from Nisan, it is likely that his successors would have done the same. I incline therefore to the view that Solomon also reckoned his years from Tishri.

The dedication of the Temple

The Temple was finished "in all its parts and according to all its specifications" (*NIV*) in Solomon's 11th year in the eighth month (1 Kings 6:38). This, as we have seen, was either six and a half years or seven and a half years after its foundation in the second month of Solomon's fourth year. The dedication took place at the feast of Tabernacles in the seventh month (1 Kings 8:2). This month being one less than that in which the Temple was finished, some writers have assumed that the dedication was celebrated before the building had been fully completed. Thus according to Clines, "it may be assumed that work was concluded in the sixth month, the temple was dedicated in the seventh month, and building was all over in the eighth month" (1974: 32 n.52). But a plain reading of the text confirms Keil's conclusion: "that Solomon dedicated the building a month before it was finished, is not only extremely improbable in itself, but is directly at variance with ch. 7:51."

There can be little doubt that the dedication was postponed for at least eleven months while Hiram the skilled worker in bronze "wrought all his work" (7:13-47). It was not until "all the work was ended" that the dedication took place (7:51; 8:1). We do not have to agree with Keil that Solomon waited thirteen years before dedicating the Temple! Most likely it took place eleven months later, in the year 3007. It only remains to note a few dates:

Accession of Saul	A.H.	2916 (Acts 13:21)
Birth of David		2926 (2 Sam. 5:4)
Accession of David		2956 (2 Sam. 5:4)
Foundation of the Temple		3000 (1 Kings 6:1)
Completion of the Temple		3006 (1 Kings 6:38)
Dedication of the Temple		3007 (1 Kings 8:2)

According to the apocryphal book of 2 Esdras (10:45 f.), "... there were 3000 years in the world wherein there was no offering as yet offered in her. And it came to pass after 3000 years that Solomon builded the city, and offered offerings." A simple addition of the dates and years given in the Bible leads unavoidably to the year 3000 for the finishing of the Temple, if not its foundation. It was, I believe, after exactly 3000 years that the foundation stones of Solomon's Temple were laid.

Summary

The period from the Exodus to the Temple was 480 years according to 1 Kings 6:1. This number is crucial to the continuation of the chronology. All attempts therefore to undermine it must be firmly resisted. Some archaeologists have already revised their dating upward bringing it more in line with the Bible, but many others are still committed to a thirteenth century Exodus which is irreconcilable with this datum.

Aaron, Miriam and Moses all died in the fortieth year of the Exodus before the nation entered the Promised Land. The division of the Land took place six years after their entering Canaan as shown by Caleb's ages in Joshua 14:6-10.

The 450 years of Acts 13:20 draw a line at the point when God gave them their land as an inheritance. If the starting point is the same as the 400 years of Genesis 15:13, they are probably made up as follows: 400 + 40 (in the wilderness) + 6 (for the conquest) + 4 (when the Lord had given rest to Israel, Joshua 23:1).

The chronology of the Judges was considered under seven propositions as follows: **(1)** Samson was born after the beginning of the Philistine Servitude as implied by Judges 13:5. His 20-year judgeship corresponded therefore with the second half of the 40-year servitude. **(2)** The Philistine Servitude came to an end at Ebenezer in 1 Samuel 7. **(3)** Samson's judgeship must coincide with the 20 years of 1 Samuel 7:2 while the ark of the covenant remained at Kiriath Jearim.

4) The Philistine and Ammonite servitudes began in the same year – "that year", Judges 10:7-8. **(5)** Eli's 40 years coincided with the 22 years of Jair followed by the 18 years of the Ammonite Servitude. The judgeship divided after the death of Tola. On the east of the Jordan and in the north were Jair, Jephthah, Ibzan, Elon, and Abdon. In the west were Eli, Samson, and Samuel. They were united again after Samuel had judged Israel for nine years.

6) The chronology is tied down by the 300 years of Judges 11:26, and (7) the 40 years which followed Barak's victory are the same as the 40 years associated with Gideon. A diagram provides a visual aid to the understanding of this period.

The text which should have told us how long Saul reigned, namely 1 Samuel 13:1, is regrettably shorn of its numbers. Providentially the required information is given in Acts 13:21. Saul reigned for 40 years like his successors David and Solomon. This is confirmed by the detail that Ishbosheth, Saul's son and heir, was 40 years old when he began to reign (2 Sam. 2:10). Ishbosheth is not included among Saul's sons in 1 Samuel 14:49, so he must have been born after Saul became king, very soon after it would seem.

David reigned for 40 years and six months, but 40 years in terms of calendar years. He must therefore have died later in the year than the sixth month. Solomon's reign is reckoned from either Tishri or from a month later than Tishri when he began to reign. It is probable that his reign is reckoned from Tishri since that is the month chosen by his successors in Judah.

Again, there is some doubt whether the Temple was 6.5 years in building or 7.5 years. Either way, the dedication was postponed for about eleven months until "all the work was finished."

Chapter Three

The New Year for Kings

The chronology of the Divided Kingdom has been the barrier reef on which most chronological schemes have come to grief. If we are to avoid the same fate, it is imperative to establish sound principles of interpretation before proceeding any further. Specifically we need to be clear on two related points. From what month of the year, Nisan or Tishri, did the respective kingdoms reckon their regnal years? And, secondly, what mode of reckoning did they use - the so-called "accession-year" (or postdating) system, or the so-called "nonaccession-year"(or antedating) system? Only after we have cracked these two nuts will we have a sure foundation on which to tackle the chronology of the Divided Kingdom.

It is stated in the Mishnah, treatise *Rosh Hashanah* 1.1, that "On the first day of Nisan is a new year for the computations of the reigns of kings and festivals." This has been uncritically accepted by many scholars. Faulstich actually dismisses the Tishri view with the remark: "There is little evidence, Biblical or ancient extra-biblical, which would indicate that the kingdom of Judah reckoned kings from a Tishri point of view" (1986: 15). It is clear however from the discussion on this passage in the Talmud itself that even the rabbis were not all of the same mind. Some of them urged that the years of (at least) non-Israelite kings were reckoned from Tishri, citing Nehemiah 1:1 and 2:1 in support.

Others have dismissed the Mishnah as preserving only a late tradition after "all memory of the exact chronological arrangements of the Hebrew kings had disappeared" (Thiele: 51). I would certainly agree that the Mishnah is largely irrelevant. This problem, as with all problems of interpretation, needs to be solved from the Bible, not by quoting authorities ancient or modern. There is in fact overwhelming evidence in the Old Testament that a Tishri-to-Tishri year operated in the Southern Kingdom. As for the Mishnah, it probably enshrines a true tradition of the custom in vogue in the Northern Kingdom, or in Judea at the time of Herod the Great and his successors. It is known that they reckoned their years from Nisan and there is evidence for Nisan reckoning in the Northern Kingdom as well. But for a start I will present the evidence for Tishri reckoning in the Southern Kingdom of Judah.

Before embarking on this I would mention in passing Christine Tetley's view. According to her the reigns of both kingdoms are reckoned from the true date of accession, from the month in which each king came to power, and their lengths of reign are rounded off to the nearest year. But, if this were the case, one would need to know the precise month when each king began to reign in order to work out an exact chronology. Since this information is not provided, I can only conclude that it is not needed and, consequently, that each reign is reckoned from the beginning of the year, be it Tishri or Nisan, not from the precise month of accession.

Two calendars

It is generally accepted that the Hebrews made use of two calendars, beginning respectively in the spring and the autumn. The employment of a year beginning in the autumn may not be expressly mentioned in the patriarchal narrative, but we do have an express command to Moses with respect to the month Abib (or Nisan as it was later called), "This month shall be unto you the beginning of months: it shall be the first month of the year to you" (Exod. 12:2). H. Kosmala must be right when he says, "The announcement in this form and in this place makes sense only if it was to replace an earlier and different counting of the months and beginning of the year" (1964: 505f.). In other words, the year had originally begun with the month Tishri, but at the time of the Exodus the first month was transferred by divine command to Nisan, which became henceforth "the beginning of months, the first month of the year."

The existence of two calendars side by side, a spring Nisan calendar used for religious purposes and an autumn Tishri calendar used for civil purposes, gives no cause for surprise. We have ourselves an ecclesiastical year which is different from the calendar year, as well as fiscal and academic years. But just as our months are always numbered from January, so it was in Israel: from the Exodus onwards the months are always numbered from Nisan regardless of which type of year is currently in view.

The following are the Jewish months, each with its number, name or names, and approximate modern equivalent:-

1st	Nisan (Abib)	Mar/Apr	7th	Tishri (Ethanim)	Sept/Oct
2nd	Iyyar (Ziv)	Apr/May	8th	Marchesvan (Bul)	Oct/Nov
3rd	Sivan	May/June	9th	Kislev	Nov/Dec
4th	Tammuz	June/July	10th	Tebeth	Dec/Jan
5th	Ab	July/Aug	11th	Shebat	Jan/Feb
6th	Elul	Aug/Sept	12th	Adar	Feb/Mar

Ezekiel 24:1 and 33:21

Of the various indications of Tishri reckoning for the later kings of Judah, perhaps the most persuasive comes from a comparison of two verses in Ezekiel, 24:1,2 and 33:21. In the first of these passages we are distinctly informed that the king of Babylon laid siege to Jerusalem on 10 Tebeth (the tenth month) in the ninth year (of the Exile). And this is confirmed by 2 Kings 25:1 where the year is identified with the ninth year of Zedekiah's reign. In the second passage we learn that news of Jerusalem's fall was conveyed to the prophet by a fugitive from the stricken city on 5 Tebeth in the twelfth year of the Exile. It was in fact in the fifth month of Zedekiah's *eleventh* year that the city was entered by Nebuchadnezzar and his victorious army (2 Kings 25:8). From Jerusalem to Babylon was a journey of about five months, not seventeen (!). Ezra, in more favourable circumstances, made the equivalent journey in four months flat (Ezra 7:9).

The era of the Exile is reckoned in Ezekiel from Nisan 597 BC (as will be explained in due course), and its years therefore coincide with the calendar year. Hence, between the siege of Jerusalem in the ninth year of the Exile and its surrender in the twelfth year, three calendar years must have elapsed. Only however on Tishri-to-Tishri reckoning are there three calendar years between the tenth month of Zedekiah's ninth year (the date of the siege) and the fifth month of his eleventh year (the date of surrender). This goes to show that Zedekiah's regnal years are reckoned from Tishri rather than Nisan:-

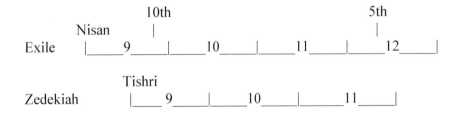

D.J.A. Clines has questioned this result on the grounds of a variant reading in Ezekiel 33:21. There is sufficient evidence, he thinks, for treating "eleventh year of our exile" as a serious alternative to the reading "twelfth year of our exile" (1972:19f.). This reading is to be found in eight Hebrew manuscripts, the Greek Lucianic recension and the Syriac. The reading "twelfth year" should nevertheless be retained, first in having the stronger manuscript support and secondly in being the more difficult reading. There can be little doubt that twelfth was changed to eleventh because of the imagined chronological problem which "twelfth" seemed to present. This agrees with the well-known harmonizing tendencies of the Greek and Syriac versions.

2 Kings 22-23

Another passage which points in the same direction is 2 Kings 22 and 23. We read there that Josiah, in the eighteenth year of his reign, sent Shaphan to the Temple where, shortly after, the book of the Law was found by Hilkiah the high priest (22:3-8). But it was also in his eighteenth year that the Passover was celebrated as recorded in the next chapter (23:21-23). This means, if Josiah's year 18 began on 1st Nisan, that the intervening events transpired in less than a fortnight.

Between the reading of the newly discovered book of the Law and the command to keep the Passover, 2 Kings gives a catalogue of Josiah's reforms (23:4-20). These include the cleansing of the Temple and priesthood, the defilement of the high places from Geba to Beersheba, the demolition of the idolatrous altars and images set up by previous kings of Judah, the destruction of the high place at Bethel, and of all the high places in the cities of Samaria. It is not to be inferred that all these reforms were carried out between the discovery of the Law-book and the Passover. It was purely for schematic reasons that the historian listed at this point the whole gamut of Josiah's reforms. In fact we know from 2 Chronicles that most of them occurred between Josiah's years 12 and 17, and others later in his reign (verse 33).

Nevertheless, even without the reforms, the other events recorded must have taken more than a fortnight. These were as follows: Shaphan was sent to the house of the Lord; the Temple money was collected from Hilkiah and given to the skilled workmen for the work of repair; while in the Temple Hilkiah found the book of the Law; he gave it to Shaphan who read it; the King is told of the book which was read to him as well; they consult the prophetess Huldah who declared to them the word of the Lord; all the elders of Judah and Jerusalem are gathered; a great convocation is held in the Temple and the book is read again; the King made a covenant before the Lord to keep His commandments. All this would have taken a few weeks rather than a few days. It must surely be admitted that the Tishri dating is more probable in this instance.

Josiah's programme of "root and branch" reform began at the time of "the second order" (2 Kings 23:4). The reference is to the second of the 24 priestly orders (or courses) which rotated through the year, each term lasting for one week from one Sabbath to the next (1 Chron. 24:1-19; 2 Chron. 23:8). There are different views on how the courses operated, but the view which seems most likely is that the 24 courses completed two cycles in the course of the year beginning respectively in Nisan and Tishri. The second order would have officiated in both the second week of Nisan and the second week of Tishri.

Dr Jones thinks that all the reforms listed in 2 Kings 23:4-20 were carried out in their entirety by the "enormous manpower pool at Josiah's disposal" during the second week of Nisan prior to the Passover on the 14th. Here is proof, he thinks, that Judah's kings counted their regnal years from Nisan rather than Tishri. But this is farfetched in the extreme. It must have been in Tishri that the reformation began, doubtless in the second week when the second order was in office.

Jeremiah 36:1-9

Another passage to which reference is made is Jeremiah 36:1-9. It was in the fourth year of King Jehoiakim that Baruch the scribe began to write out at Jeremiah's dictation all the words that the Lord had given him, and in the ninth month of Jehoiakim's fifth year that he read them out in the hearing of all the people. On this passage Julian Morgenstern has written, "Unless we may assume that the copying of Jeremiah's words required at least ten full months to complete, an assumption hardly probable, we must conclude that the transition from Jehoiakim's fourth year to his fifth year took place not very long before month IX" (1936: 442f.).

D.J.A. Clines is not convinced by this argument. "If Jeremiah could wait three months, he could wait nine months," he says. "All that is demanded is the postulation of an appropriate historical stimulus for the writing of the book, and such is provided by the events of 605 as well as by those of mid 604" (1974: 34). He is apparently unimpressed by E. Auerbach's affirmation that "Such a bombshell of a book-roll the prophet would not have laid up on ice for 9-10 months!" (1959: 116, "Eine Bombe wie die Buchrolle legt der Prophet nicht fur 9-10 monate auf Eis!"). In our view an interval of three months is altogether more appropriate.

Daniel 1:1

According to Daniel 1:1, "In the third year of the reign of Jehoiakim king of Judah, Nebuchadnezzar king of Babylon came to Jerusalem and besieged it." Nebuchadnezzar's conquest of Syria and Palestine followed on from the battle of Carchemish in May/June 605 when the Egyptian army camped by the river Euphrates was decisively beaten by the young Crown Prince of Babylon. It was in the summer of 605, near the close of his third year of reign (on Tishri reckoning), that Jehoiakim submitted to Nebuchadnezzar. Clines admits that "only on a Tishri reckoning of Jehoiakim's regnal years can a siege by Nebuchadrezzar have occurred in Jehoiakim's 3rd year." He concludes that "the date given (in Dan. 1:1) must be viewed with reserve"! (1972: 20,21,28)

Jeremiah 1:3

A further indication that Zedekiah's years are reckoned from Tishri is provided by Jeremiah's statement that the word of the Lord came to him "until the end of the eleventh year of Zedekiah ... until the captivity of Jerusalem in the fifth month" (Jer. 1:3). On Nisan reckoning the fifth month would have been nowhere near the end of Zedekiah's eleventh year, whereas on Tishri reckoning it was the last month but one. It could however be argued that Zedekiah's eleventh year had already come to an end although only four months of it had run their course.

Ezekiel 40:1

10 Nisan in year 25 of the Exile is here equated with the fourteenth year from the fall of Jerusalem. Year 25 of the Exile began in Nisan 573 BC, which was in fact the fourteenth year after the fall of Jerusalem if that occurred in 586 BC. But only on Tishri reckoning did Jerusalem fall in 586 (see above on Ezekiel 24:1 and 33:21). On Nisan reckoning it fell on 7 Ab 587.

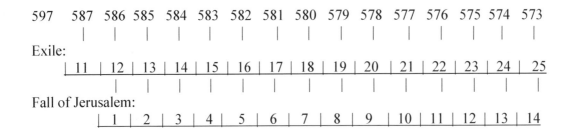

Nehemiah 1:1 and 2:1

Nehemiah mentions the month Kislev (November) and the following Nisan (March) as being both in the same year, the twentieth, of Artaxerxes' reign. From this it follows that Nehemiah reckoned the years of this Persian king by the Jewish Tishri-to-Tishri method, and not by the Persian Nisan-to-Nisan method.

Once again Clines is forced to the view that "the text of Neh.1:1 is not above suspicion." He thinks it "remarkable if Nehemiah in composing his memoirs ca. 430 BC had persisted in painfully translating the legal dates of the beneficent Persian ruler into a Judean system which most agree had been abandoned by the end of the seventh century in Judah" (1974: 34f.). This however was the method used by Jeremiah in reckoning the years of Nebuchadnezzar, and the same custom persisted in both Egypt and Syria at a much later date. I can see no reason why Nehemiah, intense patriot as he was, should not have carried on the same tradition.

These texts in Nehemiah do admit of another interpretation, namely that Artaxerxes' reign is reckoned from his actual date of accession in Ab 465 BC. In this case his 20th year would have run from Ab 446 to Ab 445. This has the support of Christine Tetley (2005: 106). But reckoning from the true date of accession does not seem to have been widely practised. Nebuchadnezzar's reign is not reckoned in this way either in Babylon or in Israel. In Ezra Artaxerxes' seventh year includes the fifth month (Ab) as well as the preceding first month (Ezra 7:7-9). This allows for Artaxerxes' reign to be reckoned either from Nisan or from the previous Tishri, but not from Ab when he ascended the throne.

1 Kings 6:37-38

E.R. Thiele found the strongest indication of a Tishri mode of reckoning in the biblical data respecting the building of the Temple (1965: 28f.). The Temple was founded in the second month of Solomon's fourth year and was finished in the eighth month of his eleventh year, having been seven years in building (1 Kings 6:37 f.). Thiele points out that on Nisan reckoning, from the second month of Solomon's fourth year to the eighth month of his eleventh year would have been seven years and six months, but on Tishri reckoning only six years and six months. Only therefore on Tishri reckoning were there seven years inclusively reckoned.

All this is true, but it does not prove that Solomon's years are reckoned from Tishri. David reigned for 40 years and six months, but the total is given as 40 years, not 41 (2 Sam. 5:4). It could be the same with the Temple: it really took seven and a half years to build, but the total is still seven. I nevertheless incline to the view (as explained in the last chapter) that in point of fact Solomon's regnal years were reckoned from Tishri, as undoubtedly were those of his successors in the southern kingdom of Judah.

Jeremiah 46:2

The evidence for Tishri reckoning in Judah is of a cumulative nature. There are several passages which cannot be explained otherwise, and none at all which are incompatible with this mode of reckoning. Or have I spoken too soon? Is not Jeremiah 46:2 a clear example of Nisan dating? According to Clines, "Jer. 46:2 provides in fact the clearest piece of chronological data relevant to this period, and its witness to a Nisan system of reckoning can hardly be challenged" (1972: 29). It would be truer to say that Jeremiah 46:2 provides the *only* piece of contrary data. For A. Malamat it is "the only real difficulty for a Tishri reckoning" (1968: 147).

This verse, translated word for word, runs like this: "Concerning Egypt: against the army of Pharaoh Necho king of Egypt, which was by the river Euphrates in Carchemish, which

Nebuchadrezzar king of Babylon smote in the fourth year of Jehoiakim son of Josiah king of Judah." Punctuated thus, it clearly states that the battle of Carchemish when Pharaoh Necho was defeated by Nebuchadnezzar took place in the fourth year of Jehoiakim. This battle took place in May/June 605, about three months before the close of Jehoiakim's *third* year on Tishri dating, and with this Daniel 1:1 agrees. If the battle really fell in Jehoiakim's fourth year according to Jeremiah 46:2, we should have to conclude (with E.R. Thiele) that the system of dating in Jeremiah is different from that in Daniel and Kings.

In Thiele's view, the royal years are reckoned from Tishri in Daniel and Kings, but in Jeremiah they are reckoned from the preceding Nisan. Hence, in Jeremiah the fourth year of Jehoiakim began in Nisan 605 and would have encompassed the battle of Carchemish in May or June of that year (1965: 161 ff.). If that is the case, Jeremiah is inconsistent in his dating. The siege and capitulation of Jerusalem - the one taking place in the first half of Zedekiah's ninth year and the other in the second half of Zedekiah's eleventh year - are uniformly dated in Jeremiah and Kings (Jer. 52:4,5,12; 2 Kings 25:1,2,8). These verses are cited by Thiele as proof of Jeremiah's inconsistency, but for us they prove the opposite: that Jeremiah's dating of regnal years is exactly the same as in Kings, proof in fact of his consistency.

Jeremiah 46:2 only presents a problem if punctuated as above. The solution which commends itself is that the central clauses of this passage are parenthetical. As S.H. Horn observes, "If the portion of the verse referring to the Battle of Carchemish is considered a parenthetical clause, all chronological difficulties are removed, and this passage falls in line with the rest of the dated historical statements of Jeremiah mentioning Nebuchadrezzar" (1967: 25f.). He would punctuate the passage as follows:

> "About Egypt: concerning the army of Pharaoh Necho king of Egypt (which was by the river Euphrates at Carchemish, which Nebuchadrezzar king of Babylon defeated) in the fourth year of Jehoiakim the son of Josiah king of Judah."

It was therefore the revelation of the oracle to Jeremiah, not the defeat of Pharaoh Necho, which took place in Jehoiakim's fourth year. In Clines' view, "the postulation of a very large parenthesis in the text (is) contrary to the plain sense." But in reality parentheses, even large ones, are quite common in verses of a chronological nature. Of this sort are Genesis 15:13 and Exodus 12:40. Our own language is an unreliable guide since ancient languages had different stylistic conventions. Although there are no other verses exactly parallel to this one, it is nevertheless true that with all the headings in Jeremiah it is the prophecy which is dated, never the event which occasioned the prophecy - except (as in 45:1 and 51:59) where they happen to coincide.

Ezekiel 26:1-2

According to Clines, the oracle against Tyre in Ezekiel 26 makes no sense unless Jerusalem had already fallen. This oracle is dated to the eleventh year of the Exile, 587 BC, but Jerusalem did not fall until 586 on a Tishri reckoning of Zedekiah's reign. Tyre is here represented as saying, "Aha, the gate of the peoples is broken, it has swung open to us; I shall be replenished, now that she is laid waste" (verse 2). The reference is not exclusively to Jerusalem, but to Judea as a whole. By 587 the land was almost totally overrun (see Jer. 34:6,7), Jerusalem had been under siege for over a year and her eventual surrender was a foregone conclusion. In this situation Tyre had every reason to exult over Judah's downfall. There is certainly no cause for emending "eleventh" to "twelfth" with Eichrodt and others. This is just another harmonizing device to be found in some Greek manuscripts.

Haggai and Ezra

Only in Haggai is there indisputable evidence of Nisan reckoning. This is not in connection with any Israelite king, but the Persian king Darius I. The book of Haggai is constructed round the following four chronological notices:-

1:1:   The 1st day of the 6th month in Darius' 2nd year
1:15:   The 24th day of the 6th month
2:1:   The 21st day of the 7th month
2:10:   The 24th day of the 9th month in Darius' 2nd year

On Tishri reckoning the seventh month would mark the beginning of a new regnal year. But in Haggai there is no change of year between the sixth and seventh months, which goes to show that Darius' reign is here reckoned from Nisan as was the custom in Persia.

Likewise in Ezra, Darius' years are reckoned from Nisan, for there also work on the Temple is said to have been resumed in Darius' second year (Ezra 4:24). The exact date is given in Haggai as the 24th day of the ninth month (2:18). But on Tishri reckoning, the months seven to twelve of Darius' second year would be reckoned to Darius' third year, not his second.

The facts are not in dispute. On the one hand, in Haggai and Ezra the second year of Darius (520 BC) and the seventh of Artaxerxes (458), are reckoned from Nisan as was the custom in Persia. On the other hand, in Nehemiah the twentieth year of Artaxerxes (445) is reckoned from Tishri after the Jewish custom (Neh.1:1 with 2:1). How are these facts to be explained?

There can be little doubt that the normal Jewish practice was to reckon the years of foreign kings according to the Hebrew mode of reckoning. This is how they computed the years of Nebuchadnezzar, whose first year of reign is equated with the fourth of Jehoiakim (Jer.25:1). But with the suspension of their national life this practice fell temporarily into abeyance, resulting in their adoption of the Babylonian/Persian practice. However, with the restoration of their Temple and City they joyfully reverted to their former custom as Nehemiah bears witness.

Nebuchadnezzar

Nebuchadnezzar's first year of reign was reckoned in Babylon from Nisan 604. By the Jews, however, it was antedated to Tishri 605, and so brought into exact correspondence with the fourth year of Jehoiakim (Jer. 25:1). This was the method used in the case of the Persian king Artaxerxes, and the presumption is that Nebuchadnezzar's reign was treated in the same way. There may be an indication of this in the fact that King Jehoiachin's Captivity is ascribed to Nebuchadnezzar's eighth year in the Bible (2 Kings 24:12), but to his seventh year in the Babylonian Chronicle (Wiseman: 33). S.H. Horn explains: "The 7th year of Nebuchadnezzar according to the Babylonian spring calendar lasted from March 27, 598 to April 12, 597, but according to the Jewish autumn calendar it had already ended in the autumn of 598 when Nebuchadnezzar's 8th year had begun" (1967: 20).

According to 2 Chronicles 36:10 it was "at the return of the year" that Nebuchadnezzar sent and brought Jehoiachin to Babylon. This Hebrew phrase occurs five times in the Old Testament and means simply "the spring", the time when kings went forth to battle (2 Sam. 11:1; 1 Kings 20:22,26; 1 Chron. 20:1). The precise date is now known from the Babylonian Chronicle. It is there recorded that "on the second day of the month Adar he captured the city (and) seized (its) king." This corresponds on Julian dating to 16 March, 597. In both Israel and Babylon Adar(u) was the last month in the year. It was the last month of Nebuchadnezzar's seventh year in Babylon, and the sixth month of his eighth year in Israel.

E.R. Thiele is very positive that Jehoiachin was taken captive on 10 Nisan 597, a few weeks after the capture of the city on 2 Adar. This is proved, he thinks, by Ezekiel 40:1 where we read, "In the 25th year of our exile, at the beginning of the year, on the tenth day of the month ... *on that very day*, the hand of the Lord was upon me." If it was the very same day, it must have been the 25th anniversary of King Jehoiachin's captivity, argues Thiele. But it must be questioned whether this is the intended meaning. Already in our discussion of Exodus 12:40,41 the import of this expression has been examined, and I there concluded that it simply looked back and focused attention on the date already mentioned. It was therefore on that very day, tenth Nisan of the 25th year of the Exile, that the hand of the Lord was laid upon Ezekiel. It is nevertheless true that the era of the Exile is reckoned in Ezekiel from Nisan 597, though it may have actually begun three or four weeks earlier.

Daniel

In the book of Daniel, as in Haggai and Ezra, the reigns of foreign kings are reckoned from Nisan, as was the practice in Babylon and Persia. Thus Nebuchadnezzar's *second* year, when he had his famous dream of the Great Image (Dan. 2:1), must have commenced in 603 rather than 604. This we know from the fact that Daniel's three years of apprenticeship (1:5) could not have expired, on inclusive reckoning, before the autumn of 603.

Daniel was taken captive soon after the Babylonian victory at Carchemish in May or June 605. A few weeks later, on 8 Ab (16 August), Nebuchadnezzar's father died, and it was 1st Elul (7 September) before he arrived back in Babylon to claim his father's throne. Daniel's apprenticeship cannot have begun before that date. But the months Elul to Adar 603 belonged to Nebuchadnezzar's second year only in Babylon; in Israel they would have fallen to his third year of reign. It must therefore be the Babylonian mode of reckoning which is found in Daniel. An approximate chronology may be tabulated as follows:-

May/June	605:	The Egyptians are decisively defeated at Carchemish
August	605:	Nebuchadnezzar's father died
September	605:	Nebuchadnezzar, back in Babylon, claimed the throne
October	605:	Daniel's three year apprenticeship began
March	604:	Nebuchadnezzar's 1st year of reign began
March	603:	His second year bega
October	603:	Daniel's apprenticeship finished around this time. After this but before the following March the King had his dream.

The Northern Kingdom

The evidence is strong that a Tishri mode of reckoning was that in use in the Southern Kingdom of Judah. But what about the Northern Kingdom of Israel? In view of the apparent absence of evidence to the contrary, it would seem a natural assumption that Tishri reckoning applied there as well. That indeed was the view I took myself until it came to my notice that a uniform Tishri dating fails to account for the peculiarities of the text in certain places.

Evidence for this is provided by the very first synchronism in 1 Kings. Rehoboam died after reigning for 17 years, but his successor Abijam began to reign in year 18 of Jeroboam. This proves that Rehoboam died after Jeroboam's 18th had begun and consequently that his reign began later than Jeroboam's. Again, Hezekiah began to reign in Hoshea's third year (2 Kings 18:1). Yet his fourth year was Hoshea's seventh and his sixth year Hoshea's ninth (18:9-10). This shows that Hezekiah's first year must have straddled Hoshea's years 3-4, and his fourth year Hoshea's years 6-7. (See below, page 86)

There are several other examples which will come to light as we work through the Divided Kingdom.

Accession year and Nonaccession year

Accession year and nonaccession year are the terms used to describe the two systems of dating royal years in vogue in the ancient world. The great nations to the north and east of Israel - Assyria, Babylonia and Persia - employed the accession-year system. That is, the king's first year of reign was *postdated* to the New Year's Day (1st Nisan) following his actual date of accession. The intervening weeks or months were called his accession year and were counted to the last year of reign of the outgoing king. Egypt on the other hand, the great nation to the south of Israel, used the nonaccession-year system, whereby the king's first year was *antedated* to the preceding New Year's Day (1st Thoth). The year of transition was reckoned to both the out-going king and the new one.

The question is, which system was in use in each of the two kingdoms of Israel? Some scholars like to make it as complicated as possible. In the opinion of Thiele, for example, the kings of Judah followed the accession-year system from Rehoboam to Jehoshaphat, the nonaccession-year system from Jehoram to Joash, and the accession-year system from Amaziah to Zedekiah, while the kings of Israel followed the nonaccession-year system from Jeroboam to Jehoahaz and the accession-year system from Jehoash to Hoshea. A scheme which has constantly to be changed in order to avoid irreparable breakdown is surely self-condemned. Thiele's system demonstrates one thing only: his own failure to solve the problem. Even one change of system would be enough to arouse suspicion. What is needed is one overall scheme which accounts for all the evidence.

It is often thought that the accession-year system was that in general use in Judah, and the nonaccession-year system that in use in Israel. This is the view of Gershon Galil, and it works quite well for the first series of kings, Rehoboam/ Jeroboam down to Jehu's seizure of the throne. But it breaks down completely with Jehu and Joash. Joash began to reign in year 7 of Jehu and Jehu's successor Jehoahaz in year 23 of Joash. Jehu however, if his regnal years preceded those of Joash, would already have died in the previous year, year 21/22 of Joash. Only if Jehu's 28-year reign followed those of Joash by six months is it possible for Jehoahaz to succeed Jehu in Joash's year 23. Here also we have another indication that Nisan dating operated in Israel, but Tishri dating in Judah.

Conclusion

The scheme which works with least complication is this: Tishri dating in Judah and Nisan dating in Israel, with the nonaccession-year system operating in both kingdoms. Every regular succession conforms to this scheme. Before embarking on a more detailed examination of the reigns of the Divided Kingdom, here briefly are the principles which I have found to work without a hitch.

1) The kings of Judah reckoned their reigns from Tishri as various passages bear witness.

2) The kings of Israel however reckoned their reigns from Nisan as shown above.

3) Both kingdoms used the *nonaccession* year system, antedating their first year of reign to the preceding Nisan or Tishri as the case may be.

4) Some of the kings crowned their sons in their lifetime in order to secure the succession or because they were too infirm to rule themselves.

5) The reign-lengths are counted from the cross-references in accordance with the plain sense of the passage. Thus, in the case of the controversial Omri, we read, "In the year 31 of Asa king of Judah, Omri reigned over Israel, 12 years" (1 Kings 16:23). The obvious sense is that Omri reigned for twelve years starting at year 31 of Asa - not from year 27 of Asa when his predecessor died as is generally assumed. This is the most important principle of all because it closes the door on most of the juggling with numbers and manipulation in which scholars indulge, and ensures a firm interlocking chain of reigns which is almost incapable of change. It may of course be difficult to reconcile in places with the Assyrian Eponym Canon, but that is a problem we can shelve for the time being. Our present purpose is to discover the dates which the Bible itself demands without interference from outside: without, that is, constantly looking over our metaphorical shoulder to get the nod of approval from the Assyrian master of ceremonies.

Chapter Four

The Divided Kingdom

The chronology of the Kings of Israel and Judah presents considerable difficulty when it comes to reconciling the biblical dates with those of the Assyrian Empire. It is proposed therefore to postpone all discussion of the Assyrian evidence until a later chapter, devoting this one to an independent treatment of the biblical data. This is the only possible procedure, methodologically speaking, if our chronology is to remain a truly biblical one. Only thus can we stay true to the principles of sound exegesis, unadulterated by pressures from outside. The penalty for such faithfulness may be a scheme that is difficult to square with the record of the monuments. That is a problem we will face up to in its proper place, after the biblical evidence has been examined.

The view is often expressed that the internal chronology of the books of Kings is a mess compared with the far more reliable scheme derived from the Assyrian Eponym Canon. Statements to the effect that the "internal contradictions are legion" are frequently found. But in fact the books of Kings and Chronicles contain all the hallmarks of a reliable history. Their material is not derived from oral tradition and hearsay but from written source books contemporary with the events recorded. In 1 Kings 11:41 we hear of "the book of the acts of Solomon", evidently a contemporary record of Solomon's affairs written up during his reign. There are twelve references to "the book of the chronicles (lit. "daily events") of the kings of Israel" and fourteen to "the book of the chronicles of the kings of Judah." In addition there are seven references in Chronicles to "the book of the kings of Israel and Judah", two to "the book of the kings of Israel" and one to "the story (*midrash*) of the book of the kings" (2 Chron. 24:27). All this points to a history which had been faithfully updated from generation to generation.

Moreover, no attempt is made to glorify the kings of Judah, to magnify their achievements or to gloss over their faults and failures. Of more than half it is said that they did what was evil in the sight of the Lord. Only two (Hezekiah and Josiah) are given unqualified praise, but even they come across as fallible human beings lacking in judgment and resolution. Their Assyrian counterparts, on the other hand, come across as semi-divine (or diabolical) beings who are always victorious in battle and unerringly successful in everything they do. Unquestionably the biblical history is the more objective and reliable of the two. We are right therefore to give precedence to the biblical account.

The structure of the books of Kings

As with the book of Judges, our first consideration is the structure of the books of Kings. These two books are really one, as they are in the Hebrew canon, the division into two being an arbitrary innovation of the Septuagint translators which cuts up the history of Ahaziah and Elijah. The main body of the book (1 Kings 2:13 to 2 Kings 25:7) consists of 39 sections dealing with the reigns of 39 kings. Of the nineteen kings of Israel, from Jeroboam to Hoshea, it is not stated of a single one that he did that which was right in the eyes of the Lord, whereas only nine of the twenty kings of Judah, from Solomon to Zedekiah, are stated to have done in some measure that which was right. Altogether, starting with David, there were forty kings in the two kingdoms, but David's reign is outside the scope of the books of Kings. What is said about him there is merely introductory to the reign of Solomon, showing how it was that Solomon, and not Adonijah or some other son of David, succeeded to the throne.

The thirty-nine sections which make up the body of the books of Kings are constructed for the most part on a fixed pattern. This is twofold. They each open with a chronological notice, and they each include a reference to "the book of the Chronicles" of the kings of Israel or Judah. So far as the sections on the kings of Israel are concerned, the chronological notices consist of the name of the king, a cross reference to the year of the reigning king of Judah, and a statement of the length of his reign. The only exceptions are the sections on Jeroboam and Jehu, where the chronological notices are omitted. Jeroboam and Jehu are the first kings respectively of the two great series of kings which constitute the history of the Divided Kingdom.

So far as the sections on the kings of Judah are concerned, the chronological notice in its fullest form consists of the name of the king, his age at accession, a cross reference to the king of Israel, the length of his reign, and the name of his mother. But many of the references are not so full. With Abijam and Asa the king's age is omitted; with Jehoram and Ahaz the king's mother is omitted; with Rehoboam and the last seven kings a cross reference to the king of Israel does not apply. For Solomon there is no chronological notice at all, while the notice for Joash is not at the beginning of his section, for the six year usurpation of his grandmother Athaliah is included in the same section.

In the case of six kings there is no mention of the book of the Chronicles. All these were either slain in battle or taken captive. They are Joram son of Ahab and Ahaziah of Judah, the last two kings of the first great series of kings, whom Jehu slew on the same day; Hoshea, the last king of Israel; and Jehoahaz, Jehoiachin and Zedekiah, three of the last four kings of Judah, all of whom were taken captive. Apart from these minor variations and omissions the pattern is sustained throughout. The structure is as follows:-

 A. 1 Kings 1:1-2:12. Introduction
  B. 2:13-11:43. The United Kingdom
   C. 12:1-2 Kings 9:29. The Divided Kingdom. First part: 15 kings
   C. 9:30-17:41. The Divided Kingdom. Second part: 15 kings
  B. 18:1-25:7. The Single Kingdom
 A. 25:8-30. Conclusion

The history of the Divided Kingdom consists of two parts, each comprising fifteen kings. The first part extends from the disruption after the death of Solomon to the deaths of Joram and Ahaziah, slain by Jehu on the same day. The second part continues the history to the end of the Northern Kingdom.

A notable correspondence is apparent between the careers of Jeroboam and Jehu. Both men were appointed to be king by a prophet - Jeroboam by Ahijah and Jehu by Elisha. At both times it was the Lord's intention to purge the kingdom of idolaters and to establish a new dynasty of God-fearing kings over the ten tribes. Both kings however were dismal failures. This correspondence manifests itself in the more detailed expansion of the Divided Kingdom. This expansion is dynastic. It depends on the number of kings, of Judah as well as Israel, who reigned during the successive dynasties of the kings of Israel. For example, there were seven kings who reigned during the period spanned by the dynasty of Omri. For the purposes of this structure, Jeroboam and Jehu are treated as separate entities, as distinct from the dynasties they founded:-

 A. 1 Kings 12:1-14:20. Jeroboam
  B. 14:21-15:32. Rehoboam to Nadab son of Jeroboam: 4 kings
   C. 15:33-16:14. Baasha dynasty: 2 kings
    D. 16:15-22. Zimri: a week
     E. 16:23-2 Kings 9:29. Omri dynasty: 7 kings

A. 9:30-10:36. Jehu
      E. 11:1-15:12. To end of Jehu's dynasty: 7 kings
    D. 15:13-16. Shallum: a month
  C. 15:17-26. Menahem dynasty: 2 kings
 B. 15:27-17:41. The remainder: 4 kings

Rules of operation

We may now proceed to an examination of the chronology of the Divided Kingdom. The principles we shall work on, assuming they are correct, will give minimal scope for error. These principles are) **(1)** The reigns of the kings of Israel are reckoned from Nisan, but those of the kings of Judah from Tishri. **(2)** The nonaccession-year system is applied to both kingdoms, that is to say, their regnal years are antedated to the preceding New Year's Day, be it Nisan or Tishri. **(3)** The cross references are invariably taken at their face value. In other words, the length of reign is always counted from the regnal year of the opposing king provided by the cross-reference. Most other chronologists have allowed themselves the liberty of counting the king's years from any point they find convenient in total disregard of the beginning of reign stated in the text. This has given them a great deal of latitude and has usually resulted in a chronology about forty years shorter than the one provided by a straightforward reading of the text. It is not latitude I shall be looking for, but interlocking certainty, and that is best achieved by a strict application of the principles just stated.

There are a few scholars, notably Shenkel and Tetley, who believe the chronology of the Old Greek and Lucianic texts is preferable to that of the Hebrew, or at least of equal value. As already stated I do not share that view. It becomes very subjective to pick and choose between the various numbers on offer, always choosing the one that seems to provide the smoothest reading. Tetley for example does not believe in co-regencies or interregna. Hence she invariably chooses the text which gives a regular succession.

It is quite possible of course that the Greek texts do have some original readings, but how are we to know which they are? If the Hebrew seems rough in places, that does not prove it is wrong. It may in fact prove the opposite. Every state passes through periods of turbulence and instability. This is sure to be reflected in the contemporary records assuming they present an accurate picture of what really took place. I shall not therefore be looking for alternative readings every time some awkward statement or number turns up in the text of Kings. In the following survey I shall stick close to the Hebrew figures while admitting in two or three places that the text may have suffered in transmission. These however do not affect the chronology as a whole.

How can Christine Tetley be sure that it was not an accepted practice in ancient Israel for a king to share the throne with his heir apparent near the end of his reign, thereby giving his son valuable training in kingship, and more importantly ensuring a smooth succession to the throne? It is an undeniable fact that Solomon was crowned king while David was still alive (1 Kings 1:28-40). David acted decisively to make sure that Solomon succeeded to the throne in the face of Adonijah's proclamation of himself as king. If David found it necessary to act in this way, we should not be surprised if several of his successors found themselves under the same necessity. In the case of Jehoshaphat's son Jehoram we are specifically informed that Jehoshaphat was still king of Judah (2 Kings 8:16). There were in fact seven kings who co-reigned with their fathers for short periods, three in Judah and four in Israel. The reason was often to secure the succession (especially in the Northern Kingdom), but sometimes for other reasons, such as the king's infirmity in old age.

There are, it is true, quite a number of apparent anomalies and ambiguities, but these can usually be resolved by a careful reading of the text. Dr. Lightfoot, the seventeenth century divine, entertained no doubts on this matter, and his words are as true today as when he wrote them. "For resolution of such ambiguities," he said, "when you have found them, the text will do it, if it be well searched.... Admirable it is to see, how the Holy Spirit of God in discords hath showed the sweet music. But few mark this, because few take a right course in reading of Scripture. Hence, when men are brought to see flat contradictions (as unreconciled there be many in it), they are at amaze, and ready to deny their Bible. A little pains right spent will soon amend their wavering, and settle men upon the Rock; whereon to be built is to be sure" (Lightfoot, II, 8f.). Fine words!

If it was true in the seventeenth century it is even more true today that few take a right course in the reading of Scripture. It is especially in the period of the Kings that a wrong course has been taken by our scholars in their endeavour to regiment the kings of Israel and Judah behind their Assyrian overlords. These kings still refuse to fall into line as they did in their lifetimes, and no amount of pushing and shoving will force them to do so. At the end of the day it may be the Assyrian kings who will have to submit, not the Israelite!

Jeroboam to Nadab

Jeroboam (Israel),		22 years	(1 Kings 14:20)
Rehoboam (Judah),		17 years	(14:21)
Abijam (Judah),	18th Jeroboam,	3 years	(15:1)
Asa (Judah),	20th Jeroboam,	41 years	(15:9,10)
Nadab (Israel),	2nd Asa,	2 years	(15:25)
Baasha (Israel),	3rd Asa,	24 years	(15:33)

Jeroboam 1	3036	
		1 Rehoboam

17	3052	17 1 Abijam
18	3053	2
19	3054	3 1 Asa
20	3055	2
Nadab 1 21	3056	3
Baasha 1 2 22	3057	

Further proof of a Nisan mode of reckoning in Israel is provided by the very first synchronism in 1 Kings. For if the years of Rehoboam and Jeroboam were allowed to run parallel, year 18 of Jeroboam, when Abijam began to reign, would fall in the year after Rehoboam's death in his year 17, and Abijam's reign would start in the year after his father's death.

The need to reckon Jeroboam's reign prior to Rehoboam's was recognised by Henry Browne back in 1844. He had this to say, "There is therefore no other way of reconciling the different notes of time, but to suppose that the epoch of Jeroboam's reign is earlier than that of Rehoboam: a supposition which will be found nowise incredible, when it is considered that the kingdom was solemnly conferred upon Jeroboam in the name of the Lord by the prophet Ahijah in the lifetime of Solomon, and apparently just at the end of his reign. 1 Kings 11:29-40" (Browne: 224).

Jeroboam's *de facto* reign began slightly later than Rehoboam's according to the narrative of 1 Kings 12, but *de jure* it began six months earlier, being antedated to 1st Nisan preceding. The various changes which Jeroboam introduced were designed, as Galil explains, "to emphasize the independent status of the kingdom of Israel; and to deepen the division between Israel and Judah, to enable the creation of two distinct entities with different cultic centers and ritual symbols which would develop disparate primal traditions, celebrate their festivals at different times, and live their daily lives in accordance with different calendars" (1996: 15).

Thiele also reckons Jeroboam's first year of reign from Nisan, six months prior to Rehoboam's first year. But he complicates matters by insisting that Jeroboam's reign is reckoned according to the accession-year system in Judah in references relating to kings of Judah, but the nonaccession-year system in Israel in references relating to the kings of Israel; and likewise Rehoboam and his successors except in reverse! (Thiele: 31) Gershon Galil quite rightly rejects all this. "His hypothesis is too complicated," he says, "and is improbable. It is difficult to assume that in each kingdom the years of reign of the other kingdom were counted in accordance with the local system" (1996: 38).

Thiele's chronology has been regarded as the best available by the majority of scholars, with veneration by many. But there are few today who are satisfied with a scheme so complicated and changeable. My own view is closer to that of Steven J. Robinson who has said, "The complexity of the scheme strains belief. No nation has ever exhibited such changefulness in its reckoning of time, and in reality Thiele's imputation of inconsistent usage to the Hebrew is but an inversion of his own failure to establish a consistent explanation" (1991/2: 90).

Taking the cross references at their face value, we are left with an overlap of two years between Jeroboam and Nadab, father and son both dying in the same calendar year. One can think of two good reasons why Jeroboam might have associated his son with him on the throne of Israel. First there was the illness with which the Lord afflicted him before he died (2 Chron. 13:20), possibly rendering him incapable of effectual rule. Secondly there was the prophecy of Ahijah the Shilonite that the house of Jeroboam would be swept away (1 Kings 14:10,11). In the circumstances Jeroboam was likely to do everything possible to ensure the continuation of his dynasty.

So far as the synchronism is concerned, Nadab's reign might have begun in either 3055 or 3056, depending on whether he began to reign in the first half or the second half of Asa's second year. If reckoned from 3055, however, he would not have outlived his father Jeroboam. But it is clear from 1 Kings 15:27-29 that Jeroboam was already dead at the time of Baasha's conspiracy.

In the Old Greek and Lucianic texts Abijam is said to reign for six years instead of three, and Jeroboam for 24 years instead of 22. Christine Tetley prefers the Greek version (p.180), but to my way of thinking it is more easily explained as a harmonising device aimed at avoiding the co-regency between Jeroboam and Nadab. Nadab now starts to reign in the year his father died, and Abijam's reign is lengthened accordingly. In order to allow Abijam to reign six years, Asa's reign now begins in Jeroboam's 24th year instead of his 20th. Why this text should be considered preferable to the MT, the Masoretic Text, I am unable to understand. Tetley's reasoning is often difficult to follow, her conclusions even harder to accept.

Shishak king of Egypt

In the fifth year of his reign Rehoboam was punished for the detestable practices (idolatry and sodomy) which were rife in the land with an invasion by "Shishak king of Egypt" (2 Chron. 12:1-12). This king has been traditionally identified with Pharaoh Shoshenk I, the Libyan founder of the 22nd Dynasty. Indeed this identification has been one of the cornerstones of modern Egyptian chronology, the date assigned to the invasion being 925 BC on the strength of E.R. Thiele's much-acclaimed (though untenable) dating of the Hebrew kings. All this, however, has been thrown into doubt by David Rohl and Roger Henry to mention only two.

"The whole situation is topsy-turvy," says Rohl, " whilst Shishak attacks Judah and enters Jerusalem to plunder the Temple of Yahweh, Shoshenk attacks Israel and does not mention Jerusalem as one of the defeated cities in his campaign record; Shishak is allied to Israel and subjugates Judah whilst Shoshenk subjugates Israel and avoids confrontation with Judah!" (Rohl: 127)

Shishak is identified by David Rohl with Ramesses II, the pharaoh often associated with the Exodus, but by Henry he is identified with Thutmose III who is usually placed in the 15th century. Thutmose III was the resentful half-brother of Queen Hatshepsut whom Henry identifies with the Queen of Sheba. There is at least evidence that Ramesses did undertake a campaign into the hill country of Judah, and did reach Jerusalem, based on the campaign relief at the Ramesseum (the mortuary temple of Ramesses II) which states that Ramesses defeated a city called Shalem in his eighth year. Thutmose III gained a significant victory at Megiddo in the second year of his independent reign. "In all, Thutmose lists 119 cities captured in Palestine, many of them founded only in Hebrew times – an uncomfortable fact ignored by those who follow the Conventional Chronology" (Henry: 63).

There is no unanimity on the true identity of Shishak. Whoever it was, the Egyptian army was enormous, consisting of foreign mercenaries as well as 1,200 chariots and 60,000 horsemen (2 Chron. 12:3). They easily overwhelmed the strongholds which Rehoboam had fortified with this eventuality in mind, and stood outside the walls of Jerusalem. When however the king and princes humbled themselves, the Lord spared Jerusalem. Shishak carried off the Temple and palace treasures and then departed.

Baasha to Omri

Baasha	(Israel),	3rd Asa,	24 years	(1 Kings 15:33)
Elah	(Israel),	26th Asa,	2 years	(16:8)
Zimri	(Israel),	27th Asa,	7 days	(16:15)
Omri	(Israel),	31st Asa,	12 years	(16:23)

				26	Asa
Baasha		24	3080		
Elah		1		27	
Zimri	1	2	3081	28	
			3082	29	
			3083	30	
Omri		1	3084	31	

One disadvantage of reckoning the reigns of Israel and Judah from different calendar months is the doubt which it permits in the dating of certain kings. Omri began to reign in 31 Asa, but should his reign be reckoned from 3084 or 3085? Zimri, his predecessor, reigned for only seven days in 27 Asa. For the next four years the nation was divided in its loyalty between Tibni and Omri (1 Kings 16:21-23). Omri was declared king by his own party on the death of Elah in 27 Asa (verse 16), but it was not until 31 Asa that he defeated his rival and began his official reign. In this instance it is not important from which year his reign is reckoned (3084 or 3085), since no succeeding reign depends on Omri's years. It is simply for convenience that I have noted his reign to 3084.

Almost without exception chronologists have been wont to number Omri's 12-year reign from 27 Asa in preference to 31 Asa. By this means he is conveniently made to die in the year of Ahab's accession (see below). It is nigh universally taken for granted that the reign-lengths of specific kings are in no way tied to the accompanying synchronisms. For Thiele in particular this is a fixed principle. Hence the beginning of the king's co-regency (real or invented) or the death of his predecessor has an equal claim to be regarded as the point from which the regnal years are numbered. Even Dr. Lightfoot, who cannot be faulted anywhere else, slips up at this point. By him also Omri's reign is reckoned from the death of Elah in 27 Asa, rather than the given synchronism in 31 Asa.

It is not true, as maintained by Galil, that Omri was crowned in year 27 of Asa according to the Hebrew text. It does say that "all Israel" made him king on the death of Elah, but in fact the nation was divided. Half the people wanted Tibni son of Ginath to be king and half wanted Omri. It was not until year 31 of Asa that the matter was resolved and it was then that Omri was crowned king. Asa's year 27 is not even mentioned in this section of Kings and cannot therefore be considered the first year of Omri's reign.

J.D. Shenkel is perfectly right when he says, "This procedure of reckoning the years before a king's official succession as part of his regnal years is completely anomalous, having no parallel elsewhere in Kings" (1968: 40). It should be sufficient to heed the plain sense of 1 Kings 16:23, "In the thirty-first year of Asa king of Judah began Omri to reign over Israel, twelve years." If Omri's twelve years are not counted from 31 Asa, the door is opened to endless variations on the chronology, and our aspiration to obtain an exact dating for the kings of Israel and Judah becomes an increasingly hopeless cause.

The Old Greek and Lucianic texts have Omri reign 12 years from 31st Asa as in the Masoretic Text. But in order to give him a full 12 years Ahab is made to succeed him in the 2nd year of Jehoshaphat instead of 38th Asa. Prior to that there is some confusion. In both texts Elah begins to reign in 20th Asa (instead of 26th) and was succeeded by Zimri in 22nd Asa (instead of 27th). Zimri reigns for 7 years in OG and for 7 days in L. But this leaves a hiatus of nine years in L and two in OG. Even if Omri is given an additional six years in Tirzah there is still an interval. Tetley's diagram on page 121 does not seem to agree with the information she gives on pages 35-36. A text which leaves unexplained gaps in the chronology hardly inspires confidence.

Asa's 36th year

In this section we meet with the first of those anomalies or ambiguities to which reference has been made. It is written in 2 Chronicles 16:1 that Baasha king of Israel came up against Judah and fortified Ramah in the year 36 of Asa's reign. But Baasha died in Asa's year 26, and so could not have invaded Judah in year 36. There are two explanations to this problem currently on offer, and it will be clear from what follows which of the two I prefer.

On the assumption that the text has suffered in transmission, there are several possibilities which have been suggested from time to time. One of the more persuasive is that of C.F. Keil that Asa's year 35 (in 2 Chron. 15:19) and year 36 (in 2 Chron. 16:1) should be changed to years

15 and 16 respectively. Keil observes that *Lamed* and *Yod*, the letter standing for 30 and 10, "are somewhat similar in the ancient Hebrew characters." If this is correct Asa's reign divides into the following sections: ten years of peace (14:1-8), the invasion and defeat of Zerah the Ethiopian (14:9-15), the covenant to seek the Lord in Asa's fifteenth year (15:10-15), followed by Baasha's rebuilding of Ramah in Asa's sixteenth year (16:1). Baasha's object was to stem the exodus of his own subjects to Judah for, as already stated, "great numbers had deserted to him (Asa) from Israel when they saw that the Lord his God was with him" (14:9). This would naturally follow the desertion of his subjects in Asa's 15th year, and so confirms the correctness of the emendation to 16th in 2 Chronicles 16:1.

There is still a problem however with 15:19. If this is emended to "fifteenth year" with Keil, we have a statement to the effect that there was no more war until Asa's fifteenth year, uttered when? - in Asa's fifteenth year (v.10)! Since that would reduce the text to nonsense, it looks very much as if "thirty-fifth" may be right after all.

There is in fact no need to emend this reference. We are here told that there was no more war until Asa's 35th year. So long as this is understood of declared war, there is no contradiction with e.g.16:9, "From now on you will have wars." Apart from sporadic skirmishes and border raids there were no more open hostilities until Asa's 35th year.

Having written "year 35", it would have been easy for the scribe to have written "year 36" in the very next verse, on the assumption that the numbers were in chronological order and that what he was about to describe amounted to war with Baasha. This not only provides a solution to the unintelligible "year 36", but also (which is just as important) explains how the error arose. In this year, year 16 if we are right, there was no open warfare on the part of Asa since he hired the king of Aram to do the dirty work for him.

The alternative solution has the support of E.R. Thiele and is in fact the traditional harmonisation of Kings and Chronicles in this place. It is that the years 35 and 36 of Asa are here reckoned from the disruption of the kingdom, corresponding on Thiele's chronology to years 15 and 16 of Asa's reign. "When would this building of Ramah take place?" asks Thiele, "- in Asa's sixteenth year, immediately after the great influx to Judah of Baasha's subjects from Israel or twenty years thereafter?" In his view, "the picture secured when 2 Chron. 15:19 and 16:1 are reckoned not as the years of Asa but years since the establishment of the divided monarchies gives both historical and chronological harmony" (Thiele: 60).

Thiele is right that "sixteenth" is the number required in 16:1, but his dating of these references from the disruption of the kingdom is opposed to the grammar. The words "of Asa's reign"(*le-malkut 'Asa*) are the same in 15:10,19; 16:1 and 12. If two of them are to be reckoned from the disruption of the kingdom, so should the others as well.

Galil is right in saying, "This hypothesis is difficult and should not be accepted, for it is stated explicitly that this count is 'of the reign of Asa,' and there is no support for the assumption that there was a count from the schism" (1996: 19).

Ahab to Joram

Ahab	(Israel),	38th Asa,	22 years	(1 Kings 16:29)
Jehoshaphat	(Judah),	4th Ahab,	25 years	(22:41,42)
Ahaziah	(Israel),	17th Jehoshaphat,	2 years	(22:51)
Joram	(Israel),	18th Jehoshaphat,	12 years	(2 Kings 3:1)
Joram	(Israel),	2nd Jehoram		(2 Kings 1:17)

Omri	Ahab 1	8	3091			
	2	9	3092	38		Asa
	3	10	3093	39		
	4	11	3094	40		
	5	12	3095	41	1	Jehoshaphat

Ahab		20		3110		
Ahaziah		21	1	3111	(1) 17	Jehoram
Joram	1	22	2	3112	(2) 18	

The Bible is more interested in Omri's moral defects than his political achievements. But it does say that he bought the hill of Samaria and built there a city which became the capital of Israel in place of Tirzah. This site, 11 km. north-west of Shechem, had a strategic position both militarily and commercially. It commanded the trade routes and was virtually impregnable. Omri must have impressed himself on the surrounding nations since the land of Israel, so far as the Assyrians were concerned, became thereafter *mat-Humri*, the land of Omri, and every succeeding king of Israel was a *bit-Humri*, a son of Omri. Even Jehu who destroyed the house of Omri to the last man was a *bit-Humri!* The references to Jehu in the Assyrian records will be discussed in the next chapter but one.

In a determined effort to ensure the succession Omri had his son Ahab to reign with him for the last five years of his reign. Jehoshaphat did the same, though for a different reason. His son Jehoram reigned officially for three years before his father's death and unofficially for five additional years. It is interesting to observe that even if Omri's years are counted from 27 Asa (as is usually done), a co-regency of one year between Omri and Ahab is still indicated on the chart. For if 3081 was Omri's first year of reign, his twelfth and last would be 3092, whereas Ahab began to reign in 3091. Admittedly 3092 is also covered by Asa's year 38, but if Ahab's reign is counted from 3092 he would have outlived his son Ahaziah. This however is forbidden by the fact that Jehoshaphat made an alliance with Ahaziah after Ahab's death (2 Chron. 20:35). This is another significant pointer that the reigns of the two kingdoms are reckoned from different months in the calendar year.

If Ahab's first year of reign is secured by the requirement that he should not outlive his son Ahaziah, so too is Ahaziah's reign secured by a similar requirement. He came to the throne in his father's penultimate year and died a few months after his father in the following year. Also in the same year Joram, Ahaziah's brother, ascended the throne of Israel because Ahaziah had no son of his own (2 Kings 1:17). That not many months elapsed between Ahab's death and Joram's accession is confirmed by 2 Kings 3:5,6. We read there (as we have already seen) that Ahab's death sparked off a rebellion by his vassal the king of Moab. It was however Joram (not Ahaziah) who mustered all Israel in response to this threat.

It is likely that Ahab, in the penultimate year of his reign, was involved in the Western alliance which confronted Shalmaneser III at Qarqar. This would explain why his son Ahaziah was raised to the throne in that year. Ahaziah outlived his father by only a few months and was succeeded by his brother Joram "in the second year of Jehoram son of Jehoshaphat king of Judah" (2 Kings 1:17). This unexpected cross-reference to Jehoram's second year would seem to indicate that Jehoshaphat, in the previous year (year 17 of his reign), had raised his son to the throne in association with himself in an unofficial capacity. His reason for doing so is not entirely clear. Jehoram, egged on by his wife (Athaliah, daughter of Jezebel), may have forced him into it. This unofficial co-regency was made official five years later, "Jehoshaphat being (still) king of Israel" (2 Kings 8:16). By this time Jehoshaphat would have been 57 years old and may have felt that the time had come to hand over the reins of government to his son.

The Moabite Stone

2 Kings 3 gives the true biblical version of the victory of the three kings (of Israel, Judah and Edom) over the rebellious Mesha, king of Moab, who had rebelled against the king of Israel after the death of Ahab. When the allies were dying of thirst the Lord miraculously provided them with flowing water which, at sunrise, looked just like red blood to the Moabites. Assuming that the three kings had slaughtered one another, they ran eagerly for the spoil, only to be slaughtered themselves as a result. The fighting went well for the allies until Mesha, in desperation, offered his son and heir as a sacrifice on the city wall. After that the tables were turned, and "the fury against Israel was great."

Israel had overstepped the mark. They had thrown stones on every good piece of land, stopped every spring of water, and felled all the good trees (3:25). God had promised to give Moab into their hands (3:18), but it was never His intention that the allies should act with inhuman brutality towards a brother nation with whom they had historic ties. He had indeed predicted that they would do so (3:19), but that was no part of the promise (in verses 17-18). The allies drove the king of Moab to the desperate act of sacrificing his son and heir on the city wall, by which he hoped to placate Chemosh, the vindictive god of the Moabites. This aroused God's anger against the allies whose unrestrained cruelty had led to this appalling deed.

The Moabite Stone, discovered by a missionary F.A. Klein in 1868, gives a different slant to the same sequence of events. The general picture is given in the opening lines:-

> I am Mesha, son of Chemosh-... , king of Moab, the Dibonite. My father was King over Moab thirty years and I became king after my father. And I made this sanctuary for Chemosh at Qrchh, [a sanctuary of] salvation; for he saved me from all the kings and let me see my desire upon my adversaries. Omri, king of Israel, he oppressed Moab many days, for Chemosh was angry with his land. And his son succeeded him and he too said, 'I will oppress Moab.' In my days he spoke (thus), and I saw my desire upon him and upon his house, when Israel perished utterly for ever. And Omri had taken possession of the land of Medeba and [Israel] dwelt in it his days and half the days of his son, forty years; but Chemosh dwelt in it in my days....

According to this version of events, Omri had taken possession of Medeba, a district north of the river Arnon allotted to the tribe of Reuben, and had dwelt there in his days and half the days of his son (Ahab), for all of 40 years. According to 2 Kings 1:1 and 3:5 it was *after* Ahab's death that Moab rebelled, and it was Joram, in association with Jehoshaphat, who took remedial action to stop him. Mesha is evidently uncertain of his facts or has deliberately distorted them. Omri's and Ahab's combined reigns come to only 28 years. If indeed it was for 40 years that Israel took possession of Medeba, it must have begun long before the accession of Omri. It is also possible that Ahab had already lost effective control of this area some years before the end of his reign. So there may be some truth in what Mesha says.

Mesha, it seems, won back all the territory north of the Arnon and fortified many of the cities in that area against future invasion from Israel. Twelve towns are mentioned by name. He massacred the Israelite population at Ataroth and Nebo. He captured Jahaz and settled there two hundred Moabite noblemen. He also rebuilt other towns with a task-force of Israelite captives. Qarhoh, Aroer and Bezer are mentioned. Altogether he claims to have added one hundred towns to his territory. Israelite control over that area was permanently lost, it seems, though it may have been many years before this was accomplished.

Jehoram to Ahaziah

Jehoram	(Judah),	5th Joram, 8 years	(2 Kings 8:16,17)
Ahaziah	(Judah),	11th Joram	(9:29)
Ahaziah	(Judah),	12th Joram, 1 year	(8:25,26)

Joram			
4	3115	22 Jehoshaphat
5	3116	1 Jehoram
6	3117	2 23
7	3118	3 24
8	3119	4 25
9	3120	5
10	3121	6
11	3122	7
12	3123	8 1 Ahaziah

Jehoram began his official reign in 3116, his father "Jehoshaphat being (still) king of Israel", as explicitly stated in 2 Kings 8:16. The situation is illumined to some extent by the record in 2 Chronicles 21. We read in verse 3 that Jehoshaphat gave gifts to all his sons, "but the kingdom he gave to Jehoram because he was the firstborn." Jehoshaphat evidently admitted his son into official partnership with himself on the throne of Judah. Jehoram however was totally unworthy of the trust bestowed on him. Soon after his father's death, when he was firmly established on the throne, he murdered all his brothers along with some of the princes of the land (verse 4). In this act of wanton cruelty he was doubtless encouraged by his unscrupulous wife, Athaliah daughter of Jezebel. When not forty years old he was afflicted by the Lord with a disease of the bowels from which he died two years later in great pain (21:18,19). This explains Ahaziah's unofficial co-regency with his father for about six months (2 Kings 9:29).

A minor discrepancy

Ahaziah was 22 years old when he began to reign (8:26). In 2 Chronicles 22:2, however, his age is given as 42. Here also it is added, "His mother's name was Athaliah, the (grand)daughter of Omri." That the statement in Kings is historically correct is proved by the fact that Jehoram was only in his fortieth year when he died, and so could not have had a son of 42. It is usual to dismiss the larger number as a textual error: 42 for 22. But we should always think twice before assuming an error in the text.

The explanation which has found acceptance in some quarters is that Ahaziah's age is backdated in Chronicles to the beginning of the reign of Omri, that is from 3081, the year in which Elah died and "all Israel made Omri, the captain of the host, king over Israel" (1 Kings 16:16). In the words of Martin Anstey, "But the Holy Ghost will not have him (Ahaziah) for a son of David's line at all. He is the son of Athaliah, the daughter of Omri and Jezebel. He is no seed of David. He is an imp of the house of Ahab, a son of the house of Omri, and as such a 'son of 42 years', for the dynasty of the house of Omri was exactly 42 years old" (Anstey: 182).

Anstey finds confirmation of this in the genealogy of our Lord in Matthew 1. There three names are omitted, Ahaziah, Joash and Amaziah, for it says "Jehoram begat Uzziah", his great-great-grandson. "St. Matthew will have it that from David to the carrying away to Babylon are 14 generations, not 17, and that these three men are no seed of the royal line of David. Their ancestry must be traced to the house of Omri." So it is in 2 Chronicles 22:2, Ahaziah's age is that of the house of Omri, the family to which he belonged. This solution is tempting, but for me unconvincing. There are quite a number of textual errors where numbers are concerned, and this most probably is one of them.

This brings us to the end of the first part of the Divided Kingdom. Joram of Israel and his nephew Ahaziah of Judah were both killed by Jehu on the same day (2 Kings 9:14-28). This must have taken place in the spring or early summer of 3123 since Joram had just returned, in company with his nephew Ahaziah of Judah, from fighting against Hazael king of Syria, and had retired to Jezreel to recover from his wounds. It was thither that Jehu drove furiously to seize the throne. Jehu now founded a new dynasty in Israel, but the throne in Judah was seized by Ahaziah's mother, Athaliah daughter of the infamous Jezebel (11:1-3).

Jehu to Jeroboam II

Jehu	(Israel),		28 years	(2 Kings 10:36)
Queen Athaliah	(Judah),		6 years	(11:3)
Joash	(Judah),	7th Jehu,	40 years	(12:1)
Jehoahaz	(Israel),	23rd Joash,	17 years	(13:1)
Jehoash	(Israel),	37th Joash,	16 years	(13:10)
Amaziah	(Judah),	2nd Jehoash,	29 years	(14:1,2)
Jeroboam	(Israel),	15th Amaziah,	41 years	(14:23)

Jehu	1	3123	Athaliah

Jehu	7	3129	1	Joash
			2	

Jehoahaz	1 28	3150	23	Joash
	2	3151		

Jehoash	16	1	3165	37	Joash
	17	2	3166	38	
		3	3167	39 1	Amaziah
		4	3168	40 2	

			14	Amaziah
Jeroboam	1 16	3180	15	

Athaliah ruled the land for six years, but this is not counted as an official reign. They are simply calendar years, 3123 to 3129. Jehoahaz began to reign in 23 Joash. On a simple Tishri (or Nisan) system of dating this would correspond to the year after Jehu's death:-

> 7th Jehu ....1st Joash
> 28th Jehu..................22nd Joash
> 1st Jehoahaz.............23rd Joash

Once again the twofold system is preferable in that it permits Jehoahaz to succeed his father in a regular manner. According to Galil, Joash's reign would have been reckoned from the death of his father rather than the seventh of Jehu. "It is hardly conceivable," he says, "that the insurgents counted the years of Joash from the murder of Athaliah, thus acknowledging the legality of her reign" (1996: 47).

This, it is true, is how a modern king would have reckoned his reign. Charles II of England, I am told, counted his reign from his father's execution rather than from his own restoration in 1660. Without exception, however, historians measure his reign from the Restoration, not from his father's execution. Here also, the inspired historian has counted Joash's reign from the seventh year of Jehu rather than from his father's death. 2 Kings 12:1 is perfectly clear, "In year 7 to Jehu Joash reigned, and he reigned 40 years in Jerusalem." This is confirmed by Jehoahaz' accession in year 23 of Joash, the very year his father Jehu died, and by Jehoash's accession in year 37 of Joash, one year before his father died.

Jehoash began to reign in 37th Joash. This points to a co-regency between Jehoash and his father Jehoahaz, due possibly to the father's absence on his Syrian wars (2 Kings 13:24,25). But is Jehoash's reign to be reckoned from 3164 or 3165? It must be admitted that either is possible. Here I have chosen the later date in the interests of a shorter co-regency. This is virtually the only place where an adjustment is possible. Otherwise the dating would seem to be fixed, assuming that our methodology is sound.

Amaziah began to reign in second Jehoash. Here also a one-year co-regency is indicated between Amaziah and his father Joash. Joash was severely wounded while fighting the Syrians (2 Chron. 24:25). Soon after he was murdered by two of his officials, but before this conspiracy he must have appointed his son as coregent. The relative position of Amaziah in Judah over against Jehoash in Israel is secured by the datum that Amaziah outlived Jehoash by fifteen years (2 Kings 14:17; 2 Chron. 25:25). Jehoash died in 3180 and Amaziah in 3194, fifteen years inclusively reckoned. This would not work out if Amaziah's reign was reckoned a year earlier, as otherwise it might.

Azariah and Zechariah

Azariah   (Judah),   27th Jeroboam,   52 years   (2 Kings 15:1,2)
Zechariah (Israel),   38th Azariah,   6 months (2 Kings 15:8)

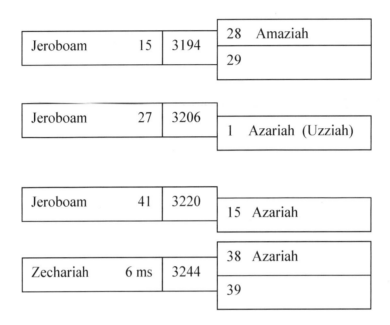

Azariah was 16 years old when he ascended the throne in 27th Jeroboam. But this was no normal succession. If he was raised to the throne in Tishri 3206 he could only have been four years old when his father died in 3194. A twelve year regency during Azariah's minority is the clear implication of the text as recorded.

Most students of chronology (since Archbishop Ussher) have taken exception to this interregnum and taken measures to eliminate it. Keil for example says "Azariah (Uzziah) must have become king in the fifteenth year of Jeroboam, since, according to ch.14:21, the people made him king after the murder of his father, which precludes the supposition of an interregnum." According to him, the Hebrew letters standing for 27 are similar in appearance to those standing for 15, and in this way the error arose. Even if this were the case it does not explain how a perfectly regular cross-reference could have been mistaken by the scribe for a totally irregular one without apparently anyone noticing. It is true 2 Kings 14:21 gives no hint of an interregnum, but to say that it precludes the supposition is to overstate the case. It is, I admit, unusual that no explicit reason is given for Azariah's delayed accession.

Likewise Zechariah's brief enthronement did not occur until 38th Azariah, twenty-four years after his father's death in 3220. He began to reign in Azariah's year 38 and died in year 39, that is from spring to autumn (or summer to winter) in the same calendar year. It has to be assumed that a period of civil war followed Jeroboam's long and stable reign while such men as Zachariah, Shallum and Menahem contended for the throne.

In this instance it is not Zechariah on his own, but his successors Shallum, Menahem, Pekahiah and Pekah, all of whose reigns are dated against Azariah's reign. All five stand or fall together. There can be no question but that all these kings are correctly placed with reference to the reign of Azariah. Even if Azariah's reign is reckoned from his father's death there is still an interregnum of 12 years between Jeroboam's death and the accession of his son. At most the chronology can be reduced by 12 years at this juncture, but this is far too short for the convenience of those who are looking for harmony between Israel's chronology and that of Assyria. To satisfy them a reduction of 40 years is required, but there is no way that can be achieved within the framework of 1 and 2 Kings without making all sorts of unwarranted assumptions.

These two interregna, one of twelve years and the other of twenty-four, have been regarded with suspicion and disbelief since at least the time of Josephus. To all who would remove these interregna I would quote the plain statement of Scripture: "In year 27 of Jeroboam king of Israel began Azariah son of Amaziah king of Judah to reign. Sixteen years old was he when he began to reign, and he reigned 52 years in Jerusalem." If his 52 years are not reckoned from 27th Jeroboam, or if 27th Jeroboam is not reckoned from the beginning of his reign in 15th Amaziah, there is an inexplicable lacuna in the text which is calculated to frustrate the whole pursuit of chronology. In our opinion this consideration alone is sufficient to overrule the objections that have been raised and continue to be raised.

Thiele in particular does not believe in interregna. He writes as follows:-

... in the history of nations there are few records of states passing through periods when they were without rulers. Even in times of trouble and crisis nations had their rulers, and at such periods those who would exercise control were usually present in increased numbers. History has indeed shown that periods of political weakness and chaos have usually resulted in a multiplication of rulers rather than in a cessation of rulership. The invention of interregna for the sake of endeavouring to clear up certain seeming chronological discrepancies is something which must therefore be approached with extreme caution. When interregna are invented and inserted where they ought not to be, it is only to be expected that the resultant chronological pattern will be drawn out beyond the years of contemporary nations and beyond the terms of absolute chronology (1965: 21).

It is surely very cavalier of Thiele to reject a priori the very possibility of interregna. Only the Bible can determine whether interregna occurred in Israel's royal succession, not the records of contemporary nations. In any event, it is not we who have *invented* interregna in order to clear up an apparent discrepancy, it is he who has deliberately excised them in order to harmonize Israel's chronology with that of Assyria. No one in his senses would invent or insert intervals of twelve and twenty-four years respectively, but when the text of Scripture indicates interregna of these dimensions, what else can we do than humbly accept what is written?

Before rejecting these (and other) interregna in Israel's history, it is only proper to investigate the conventions observed in the books of Kings in the matter of reckoning reigns. The best indication is provided by the example of Omri. Omri was made king by the army in 27 Asa when news reached the troops that "Zimri has conspired, and he has killed the king." For the next four years, however, Omri was not the only king in Israel, for "the people of Israel were divided into two parts; half the people followed Tibni the son of Ginath, to make him king, and half followed Omri" (1 Kings 16:21). It was not until 31 Asa that Omri finally prevailed over his rival and became sole king in Israel. It is moreover from this year that his twelve-year reign is reckoned. From this we learn that the normal practice was to reckon the king's reign, not from his own assumption of royal status, but only from such time as he was universally recognised as king by the nation at large. Thiele is doubtless correct that "periods of political weakness and chaos have usually resulted in a multiplication of rulers." It is precisely for this reason that no one king is recognised in Scripture during these periods of divided rule.

Also in the case of Joash. Though "hardly conceivable" in the opinion of Galil, his reign is clearly reckoned from his own installation and not from the death of his father. Interestingly,

Thiele here follows the Bible contrary to his own principles.

Both Thiele and Faulstich argue that the people of Judah raised the youthful Azariah to the throne when his father Amaziah was taken prisoner of war by the king of Israel (2 Kings 14:13; 2 Chron. 25:23). Azariah, they say, was sixteen years old on becoming regent for his father Amaziah, not when he was raised to the throne after his father's death as stated in 2 Kings 14:21. But the Bible does not support this theory. According to 2 Chronicles 25:23 "Jehoash brought him (Amaziah) to Jerusalem", where presumably he continued to reign under the watchful eye of Jehoash. T.R. Hobbs observes, "the evidence for such a co-regency is lacking ... there is no suggestion that Amaziah was held captive for any long period of time. If the hostages taken from Jerusalem had included the king then it would have been stated." Again, "14:17 clearly states that Amaziah lived for fifteen years after the death of Joash, and there is no hint at all that this period was one spent in captivity" (1985: 185).

Thiele, however, calls attention to the statement in 2 Kings 14:22: "He built Elath and restored it to Judah, after the king slept with his fathers." He then quotes W.G. Sumner to the effect that this verse "is either a most idle and meaningless statement, or else it has a significance which has not yet been perceived. It is difficult to avoid the suspicion that it alludes to the fact that Azariah was made king after his father was captured by Jehoash, and before he was released, and that he did this after his father's release and death" (Thiele: 85).

If 2 Kings 14:22 is speaking of Azariah (as everyone assumes), it is certainly a surprising statement. It can only mean that Azariah rebuilt Elath when still a minor following his father's death. But maybe this verse does have a significance which has not yet been perceived. Can we be sure that it refers to Azariah at all? It is self-evident that this section of 2 Kings (namely, 14:1-22) concerns *Amaziah*, not Azariah. Moreover, the last word of verse 21 is "Amaziah", and it is followed by "He". *He* (Amaziah) was the one who rebuilt Elath and restored it to Judah "after the king slept with his fathers". That is, after the death of Jehoash king of Israel whose death is recorded in precisely the same way in verse 16. It was therefore Amaziah who rebuilt Elath during the 15 years that he outlived Jehoash.

It is clearly implied that Amaziah, so long as Jehoash was alive, was under the thumb of the Israelite king. So severely restricted were his movements that Jehoash was effectually king in Jerusalem. This explains the unexpected repetition in verses 15,16 of the concluding formula to Jehoash's reign (repeated from 13:12,13, its rightful place). Only after Jehoash's death was Amaziah able, in some degree, to strike an independent line. Notable among his achievements after Jehoash's death was to re-establish Judah's control over Elath (=Ezion-geber), now rebuilt and restored to Judah.

Others have felt it incongruous that Azariah should have had to wait until he was sixteen before being allowed to reign. We read of Joash becoming king at 7, Josiah at 8, and Manasseh at 12. So why was Azariah kept waiting so long? The text, brief as it is, is not without pointers as to what really happened.

During the previous reign Jehoash had been in virtual control of Judah (2 Kings 14:13-14). Now it was the turn of his son, Jeroboam (II). Jeroboam, we are told, "restored the borders of Israel from Lebo (the entrance to) Hamath as far as the Sea of Arabah (the Dead Sea)" (14:25). Israel's borders were now comparable to what they had been in the days of Solomon (1 Kings 8:65, cp. Amos 6:14). Jeroboam, it seems, had taken over the whole of the southern kingdom of Judah as far as the Dead Sea. But this he had accomplished not as conqueror, but as saviour. Israel's affliction was very bitter due to harassment from their neighbours presumably, but the Lord saved them by the hand of Jeroboam the son of Jehoash (14:26-27). Evidently Jeroboam's suzerainty was accepted by the people of Judah because he had brought welcome relief in their time of need.

In 14:28 the enigmatic statement is found that Jeroboam "restored Damascus and Hamath to Judah in Israel" (see *ESV*). The text as it stands is difficult to understand. It has been suggested however that we should read "to Judah *and* Israel", by the change of the letter *Beth* to the like-sounding *Waw* or *Vav* (see Hobbs: 184), thereby implying that Judah and Israel became jointly the overlords of Damascus and Hamath.

The clear implication is that Jeroboam, after the murder of Amaziah, became effectual ruler in Judah. What part he may have had in his murder, if any, is not revealed. We may guess however that he remained in control of Judah throughout Azariah's minority. It was not until Azariah was 16 years old that "the people of Judah" felt strong enough to dismiss Jeroboam's ruling junta in Jerusalem and to make Azariah king in place of his father Amaziah (14:21).

"This body, loyal to the Davidic line," writes Malamat, "normally came into play in times of crisis, especially when the continuity of the line was in question" (1968: 140). Otherwise called *'am ha'arets*, the people of the land, this group was instrumental in the overthrow of Athaliah and in restoring Joash to the throne (2 Kings 11:18-20). When Amon was murdered by his courtiers the *'am ha'arets* were quick to take action. The conspirators were punished and Josiah was placed on the throne (21:24). When Josiah was himself killed at Megiddo, the *'am ha'arets* intervened to make Josiah's *younger* son king in his place. Jehoahaz, 23 years old, represented his father's anti-Egyptian policy. The situation at the time of Azariah's accession was sufficiently grave to call for direct action by the people of Judah.

S. Talmon, one of many who have written on this subject, has this to say: "It would appear that in the period we have covered so far, i.e. the second half of the ninth century and the first half of the eighth, the Davidic dynasty repeatedly was threatened by internal rift, and that for this reason the *'am ha'arets* time and again had to put into effect its protective power" (1967: 74).

In the case of Zechariah there can be little doubt that civil war enveloped the land after the death of Jeroboam, while the various contenders vied for the throne. One of these, Zechariah, had a mandate from the Lord to be ruler in Israel because Jehu had been promised that his descendants would have the throne to the fourth generation (2 Kings 10:30). Zechariah was in fact the fourth in succession (cp. 15:12). Very probably he had already been reigning over part (perhaps the greater part) of Israel for the previous 24 years, though it was only for the concluding six months that he achieved universal recognition. It is only the final six months that are recognised in accordance with the conventions of the time in reckoning the lengths of reigns.

Thiele disposes of this interregnum in the same way as the previous one. He eliminated the twelve-year interregnum between Amaziah and Azariah by imposing a co-regency of that number of years between Jeroboam and his father Jehoash. He then eliminates the interregnum between Jeroboam and Zechariah by assuming a co-regency of 23 years between Azariah and his father Amaziah. So the troubles of one kingdom are thrust on to the other, and interregna are exchanged for co-regencies!

But the Bible is innocent of this chicanery. There Jeroboam succeeds his father, Jehoash, with complete regularity, and there is no justifiable reason why his reign should be reckoned from any other point. This being the case, an interregnum between Amaziah's assassination and Azariah's accession cannot be avoided. But even this is quite in order seeing that Azariah was only four years old and Jeroboam had extended his rule as far south as the Dead Sea. Azariah's years are counted in 2 Kings from his true accession at the age of sixteen, but even if they are antedated to the year his father died (the only other feasible starting-point), we still have a long interregnum (twelve years) between Jeroboam and Zechariah. A few years could be removed in this way, but not enough to satisfy the harmonists and at the expense of breaking up a standard chronological link (2 Kings 15:1-2). Proverbially a chain is as strong as its weakest link.

Simply to emend the text, as is the custom of some, is just not good enough. One must also explain how the errors arose. It is hardly conceivable that anyone would deliberately create gaps in the succession, so they must have come about through careless transmission. Numbers are of course notoriously susceptible to corruption, but only if the numbers are similar in appearance or for some other recognised cause. We have also to contend with Zechariah's four successors,

Shallum, Menahem, Pekahiah, and Pekah, all of which are dated by reference to Azariah's reign. We are faced here, not with one emendation, but five!

Shallum to Ahaz

Shallum   (Israel),   39th Azariah,   1 month   (2 Kings 15:13)
Menahem (Israel),   39th Azariah,   10 years   (15:17)
Pekahiah (Israel),   50th Azariah,   2 years   (15:23)
Pekah   (Israel),   52nd Azariah,   20 years   (15:27)
Jotham   (Judah),   2nd Pekah,   16 years   (15:32,33)
Ahaz   (Judah),   17th Pekah,   16 years   (16:1,2)
Jotham still alive in his 20th year   (15:30)

			47 Azariah
Zechariah		3244	39
Shallum Menahem	1	3245	40

Menahem	9	3253	
	10	3254	48 Azariah
		3255	49
Pekahiah	1	3256	50
Pekah	1 2	3257	51
	2	3258	52 1 Jotham

			1 16 Jotham Ahaz
Pekah	17	3273	2 (17)
	18	3274	3 (18)
	19	3275	4 (19)
	20	3276	5 (20)

Zechariah began to reign in 38th Azariah, his successors Shallum and Menahem in 39th Azariah. Zechariah's six-month reign must have crossed the dividing line between Azariah's years 38 and

39. From this point on, the Israelite succession gives rise to regular breaks. After the death of Menaham a break of two years is indicated, and another of eight years after the death of Pekah. There can be no mistake here seeing that all these kings are cross-referenced to the reign of Azariah. Evidently Pekahiah and Hoshea had serious opposition to overcome during this terminal period of Israel's monarchy. These periods of strife are not counted in the tale of regnal years and thus take on the appearance of interregna.

It was quite usual for Hellenistic kings to grant themselves additional years to which they were not really entitled. The Bible however leans in the opposite direction. The kings of Israel and Judah were only recognised as reigning when their position was accepted by the nation. This explains why periods of civil war and divided rule are not included in the official reign of the victorious contender. We do not know how kings such as Zechariah and Hoshea reckoned their own reigns, but we do know how the inspired editor of the books of Kings reckoned them. As might be expected, this was the truthful de facto reckoning.

Furthermore, the reigns of Zechariah, Shallum, Menaham, Pekahiah and Pekah are all cross-referenced to the reign of Azariah. Hence they are all fixed in relation to one another. There can be no justification for reckoning Pekah's reign (in Gilead according to Thiele) from the same point as Menaham's, and Jotham's reign from the second year of Pekah's alleged co-regency with Menaham. The whole scheme as devised by Thiele is artificial and contrived, and quite contrary to what the Bible plainly requires.

Most modern chronologists of the Divided Kingdom find it necessary to reduce Pekah's official reign. Thiele reduces it to eight years and Galil to five (at most). This is because Tiglath-pileser III claims to have received tribute from Menaham in c.738 BC. Gershon Galil's comment is typical: "Pekah undoubtedly did not reign for 20 years as a sole monarch, since ca. 7 years elapsed between the giving of tribute by Menaham (year 8 of Tiglath-pileser III - 738) and by Hoshea in year 15 of Tiglath-pileser III (731), and therefore it is perfectly clear that Pekah could not have reigned as sole monarch for two decades" (1996: 65). Or Miller and Hayes: "It is, of course, impossible to fit a reign of twenty years in Samaria by Pekah into the firm chronology established on the basis of the Assyrian inscriptions" (1986: 323).

But note how comfortably Pekah's reign rests in the space allotted to it in the Bible. He came to the throne in the year his predecessor died. In his second year Jotham became king in Judah, at exactly the right time in the year his father Azariah died. In his seventeenth year Ahaz became king, again at the right time when his father's official reign concluded. And he died in year 20 of Jotham, who was evidently still alive though forced into retirement after 16 years of reign. No king fits more neatly into his allocated place than Pekah. To tear him from that place and dump him on top of his predecessors, or arbitrarily to reduce his length of reign, is chronological vandalism. One does not tear up a section of rail track, carefully laid and interlocked, and fling it on top of an adjacent section - not without derailing the entire network! But these scholars will stop at nothing to bring the Bible into line with the supposed requirements of two or three mutilated and possibly mistaken Assyrian inscriptions. These we will look at in the next chapter but one.

Jotham reigned for 16 years, but in fact he was still alive four years later. This we know from the statement that Pekah was murdered in year 20 of Jotham (2 Kings 15:30). The circumstances in which Ahaz took over the throne are not stated in so many words, but almost certainly they were connected with the threat of imminent invasion from the hostile alliance of Israel and Syria. This war had already assumed serious proportions while Jotham was still on the throne (15:37), and the situation became critical soon after Ahaz' elevation (16:5-9; 2 Chron. 28:5-21; Isaiah 7-8). There can be little doubt that Ahaz was put on the throne by the pro-Assyrian party to cope with the mounting crisis. An appeal to Assyria seemed to them the only hope of national survival, but this was something which the godly Jotham was unwilling to do. Jotham, therefore, was forced into retirement in favour of his less scrupulous son.

Hoshea and Hezekiah

Hoshea   (Israel),   12th Ahaz   9 years   (2 Kings 17:1)
Hezekiah (Judah),   3 rd Hoshea,   29 years (18:1,2)

Hoshea				
Hoshea	1	3284	12	Ahaz
	2	3285	13	
	3	3286	14	
	4	3287	15 1	Hezekiah
	5	3288	16 2	
	6	3289	3	
Samaria besieged	7	3290	4	
	8	3291	5	
Samaria captured	9	3292	6	

The chronology indicates an interval of eight years between the death of Pekah and Hoshea's official beginning of reign. Unofficially he had started to reign in the twentieth year of Jotham after killing his predecessor (2 Kings 15:30), but the chronicler chooses to count his years from 12th Ahaz when his position was established by the Assyrian king.

There are significant pointers in the Bible that Ahaz, in recognition of his collaboration with the Assyrian king, was given by him authority over the remaining portion of the Northern Kingdom after he, Tiglath-pileser, had conquered the rest of the land. This kingdom, as Dr Jones points out, had been reduced by nearly 75 percent, and the remaining portion left to Samaria was a mere 35 miles wide by 45 miles long. If Ahaz was granted royal authority over this remnant it would explain why he is called "king of Israel" in 2 Chronicles 28:19. It would also explain some interesting additions to the text of Chronicles as compared with 2 Kings. Compare the following:

2 Kings 16:19-20: "Now the rest of the acts of Ahaz that he did, are they not written in the Book of the Chronicles of the Kings of Judah? And Ahaz slept with his fathers and was buried with his fathers in the city of David, and Hezekiah his son reigned in his place."

2 Chronicles 28:26-27: "Now the rest of his acts and all his ways, from first to last, behold, they are written in the Book of the Kings of Judah *and Israel.* And Ahaz slept with his fathers, and they buried him in the city, in Jerusalem, *for they did not bring him into the tombs of the kings of Israel.* And Hezekiah his son reigned in his place."

If Ahaz was king of Israel as well as Judah at this time, it would explain the apparent interregnum in Israel between Pekah and Hoshea. While Ahaz remained in Jerusalem, it is likely (as Dr Jones suggests) that "Hoshea functioned as the 'on site' overseer in Samaria." Eventually, in Ahaz 12th year, Hoshea was made official king. Tiglath-pileser claims to have appointed him himself: "Pakaha, their king they deposed and I placed Ausi' (Hoshea) over them as king."

Jotham and Hezekiah

Thiele gets rid of the interregnum between Pekah and Hoshea in the usual way, by exchanging it for a co-regency between Jotham and Azariah. In the Bible, however, Jotham succeeds his father in a perfectly regular fashion. His accession is synchronised with second Pekah, the very year his father died. In this case, it is true, his reign might easily have been reckoned from an earlier point. Azariah, we are told, was afflicted with leprosy and lived in a separate house. Moreover, "Jotham the king's son was over the house, judging the people of the land" (2 Kings 15:5). There was in effect a handover of royal authority, but interestingly the chronicler does not include this co-regency in Jotham's reign. Without any manipulation Jotham's reign begins in the very year his father died.

According to J. Hughes (*Secrets of the Times*: 105f.), "This must make it extremely doubtful that co-regencies ever existed as a possible form of government in Israel or Judah." But one can think of other reasons why this co-regency was not officially recognised. Jotham, a devout and loyal son, may have hesitated to take advantage of his ailing father by assuming royal status while his father was still alive. Compared with Azariah, the much loved and longest reigning king of Judah, Jotham must have felt inadequate and unqualified to step into his father's shoes. It was therefore out of deference for his father that Jotham declined to be called king.

Hezekiah began his reign in third Hoshea. He must therefore have co-reigned with his father for one year. Yet Hezekiah's programme for reform was commenced on 1st Nisan in his first year of reign according to 2 Chronicles 29:3,17. Dr. Lightfoot dares to think that Hezekiah "even in the lifetime of Ahaz, casteth out those defilements, that Ahaz had brought into the temple." If that were so, Ahaz must have been thoroughly disgraced. Realistically, it is most unlikely that Hezekiah would have taken this initiative while his father was still on the throne. Hence it is more probable that this was the first year of his sole reign, his father Ahaz having recently died. The month was Nisan, 3288.

That Ahaz was already dead is presupposed by the words of the priests when they reported back to Hezekiah: "We have cleansed all the house of the Lord... All the utensils which King Ahaz discarded in his reign when he was faithless, we have made ready and sanctified" (29:18,19). This is the only event of Hezekiah's reign which is dated in Chronicles, and the date is one year lower than in Kings. The sanctuary was cleansed in just sixteen days. But it was now too late to observe the Passover in the first month, so they observed it in the second month instead, for which provision was made in the law (Num. 9:10,11). There had been no Passover like that one since the days of Solomon! (2 Chron. 30:26)

The interregnum between Pekah and Hoshea is routinely eliminated by recent chronologists, but note how well Hoshea fits into the space allotted him. In his third year Hezekiah begins to reign, one year before the death of his father. But if the interregnum is removed, Hoshea's reign is pushed back eight years and, consistent with the revealed data, Hezekiah's reign is likewise pushed back eight years and made to overlap with that of his father Ahaz. According to *The New Bible Dictionary*, Ahaz and Hezekiah reigned together for thirteen years. But consider for a moment what anomalies that gives rise to. Hezekiah, the most righteous king since David, is made to co-reign with Ahaz, one of the worst. How could Hezekiah have reigned together with his father without being tarred with the same brush, without being guilty by association of his father's excesses? It is morally impossible for these two kings to have reigned together for any length of time.

Samaria was besieged by the Assyrian army in that part of Hezekiah's fourth year which corresponds to Hoshea's seventh, and was captured in that part of Hezekiah's sixth year which corresponds to Hoshea's ninth, being three years inclusive (2 Kings 18:9,10). Here again we have proof that Hezekiah's and Hoshea's reigns are reckoned from different calendar months. If Hezekiah's first year ran parallel to Hoshea's third, then his fourth year would parallel Hoshea's sixth, and his sixth year Hoshea's eighth. No part of his fourth year would have coincided with Hoshea's seventh, or his sixth year with Hoshea's ninth.

Another minor discrepancy

A problem arises in connection with Hezekiah's age on his accession to the throne. According to both Kings and Chronicles he was 25 in Hoshea's third year, yet his father Ahaz was 20 years old only thirteen years before (2 Kings 16:2; 2 Chron. 28:1). At the age of 33 Ahaz had a son of 25(!), only eight years old at the birth of Hezekiah. Certainly young marriages were not uncommon. Amon was only 15 at the birth of Josiah, Josiah himself only 14 at the birth of Jehoiakim and 15 at the birth of Jehoahaz. Eight however defies all probability. This is another example of textual error where numbers are concerned. Either Ahaz was really 25 years old (so the Greek and Syriac in 2 Chron. 28:1), or Hezekiah was only 20 or even 15.

There is a curious parallel between Hezekiah and Amaziah. According to the received text both were 25 when their reigns began, both reigned for 29 years, and both were granted 15 years of grace at the end of their reigns (14:17; 20:6). The scribe may have been thinking of Amaziah when he wrote 25, when Hezekiah's true age was really 15. Jotham was also 25 when he began to reign.

Summary

The structure of the books of Kings shows the orderly nature of the material. Every section is balanced by another in a manner which clearly shows orderliness and design.

The rules of operation are straightforward. In the Northern Kingdom reigns are reckoned from Nisan, in the Southern Kingdom from Tishri, both in accordance with the nonaccession-year system of dating. The cross-reference marks the beginning of the king's reign and his reign-length should always be counted from that point, not from some other point at the whim of the expositor.

Jeroboam's *de facto* reign began slightly later than Rehoboam's, but *de jure* it began six months earlier, being antedated to Nisan. Further proof of a Nisan mode of reckoning in Israel is provided by the first synchronism in 1 Kings 15:1: Abijam began to reign in 18th Jeroboam, the year after his father's death.

The Greek text for these reigns is preferred by Christine Tetley, but the differences found there can more easily be explained as a harmonising device aimed at avoiding the necessity of a co-regency between Jeroboam and Nadab.

Rehoboam was invaded by Shishak king of Egypt in the fifth year of his reign. Shishak is usually identified with Sheshonk I, the Libyan founder of the 22nd dynasty. This however has been disputed by David Rohl and Roger Henry, but they are not agreed as to who this king really was.

Omri's reign is cross-referenced to 31st Asa in 1 Kings 16:23, but almost every writer on the subject begins his reign in 27th Asa when his predecessor died. A smooth succession for Ahab is ensured by this means. This is something of a test case. If this synchronism does not prove to be firm, there is no guarantee that any others are firm. For this reason it is crucial that Omri's years are counted from 31st Asa.

The reference to Asa's 36th year to the effect that Baasha came up against Israel (in 2 Chronicles 16:1) creates a problem in that Baasha died in Asa's 26th year. Many have supposed that Asa's reign is here reckoned from the disruption of the kingdom under Jeroboam. This however is quite contrary to the plain sense. It is far more likely to be a textual error for 16th Asa. The error arose from the fact that Asa's 35th year is mentioned in the previous verse.

It was Omri who built Samaria and made it his capital. His son Ahab reigned with him for the last five years of his reign. A similar situation arose in Judah. Jehoram, son of Jehoshaphat, co-reigned with his father officially for three years and unofficially for another five.

When Ahab died his vassal Mesha king of Moab withheld tribute and rebelled (2 Kings 3). Joram joined forces with Jehoshaphat of Judah and the king of Edom and invaded Moab. By the Lord's intervention they won a signal victory. But great wrath came upon Israel when they drove the king of Moab to the desperate expedient of sacrificing his eldest son on the city wall. Mesha's version of the story is to be found on the Mesha stone. He claims to have driven Israel right out of his land, so much so that "Israel perished utterly for ever."

Ahaziah, son of Jehoram, was 22 when he began to reign (2 Kings 8:26), but in Chronicles his age is given as 42. Some have argued that Ahaziah's age is here backdated to the beginning of the reign of Omri. But a copyist's error is far more likely.

The reigns of Azariah in Judah and Zechariah in Israel present an interesting problem. The text as it stands clearly implies a twelve-year gap during Azariah's minority and a 24-year 'interregnum' prior to Zechariah's accession. These apparent interregna are routinely eliminated by scholars, but the text as received appears to be correct. An interregnum prior to Zechariah cannot be avoided since Zechariah himself and his successors Shallum, Mehahem, Pekahiah and Pekah are all synchronised with Azariah's reign. Azariah himself was only four years old when his father Amaziah was murdered, and Judah itself was "saved" by Jeroboam the son of Jehoash, who restored the border of Israel from Lebo-Hamath as far as the Dead Sea. Jeroboam was now king of Judah as well as Israel, and that is how it remained for the next twelve years.

Israel's succession gives rise to regular breaks from this point onwards. After the death of Menahem there is a break of two years, and another of eight years after the death of Pekah. Nearly all modern scholars find it necessary to cut back Pekah's official reign of 20 years. Thiele reduces it to eight years, Galil to five. Pekah however fits perfectly into the space allocated to him. No king fits better.

When Azariah was afflicted with leprosy and lived in a separate house, he handed over the reins of government to his son Jotham. But interestingly Jotham was not recognised as king until after his father's death. He was reluctant, it seems, to step into his father's illustrious shoes while his father was still alive.

Jotham reigned for 16 years, but he was still alive four years later as shown by the notice that Pekah was murdered in Jotham's twentieth year. Ahaz, it seems, was raised to the throne by the dominant pro-Assyrian party and Jotham forced into retirement.

Hezekiah's reformation commenced on 1st Nisan in his first year of reign according to 2 Chronicles. His reign is here reckoned from his father's death though in 2 Kings he starts to reign one year earlier. His age presents another minor discrepancy. He cannot have been 25 when he began to reign seeing that his father was 20 years old only thirteen years before. More probably he was 15.

Samaria was besieged in Hoshea's seventh year and fell in his ninth, corresponding to Hezekiah's fourth and sixth years (2 Kings 18:9-10). Here again we have proof that the reigns in Israel and Judah are reckoned from different calendar months.

The Kings of the Divided Kingdom

ISRAEL		JUDAH	
Jeroboam	3036 – 3057	Rehoboam	3036 - 3053
Nadab	3056 - 3057	Abijam	3053 - 3055
Baasha	3057 - 3080	Asa	3055 - 3094
Elah	3080 - 3081	Jehoshaphat	3094 - 3118
Zimri	3081	Jehoram	3116 - 3123
Omri	3084 - 3095	Ahaziah	3123
Ahab	3091 - 3112	(Athaliah)	3123 - 3129
Ahaziah	3111 –3112	Joash	3129 - 3168
Joram	3112 - 3123	Amaziah	3166 - 3194
Jehu	3123 - 3150	Azariah	3206 - 3258
Jehoahaz	3150 - 3166	Jotham	3258 - 3273
Jehoash	3165 - 3180	Ahaz	3273 - 3287
Jeroboam	3180 - 3220	Hezekiah	3286 - 3314
Zechariah	3244		
Shallum	3245		
Menahem	3245 - 3254		
Pekahiah	3256 - 3257		
Pekah	3257 - 3276		
Hoshea	3284 - 3292		

The reigns of the Divided Kingdom are set out in full at the end of the book with their dates BC as well as AH.

Chapter Five

The Single Kingdom

> A. 2 Kings 18:1-20:21. Hezekiah: a good king
>   B. 21:1-18. Manasseh: wicked   Independent
>   *B*. 21:19-26. Amon: wicked
> *A*. 22:1-23:30. Josiah: a good king
>
>   C. 23:31-35. Jehoahaz: three months
>   D. 23:36-24:7. Jehoiakim: eleven years
>   Appointed by Pharaoh Necho   Vassal
>   *C*. 24:8-17. Jehoiachin: three months
>   *D*. 24:18-25:7. Zedekiah: eleven years
>   Appointed by Nebuchadnezzar

After the collapse of the Northern Kingdom there still remained eight kings to run their course before the kingdom of Judah also fell victim to the northern invader. These are the kings of the Single Kingdom and their interrelation is shown above.

Of all the successors of King David on the throne of Judah, Hezekiah and Josiah alone approached him in faithfulness and integrity. Of Hezekiah it is written, "He trusted in the Lord God of Israel; so that after him was none like him among all the kings of Judah, nor any that were before him" (2 Kings 18:5). And similar praise is accorded to Josiah, "And like unto him was there no king before him, that turned to the Lord with all his heart, and with all his soul, and with all his might, according to all the law of Moses; neither after him arose there any like him" (23:25). These two kings alone are given unqualified praise, it not being said of them, "but the high places were not removed". Furthermore, Hezekiah was the fourteenth king and fourteenth generation from David. Likewise Josiah was the fourteenth king and generation from David according to the shortened genealogy of Matthew 1.

If Hezekiah and Josiah were the two most faithful kings, Manasseh and Amon were among the most wicked. It was the wickedness of Manasseh which brought down on Jerusalem the threat of desolation (21:10-15; 23:26; 24:3); while Amon, we are told, "walked in all the way that his father walked in, and served the idols that his father served, and worshipped them" (21:21).

The independent kingdom of Judah ended with the death of Josiah at Megiddo. Thereafter it was tributary, first to Egypt and then to Babylon. Hence the last four kings form a group on their own. The two who succeeded their fathers in the normal way were both removed by foreign powers after three months on the throne, and their successors appointed by these kings.

Hezekiah to Josiah

Hezekiah,	3rd Hoshea,	29 years	(2 Kings 18:1,2)
Manasseh,		55 years	(21:1)
Amon,		2 years	(21:19)
Josiah,		31 years	(22:1)

Hezekiah came to the throne in the year 3286 and reigned 29 years. He died therefore in 3314. From this point onwards there are no more cross references for nearly a hundred years. In this situation the only credible way forward is to assume a normal succession for each king. Any other recourse would be entirely subjective and invite wholesale condemnation. Assuming therefore normal successions and according each king one year less than the total given him, we arrive at the following dates:

Hezekiah (29 years).....	3286 - 3314
Manasseh (55)	3314 - 3368
Amon (2)	3368 - 3369
Josiah (31)	3369 - 3399/3400
Jehoahaz (3 months)	3400

Josiah, it would appear, died in the year 3400, exactly 400 years after the foundation of Solomon's Temple. The independent kingdom of Judah expired on the plains of Megiddo, thereafter it was tributary first to Egypt and then to Babylon. We move on now to the remaining kings of Judah and here we are assisted by the cross references to the reign of Nebuchadnezzar, king of Babylon.

Nebuchadnezzar

The first year of Nebuchadnezzar represents a turning point in Bible chronology. From this point onwards dates are given in terms of Gentile kings, a practice which is continued in the New Testament (Luke 3:1). The explanation is not far to seek: it is that the times of the Gentiles began in Nebuchadnezzar's first year. In this year God took away the privilege of national autonomy from Judah and gave over their land to a series of Gentile overlords of which Babylon was the first (Jer. 25:1-11; 27:1-11; Dan. 2:37,38). One of the penalties of the times of the Gentiles is that dates are given in terms of Gentile kings. It is providential that general unanimity exists as to the dates of Nebuchadnezzar and his successors.

Traditionally these dates have relied heavily on the Canon of Ptolemy. It is true there have been some notable dissidents. Dr. Robert R. Newton in particular has questioned the reliability of the astronomical observations recorded by Ptolemy, and much else besides. Even Faulstich is not persuaded of the complete accuracy of Ptolemy's canon. Thus his date for Nebuchadnezzar's first year is 606 BC, rather than 604, and for the fall of Jerusalem 588 instead of 586 or 587. Rolf Furuli would go even further. He has no use whatsoever for Ptolemy's Canon, his date for Nebuchadnezzar's accession being 625 and for the fall of Jerusalem 607. Anyone who has doubts on this matter should consult Carl Olof Jonsson's definitive work *The Gentile Times Reconsidered* (1998). This book provides us with a massive vindication of the accepted chronology of the reigns of Nebuchadnezzar and his successors.

It needs to be emphasized that neither Ptolemy's Canon nor the astronomical observations in the Almagest are important any more. Jonsson is very clear on this point. "The question of the length of the Neo-Babylonian era", he says, "may be definitely solved without the aid of Ptolemy's canon or the observations in Ptolemy's Almagest. In regard to Neo-Babylonian chronology, Claudius Ptolemy is of very little concern today." This is because the required information is already supplied in abundance by cuneiform texts and king-lists contemporary with the events. Indeed, "The canon, or king-list, was in use centuries before Claudius Ptolemy. It was inherited and brought up-to-date from one generation of scholars to the next." Likewise "The Persian and Greek eras are covered by numerous documents that similarly uphold the chronology of Ptolemy's canon" (Jonsson: 28-32).

This accuracy is confirmed by fourteen lines of evidence in Jonsson's work. These include: Ancient historians such as Berossus; Ptolemy's Canon; Neo-Babylonian Chronicles; synchronisms with the chronology of Egypt; Babylonian King lists; Royal Inscriptions; administrative and legal documents; and Babylonian astronomical documents, where seven important tablets are considered. "Few reigns," he says, "in ancient history may be dated with such conclusiveness as that of the Neo-Babylonian king Nebuchadnezzar ... not just two or three but as many as fourteen independent evidences have been presented, and all of them point to the year 587/86 BCE as the date of Nebuchadnezzar's eighteenth year" (Jonsson: 189f.).

I take my stand on Jonsson's work which only confirms the position upheld by the majority of modern researchers. It is a matter of no small encouragement to find ourselves on terra firma when the internal biblical dating fails us. We could so easily have been cast on the open sea with no compass to guide us, but instead all is fixed and certain!

Nebuchadnezzar's first year according to the Babylonian accession-year system (beginning in Nisan) was 604 BC. There is reason to believe however that the Jews used to reckon the years of foreign kings by their own system. This was certainly the case with the Persian king Artaxerxes whose twentieth year included both Kislev (the ninth month) and the following Nisan (Neh. 1:1; 2:1), and the presumption is that Nebuchadnezzar's years were similarly reckoned. This being the case, his first year would have been antedated to Tishri 605, and so brought into exact agreement with the fourth year of Jehoiakim (so Jer. 25:1).

The following are the dates of the last three kings of Judah as determined by cross reference with the regnal years of Nebuchadnezzar:-

Jehoiakim, 11 years (2 Kings 23:36)	608 BC
Servitude to Babylon, 3rd Jehoiakim (Dan.1:1)....	605 (July or August)
1st Nebuchadnezzar, 4th Jehoiakim (Jer.25:1)	605/4
Jehoiachin, 3 months and 10 days (2 Chron.36:9)	598
The Exile, 8th Nebuchadnezzar (2 Kings 24:12)	598/7
Zedekiah, 11 years (24:18)	597
Jerusalem besieged, 9th Zed., 10th month (25:1) ...	589
Jerusalem captured, 19th Neb., 5th month (25:8)....	586

The judgment of Servitude

The judgment of Servitude took place in Jehoiakim's third year, 606-5 BC (Dan. 1:1). Nebuchadnezzar, crown prince of Babylon, having besieged and captured Jerusalem, was content to carry away some of the vessels of the Temple and some youths of the seed royal and nobility, including Daniel and his companions. This event cannot have taken place before July 605, since it was preceded by the famous battle of Carchemish in May or June of that year in which the Egyptians were decisively defeated and their aspirations in the Euphrates area silenced for ever. This battle opened up Syria and Palestine to the victorious Babylonian army. The judgment of Servitude is also mentioned in 2 Kings 24:1 and 2 Chronicles 36:6,7, but its date is given only in Daniel.

According to 2 Chronicles 36:6-7, as well as taking vessels from the house of the Lord, Nebuchadnezzar bound the king, Jehoiakim, with bronze shackles with the intention of taking him to Babylon. One would assume that he carried out his intention though 2 Chronicles does not actually say so. In Daniel too there is more than a hint that Jehoiakim was also taken to Babylon on this occasion. Daniel 1:2, simply translated, says, "And the Lord gave into his (Nebuchadnezzar's) hand Jehoiakim king of Judah and a part of the vessels of the house of God, and he brought them to the land of Shinar to the house of his god, and the vessels he brought to the treasure house of his god."

This is how E.J.Young translates the verse. In view of the adversative force of the phrase "and the vessels", Young thinks that the the suffix "them" ("and he brought *them*") is best referred to both the king and the vessels. It has been suggested that Jehoiakim may have personally required to go to Babylon to take part in the victory celebrations as a conquered and vassal king, as was Manasseh in the days of Esarhaddon (2 Chron. 33:11). He may even have been brought to the house of Nebuchadnezzar's god in order to witness the humiliation and impotence of his own God, Yahweh, as the vessels from the house of God were placed alongside those of other conquered nations. But he was not kept prisoner in Babylon for long. Having been thoroughly humiliated, he was restored to his throne on promising abject obedience to the Babylonian king.

It was shortly after this, on 8 Ab 605 (15/16 August), that Nebuchadnezzar's father died. On hearing the news Nebuchadnezzar hurried back to Babylon to claim his father's throne, which he did on 1st Elul, only twenty-two days later. How the news of his father's death reached Nebuchadnezzar is not entirely clear. Fire and smoke signals were certainly used on occasions. "Nevertheless," says Wiseman, "with the long desert crossing from the R. Euphrates such a system is less likely than the use of a series of fast couriers" (1985:17). It was "on the first day of Elul (6/7 Sept.)" that "he sat on the throne of Babylon." Assuming it was from Riblah that he set out, he would have travelled about 580 miles in 12 to 15 days. The young king with his escort could easily have covered fifty miles in a day riding on horseback assuming that fresh steeds were provided at regular interval. His first year is reckoned in the Bible from the next month, 1st Tishri, 605, and by the Babylonians from the following new year, 1st Nisan, 604. From this date, 604 BC, are reckoned the times of the Gentiles, a prophetic time-period of great importance, which spans the centuries from 600 BC to the present day.

But when was it that Daniel was captured and taken to Babylon? Was it before the death of Nabopolassar or after? We know it took place in Jehoiakim's third regnal year, so before the end of Elul 605. According to Berosus, as quoted by Josephus in *Contra Apionem* I.19:136-138, Nebuchadnezzar, when he heard of his father's death, "set the affairs of Egypt and the other countries in order, and committed the captives he had taken from the Jews, and Phoenicians, and Syrians, and of the nations belonging to Egypt, to some of his friends, that they might conduct that part of the forces that had on heavy armour, with the rest of his baggage, to Babylonia; while he went in haste, having but a few with him, to Babylon."

Daniel's three year training course in Babylon (Dan. 1:5) can hardly have begun any later than the autumn of 605, since it was already completed before the end of Nebuchadnezzar's second year (Dan.2:1), in Adar 603 (=March 602). Not until the course was over would Daniel have been permitted to "stand before the king" (1:5), and this is precisely what he did in Daniel 2. In practice the course cannot have been much more than two calendar years, or three on inclusive reckoning.

The Captivity

Far more drastic than the Servitude was the judgment of Captivity (or *Exile*) seven years later. From the Babylonian point of view open rebellion had to be punished (2 Kings 24:1). Jehoiakim had not only rebelled against Babylonian rule, but against God's decree committing to Nebuchadnezzar supremacy over the nations. This time the city was ransacked of everything of value, and all Jerusalem was taken captive, leaving none but the poorest class in the land (24:10-14). This judgment took place in Nebuchadnezzar's eighth year, 598/97 on Jewish reckoning (24:12). The precise date is now known from the Babylonian Chronicle. The city was captured on 2 Adar 598, corresponding in Julian dating to 15/16 March 597. A short while later, after the year had expired (2 Chron. 36:10), Nebuchadnezzar "sent" and brought King Jehoiachin to Babylon. Hence it is from Nisan 597 that the era of the Exile is reckoned in Ezekiel.

Wiseman says, "That a specific date for the capture of Jerusalem is given (15/16 March 597 B.C.) shows its importance in Babylonian eyes. The Chronicle had given a precise date for the taking of the lesser towns of Rahilu and Ruggulitu, but only elsewhere, in this Chronicle, for the death of Nabopolassar and for Nebuchadnezzar's accession to the throne" (1985: 32).

We can agree with Gershon Galil that "This unique date [2 Adar 598/597] is undoubtedly the most precise in Israelite history during the biblical period and constitutes one of the cornerstones of the biblical chronology" (1996:108). But it cannot be taken for granted that Israel's calendar was always in exact agreement with the Babylonian calendar. Galil confirms : "there is no proof for the presumed correspondence between the calendars. To the contrary, since there was no intercalation of years in Babylonia, it is certainly possible that at times the calendars diverged" (1996:113). There was no fixed intercalation in Israel either for that matter. Neither their leap years nor their new year days were necessarily the same as in Babylonia.

Nisan 597 began in Babylon on 13 April, but in Israel it could well have been a month earlier, 15 March. In that case 2 Adar 598 in Babylon would correspond to 2 Nisan 597 in Israel. This might explain why the era of the Captivity (or Exile) is reckoned from 1st Nisan 597 in Ezekiel. For Israel the state of the crops and the size of the lambs were far more potent considerations than the date of the spring equinox which was all-important in Babylon. And there were other variables in the Hebrew calendar (such as certain days being taboo for specific occasions) which cast doubt on the equations that are usually cited as certainties. It is with these reservations that the correspondence 2 Adar 598 equals 16 March 597, and others like it, are quoted in this work.

If it was on 2 Adar that Jerusalem was captured, this was presumably the day on which Jehoiachin's one hundred-day reign came to its inglorious end. In that case his father Jehoiakim would have died on 21 Marchesvan, corresponding probably to 9 December. Thiele has pointed out how well this agrees with Jeremiah 36:30, where we find Jeremiah's prediction, uttered six years earlier, that Jehoiakim's dead body would be "cast out to the heat by day and the frost by night." Only in the winter months would there have been frost by night.

Jehoiachin was succeeded by his uncle Zedekiah. He however, as the cross references show, did not commence his reign until Tishri 597. This would suggest an interregnum of six months between Jehoiachin's exile and Zedekiah's accession. This may look like an "accession year", but no solid evidence has yet been found for the employment of an accession-year in Judah.

The editor of the books of Kings was always careful to note any delay in the *de facto* beginning of a king's reign, and here a delay of six months is tacitly acknowledged. This is best explained by the extensive deportation of Judah's population leaving none "save the poorest sort of the people of the land." The wholesale deportation of ten thousand men of substance, not counting women and children, must have taken some months (2 Kings 24:14-17). It was the Babylonians who rounded up the population and occupied the land. Zedekiah could only sit back and watch helplessly while this exodus took place. His reign could not begin in any meaningful way until after the Babylonians had left. And there may have been other time-consuming formalities such as Zedekiah going to Babylon to pay homage to Nebuchadnezzar (cp. Jer. 51:59). The Babylonian Chronicle, BM 21946, explains these events as follows:-

> In the seventh year (of Nebuchadnezzar's reign, 598-597), the month of Kislev (Dec/Jan), the king of Akkad mustered his troops, marched to the Hatti-land, and encamped against (besieged) the city of Judah (Jerusalem) and on the second day of the month of Adar (16 March, 597) he seized the city and captured the king (Jehoiachin). He appointed there a king of his own choice (Zedekiah), received its heavy tribute and sent (them) to Babylon.

In the Babylonian Chronicle the exile of King Jehoiachin is reckoned to Nebuchadnezzar's *seventh* year, rather than his eighth. This is because the king's eighth year was reckoned from Tishri in Judah, six months earlier than in Babylon. Adar was the last month of the King's seventh year in Babylon, though nearly half way through his eighth year in Israel. Alberto Green comments: "The appointment of Zedekiah as king by Nebuchadrezzar must have come immediately after the fall of the city, if time must be allowed for him to make the fast trip back to Babylon in time for the New Year. Zedekiah's accession would clearly be during Nebuchadrezzar's seventh Babylonian regnal year, where the Chronicle puts it" (1982: 60).

It was in the spring of 597 that Nebuchadnezzar sent and brought Jehoiachin to Babylon. This month (Nisan) was the king's eighth year of reign in both Babylon and Israel.

The judgment of Desolation

The last and severest judgment which befell the unhappy city was its siege and eventual surrender in the ninth and eleventh years of Zedekiah. The city was besieged on the 10th day of the 10th month, 589 BC, and it is this event rather than the fall of the city two and a half years later which is emphasized in the Bible. This is the day which Ezekiel was urgently commanded to write down: "Son of man, write down the name of this day, this very day. The king of Babylon has laid siege to Jerusalem this very day" (Ezek. 24:1,2). It is also the point from which the 70 years of indignation are reckoned in Zechariah 1:12. Sir Robert Anderson once wrote:

> The essential element in the judgment was, not a ruined city, but a land laid desolate by the terrible scourge of a hostile invasion (Jer. 27:13;Hag. 2:17), the effects of which were perpetuated by famine and pestilence, the continuing proof of the Divine displeasure. It is obvious therefore, that the true epoch of the judgment is not, as has been generally assumed, the capture of Jerusalem, but the invasion of Judea. From the time the Babylonian armies entered the land, all agricultural pursuits were suspended, and therefore the desolations may be reckoned from the day the capital was invested, namely, the tenth day of the tenth month in the ninth year of Zedekiah. This was the epoch as revealed to Ezekiel the prophet in his exile on the banks of the Euphrates (Ezek. 24:1,2), and for twenty-four centuries the day has been observed as a fast by the Jews in every land (*The Coming Prince*: 69-70).

A breach was made in the city wall on the 9th day of the 4th month in Zedekiah's year 11 (2 Kings 25:2 ff.). This was in the last quarter of Zedekiah's eleventh year and corresponds probably to 18 July 586 BC. That three calendar years elapsed between the siege and surrender of Jerusalem is confirmed by Ezekiel 24:1,2 and 33:21, as has already been explained. These events are placed there respectively in the ninth and twelfth years of the Exile.

Jeremiah 52:28-30

Besides the two main captivities in 597 and 586, three minor deportations are noted in Jeremiah 52:28-30, occurring in Nebuchadnezzar's years 7, 18, and 23. The very small numbers involved, 3,023, 832 and 745, confirm that these captivities were either preliminary or additional to the two major captivities. These deportations may be explained as follows. Nebuchadnezzar's seventh year, Jewish style, ran from Tishri 599 to Tishri 598, corresponding in part with his sixth year, Babylonian style, Nisan 599 to Nisan 598. The Chronicle records that near the end of his sixth year, between Kislev and Adar 599, Nebuchadnezzar conducted a campaign against the Arabs, using the Hatti-land as his base. It was probably at this time that he took captive 3,023 *Yehudim* (provincial Jews) from locations in Judah. The harassment of Jehoiakim by "bands of Chaldeans" is mentioned in 2 Kings 24:2.

These *Yehudim* stand in contrast with the 832 captives "from Jerusalem". These were taken captive during the siege itself and may have included some who deserted to the Babylonians in compliance with Jeremiah's advice (Jer. 21:9; 38:2). Again, some more *Yehudim* were captured in Nebuchadnezzar's year 23, 583/2 BC. These 745 must have been some loyal citizens who remained behind when the majority went down to Egypt. For an explanation of these minor captivities, see Alberto Green (1982: 63-66) and Jones (p.127).

The year of Josiah's death

To the chronology of the last three kings of Judah may now be added the reigns of Josiah and Jehoahaz. The information is provided by Jeremiah in the fourth year of Jehoiakim: "from the thirteenth year of Josiah the son of Amon, king of Judah, even unto this day, *these three and twenty years*, the word of the Lord hath come unto me" (Jer. 25:1-3). So from fourth Jehoiakim back to thirteenth Josiah was a period of 23 years.

If this period is reckoned inclusively as one would expect, then Josiah's year 13 would work out at 627/6 BC (627-22=605), and his first year at 639/8 . In this case his 31st and last year would be 609/8 . The battle in which Josiah was fatally wounded would have taken place in the spring or early summer. Hence Josiah must have died in the spring or early summer of 608. Josiah by popular acclaim was succeeded by his younger son Jehoahaz, but only three months later Pharaoh Necho, on his return journey from Assyria, incarcerated Jehoahaz at Riblah in Syria and placed on the throne his half-brother Eliakim, whose name he changed to Jehoiakim (2 Kings 23:30-34). By this time the month of Tishri would have nearly, if not fully, arrived, and consequently Jehoiakim's reign is counted from Tishri 608. This in fact is what the chronology requires as shown above.

The dissatisfaction of scholars

There was a time when the majority of scholars were happy to accept that Josiah had died in 608. However, with the publication of the Babylonian Chronicle BM 22047 by Professor D.J. Wiseman in 1956, the scholarly world shifted its position. With all but total unanimity it is now maintained that Josiah must have died in 609, notwithstanding the fact that Jehoiakim's first year of reign cannot have begun before Tishri 608.

The destruction of Nineveh by the Medes and Babylonians took place in 612 BC. The reigning king of Assyria, Sin-shar-ishkun, seems to have died in the flames of his burning palace. But a makeshift government was set up at Harran by Ashur-uballit II. However, in 610 Ashur-uballit and his Egyptian helpers were obliged to abandon Harran on the approach of the combined forces of the Babylonians and Umman-manda, leaving the city to the mercy of the invaders. This brings us to 609 the year in which Josiah is supposed to have died in a vain attempt to intercept the Egyptian army at Megiddo (2 Kings 23:29; 2 Chron. 35:20-24).

According to the Fall of Nineveh Chronicle BM 21901, in Tammuz (June/ July), year 17 of Nabopolassar king of Babylon (609), "a great Egyptian army" in conjunction with the Assyrians crossed the Euphrates with the intention of recapturing Harran. Their efforts seem to have met with some initial success, and they maintained the siege for almost two months, until Elul (August/ September). But when Nabopolassar marched to the aid of his beleaguered troops an attack was apparently unnecessary, for he went off immediately to the hilly district of Izalla to the north-east of the city. This is the last we hear of Ashur-uballit or of an Assyrian stand.

The catchline at the conclusion of this tablet, "In the [18th] year (608): in the month Elul the king of Akkad mustered his army...", was thought by C.J. Gadd to introduce an encounter with the Egyptians in the year 608. But Chronicle BM 22047 proved Gadd to be wrong. The campaign of 608 was directed against Urartu in the north, not against the Egyptians. It is nevertheless true that the Egyptians, encamped at Carchemish, held Syria for another four years, and still in 606 inflicted a defeat on Nabopolassar. Their final defeat at Carchemish and expulsion from Syria took place in May/June 605.

The Chronicle makes no mention of either the Egyptians or the Assyrians in the year 608, and this fact more than anything else has convinced the scholarly world that Josiah must have died in 609. One solution, championed by Malamat and Alberto Green among others, assumes a consistent application of post-dating on the part of the Jews. Jehoiakim, it is argued, must have been installed as king after 1st Tishri 609. The succeeding eleven months or more were counted as his accession year and his first year of reign began in Tishri 608. This, they say, is borne out by subsequent reigns. Nebuchadnezzar succeeded his father in Ab 605. Again, by postdating, his first year is reckoned by the Jews from Tishri 605 (and by the Babylonians from Nisan 604). Zedekiah was appointed king by Nebuchadnezzar in Adar 598, but his first year of reign was postdated to Tishri 597.

But are they justified in assuming an accession year at all? Down to this point the kings of Judah have consistently employed the nonaccession-year system. What reason had Jehoiakim for changing this time-honoured custom? If his Egyptian overlord had made use of an accession year Jehoiakim might have done the same in deference to his royal overlord. But the Egyptians employed the nonaccession-year system the same as in Israel. Jehoiakim had no reason for acting any differently from his forefathers nor, I believe, did his few remaining successors.

Notwithstanding the silence of the Babylonian Chronicle, the year 608 for Josiah's death is undoubtedly that which best accords with the biblical evidence. An Egyptian presence in Assyria is mentioned for both 610 and 609. Though not explicitly mentioned, their presence there in 608 as well cannot be excluded. E.R. Thiele, in the first edition of his *Mysterious Numbers*, took the view that Josiah died in 608, and even after the publication of the Babylonian Chronicle in 1956 he still regarded this as a feasible alternative. Writing in October of that year he said, "With the forces of Egypt so active in the Euphrates area, the possibility of Necho making an appearance there in 608, although not expressly mentioned, cannot be categorically dismissed" (1956: 143). We may infer that Pharaoh Necho on this occasion avoided any clash with the Babylonian army, and for this reason the expedition is passed over in silence in the Babylonian Chronicle.

What was Josiah playing at?

But what reason do we give for Josiah's fatal intervention at Megiddo, or indeed for Egypt's apparent concern for Assyria's survival? The usual explanation is that Josiah's action was part of a concerted attempt to pin down the Egyptian forces while the Medo-Babylonian army disposed of the hated Assyrian. A better assessment of the situation is given by A. Malamat (1973: 267-79). According to him the political vacuum left by the retreating Assyrians was the subject of rivalry between Egypt and Judah. Josiah had already extended his rule over districts coinciding more or less with the former Assyrian province of Samerina. What he wished to avoid was an Egyptian takeover in the still unclaimed districts in the former province of Magiddu, comprising the Jezreel valley and Galilee. Egypt, likewise, was chiefly interested in implementing its own territorial ambitions at the expense of the retreating Assyrians (and the invading Babylonians). Hence the Bible is not so wide of the mark when it implies that Pharaoh Necho was marching *against* the last king of Assyria, rather than to his support (2 Kings 23:29 *KJV*). It was not until 605 that Egypt's aspirations in this region were finally halted. Josiah's action was politically astute, but it was not in accord with the will of God as put in the mouth of the Egyptian pharaoh (2 Chron. 35:21,22).

It must be admitted that a great deal of uncertainty attends the circumstances of Josiah's intervention and death. According to Miller and Hayes, "Any proposed scenario about why and how Josiah was killed at Megiddo must be based on speculation" (1986: 402). In view of this uncertainty, the dogmatism of scholars that Josiah can only have died in 609 is inappropriate.

It is not impossible that the king of Assyria referred to in 2 Kings 23:29 is the Babylonian conqueror, Nabopolassar. Having conquered Assyria he would naturally assume the title of the defeated king. Pharaoh Necho's real enemy was Babylon, not Assyria. Babylon now threatened to take over former Egyptian territory in Syria and Palestine and this is what Necho was determined to prevent. There is no doubt whatsoever that "against" is the correct translation of the preposition *'al* in this verse ("Pharaoh Necho king of Egypt went up *against* the king of Assyria", *KJV*). If it can be assumed that Nabopolassar is the new king of Assyria (rather than the defunct Ashur-uballit), the problem is solved once and for all.

The beginning of reign

Some have thought that the expression "in the beginning of the reign", *bereshit mamlekhet* (or *mamlekhut*), as applied to Jehoiakim (in Jer. 26:1) and to Zedekiah (in Jer. 27:1; 28:1; 49:34), indicates an accession year, on the analogy of the Assyrian *resh sharruti*. But that is clearly not the case, since in Jeremiah 28:1 Zedekiah's "beginning of reign" is further defined as the fifth month of his fourth year! The expression only means "the early part of his reign". Keil explains, "The reign of Zedekiah is divided into two halves: the first period, or beginning, when he was elevated by Nebuchadnezzar and remained subject to him, and after or last period, when he had rebelled against his liege lord." The same applies to Jehoiakim as 2 Kings 24:1 bears witness.

   The only other occurrence of this expression is in Genesis 10:10 with reference to Nimrod. In none of these places is there any allusion to an accession year.

Jeremiah 46:2

This verse has already been mentioned in Chapter 3. I said there that it was the only verse which presented a problem to a Tishri dating of the reigns of the kings of Judah. I will here repeat briefly what I have said already. In this verse there appears to be an unequivocal statement to the effect that Nebuchadnezzar defeated the king of Egypt at Carchemish in the fourth year of Jehoiakim. Quite literally it says:

> What was the word of the Lord to Jeremiah against the nations: concerning Egypt, against the army of Pharaoh Necho king of Egypt, which was by the river Euphrates in Carchemish, which Nebuchadrezzar king of Babylon smote, in the fourth year of Jehoiakim, son of Josiah, king of Judah.

This statement, taken at face value, presents a serious problem for our dating since Jehoiakim's fourth year had not yet begun when Pharaoh Necho was defeated at Carchemish. That battle took place in the spring or early summer of 605, during the second half of Jehoiakim's *third* year, and it was still Jehoiakim's third year when Nebuchadnezzar besieged Jerusalem a month or two later, as Daniel 1:1 correctly records. What therefore are we to do with Jeremiah 46:2?

   Many suggestions have been made, most of them unworthy of serious consideration. The only one which commends itself is that of S. H. Horn who considers the central clauses to be parenthetical. He would translate:

> The word of Yahweh which came to Jeremiah the prophet, against the nations; about Egypt: against the army of Pharaoh Neco, king of Egypt (which had been at the river Euphrates at Carchemish which Nebuchadrezzar king of Babylon had defeated) in the fourth year of Jehoiakim son of Josiah, king of Judah. (1967: 26)

Actually the parenthesis need include no more than the six words "which Nebuchadrezzar king of Babylon defeated." But either way, it is the oracle, the word of the Lord to Jeremiah, which came to him in the fourth year of Jehoiakim, not the defeat of Pharaoh Necho at Carchemish.

Some may regard this as "artificial and unnatural", but in fact it is no different from several other verses of a similar construction which we have already seen or will shortly see. Compare:

Genesis 15:13: "Know of a surety that thy seed shall be a stranger in a land that is not theirs (and they shall serve them and they shall afflict them) 400 years."
Exodus 12:40: "Now the sojourning of the children of Israel (who dwelt in Egypt) was 430 years."
2 Chronicles 36:21: "to fulfil the word of the Lord by Jeremiah (until the land had enjoyed her sabbaths: for as long as she lay desolate she kept sabbath) to fulfil 70 years."

Not so different is Jeremiah 45:1: "The word that Jeremiah the prophet spoke to Baruch the son of Neriah (when he had written these words in a book at the mouth of Jeremiah), in the fourth year of Jehoiakim the son of Josiah king of Judah, saying ..." Also Jeremiah 51:59.

All these verses, taken in isolation, might be interpreted differently but, taken in context, no other interpretation is possible. It is the same with Jeremiah 46:2. Taken in context it cannot mean that the battle of Carchemish took place in Jehoiakim's fourth year. We know that his fourth year did not begin until Tishri 605, and that was four or five months after the Egyptian defeat at Carchemish. Better far to accept a short parenthesis than to throw the entire chronology into disarray as all other solutions do!

Nebuchadnezzar's reign in Judah and Babylon

Nebuchadnezzar's regnal years were reckoned in Babylon from Nisan in agreement with the calendar year, as shown on the left of the diagram. In Judah, however, they were reckoned from the preceding Tishri, in line with the regnal years of their own kings, as shown on the right. Hence Jerusalem was captured in Nebuchadnezzar's seventh year, Babylonian style, but in his eighth year as reckoned in Judah.

Nabopolassar	18	608 BC (3400)	1 Jehoiakim
	19	607 (3401)	2
	20	606 (3402)	3
21 Nebuchadnezzar acc.year	605 (3403)	Daniel and co. taken captive
			4 1 Nebuchadnezzar
Nebuchadnezzar 1	604 (3404)	

			7 Nebuchadnezzar
			10 Jehoiakim
Nebuchadnezzar 7 Jerusalem taken, 2 Adar	598 (3410)	11 3 ms. Jehoiachin. Exiled at the turn of yr., 2Chr.36:10
8 First year of the Exile	597 (3411)	Depopulation of Judah
			1 Zedekiah
9	596 (3412)	

		8 Zedekiah
Nebuchadnezzar 16 Ninth year of the Exile	589 (3419)	9 Jerusalem besieged, 10th Tebeth, Ezek.24:1,2
17	588 (3420)	10
18	587 (3421)	11 Jerusalem falls, 9th Tammuz
19	586 (3422	

Actually Nebuchadnezzar's father died on 8 Ab 605 and the new king claimed his father's throne back in Babylon on 1st Elul. This is one month before Tishri 605, the month from which the Bible reckons Nebuchadnezzar's first year. So what we find is the Jews antedating the king's reign, not from his actual accession month, but from the following Nisan when his first year began in Babylon. This brought Nebuchadnezzar's first year into line with Jehoiakim's fourth (Jer.25:1) and his 18th year into line with Zedekiah's tenth (32:1), but always six months ahead of the equivalent year as reckoned in Babylon.

This is very similar to what occurs in the Canon of Ptolemy. There also the reigns of Babylonian and Persian kings are antedated from their postdated first year of reign. In their case they are antedated to 1st Thoth, the Egyptian New Year's Day. Depuydt calls this "predating of postdating" – "a zigzag procedure consisting of two movements in opposite directions: postdating forward from the actual beginning of reign to the first Babylonian new year, that is, the beginning of the Babylonian Year 1, which always falls around the spring equinox, and predating backward from the beginning of the Babylonian year 1 to the Egyptian new year" (Depuydt: 115).

2 Kings 25:27

According to 2 Kings 25:27 and Jeremiah 52:31, it was in year 37 of the Exile that Evil-Merodach (Amel-Marduk, son and successor of Nebuchadnezzar) "in the year of his reigning" lifted up the head of King Jehoiachin, that is released him from prison. And this was on the 27th day (25th in Jeremiah) of Adar, the twelfth month. The phrase "year of his reigning" is usually taken to mean Amel-Marduk's accession year, 562 BC. If however the years of the Exile are here reckoned from Nisan 597 (as in Ezekiel), the year 37 would be 561/60, near the end of Amel-Marduk's first year of reign. Hence Finegan believes the phrase should be translated "in the first year of his reign" (para 449).

However, in the view of Gershon Galil, it is unreasonable to suppose that Jehoiachin was released at the end of Amel-Marduk's first year of reign. "It cannot be assumed", he says, "that Jehoiachin was released at the end of the first year of Amel-Marduk, i.e. more than twenty months after his coronation. To the contrary, it may reasonably be supposed that Amel-Marduk, like many kings in the ancient Near East, released Jehoiachin within the context of a *duraru* [amnesty] he probably proclaimed close to his coronation" (1996: 117n).

T.R. Hobbs correctly translates the Hebrew expression "in the very year he began to reign", but he then gives the precise date as 12 March 560. That, however, would be the end of Amel-Marduk's first year, not the very year he began to reign. Possibly the Exile is reckoned in 2

Kings on a factual basis from the exact month (Adar 598) that Jehoiachin was taken captive. Reckoned from Adar 598, the thirty-seventh year would have begun in Adar 562, a short while before the close of Amel-Marduk's accession year. 2nd Adar 562 corresponds to 8th March 561, about three weeks before Jehoiachin's release.

King Jehoiachin was released a few days before the first new year's day of Amel Marduk's reign when his first year of reign began. It was doubtless in prospect of this joyful occasion that this act of clemency was designed. Along with other liberated kings, Jehoiachin was privileged to have a part in the celebrations that marked this occasion.

Amel-Marduk began to reign on 5 Tammuz 562 (probably 19 July - BM 65270), and his accession year lasted about nine months. When Jehoiachin was released he put off his prison garments and was given even a higher status than the other kings who ate regularly at the king's table. D.J. Wiseman says, "'To eat at the king's table' is explained as the receipt of regular royal allowances (v.30). These were usually of wheat, barley, and oil and occasionally, meat, ointment and clothing. They were handed by the administration to a dependant and not necessarily consumed in the palace itself" (1985: 82).

It is interesting to observe the very different treatment meted out to King Jehoiachin and his successor Zedekiah. While Zedekiah languished blinded in some adjacent prison, Jehoiachin was regarded as something more than the titular head of the Jewish diaspora. As Wiseman points out, "Texts from the Southern Palace show that in 592/1-569/8 Nebuchadrezzar granted Jehoiachin of Judah (*Yaukin sar (mat) Yaudaya*) oil from the royal stores. Supplies were granted also to his five sons who were in the care of a Babylonian appointee one Qana'ama, possibly a Jew (*Qana-yau*). This may indicate that the family as a whole was held not merely as royal hostages to be displayed on state occasions but to be trained for eventual return to their land as loyal supporters of the Babylonian regime" (1985: 81).

In this connection it is interesting to note that Zerubbabel, leader of the returning exiles, was a grandson of Jehoiachin (1 Chron. 3:17-19). This agrees well with Jeremiah's assessment of those carried away with Jehoiachin as "very good figs, even like the figs that are first ripe", in marked contrast with the residue left behind with Zedekiah who were "evil figs which cannot be eaten, they are so evil" (Jer. 24:1-8)! Of the captives under Jehoiachin the Lord says, "I will set my eyes upon them for good, and I will bring them again to this land" (v.6).

Daniel 1:1

According to Daniel 1:1 it was in the third year of King Jehoiakim that Nebuchadnezzar besieged Jerusalem and carried off certain Israelites from the royal family and the nobility, including Daniel and his companions. It was in the summer of 605, soon after the battle of Carchemish, that the king of Babylon besieged Jerusalem, Jehoiakim's third year being still in progress. His fourth year began in Tishri (Sept/Oct) of the same year.

The Babylonian Chronicle is quite succinct: "At that time (after defeating the Egyptians at Carchemish) Nebuchadrezzar conquered the whole land of Hatti", meaning Syria/Palestine. But some scholars believe this to be wrongly translated. According to them it should read "the entire land of Ha[ma]th", not "the entire land of Hatti." A. Malamat for example says that Judah submitted to Nebuchadrezzar in December 604 (over a year later) when the king of Babylon devastated Ashkelon in Kislev of his first year of reign, and that the reference in Daniel is in error. But Daniel's version is confirmed by Josephus who says that Judean captives, among others, were carried off to Babylon after the victory at Carchemish (*Ant*.X.11.1).

Sabbatical and Jubilee years

Both Jonsson and Faulstich attach considerable importance to the recurring cycles of Sabbatical and Jubilee years. Both writers think they can identify some of these and believe that their own chronology is confirmed by its agreement with these recurring fixtures. From the study of post-biblical Jewish texts a number of Sabbatical years have been identified from 331 BC onwards. Working backwards from these, the dates of Old Testament Sabbatical and Jubilee years can also be identified, or so it is claimed (Jonsson: *Supplement*, 56-60). One such Sabbatical year, argues Jonsson, was 590/89, his year for the siege of Jerusalem in the ninth year of Zedekiah. This, he says, is confirmed by Jeremiah 34 which speaks of the liberation of slaves. Another, according to Faulstich (using a different calculation), was the fall of Jerusalem in 588. Since however both these dates are demonstrably wrong, I am not exactly impressed by this method of settling the chronology!

The Sabbath year was ordained every seventh year. It only concerned the land, being "a Sabbath of solemn rest for the land". Its purpose was to give the land a complete rest from agricultural pursuits one year in seven (Lev.25:1-7). The Jubilee year was ordained every fiftieth year. It began on the Day of Atonement on the tenth day of the seventh month. In this year every holding was restored to its former owner so that no family would permanently forfeit its allotment in the promised land (Lev.25:8-17). In the Sabbath year there was also a release of all debts. Every creditor waived his rights in this regard and every debtor was released from what he owed (Deut.15:1-6).

It has been inferred from Deuteronomy 31:10-11 that the Sabbath year ran from Tishri to Tishri, as did the year of Jubilee. It is here implied that "the end of every seven years" coincided with the Feast of Booths. Others however (e.g. Dr Jones, p.288) have argued that the Jubilee year straddled the 49th and 50th years, six months (Tishri to Adar) in one year and six months (Nisan to Elul) in the next. In that case there were 49 years from one Jubilee to the next, and the Sabbath year ran from Nisan to Nisan. Probably the Tishri option should be accepted, but even the ancient authorities were undecided on how it worked. Maimonides, quoted by Finegan (para 232) said, "The Jubilee year is not included in the number of the seven-year periods; the forty-ninth is Shemittah, the fiftieth year is Jubilee, and the fifty-first year is the beginning of the (new) seven-year periods." But the book of Jubilees (about 160-150 BC) has Jubilee periods of 49 years, and this is accepted by modern scholars such as Ben Zion Wacholder.

The usual practice is to reckon retrospectively from known Jubilee or Sabbatical years in Israel's history, such as 163 BC (see 1 Macc. 6:20,49,53) or 135 (1 Macc. 16:14-17). But this only works on the assumption that the system continued without a break (or was resumed as if there had been none) during and after the Exile. Nehemiah bound himself and the people "to walk in God's law that was given by Moses the servant of God … we will (he said) forego the crops of the seventh year and the exaction of every debt" (Neh.10:29-31). His words imply that hitherto that had not been the case. Finegan (para 224) quotes the Jewish tractate *Seder 'Olam Rabbah* 30:31-37: "Just as at their incoming in the time of Joshua they became subject to tithes, Sabbatical years and Jubilees … so too at their incoming in the time of Ezra." Hence it seems likely that a fresh start was made after the Exile as suggested by Nehemiah 10:31.

The alternative is to calculate prospectively from Joshua's conquest of the promised land. But this again involves unproven assumptions. It assumes that one's own chronology is completely correct and that the system operated without a fault throughout the era of the Judges when widespread lawlessness prevailed and "every man did that which was right in his own eyes." I would not consider that a safe procedure either.

In Jeremiah 34 Zedekiah made a covenant with all the people in Judah to proclaim freedom of their slaves. Since this was a feature of the year of Jubilee, it is concluded that this, the year of the siege, was a Jubilee or Sabbatical year. In Jonsson's view this confirms his date, 590/89, for the siege of Jerusalem. He dismisses the view of "some Bible commentators" that Zedekiah called for the freedom of slaves simply to avert disaster, not because it was a Sabbatical year. What Zedekiah did, he argues, is in agreement with the legal provisions set forth in Deuteronomy 15:12-18. It is not certain however that Deuteronomy here is referring to the Sabbatical year at all. A Hebrew slave was to be set free in the seventh year of service. It was only in the year of Jubilee that Hebrew slaves were supposed to be released *en masse* (Lev.25:10), and 590/89 was not a Jubilee year (Finegan, para 235).

The expression "proclaim liberty" (*qara deror*) occurs four times in Jeremiah 34 (verses 8,15,17), and elsewhere only in Leviticus 25:10 and Isaiah 61:1. It is a technical term linking Jeremiah 34 with the manumission of slaves as required in the year of Jubilee. However, it is obvious from reading this chapter that the manumission of slaves as required by the law had not been observed for a long time. So, once again, it would be hazardous to draw any far-reaching conclusions.

Another passage which has marked Sabbatical overtones is 2 Kings 19:29. Here we have the sign which Isaiah conveyed to Hezekiah that the Assyrian king was about to be led away like a stubborn and wayward ox with a bit and a hook in his nose. "This year eat what grows of itself, and in the second year what springs of the same. Then in the third year sow and reap and plant vineyards, and eat their fruit."

The word translated "what grows of itself" occurs in this sense only here, Psalm 37:30 and Leviticus 25:5,11. The three years mentioned in 2 Kings are the same as the seventh, eighth and ninth years mentioned in Leviticus 25:21-22 in connection with the year of Jubilee. For this reason Dr Floyd Jones places the Assyrian invasion (the second of the two invasions he proposes) in 609/8 because he reckons that was a Jubilee year. My date is also 609/8 but not for that reason. It just so happens that 609/8 is the year that my chronology requires.

In year 14 of his reign Hezekiah received the promise, "This year you will eat what grows by itself, and the second year what springs from the same. But in the third year sow and reap, plant vineyards and eat their fruit" (2 Kings 19:29). This is precisely what is promised in connection with the year of Jubilee in Leviticus 25:20-22, though it would apply equally to the Sabbatical year (vv. 4,5). My date for Hezekiah's year 14 is 709/8. This could have been a Sabbatical year (709-8). But the Lord's promise in this instance has more to do with the devastation of the land by the Assyrians than the observance of a Sabbatical year. Although cultivation had not been possible for two successive seasons, it is implied, this was not set to continue: in the third year everything would be back to normal.

In Leviticus 26 the people are warned of the dire consequences resulting from their failure to keep these commandments. The catalogue of penalties reaches its climax in verse 33 with the threat of total desolation of both their land and their cities. Then, verse 34, "the land shall enjoy its Sabbaths as long as it lies desolate.... As long as it lies desolate it shall have rest, *the rest that it did not have on your Sabbaths when you were dwelling in it.*" The sad truth is that the Sabbath years were *never* observed until after the Exile. It is rather pointless therefore calculating when they might have occurred.

Ezekiel's "thirtieth year"

In the opening verse of Ezekiel there is a reference to "the thirtieth year", but without explaining the nature of the era concerned. The same year is also defined as "the fifth year of King Jehoiachin's captivity", that is 593 BC.

This enigmatic reference to the thirtieth year has nothing to do with "the twenty-seventh" year of Ezekiel 29:17, where undoubtedly the Exile should be understood. Nor is it to be explained as Ezekiel's age on being appointed to the office of priest, for Numbers 4:3 required a full thirty years to which Ezekiel would not have attained. It cannot even be explained as the thirtieth year of the Neo-Babylonian Kingdom, for that was founded in 626 BC, four years too early for the era in question. It must therefore be a cross date to some event in Jewish history thirty years before the fifth year of the Exile. This fixes it as the epoch-making year of the finding of the Book of the Law in year 18 of Josiah's reign (2 Kings 22; 2 Chron. 34). Josiah's year 18 began in Tishri 622, and taking this as the starting point we arrive at the required date, 593.

What heart-searching, repentance, and dedication the finding of the Law had engendered in the reign of Josiah! What a reformation it had produced, a clean sweep of all the accumulated abominations of centuries! What a Passover was celebrated the following year - there had been nothing like it since the days of the Judges! But how greatly had the situation changed by 593, the fifth year of the Exile of King Jehoiachin and the fifth year of the reign of King Zedekiah. The nation was now a fraction of its former size and about to plunge into the abyss. And the reason - they had not obeyed the Book of the Law, the very same found in the Temple in the eighteenth year of Josiah. By the standard set by that Law the nation was doomed, but by the standard of God's grace which only a prophet like Ezekiel could discern, there was still the hope of a glorious future when the judgment had spent itself and the nation was cleansed of its habitual defilement and disobedience.

The pious in Israel must have looked back nostalgically to the time of Josiah's famous reform and even regarded it as the beginning of a new era. According to Hayes and Hooker (1988: 86) the royal calendar was changed in this year from one beginning in Tishri to one beginning in Nisan. For this there is no evidence whatsoever. We may however agree with them that Josiah's reform was regarded by the faithful as the beginning of a new era.

Forty years and 390 years

The prophecy comes in Ezekiel 4. Ezekiel is commanded to depict Jerusalem on a clay tablet such as were in common use in Babylonia. He was then to lay siege to it with miniature siege engines, a ramp and model battering-rams. Not only so, he was himself to bear the iniquity of the houses of Israel, 390 days for Israel on his left side and 40 days for Judah on his right side, a day for each year of their sin. His daily fare was to be that of a people under siege (or in exile) and at the same time he was to prophesy against Israel with bared arm. This he was actually to do in literal obedience to the Lord's directions. Indeed, the Lord would bind him with invisible ropes to prevent him from turning over before the set time.

It has been well said that whatever God commands anyone to do, that thing He enables him to do. So Ezekiel was divinely enabled to carry out the seemingly impossible feat of lying on the same side for 390 days, and then on the other side for 40 days. Eichrodt remarks, "Appeals to physical impossibility are not justified by what we know of the powers of the Indian Yogis and fakirs to enter into a sustained trance" (*Ezekiel*: 83). Ezekiel however had to prepare his frugal meals and eat them at set times, so there was no opportunity for sustained trance.

The expression "to bear sin or iniquity" is a technical term in the Pentateuch for to bear the punishment due to sin or iniquity. Ezekiel was to take upon himself the consequences of Israel's sin. But the two periods of days represent not the years of punishment, but "the years of their sin" (4:5). The forty years of Judah's sin is best explained as corresponding to the ministry of Jeremiah. Jeremiah's prophetic ministry extended from the year 13 of Josiah (627-26) to the year 11 of Zedekiah (587-86), a period of 40 regnal years (Jer.1:1-3).The national guilt increased beyond measure as a result of Jeremiah's tireless exposure and condemnation of their conduct. What with Josiah as king and Jeremiah as prophet, there could be no more excuse for their continued disobedience. It is for this reason that these forty years are singled out as the period of iniquity for the house of Judah.

By many the 390 years of Israel's sin are assumed to be the years of the Northern Kingdom, beginning with the disruption of the kingdom under Jeroboam. By my reckoning, from the first year of Jeroboam to the eleventh of Zedekiah was 386 years, which Ezekiel might have rounded up to 390. But I would question whether the sins of the northern tribes in exile subsequent to the fall of Samaria can be legitimately counted. I would even question whether their sinful conduct in Tirzah and Samaria has any real bearing on the siege and surrender of Jerusalem. In my view these 390 years are more satisfactorily applied to the time when the Ephraimite tribes were dominant in Israel and Jerusalem was shared by the Jebusites and the Benjaminites (Judges 1:21). From the division of the Land to the death of King Saul was exactly 390 years. That this was a period of iniquity the books of Judges and 1 Samuel leave us in no doubt.

For Dr Floyd Jones these 390 years are "a key biblical anchor point", "the mathematical key to correctly founding the chronology of the kings of Judah and Israel." He considers Ezekiel 4:4-8 "completely apropos in assigning the 390-year prophecy to 'Israel' over a century and a quarter after that kingdom had ceased to exist as an entity" (2005: 133). He notes that there had been a mass emigration from the Northern Kingdom to the Southern Kingdom both before and after the fall of Samaria (2 Chron.15:9; 35:17-19). Hence it was quite proper to speak of Israel's sin even after the collapse of the Northern Kingdom. But Ezekiel speaks of "the house of Israel" and "the house of Judah" as two separate entities. In my judgment these terms would not apply after the house of Israel had ceased to exist as an independent kingdom, quite apart from the impropriety of reckoning Israel's sinful conduct in Samaria as contributing to the guilt of Jerusalem.

Josiah, Amon, Manasseh and Hezekiah

Josiah came to the throne in 639 BC. But what of his predecessors, Amon, Manasseh and Hezekiah, for whom there are no cross-references? As already mentioned the only safe and prudent course is to assume that they succeeded one another in a regular fashion. To assume otherwise is arbitrary and subjective, and lays one open to the charge of fixing the chronology. Assuming therefore a regular succession we arrive at the following BC dates for Josiah and his predecessors: -

> Josiah ascended the throne in 639
> Amon in .... 640 (+1)
> Manasseh in .... 694 (+54)
> Hezekiah in .... 722 (+28)

These dates will not satisfy many people. They do not sit comfortably with the received date for the fall of Samaria in Hezekiah's sixth year (2 Kings 18:10). If Samaria fell in 722 or 723 as is commonly believed, then Hezekiah must have ascended the throne in 727 or 728. But there is no way Hezekiah's accession can be pushed back to 727 without assuming an interregnum between two of his successors. There simply are not enough years to fill the gap. Even if Amon, Manasseh and Hezekiah are given their full quota of years (assuming an accession year for each of them), we only acquire an additional three years and raise Hezekiah's accession to 725. Even if Josiah came to the throne in 740, we are still one year short. But the Bible gives no hint that King Manasseh adopted the accession-year system, nor does it support the idea that Josiah's reign began in 740. We have therefore a stark choice: either we believe that Samaria fell in 722 in accord with the scholarly consensus or we accept a date a few years later (716) on the basis of an uncomplicated acceptance of the biblical data. This is admittedly a problem area which will be fully discussed in the next chapter.

By modern scholars (since Thiele) Hezekiah has been given what amounts to two reigns. In the sixth year of his first reign Samaria fell in 723/2 BC; in the fourteenth year of his second reign Sennacherib invaded in 701. The Bible, however, knows of only one reign: it began in the third year of Hoshea and lasted 29 years. Where in the Bible is there the faintest suggestion that

Hezekiah had two reigns, one as coregent with his father and another as sole king, separated by thirteen or fourteen years? The whole idea is manifestly absurd as many people would admit.

Summary

For the later kings of Judah there are no cross references with the kings of Israel to help us in our quest. To a large extent, however, this is compensated for by cross references to the reign of Nebuchadnezzar king of Babylon. We are relieved to discover that the reigns of the kings of Babylon are confirmed by an abundance of contemporary documentation which provides all the information we need.

It is only the reigns of Manasseh, Amon and Josiah for whom no cross references are available. So far as these kings are concerned, the only defensible way forward is to assume a regular succession in each case.

There were three judgments of escalating severity which came down on the kingdom of Judah in its declining years. The first of these was the Servitude in the summer of 605 BC when Daniel and his companions were carried off to Babylon. The second was the Captivity or Exile of King Jehoiachin at the end of 598 or the beginning of 597. The exact date is now known from the Babylonian Chronicle: it was 2 Adar 598 (in Babylon) corresponding to 15/16 March 597, probably 2 Nisan 597 in Israel. The third was the judgment of Desolation in the summer of 586 when the kingdom of Judah came to an end.

The occasion of Josiah's death, both its date and the circumstances attending it, has provoked a great deal of discussion. The dogmatism of scholars that 609 is the only possible date was shown to be unfounded. The date required by the Bible is undoubtedly 608.

The only verse which presents a problem to Tishri dating is Jeremiah 46:2 where the battle of Carchemish is apparently dated to the fourth year of Jehoiakim, instead of the third. The solution was found in the presence of a parenthesis. The fourth year of Jehoiakim is the date of the oracle, not the date of the battle of Carchemish.

The significance of King Jehoiachin's release from prison at the beginning of the reign of Evil Merodach (Amel Marduk) in 562 BC was considered. This was found to be more than an act of clemency on the part of the Babylonian king. It was a step toward restoring him (or one of his descendants) to eventual governmental responsibility in Judah.

The question about Sabbatical and Jubilee years, on which some scholars have placed a great deal of reliance, was found to be largely irrelevant. There is no evidence that these were observed at all, not at least on a regular basis, in pre-exilic times. One purpose of the judgment of Desolation was to give the land a much needed time of rest, the Israelites having failed to observe the prescribed Sabbatical and Jubilee years for a very long time.

Finally, references in Ezekiel to the thirtieth year (1:1) and to 40 and 390 years in chapter 4, were briefly examined.

Chapter Six

The Assyrian Problem – Toward a Solution

A handful of Assyro-Israelite contacts, apparently fixed and certain as to their dates, have furnished the framework of almost every chronological scheme devised in recent years for the period of the Kings. Ahab's participation in the battle of Qarqar in 853 BC, Jehu's payment of tribute to Shalmameser III in 841, Menahem's encounter with Tiglath-pileser III in about 740, Pekah's replacement by Hoshea in 732, the fall of Samaria in 722 or 721, and Hezekiah's encounter with Sennacherib in 701 - these are the supposedly fixed points around which the biblical data have been judiciously arranged.

It is hardly surprising in view of the method employed that the resultant schemes have shown a very close agreement with the Assyrian material as commonly interpreted. But their treatment of the biblical material has been far less satisfactory. In order to ensure the coincidence of these synchronisms it has been necessary to compress the biblical data in the most arbitrary manner. Whereas the older chronologists freely emended the text to make it agree, the method today is to explain the figures as they stand (so far as that is possible), but in such a way as to fit in with the preconceived framework. A semblance of fidelity to Scripture is thereby preserved. It is however only a semblance, for it is evident that the Bible has not been interpreted in a natural or grammatical way in accord with sound principles of exegesis.

A traditional chronology derived from the Bible is no longer entertained in scholarly circles. It is even asserted that the Bible has no chronology of its own at all, and that the only system available is that of Assyria. The Hebrew kings are still made to submit to their Assyrian overlords as they did in their lifetime. The scorn of scholars is immediately aroused if one dares to question the integrity of the Assyrian Eponym Canon or the accuracy of the Assyrian inscriptions. But we need to get our priorities right. To which do we give precedence, the Bible or the Canon, the Royal Canon as found in the books of Kings and Chronicles or the Eponym Canon inscribed on clay tablets?

Different approaches

There are three approaches which have been adopted to explain the disagreement between the two schemes of chronology, the biblical and the Assyrian. These have been called the Co-reign Theory, the Gap Theory, and the Objective Theory.

The Co-reign Theory is that adopted by modern scholars. It imposes a number of overlapping reigns or co-regencies on to the kings of Israel and Judah with the purpose of reducing the biblical chronology to the pattern determined by the Assyrian Eponym Canon and the royal inscriptions. The Gap Theory, on the other hand, tackles the problem from the opposite direction. It proposes one or more gaps in the eponym record sufficient in length to draw out the Assyrian dates to the measure required by the Bible. The third approach, the so-called Objective Theory, tries to do justice to both sources of information without radical alteration to either.

This was the approach adopted by George Smith who first published the Assyrian Eponym Canon in 1875, by Otis T. Allis and others. This is "the principle of taking the Assyrian records to be correct as to Assyrian dates, and the Hebrew records as to Hebrew dates" (Smith: 185). It is the principle we should all like to be true. It does in fact work reasonably well for the later contacts, those relating to Tiglath-pileser III, Sargon and Sennacherib, but for the earlier contacts it has proved sadly inadequate. Here there is a discrepancy of more than forty years which the objective approach is unable to bridge. The Co-reign approach treats the Bible neither fairly nor faithfully, which leaves some form of Gap theory as the most likely alternative.

It is not the purpose of this chapter to rework Israel's chronology so as to arrive at a closer agreement with the Assyrian evidence. The chronology of the Kings has already been discussed and it is not my intention to make any amendments. My attention now is to look at the Assyrian material and to suggest ways in which it may be reconciled with the Bible. Other writers have done the same and I am indebted to their input. I think in particular of Christine Tetley's courageous contribution (2005). She not only recognises the need to add some 44 years to the presumed chronology derived from the Assyrian Eponym Canon (AEC), but actually suggests a couple of places where gaps may possibly be located in the eponym sequence. Others have done the same, Anstey and Jones for example, but their suggestions are not developed.

The following pages seek to highlight the problems and to offer tentative solutions. The solutions can only be tentative since the evidence is lacking for anything more definite and I am not myself an Assyriologist. I have however submitted this chapter to Professor A.R. Millard of Liverpool University whose speciality is Assyriology. I am grateful to him for many useful suggestions and for saving me from a rash of elementary blunders. He is however not at all in agreement with my approach. As an Assyriologist and an authority on the Assyrian Eponym Canon he is certain that the Assyrian dates are reliable and that the chronology of the Hebrew kings must be made to fit. For his kindness and constructive criticism however I am profoundly grateful.

The contacts with Assyria appear in two groups: those falling in the reigns of Tiglath-pileser III, Sargon and Sennacherib in the second half of the eighth century BC, and those falling in the reigns of Shalmaneser III and Adad-nirari III in the ninth century. I will begin with a brief survey of the main sources relevant to our study.

The Assyrian Eponym Canon

Undoubtedly the most important source for the establishment of Near Eastern chronology is the so-called Assyrian Eponym Canon. For Assyriologists it provides the only solid basis for the whole of Near Eastern chronology from the middle of the second millennium, though it is only reckoned to be certain from presumed 910 to 648 BC. It was the custom in Assyria to appoint for each calendar year a high official as *limmu* or eponym for that year. Events were sometimes dated by the year of the reigning monarch, but more often it is the name of the *limmu* by which events and inscriptions are defined. A number of Eponym Lists have come down to us in longer and shorter sections. Earlier classifications have now been superseded by Alan Millard's definitive edition, *The Eponyms of the Assyrian Empire 910 - 612 BC* (1994). Of special interest are the Eponym Chronicles. These furnish us not only with the names of the eponyms, but also with his official position or title and the main event (usually the destination of the anuual campaign) of the year. These entries are of prime importance for the reconstruction of the history of the period.

The eponym succession has been clamped down in terms of BC years by the note attached to the *limmu*-ship of Bur-Sagale in the tenth year of the reign of Assur-dan III: "In the month of Simanu (=Sivan) an eclipse of the sun took place." This has been identified with the eclipse of 15/16 June 763, and by this the entire list has been anchored down. It has been appropriately called "the sheet-anchor upon which depends not only the Assyrian chronology but also that of Western Asia" (Van der Meer). It is generally believed that the extant fragments offer an unbroken succession of eponyms from about 910 to 648 BC, covering the greater part of the Divided Kingdom in Israel.

It was usual for the king himself, down to and including Tiglath-pileser III, to hold the office of *limmu* in his second regnal year. He was normally followed by four or five palace officials: the *turtanu* (Commander-in-chief), *rab-shaqe* (Chief cup-bearer), *nagir ekalli* (Palace herald), and *masennu* (Chamberlain). These were followed by the provincial governors. Then, after an interval of thirty years, as in the case of Shalmaneser III, the series began again with the king as eponym.

There is every reason to believe that the Assyrian Eponym Canon is reliable back to 763 BC. For this period the reigns can be checked against the Canon of Ptolemy and the Babylonian Chronicle. But prior to 763 there are no checks on the AEC; it is simply a list of names which may or may not be complete. From our point of view there can be no doubt that the list is defective. An additional 44 years need to be found. There is at present no agreement where, at what points, these years have been lost, but Christine Tetley has made some bold suggestions.

It should be noted, however, that the eclipse of 15 June 763 is not the only one to occur in Simanu around that time. There were also eclipses on 24 June 791(+28 years), 4 June 800(+37 years), and 13 June 809(+46 years). There could in theory be a gap in the record more recently than 763, in which case a different eclipse would apply. But in my view the AEC is reliable post-763 where various checks are in place, but gaps may occur in its earlier phases where no checks exist.

The integrity of the Canon cannot be taken for granted even in its later stages if Rolf Furuli is to be believed. In his view, "The 19 lists and fragments from which the Eponym Canon was made were made from a plethora of different documents, and that would suggest that the canon contains errors and is not trustworthy in every detail" (Vol.II, 177). He proposes a radical revision of Old Testament chronology in which Samaria fell in 740 BC, Hezekiah's fourteenth year was 732 and the fourth year of Jehoiakim was 625. It is most unlikely that his revision will be accepted by anyone outside his JW clientele, but the suspicion remains that the Canon is not the seamless robe it is made out to be. There could well be hidden chasms of varying lengths. Some years may have been deliberately removed from the record (for one reason or another), and others lost through scribal error.

Royal Inscriptions

The Royal Inscriptions fall generally into two categories: (1) the Annals inscriptions (really building inscriptions) in which the king's campaigns are recorded by *palu* (year of reign) or *girru* (campaign) and concluding with the description of building operations, and (2) the Display or Summary inscriptions, in which the royal campaigns are summed up on a geographical basis for the glorification of the monarch.

The Display inscriptions are of little value as compared with the Annals, but are useful for the purpose of filling in gaps in the often fragmentary Annals inscriptions. Their purpose was not to provide a connected history of the reign, but simply to give a broad sweep of the monarch's achievements. Often, however, they are the only form of inscription we have - as with the reign of Adad-nirari III. The Annals inscriptions are generally more reliable and accurate in their relative chronology, though apart from the AEC it would not be safe to use them as a basis for an absolute chronology. They too are prone to exaggeration and distortion in the interests of an Assyrian victory and the glorification of the monarch. A.T. Olmstead describes the procedure of the Assyrian scribe as follows:-

As soon as the king had won his first important victory, the first edition of the annals was issued. With the next great victory, a new edition was made out. For the part covered by the earlier edition, an abbreviated form of this was incorporated. When the scribe reached the period not covered by the earlier document, he naturally wrote more fully, as it was more vividly in his mind and therefore seemed to him to have the greater importance. Now it would seem that all Assyriologists should have long ago recognised that any one of these editions is of value only when it is the most nearly contemporaneous of all those preserved. When it is not so contemporaneous, it has absolutely no value when we do have the original from which it was derived (Olmstead 1916: 8).

This is not quite correct, I am told, since sometimes extra material might be included in the later editions. It is nevertheless a useful observation.

The best popular edition of the Assyrian royal inscriptions is D.D. Luckenbill, *Ancient Records of Assyria and Babylonia*, 2 vols. 1926. Most of the ones of interest to us appear in J.B. Pritchard, *Ancient Near Eastern Texts* (ANET), 3rd ed. 1969, and most recently in *The Context of Scripture*, Vol. II, ed. William W. Hallo, 2000. For the most part I shall be using Hallo's edition in this chapter.

The Khorsabad and SDAS King Lists

The Khorsabad King List was found at Khorsabad, on the site of ancient Dur-Sharukin, in the course of excavations conducted there in 1932/33. The SDAS List, which is almost identical, is so called because it came into the possession of Dr. S.H. Horn of the Seventh Day Adventist Seminary in Washington DC. Both lists are published by I.J. Gelb in the *Journal of Near Eastern Studies* for 1954, pp.209-30.

The Khorsabad list bears a colophon stating that it was copied from a King list tablet in the city of Assur by a certain Kandilanu, a scribe of the temple of Arbela, in the second eponymy of Adad-bel-ukin, namely 738 BC. It ends accordingly with the ten-year reign of Assur-nirari V, the immediate predecessor of Tiglath-pileser III. The SDAS list, on the other hand, includes another two reigns, those of Tiglath-pileser (18 years) and Shalmaneser (5 years).

These lists take us through an impressive run of 107 and 109 kings respectively. For the earliest kings only their names are given, but beginning with Irishum son of Ilushuma, the 33rd king, the lists include the regnal years of each king, sometimes with short notes in explanation of the succession. Strictly speaking they do not furnish us with an independent witness to the chronology since, on their own admission, they are based on the *limmu* lists. Thus for the six kings preceding Irishum the compiler notes that no record of the relevant eponyms was extant. He is unable therefore to give the lengths of these reigns. It is a reasonable assumption that the lists essentially are a condensation of the AEC in terms of the eponym period of each king, that is the number of years between the *limmu*-ship of one king and that of his successor. They do however give some information not found in the Eponym Canon, e.g. parentage.

A detailed discussion of the Khorsabad King List is given by A. Poebel in the *Journal of Near Eastern Studies*, for 1942 and 1943.

Neo-Babylonian Chronicles

Seven chronicles in this series have been discovered. These are: Chronicle 1 which covers the period from the accession of Nabu-nasir (747 BC) to the death of Shamash-shuma-ukin (648); Chronicle 2, from the accession of Nabopolassar (626) to his third year of reign (623); Chronicle 3, from the tenth to the seventeenth years of Nabopolassar (616-609); Chronicle 4, from the eighteenth to the twentieth years of Nabopolassar (608-606); Chronicle 5, from the twenty-first year of Nabopolassar (605) to the tenth year of Nebuchadnezzar (595); Chronicle 6, concerning the third regnal year of Neriglissar (557); and Chronicle 7, the Nabonidus Chronicle, from the accession of Nabonidus in Babylon (556) to sometime after the capture of Babylon by Cyrus (539).

So far as the present chapter is concerned, it is only Chronicle 1 which is immediately relevant. The text is divided by horizontal lines into sections of unequal length, each dealing with the events within the section. The record is written from the Babylonian point of view, but apparently without partiality or distortion. In the words of A.K. Grayson, to whom we are indebted for the first complete edition of these chronicles:-

It appears that the scribes simply wished to record what had happened in and around their land. We have, therefore, what seems to be history being written for history's sake as early as the eighth century BC. Of course this history-writing is parochial. But it is not chauvinistic. That is to say, the interest of the scribes is confined to the events that concern Babylonia and her king (thus parochial), but these events are recorded dispassionately (whether shameful or honourable) without any distortion due to national pride (1975:11).

The Canon of Ptolemy

In close agreement with the Babylonian Chronicle is the Canon of Ptolemy. Ptolemy - astronomer, geographer, historian and chronologist - lived from AD 70 to 161. He began his famous canon at the same point as the Babylonian Chronicle, the accession of Nabonassar in 747 BC. He lists the kings of Babylon down to Nabonidus, the kings of Persia from Cyrus down to Darius III and Alexander the Great, the Ptolemies of Egypt to Cleopatra, and the emperors of Rome from Augustus to Antoninus Pius. He records not only the lengths of each reign but also the grand total at the end of each reign from the accession of Nabonassar.

The remarkable accuracy and reliability of Ptolemy's Canon is generally recognised, being confirmed by the astronomical material to be found in his Almagest. J.A. Brinkman says, "Careful scrutiny of its dates beginning with Nabonassar shows that these compare favourably with the best cuneiform sources. For the period under consideration here, the 'Ptolemaic Canon' is in almost total agreement with the Babylonian Chronicle, an eminently reliable document" (Brinkman 1968: 35). The contents and mechanics of the Canon are described by Leo Depuydt (1995) and its accuracy confirmed by Carl Olof Jonsson's authoritative treatise already referred to, *The Gentile Times Reconsidered*, Atlanta 1998. There are some however (e.g. Rolf Furuli) who regard it as totally worthless.

Rezin and Pekah

This may seem an unusual place to commence an examination of Assyro-Israelite contacts. I do so because we have at this point a perfect fit with the Assyrian Eponym Canon. Elsewhere agreement can only be achieved with a varying amount of special pleading, but here at least the agreement is clear and perspicuous. Dating back from the reign of Josiah, assuming a normal succession in each case, we find that Ahaz' reign began in 735 and Pekah's death in 732. This agrees perfectly with the AEC which records "to Damascus" as the destination of the Assyrian army for the years 733 and 732.

Scholars are virtually unanimous that Pekah died in 732 or 732/1. There is less agreement over the date of Ahaz's accession, but this is fixed by the Bible which has Ahaz begin his reign in year 17 of Pekah. The fact that Pekah's demise works out at exactly 732, without any of the ploys practised by modern scholars, must be accepted as a strong argument in favour of the method employed in this treatise. The terminal dates having been established, the intermediate ones are of course an integral part of the sequence. The dates for this period are as follows:

Accession of Ahaz	(3273) 735
Death of Pekah	(3276) 732
1st year Hoshea	(3284) 724
1st year Hezekiah	(3286) 722
7th Hoshea, Samaria under siege ...	(3290) 718

9th Hoshea, Samaria falls	(3292) 716
14th Hezekiah, Sennacherib invades	(3299/3300) 709/8
1st year Manasseh	(3314) 694
1st year Amon	(3368) 640
1st year Josiah	(3369) 639
31st Josiah	(3399/3400) 609/8

Ahaz, it will be remembered, appealed to the king of Assyria in defiance of Isaiah's reassuring words at the aqueduct of the Upper Pool (Isaiah 7:1-9). Soon after that Isaiah's wife gave birth to the boy who was given the ominous name of Maher-shalal-hash-baz ("Quick to the Plunder, Swift to the Spoil"). At the same time he was told by the Lord, "Before the boy knows how to say 'My father' or 'My mother' (*Avi* or *Immi*), the wealth of Damascus and the plunder of Samaria will be carried off by the king of Assyria" (8:1-4).

Isaiah's encounter with Ahaz must have taken place in the king's first year of reign. We know this because Ahaz' accession preceded Pekah's death by only three years according to the chronology of 2 Kings (15:27; 16:1). According to Isaiah (7:16; 8:4) about the same time elapsed between Isaiah's meeting with Ahaz and the devastation of the land by Tiglath-pileser, at which time Pekah was assassinated by Hoshea (2 Kings 15:29,30). Ahaz' accession in 735 is in close agreement with the despoiling of Damascus and the death of Pekah in 732.

These dates are generally accepted on the basis of the Assyrian evidence, but of greater importance for us is the fact that they are also required by the Bible. We have here a firm synchronism with the AEC which interlocks our own chronology with that of Assyria. On this basis we can proceed with some degree of confidence (or should I say trepidation?) in either direction.

According to 2 Kings, "The king of Assyria complied (with Ahaz' entreaties) by attacking Damascus and capturing it. He deported its inhabitants to Kir and put Rezin to death" (16:9). In addition, "He took Gilead and Galilee, including all the land of Naphtali, and deported the people to Assyria" (15:29). Taking advantage of Pekah's desperate predicament Hoshea son of Elah "attacked and assassinated him, and then succeeded him as king in the 20th year of Jotham son of Uzziah" (15:30). All this took place in 732, the same year as Damascus was captured by Tiglath-pileser.

Judah's conflict with Syria and Ephraim (Israel) began in the reign of Jotham (2 Kings 15:37). Their purpose may have been to force Jotham into relinquishing his hold on territory in Transjordan. In any case Jotham was evidently losing ground, and in face of the mounting threat Ahaz was raised to the throne on a wave of popular alarm. Ahaz was known for his strong pro-Assyrian sympathies in contrast with his father Jotham, and it was to Assyria (rather than to the Lord) that the people were looking for salvation.

The war rapidly escalated. The Philistines invaded the low country of Judah and seized a number of villages (2 Chron. 28:18). The Aramaeans also invaded and many prisoners were carried off to Damascus. Pekah himself inflicted a great slaughter in which the king's son was killed (28:5-7). Even Elath on the Red Sea was seized by the Aramaeans (2 Kings 16:6). In this situation Ahaz was assured by Isaiah that the two northern kingdoms would be despoiled within two or three years (Isaiah 7:16; 8:4). As it was they were only smouldering stumps of wooden pokers whose fire was already extinguished. Ahaz however did not believe him. He would not be moved from his fixed intention to appeal to the king of Assyria for help.

This came all too readily. For 734 the Eponym Canon has "to Philistia", and for 733 and 732 "to Damascus". The opposition was truly defeated. Tiglath-pileser's strategy was first to attack Philistia and then, having isolated Rezin, to turn back on Damascus. Damascus was virtually destroyed and Israel robbed of most of its territory. However, Tiglath-pileser's blessing was not sufficient to secure Hoshea's immediate acceptance by the rump kingdom of Israel. It was another eight years, as the chronology reveals, before his reign officially began.

Tiglath-pileser's Annals inscriptions relating to this campaign are few and fragmentary, and there is no certainty to which years they refer. The conquest of the Damascene region is described as follows:-

> ... That one (i.e. Rezin), in order to save his life, fled alone; and he entered the gate of his city [like] a mongoose. I impaled alive his chief ministers; and I made his country behold (them). I set up my camp around the city for 45 days; and I confined him like a bird in a cage. His gardens, [...] orchards without number I cut down; I did not leave a single one. ... the town of ...]hadara, the home of the dynasty of Rezin the Damascene, [the pl]ace where he was born, I surrounded (and) captured. 800 people with their possessions, their cattle (and) their sheep I took as spoil. I took as spoil 750 captives from the city of Kurussa (and) the city of Sama, 550 captives from the city of Metuna. I destroyed 591 cities of 16 districts of Damascus like mounds of ruins after the Deluge. (*The Context of Scripture*, II, 286)

Commenting on this passage M.F. Unger says, "Making due allowance for hyperbole on the part of the Assyrian annalists, the destruction of the Damascene region must have been terrific." (1957: 101) There are several texts which speak of the conquest of Bit-Humria (Israel), the death of Pekah and the installation of Hoshea.

Summary 4: I carried off [to] Assyria the land of Bit-Humria (Israel), [...Its] "auxiliary [army"] [...] all of its people, [...] [I/they killed] Pekah, their king, and I installed Hoshea [as king] over them. I received from them ten talents of gold, x talents of silver, [with] their [possessions] and [I car]ried the [to Assyria]. (*Context II*, 288)

Summary 9: [I captured the land of Bit-Humria] to its fu[ll extent ...] [I carried off to Assyria] ... [together with] their possessions. [...[I placed Hoshea] as king over them. [...] before me to the city of Sarrabani. (291)

Summary 13: [the land of Bit-Humria] all [of whose] cities I levelled [to the ground] in my former campaigns, [...] I plundered its livestock, and I spared only (isolated) Samaria. [I/They overthrew Pek]ah, their king. (292)

On the strength of Summary 9 (most of which is missing) Na'aman thinks the slaying of Pekah and the installation of Hoshea should be postponed till the following year, 731. The footnote in *Context II* says, "This sentence appears to mention Hoshea's (or more likely, his messengers') appearance before Tiglath-pileser with tribute at Sarrabani in southern Babylonia." This was the direction of Tiglath-pileser's campaigning in 731, but Summary 9 (supposing it is correctly restored) does not say when Pekah died. All it says is that a King of Israel appeared before Tiglath-pileser at Sarrabani. That was either Hoshea or Ahaz. As already mentioned, there is reason to believe that Ahaz was rewarded for his collaboration with Assyria with the remaining portion of the Northern Kingdom over which he now became king at the discretion of the Assyrian monarch.

A fragment of considerable interest forms part of the first Nimrud Tablet which purports to give a resume of the first 17 years of Tiglath-pileser's reign (745-729). Having recorded the conquest of the Arabian tribes and the appointment of Idibi'lu, there follows a list of rulers who paid tribute to Tiglath-pileser. Among these is "Iauhazi of the land of Judah" (*Context II*, 289). Iauhazi corresponds to Jehoahaz, which is Ahaz with the divine prefix. This form is not found in the Bible. The name means "The Lord has taken hold", but interestingly Ahaz dropped the divine component. Maybe he preferred not to know that the Lord had taken hold of him!

The Fall of Samaria

If all the synchronisms with Assyria fell into place like the one we have been considering, there would be no problems, no heart-searching. Notoriously this is not the case! One of the most problematic of all is one which most people would consider fairly certain, namely the fall of Samaria. On the strength of 2 Kings 18:9 in conjunction with the AEC this is usually placed in 722 or 721. Shalmaneser was succeeded by Sargon in 722, and it was Shalmaneser who laid siege to Samaria in the fourth year of King Hezekiah according to 2 Kings 18:9.

The death of Pekah in 732 has been doubly confirmed by both the Bible and the AEC. Here we have a reliable synchronism exactly ten years before the fall of Samaria according to the majority view. But as we have seen the Bible indicates sixteen years between the death of Pekah and the fall of Samaria. How can 16 be reduced to 10, that is the question. Most scholars do it by juggling with the numbers in 2 Kings. The interregnum between Pekah and Hoshea is eliminated, and the chronology is conveniently reduced by 8 or 9 years. But for this there is no justification so far as the Bible is concerned. Hoshea's reign is as securely placed as any other. Moreover, dating back from the death of Josiah we arrived, without any manipulation, at 735 for the first year of Ahaz and 732 for the death of Pekah, dates which are generally accepted. Not only are these dates established, but all the intervening ones as well: the fall of Samaria, the invasion of Sennacherib, the accessions of Manasseh and Josiah, etc. If by dating back from Josiah we arrive at 735 for the first year of Ahaz, by the same process we arrive at 716 for the fall of Samaria and 708 for the invasion of Sennacherib.

722 is widely accepted as the year of Samaria's fall, but as we have seen there are simply not enough regnal years between Hezekiah's 6th (when Samaria fell) and Zedekiah's 11th (when Jerusalem fell) to fill up the interval. Faulstich is only able to do it by giving each king his full number of years (contrary to established practice) and by assuming that Jerusalem fell in 588 instead of 586 (contrary to the accepted dates of Nebuchadnezzar's reign). One writer, A Jepsen, has tried to conjure up an additional three years by suggesting an interregnum during Manasseh's minority (1964: 36 f.). This is certainly possible since Manasseh was only twelve years old when he ascended the throne, but the Bible is silent respecting a regency. Taken at their face value there are six years too few if Samaria fell in 722. Hence my date for the fall of Samaria is 716 rather than 722. This is the date which the Bible most naturally suggests.

The king of Assyria who besieged and captured Samaria is not named in 2 Kings 17:5-6. I would agree with Christine Tetley that this king was Sargon II, not Shalmaneser V. In the following chapter however, where the same information is repeated with additional details, the king in question is said to be Shalmaneser (18:9).

It may seem a precarious speculation to suggest that "Shalmaneser" in 2 Kings 18:9 is no part of the original text, but has been wrongly introduced from 2 Kings 17:3. It may however be the only course open to us. Errors of transmission are not uncommon in the Bible. Numbers in particular are liable to be miscopied, but names have also been added on rare occasions. A case in point could be Matthew 27:9 where an allusion to Zechariah 11:13 is wrongly attributed to Jeremiah. It is most unlikely that any copyist would have changed Zechariah to Jeremiah, but if the prophet was unnamed he might mistakenly have supplied "Jeremiah". The text without Jeremiah is in fact attested by the Syriac version, which may preserve the original reading. This is precisely what I assume to have occurred in 2 Kings 18:9: an unnamed king of Assyria has been supplied with the wrong name.

2 Kings 18:9-10 is the only text which says that Shalmaneser was responsible for the siege and capture of Samaria. On the Assyrian side, Shalmaneser's successor Sargon II claims sole

responsibility as we shall see. In the present instance, Shalmaneser cannot be correct if Samaria fell in 716 since Shalmaneser died in 722. Hence my proposal that "Shalmaneser" has been added to the text by some scribe who thought the king of Assyria should have a name. I do however have another explanation (see below) which requires no alteration of the text. This will be more acceptable to some, but for me it is open to question, not least because it interferes with the first year of Ahaz and the last of Pekah whose dates cannot easily be moved in either direction.

The words "against Samaria" which are regularly added to the AEC for the years 725, 724 and 723 (so Thiele, Faulstich, and Floyd Jones, following Olmstead and Luckenbill) are simply not there. The tablet is broken at this point: the restoration "to Samaria" is pure conjecture and wishful thinking.

Samaria still active (and rebellious) in 720 BC

The Assyrian inscriptions lend no support to the view that Shalmaneser was in any way involved in the siege or capture of Samaria. According to them, Samaria was still active and rebellious in 720, two years into the reign of Sargon. When Ilubi'di of Hamath rebelled in Sargon's second regnal year, Samaria was also involved. According to the Asshur Charter, "He (Ilubi'di) gathered Arpad and Samarina, and he turned (them) to his side" (*Context II*, 295). Likewise in the Annals, speaking of the same event, "Damascus and Samari[a he caused to rebel against me]" (293).

Hayim Tadmor's explanation that "Samaria, evacuated by the Assyrian army on the death of Shalmaneser in 722, joined in the rebellion" (1966: 91) hardly carries conviction. Samaria would have been in no position to join a rebellion so soon (or indeed ever again) after its capture and the exile of its inhabitants.

In Tadmor's view Samaria was actually conquered twice, once near the end of Shalmaneser's reign and again by Sargon in 720 BC after the defeat of the coalition under Ilubi'di of Hamath. To this second conquest of Samaria in 720 he would refer all the references in Sargon's inscriptions to his conquest of Samaria. Bob Becking (whose full and detailed survey of all the relevant material is an invaluable resource) is substantially of the same opinion. He recognises that the biblical tradition (in 2 Kings 17:5-6 and 18:9-11) mentions only one conquest. It is possible, he thinks, that in process of transmission the account of a double conquest has merged into a single one (1992: 39). Hence he finds no objection to the view that Samaria was conquered twice.

That Samaria could have joined a new coalition after its conquest by Shalmaneser hardly seems possible. Nadav Na'aman is strongly of the same opinion. He has this to say:

Literary sources, reliefs and archaeological excavations agree that the conquest of non-submissive cities by the Assyrians was always an extremely destructive event. If Samaria was besieged for three years (with all the terrible effects of such a long siege) and then conquered by the Assyrians in 723/22 BC, one would hardly expect its weakened surviving inhabitants to be able to participate in a rebellion that broke out shortly afterwards. Yet according to Sargon's earliest inscription (the Assur charter) - from his second year - the Samarians participated in the alliance formed by the king of Hamath alongside the older provinces which had been annexed by Tiglath pileser III. Furthermore, the episode of the conquest of Samaria occupied a central place in Sargon's inscriptions composed in his later years, after he had conquered and annexed vast areas and had expanded the Assyrian empire to its maximal extent. It is thus clear that the king and his scribes regarded the former as a major event of the king's early years. The participation of the Samarians in the rebellion of 720 BC and the place of the city's conquest in Sargon's inscriptions do not accord well with the assumption that Samaria was captured by Shalmaneser after a long siege and that Sargon had recaptured a weakened, ruined city (1990: 208).

In Na'aman's view Samaria was captured only once, and that was in 720 after a siege "which apparently did not last long." But we know from the Bible that Samaria was in fact besieged for three years, and there is nothing in Sargon's inscriptions to suggest that Samaria was captured or even besieged in the year of this rebellion. It would seem that Samaria sustained only a minor defeat in 720, its true punishment postponed for a later time.

Gershon Galil avoids the unlikely situation of Samaria being conquered twice in so short a time. According to him Samaria fell in 720, after a siege of two years which had begun in the year of Shalmaneser's death. In this way he reconciles the biblical and Assyrian traditions into one harmonious event. In agreement with the Bible he attributes the siege of Samaria to Shalmaneser, and in agreement with Sargon's inscriptions he ascribes the conquest of the city to Sargon.

On the face of it this would appear a neat solution to the problem. But in fact Galil has simply replaced one unlikely situation with another equally unlikely. He asks us to believe that Samaria, while still under siege by the Assyrian army, joined another anti-Assyrian coalition under Ilubi'di. Galil plays down Samaria's involvement in the rebellion of 720. It is possible, he says, "that the Israelites, along with soldiers from the provinces of Damascus, Sumur, Arpad, and probably also Hadrach, volunteered to aid the king of Hamath in the revolt against Assyria" (1996: 93). In this case, they were inhabitants of outlying Israelite cities or the inhabitants of Samaria who had managed to extricate themselves from the blockade. But this again fails to carry conviction, especially since the king of Assyria had already overrun the entire country before besieging Samaria (2 Kings 17:5).

Sargon claims to have conquered Samaria in no less than eight of his inscriptions. These are set out in full by Becking on pages 25-38 of his work. The fullest account occurs in the Nimrud prisms IV.25-41:

> [The inhabitants of Sa]merina, who agreed [and plotted] with a king [hostile to] me, not to do service and not to bring tribute [to Assur] and who did battle, I fought against them with the power of the great gods, my lords. I counted as spoil 27,280 people, together with their chariots, and gods, in which they trusted. I formed a unit with 200 of [their] chariots for my royal force. I settled the rest of them in the midst of Assyria. I repopulated Samerina more than before. I brought into it people from countries conquered by my hands. I appointed my eunuch as governor over them. And I counted them as Assyrians. (*Context II*: 295)

The capture of Samaria's inhabitants, their exile to Assyria, and their replacement by peoples from countries conquered by Assyria are all clearly mentioned. The Nimrud prisms, like the Great Summary Inscription which recounts the fall of Samaria in similar terms, is geographical rather than annalistic in arrangement. Its disregard for chronology is exemplified in the column under discussion, where events belonging to fourteenth, fifth, second and fourth *palu*'s are found in succession.

The accepted date is given in the Asshur Charter where Ilubi'di's rebellion is placed in Sargon's second *palu* (720). The tablet is badly broken, but lines 16-20 are clear enough:

> In my second regnal year, when I had sat on the royal throne and had been cro[wned] with the crown of lordship, I smashed the forces of Humbanigas, king of Elam; I decisively defeated him. Il[ubi'di of] Hamath, not the rightful holder of the throne, not fit(?) for the palace, who in the shepherdship of his people, did [not attend to their] fate, [but] with

regard to the god Assur, his land (and) his people he sought evil, not good and he treated contemptuously. He gathered Arpad and Samerina, and he turned (them) to his side... (*Context II*: 295)

The tablet goes on to describe the conquest of Hamath and the land of Amurru, meaning the land of the west. The latter, it says, was subdued and its inhabitants brought to the city of Asshur.

In the Khorsabad annals (written probably in 707 BC), the conquest of Samaria is placed in Sargon's *resh sharruti*, his accession year (December 722 to March 721). But it is generally recognised that this arrangement is artificial. The conclusion to which scholars have arrived is that Sargon had a domestic crisis to deal with at the beginning of his reign. Owing to civil disorder at home he was unable to embark on a military campaign during his accession year and first *palu*. Sargon's scribes were anxious to cover up for this failure. Hence the Khorsabad annalists, while in general agreement with the dating of the Asshur Charter, assign a number of events, notably the conquest of Samaria, to the king's accession year and first *palu*.

Becking, however, disagrees. He thinks some other nation ending in -*ina*, other than *Samerina*, was intended in the broken text of the Khorsabad annals. A number of possibilities present themselves. If Becking is right there is no antedating of Sargon's conquest of Samaria in the annals, and the Asshur Charter is undisputed so far as the date of the rebellion is concerned.

The actual date of Samaria's fall cannot be deduced from Sargon's inscriptions. It does however occupy a prominent place in a number of them. Galil observes, "we cannot ignore the numerous testimonies to the conquest of Samaria in the time of Sargon, and assume that they are all false" (1996: 87). There is no suggestion in the Assyrian sources that any other king was involved. There is however a contrary signal in the Babylonian Chronicle.

The Babylonian Chronicle

Confirmation that Shalmaneser was involved in the siege and sack of Samaria has been found in the Babylonian Chronicle. The relevant section from the Chronicle is Column i, lines 23-32.

(23) Tiglath-pileser ascended the throne in Babylon.

---

(24) The second year: Tiglath-pileser died in the month Tebet.
(25) For <eighteen> years Tiglath-pileser reigned in Akkad and Assyria.
(26) For two of these years he ruled in Akkad.
(27) On the 25th day of the month Tebet, Shalmaneser ascended the throne in Assur
(28) <and Akkad>. He ruined (*hepu*) Samaria.

---

(29) The fifth year: Shalmaneser died in the month of Tebet.
(30) Shalmaneser ruled over Assur and Akkad for five years.
(31) On the 12th day of the month of Tebet, Sargon ascended the throne in Assur.
(32) In the month of Nisan Marduk-apla-iddina (Merodach-baladan) ascended the throne in Babylon.

Na'aman argued that the ravaging or ruination of Samaria should be assigned to Shalmaneser's accession year because "the text of the chronicle is organized throughout in a chronological order, with each and every event accurately dated within a specific year of the king of Babylonia and a transverse line marked to separate the years of reign." He also argued that the verb *hepu* means to plunder or ravage rather than the breaking of walls after a siege.

Most however would agree with Hayes and Kuan (1991) that the horizontal line in the text indicates that Samaria was ravaged at some point prior to the fifth (and last) year of Shalmaneser's reign. Na'aman makes the Chronicle far more exact than it really is. One has only to look at the material between lines 24 and 28. This includes the final year of Tiglath-pileser (727-26), as well as the accession year of Shalmaneser V (727-26) and the first four years of his reign (726-23).

"The arrest of Hoshea", say Hayes and Kuan, "was probably part of a sequence of events in 725 which included not only Shalmaneser's ravaging of the Israelite capital but also the provincialization of Samaria and, from the Assyrian point of view, the termination of Israel's independence." Samaria, they think, was besieged a year or two later, allowing them time to recoup their strength and to re-establish a monarchical government. Samaria fell in 722/21 after a three-year siege. The Samarians nevertheless "covenanted together under a king to join in rebellion against Sargon who had assumed the throne in Tebet 722-21."

Again we are asked to believe that Samaria joined the rebellion little more than a year after the fall of Samaria and the deportation of its inhabitants! Becking notes that this is the only entry in the Babylonian Chronicle which is not introduced by MU X "in the year X ..." He regards the Chronicle as an important historical source for the conquest of Samaria "at some point or other in the reign of Shalmaneser V" (p.24).

This is also the view of Gershon Galil. "This", he says, "is the only event in his reign which is mentioned, and it cannot be determined if it occurred in the beginning of, during the course of, or at the end of his reign" (1996: 89).

K. Lawson Younger, Jr. questions Na'aman's understanding of the semantic range of the verb *hepu*. "From the parallels in the royal inscriptions," he says, "it becomes clear that the verb denotes the ruination of cities and, perhaps bombastically, of whole countries, not simply the pacification of a region... It is a relatively straightforward assertion that Shalmaneser captured the city of Samaria. One should not make too much of it, nor should it be discounted" (1999: 46).

In Younger's view, Samaria fell in 722. Shalmaneser died a natural death and was succeeded by Sargon II in the midst of internal strife. In 720 Yau-bi'di of Hamath organized a coalition against Sargon which included Arpad, Simirra, Damascus, Hatarikka, and Samaria. The coalition was decisively defeated at Qarqar, the same place as Shalmaneser III's encounter with a similar coalition in 853 BC (presumed date). "Sometime soon after this battle Sargon besieged and captured Samaria. This would have been a very brief siege and a very rapid conquest of the city ... part of a much larger Blitzkrieg in which he subdued the West in 720 B.C" (471 f.).

Personally I find it incredible that Samaria could have joined a rebellion only two years after being sacked by Shalmaneser. Nor could it have joined a rebellion if it was already under siege and was suffering the privation and trauma which a prolonged siege inevitably entailed (cp. 2 Kings 6:24-30). Maybe there is more to be learned from 2 Kings 17.

2 Kings 17:3-6

Often the literal translation of the *KJV* is more faithful to the original than the less literal modern translations which all too often are influenced, consciously or unconsciously, by considerations from outside. Take for example 2 Kings 17:3 which the *KJV* translates quite literally, "Against him came up Shalmaneser king of Assyria, and Hoshea became his servant, and gave him presents." Compare with this the *NIV* translation, "Shalmaneser king of Assyria came up to attack Hoshea, who had been Shalmaneser's vassal and had paid him tribute." According to the *KJV*, Hoshea became Shalmaneser's servant as a result of the king's invasion. But the *NIV* has Shalmaneser's action to follow Hoshea's vassalage and payment of tribute.

There can be no doubt that 2 Kings 17:3-5, reveals the following sequence of events:

v.3   Shalmaneser came up against Hoshea
         Hoshea became his servant and paid tribute
v.4   The king of Assyria found treachery in Hoshea
         he constrained him and put him in prison
v.5   The king of Assyria came up through all the land
         he went up to Samaria and besieged it three years.

This is how it comes across in the *KJV* and most other versions. The construction is straightforward, a simple perfect followed by consecutives as is usual in narrative style. Becking is of the same opinion. 2 Kings 17:3-4, he says, contains a narrative chain of *wayyiqtol* forms, which describe a series of succeeding acts (p.50). If we accept the *KJV* translation, the events described may be filled out as follows:

1) At the beginning of Shalmaneser's reign, in consequence of an act of defiance on the part of Hoshea, Shalmaneser came up against Hoshea and reasserted his authority. This may have been in 727 (assuming Hoshea was already in charge of Samaria as Ahaz's deputy), soon after the death of Tiglath-pileser III when vassal kingdoms were prone to rebel.

2) After an interval Hoshea conspired with So, king of Egypt, in another bid to throw off the Assyrian yoke. At the same time he withheld the tribute which he had previously paid "year by year".

3) Shalmaneser reacted immediately. He invaded Israel, captured Hoshea and put him in prison. The absence of any reference to these events in Assyrian sources is due probably to the absence of any inscriptions for Shalmaneser's reign. But the entry in the Babylonian Chronicle to the effect that Shalmaneser "ravaged Samaria" is most probably a reference to this invasion.

4) Hoshea's release from prison and reinstatement as puppet king of Israel is presupposed in verses 5-6 where the subsequent siege and fall of Samaria are recorded. Hoshea's official reign began in 724 according to my dating; so it must have been in that year that Hoshea was appointed king in Samaria. In verses 5 and 6 "the king of Assyria" responsible for the siege and capture of Samaria is not named. This king was Sargon, Shalmaneser's successor.

Younger, in company with many modern scholars, does not agree with this reconstruction, but he does go so far as to admit that, "If vv.3 and 5 do not refer to the same event, then the reason for Shalmaneser's action against Hoshea in v.3 is unstated, and the reader must supply the notion of a rebellion after the death of Tiglath-pileser III as the cause of Shalmaneser's action" (1999: 478).

Nadav Na'amon concurs "that v.3 most probably refers to unrest and perhaps even rebellion that broke out in the West upon the death of the great emperor and the accession of his son Shalmaneser V". With this I would agree, as also with his belief that "the king of Assyria in (2 Kings 17) vv.3-4 is Shalmaneser whereas the king in vv.5-6 is Sargon, his successor." If this is correct, the Babylonian Chronicle will refer to Shalmaneser's action as described in verses 3-4, while the siege and sack of Samaria can be credited to Sargon who claims to have done this very deed in no less than eight of his inscriptions.

Hoshea's official reign, on my dating, began in 724, but prior to that he had been contending for the throne, and was in partial control, since the death of Pekah in 732. While in prison he would not have been recognised as king of Israel, so probably it was in 724 that he was released from prison and his official reign began.

2 Kings 18:9-11

2 Kings 17:3-4, the passage we have just looked at, has no parallel in the following chapter. But the next two verses, 17:5-6, are repeated almost word for word in 18:9-11. These verses repeat nearly all of 17:5-6 but with additional material. This material includes, the year in which the Assyrian king marched against Samaria and besieged it, namely the fourth year of Hezekiah (= 7th Hoshea); the name of the king of Assyria: Shalmaneser; and the length of the siege: three years (inclusively reckoned), that is from the fourth to the seventh of Hezekiah (= 7th to 9th Hoshea). The two passages are usefully placed in parallel columns by Becking (pp.47-48). Both conclude with the statement that Israel was exiled to Assyria, and were taken to Halah, Habur, the river of Gozan, and the cities of the Medes.

When?

With respect to the last of these locations Younger remarks, "These Israelites could not have been deported there before 716 BCE, simply because before that date Sargon had no 'cities of the Medes' within his provincial jurisdiction" (1998: 223). In that year Sargon marched against his rebellious vassal Ullusunnu of Manna in the north of Media. It is mentioned in Sargon's annals that the king of Assyria brought there conquered peoples from other lands (see Becking: 70). It is also mentioned in the Cyprus Stela that exiles from the land of Hattu (= Syria and Palestine) were deported to Media among other places. Becking thinks this took place most probably in 716 (p.72).

It is mentioned in 2 Kings 17:24 that the king of Assyria brought people from Babylon, Cuthah, Avva, Hamath and Sepharvaim and settled them in the towns of Samaria. In the Khorsabad annals we read also of Arab tribes-people who were settled in Samaria: the Tamudi, Ibadidi, Marsimani, and Hajapu. This took place in Sargon's 7th *palu* (= 715) according to the annals. In this year Sargon campaigned in the Sinai area and on the Egyptian border. It was probably in this year, says Becking (p.102), that Sargon sent some of the earlier-conquered Arabs to parts of Samaria.

The date of Samaria's fall cannot be decided from Sargon's fragmentary inscriptions. But if the city was still intact in 720 it cannot have fallen before 718, and my date, 716, is perfectly feasible. Sargon II, says Younger, continued the established Assyrian policy begun by Tiglath-pileser III directed at ensuring Assyrian security along the important Damascus-Megiddo-Egypt route, giving access to the Philistine states, Gaza in particular. "Sargon II continued the overarching Assyrian policy by solidifying Assyrian control over the Philistine coast through his campaigns of 720, 716, and 713-12 BCE" (1998: 225 f.). It would seem a logical move on the part of the Assyrian king to eliminate Samaria on the way, so removing a potential danger in his rear.

A possible alternative

I said above that I had an alternative solution which did not involve any emendation of 2 Kings 18:9, but that I was not prepared to endorse it. This solution requires the assumption of an interregnum or regency. Jepsen suggested a three-year regency during the minority of Manasseh. There is no evidence or likelihood of this, but the situation is very different with respect to Josiah. Josiah has undoubtedly a much stronger claim that Manasseh. Josiah was only eight years old when he ascended the throne, and his father, Amon, twenty-three when he was assassinated. Assuming a three-year or five-year regency after Amon's assassination, Josiah would have been three or five years old when his father died.

The circumstances surrounding Josiah's accession are very similar to those surrounding Azariah's when a takeover by Jeroboam is the most likely solution. Consider for a moment the parallels. Josiah's father, like Azariah's, fell prey to a conspiracy which ended his days prematurely. Azariah was only four, it seems, when his father died, and Josiah only three if a five-year regency is assumed. In both cases the people of the land/Judah intervened to put the young king on the throne, a sure sign of political unrest involving a dispute over the succession. If there was an interval in the case of Azariah before he was placed on the throne by the people of Judah, might there not also have been an interval before Josiah's investiture by the people of the land? This is an alternative scenario which some may prefer. On this assumption the dates would be as follows:-

6th Hezekiah (Fall of Samaria)	723/722
14th Hezekiah (Sennacherib's invasion)...	715/714
29th Hezekiah/ 1st Manasseh	700/699
55th Manasseh/ 1st Amon	646/645
2nd Amon (and regency)	645/644
1st Josiah	639/638

On this showing a regency of five years is indicated between the death of Amon and Josiah's accession. Amon would have been twenty years old at the birth of his son, and Josiah three when his father died. In this way the year 722 can be retained for the fall of Samaria and the integrity of 2 Kings 18:9 preserved, but only at the expense of the death of Pekah and the capture of Damascus. These events are now pushed back by six years, much too early for the dates suggested by the AEC. There is moreover nothing in the Bible to suggest a regency and nothing very remarkable about Amon having a son at the age of fifteen. Josiah himself was even younger, fourteen, at the birth of Jehoiakim, and sixteen at the birth of Jehoahaz. It is also wrong in principle to assume an interregnum or co-regency when the text neither records nor requires one. Hence I prefer myself to believe that Josiah succeeded his father without an interval, and that Samaria fell in 716 in spite of the difficulties which that involves.

Let us consider the alternative for a moment. Shalmaneser died in the winter of 722 (on 12 Tebet, according to the Babylonian Chronicle). Hence the latest point when he could have laid siege to Samaria is the summer of 722, in which event Samaria would have fallen in 720, as Na'aman and Galil believed. If Hezekiah and his successors are all given their reigns in full, we get the following result:

```
  720
  -23   (remaining years of Hezekiah)
  697
  -55   (Manasseh)
  642
   -2   (Amon)
  640
  -31   (Josiah)
  609
```

Most people think that Josiah died in 609, so in theory the gap is bridged between the fall of Samaria in 720 and the death of Josiah. But this only works on the assumption that Manasseh adopted the accession-year system in defiance of the established practice of his forefathers. Instead of reckoning his reign from Tishri 698, as we would expect, he reckoned it from Tishri 697, a novelty that was continued by his successors. But there is no reason which comes to mind why Manasseh should have departed from established custom in this respect, quite apart from the fact that there is nothing in the text to support it. Moreover, 720 is not a date favoured by scholars. Most would date the fall of Samaria to 722, a year irreconcilable with the reign-lengths of Hezekiah and his successors unless one assumes a regency as suggested above.

According to Faulstich (p.19), "After the fall of Samaria there was no Northern Kingdom (Israel) and there is no need for the subtraction of one year because cross-referencing is no longer used. The dates ascribed to the kings of Judah can be added without the loss of a year." But I cannot make any sense of this remark. If Manasseh and his successors continued to antedate, in accord with the nonaccession-year system, one year must still be deducted from their reigns. The absence of cross-referencing makes no difference whatsoever.

Another problem is that Ahaz' reign and the fall of Damascus would automatically recede by four years (if Samaria fell in 720) and by six years (if Samaria fell in 722). But these events are already correctly placed, they cannot be moved back any further. If, by way of compensation, the eight-year interregnum between Pekah and Hoshea is eliminated more problems are created. The synchronism with 12 Ahaz (the time of Hoshea's succession) is invalidated, as well as the beginning of Hezekiah's reign in the third year of Hoshea.

In the circumstances I feel justified in supposing that the mention of Shalmaneser in 2 Kings 18:9 is an intrusion, interpolated (mistakenly) from the previous chapter (17:3-4) by some scribe who thought the king of Assyria should have a name and must be the same king as previously mentioned.

Sennacherib invades Jerusalem

According to the Bible (2 Kings 18:13; Isaiah 36:1) it was in Hezekiah's year 14 that "Sennacherib, king of Assyria, attacked all the fortified cities of Judah and captured them." That was in 709/8 on my dating of Hezekiah's reign. Sennacherib gives his own account of the invasion of Judah, the capture of 46 walled towns and the investment of Jerusalem in his Annals. The earliest account is in the Rassam Cylinder written soon after the event in 700 BC, and the better known account in the Taylor Prism which was copied in 691. This event he ascribes to his third campaign which is dated to 702 by Faulstich and Jones and 701 by everyone else. The familiar passage relating to Hezekiah the Jew is given as follows in the Rassam Cylinder:-

As for Hezekiah, the Judaean, I besieged forty-six of his fortified walled cities and surrounding smaller towns, which were without number. Using packed-down ramps and applying battering rams, infantry attacks by mines, breeches, and siege machines, I conquered (them). I took out 200,150 people, young and old, male and female, horses, mules, donkeys, camels, cattle, and sheep, without number, and counted them as spoil. He himself, I locked up within Jerusalem, his royal city, like a bird in a cage. I surrounded him with earthworks, and made it unthinkable for him to exit by the city gate. His cities which I had despoiled I cut off from his land and gave them to Mitinti, king of Ashdod, Padi, king of Ekron and Silli-bel, king of Gaza, and thus diminished his land. I imposed dues and gifts for my lordship upon him, in addition to the former tribute, their yearly payment. He, Hezekiah, was overwhelmed by the awesome splendour of my lordship, and he sent me after my departure to Nineveh, my royal city, his elite troops (and) his best soldiers, which he had brought in as reinforcements to strengthen Jerusalem, with 30 talents of gold, 800 talents of silver, choice antimony, large blocks of carnelian, beds (inlaid) with ivory, armchairs (inlaid) with ivory, elephant hides,ivory, ebony-wood, boxwood, multicoloured garments, garments of linen, wool (dyed) red-purple, vessels of copper, iron, bronze and tin, chariots, siege shields, lances, armour, daggers for the belt, bows and arrows, countless trappings and implements of war, together with his daughters, his palace women, his male and female singers. He (also) dispatched his messenger to deliver the tribute and to do obeisance. (*Context II*, 303)

This account is very different from what we find in the Bible, different not only in tone (as one would expect) but also in content. This has led a number of writers to conclude that two quite separate events are being described. By many it has been supposed that the invasion described here was the first of two invasions. By E.W. Faulstich and Steven J. Robinson (1991/2), however, it is proposed that the first invasion took place in Hezekiah's 14th year, eight years after the fall of Samaria, and the second in 701 as described in the Assyrian Annals.

Advocates of this idea emphasise the divergences between the two accounts. The following have been noted by Robinson and others:

1) First and foremost the two campaigns are separated by a number of years on any straightforward reading of the relevant texts.

2) In addition to 30 talents of gold and 800 talents of silver Sennacherib claims to have received many other luxury items, not to mention Hezekiah's daughters and women of his palace. These may be included in the words "whatever you demand of me" in 2 Kings 18:14, but there is no specific mention of any of them. These items, it is mentioned, were "sent me (Sennacherib) after my departure to Nineveh", but Hezekiah would have had no need to send them at all if the Assyrian army had already been destroyed.

3) The siege of Lachish, Judah's second city, is prominent in the biblical account (see 2 Chron. 32:9). The siege of Lachish is depicted in glorious relief on the walls of Sennacherib's palace at Nineveh. There is however no mention of it in the Rassam Cylinder. Robinson comments, "It is scarcely conceivable that, while the conquest of Lachish took pride of place in the Assyrian ruler's palace, it should receive no notice at all in the annals." This fact is adequately explained if the campaign of 701 was not the only one which Sennacherib conducted in this region. If Lachish was foremost of the cities captured in the earlier campaign, there would be no occasion to mention it in the Annals account of his later campaign.

4) The Annals refer to a massive army deployed by the kings of Egypt and Ethiopia. These Sennacherib defeated prior to conquering Eltekeh, Timnah and Ekron. But the Bible refers only to the approach of an army under Taharka, the (future) king of Egypt and Ethiopia. There is no mention of a battle since that very night Sennacherib sustained a supernatural reversal in which the greater part of his army was annihilated.

According to Sennacherib, "In the plain of Eltekeh, they (that is, the kings of Egypt and Ethiopia) drew up their ranks against me and sharpened their weapons. Trusting in the god Ashur, my lord, I fought with them and inflicted a defeat upon them." William H. Shea and others find the solution in two campaigns, one in 701 and another some years later. Two campaigns, one in 701 and the other some years *earlier*, would solve the problem equally well.

5) In the same year Merodach, king of Babylon, sent envoys to Hezekiah in Jerusalem. Merodach-baladan was king of Babylon from 721 to 710. In 701 the king of Babylon was Bel-ibni.

6) The most notable variant in the opinion of Faulstich is Sennacherib's claim to have thrown up earthworks against the besieged city, contrary to Isaiah's assurance in 2 Kings 19:32, "He shall not ... cast a bank against it". However, a more correct translation of the Assyrian removes this discrepancy. As Millard points out, "Sennacherib encircles Jerusalem with watchtowers, yet does not press a siege" (1985: 70).

7) In addition both writers notice that 2 Chronicles 32:4 (and 2 Kings 19:17) speak of "the *kings* of Assyria", as if there was more than one king of Assyria at that time. Sennacherib did not become sole king until 705, but he could well have shared power with his father at an earlier date. But the reference is a general one, not to any particular kings of Assyria.

The cumulative case presented by these divergences is offered as proof that Sennacherib's first invasion, as related in 2 Kings, took place many years before the invasion of 701 (in 715 according to Faulstich, 713 according to Robinson). The theory of two campaigns, separated by a number of years, goes a long way towards solving the problem. But the notion that Hezekiah was humiliated by Sennacherib on a second occasion, not mentioned in the Bible, flies in the face of 2 Chronicles 32:26 where it is stated as a fact that "the Lord's wrath did not come upon them (again) during the days of Hezekiah." If an invasion of this severity had really taken place, the failure of the biblical writers to mention it is exceedingly difficult to explain.

The best Faulstich can offer is this: "The Scripture is probably silent concerning the second invasion by Sennacherib in 702 B.C. because it happened several years before the death of Judah's finest king since David (cf. 2 Kings 18:3; 2 Chronicles 30:26). It would not seem proper to close Hezekiah's biography on such a tragic note as a humiliation by Sennacherib." (p.109) But that is hardly a convincing argument. David himself was not let off on compassionate grounds. There was no glossing over the troubles which marred *his* later years.

The divergences enumerated are an important part of the equation, but they are nevertheless one-sided in that they ignore the equally impressive parallels between 2 Kings and Sennacherib's annals. One has only to read the account in 2 Kings to see that Sennacherib's encounter with Hezekiah was in two phases. In ch.18:13-16 the Assyrian king is successful in capturing the fortified cities of Judah. Hezekiah abjectly promises to pay whatever the king demands if only he will go away. Sennacherib's demand of 300 talents of silver (800 according to Sennacherib) and 30 talents of gold is obediently handed over. However, the Assyrian king is still not satisfied. He now sends his field-commander from Lachish and demands the total surrender of Jerusalem. Here begins the second phase of his campaign, that which ends in the annihilation of the Assyrian army, 2 Kings 18:17 to 19:37. Unsurprisingly, this phase is passed over in silence in Sennacherib's account. There is however a close agreement between the Assyrian account and the first successful phase of the Assyrian offensive. The points of agreement are as follows:-

1) According to 2 Kings Sennacherib attacked all the fortified cities of Judah and captured them. The king himself says, "I besieged 46 of his fortified walled cities and surrounding small towns."

2) In 2 Kings Hezekiah sends a message, "I have done wrong. Withdraw from me, and I will pay whatever you demand of me." Likewise in the Rassam Cylinder, "He (also) dispatched his messenger to deliver the tribute and to do obeisance."

3) According to 2 Chronicles 32:6 Hezekiah "appointed military officers over the people and assembled them before him in the square at the city gate." Sennacherib also alludes to Hezekiah's "elite troops (and) his best soldiers, which he had brought in as reinforcements to strengthen Jerusalem."

4) Hezekiah paid 300 talents of silver and thirty talents of gold. The Rassam Cylinder has 800 talents of silver and thirty talents of gold along with an assortment of exotic gifts. Sennacherib records other demands not mentioned in Kings, including Hezekiah's daughters. If Hezekiah had met these demands in full it is strange that Sennacherib did not go away. Sennacherib's continued offensive rather suggests that he was far from satisfied with Hezekiah's response.

5) Sennacherib does not claim to have captured Jerusalem. This also is in agreement with 2 Kings.

6) Lachish is not mentioned in Sennacherib's account, but his palace reliefs at Nineveh depict the king sitting on his throne outside the conquered city of Lachish receiving homage from leading dignitaries while captives are led past him in chains. This agrees with 2 Kings 18:14 where Hezekiah sends his message of surrender to the king of Assyria at Lachish.

Without a doubt the Rassam Cylinder gives the Assyrian version of Sennacherib's initial successes in 709/8, when he was acting as Commander-in-chief for Sargon, his father. But why in that case are they included in the record of his third campaign in 701? There is no need to put the Bible on the wrack in order to stretch its chronology to the required length as is usually done. Nor is anything to be gained by emending fourteenth to twenty-fourth (in 2 Kings 18:13) with George Smith, O.T. Allis, Christine Tetley and others. It was at this time that 15 years were added to Hezekiah's life (2 Kings 20:6). Hezekiah reigned for 29 years, not 39.

The account of Hezekiah's submission seems to have been added to the record of Sennacherib's third campaign for reasons of geographical affinity. On this occasion, in 701, he must have left Hezekiah well alone, the humiliating destruction of his army on a previous occasion still being fresh in his memory. But to cover up for this failure he included in this place the account of Hezekiah's submission in 709/8. A.K. Grayson has said that the Assyrian scribes sometimes garbled the narrative by changing the date of a defeat and weaving it into the account of a later battle (1980: 271). This is exactly what I believe has happened here.

John Bright correctly observes, "What is important is that 2 Kings 18:14-16 (not in Isaiah), and it alone, is remarkably corroborated and supplemented by Sennacherib's own account of the campaign of 701" (1960: 299). In his view, news of Assyrian reverses, plus the promise of aid from Egypt, prompted Hezekiah to rebel a second time in 690/89. It was this which provoked the Assyrian invasion described in 2 Kings 18:17 to 19:35. But the opening verses, 18:13-16, he is happy to leave to 701. What however the chronology requires is an *earlier* campaign, not a later one.

Dr Jones further muddies the waters by proposing *three* Assyrian invasions: the first in Hezekiah's 14th year, 2 Kings 18:13-16 and Isaiah 36:1; the second in Hezekiah's 18th year, 2 Kings 18:17-19:35 and Isaiah 36:2-37:36; and a third in 702/1 (if it occurred at all) as described in Sennacherib's own account. But no-one reading 2 Kings 18 would suspect for a moment that there is an interval of four years (thirteen according to Bright) between verse 16 and verse 17. Still less would he suspect that Hezekiah's 14th year in Isaiah 36:1 refers only to the *first* verse, whereas verses 2 and following refer to a later invasion. The only natural reading of these chapters is to view them as continuous narratives relating to Hezekiah's 14th year.

My own solution avoids these anomalies. The entire narrative in 2 Kings and Isaiah took place in Hezekiah's 14th year where the Bible puts it. When again Sennacherib invaded this outpost of his empire in 701 he was careful to leave Hezekiah well alone. He did however include in his annals, by way of compensation, a record of the opening stage of his earlier campaign in which he had successfully overrun the fortified cities of Judah and imposed a crippling indemnity on the remorseful Hezekiah. Concerning the subsequent humiliation which he sustained when his army was mysteriously decimated, he is of course completely silent. Like every other king he wanted to be remembered for his magnanimous deeds and victorious campaigns, not as someone whose army had been virtually wiped out by "an act of God"!

Alan Millard asks, "Why, then, does the report only appear in texts dated 701 and later?" "I do not know", he says, "of any comparable example of a king reporting a campaign achieved prior to his accession counting it in the achievements of his reign." The absence of an exact parallel does not prove that it could not have happened. The two-invasion theory, in one form or another, is widely accepted by scholars of very different points of view. It undoubtedly provides the best solution to the problem.

What of Merodach-baladan?

But what of Merodach-baladan, the king of Babylon who sent an embassy to Hezekiah to suss out his wealth and defences on the pretext of congratulating him on his recovery from illness (2 Kings 20:12-13)? According to the Babylonian King-list A, the royal succession was as follows: Merodach-baladan 12 years (721-10), Sargon 5 years (709-5), Sennacherib 2 years (704-3), Marduk-zakir-shumi and Merodach-baladan (again) one and nine months respectively, and Belibni 3 years (702-700). Merodach-baladan was ousted from Babylon in 710 but maintained his independence as ruler of the Chaldean district of Bit-Yakin. It was in this capacity that he tried to rally Hezekiah's support in a broad-based alliance against the Assyrian overlord. In course of Sennacherib's first campaign (703) he fled for his life into the swamps and marshes where he could not be found.

Merodach-baladan's chequered career for the years 710-707 is given as follows by Bob Becking (pp.95f.). In 710 (*palu* 12 of Sargon's reign) Sargon conquered Babylon and had himself invested as king in place of Merodach-baladan, who therewith withdrew to Dur-Jakin. In 709 (*palu* 13) Dur-Jakin was besieged but not conquered. After negotiations Merodach-baladan's life was spared. In 707 (*palu* 15) Dur-Jakin was besieged and definitively conquered. Merodach-baladan fled to the marshlands of southern Babylonia.

In 708, therefore, Merodach-baladan was still very much at large. Though no longer king of Babylon, he doubtless regarded himself as the rightful king. His purpose in visiting Hezekiah was to enlist the king's support in his own ambition to oust the Assyrians from Babylon and to recover the throne for himself. Hezekiah for his part, flattered by the personal interest shown in him by such an exalted person and elated with the feeling of his own importance, foolishly showed off all his wealth and military hardware. "There was nothing in his palace or in all his kingdom that Hezekiah did not show them" (Isaiah 39:2)!

Hezekiah showed off his storehouses full of silver and gold and his other treasures to Merodach-baladan's envoys. But how did he come by all this treasure seeing that he had just handed over to Sennacherib all the temple silver as well as the treasuries of the royal palace and had even stripped off the gold covering the doors and doorposts of the temple? (2 Kings 18:15,16). The answer may be found in 2 Chronicles 32:23. In gratitude for his part in destroying the Assyrian army and removing the Assyrian threat, Hezekiah was handsomely rewarded by the surrounding nations. There was also the plunder, which must have been considerable, captured from the 185,000 slain Assyrians and from the survivors who fled in haste after the disaster which had overtaken them.

There are some however who would place Hezekiah's illness and the visit of Merodach-baladan's envoys *before* Sennacherib's invasion. This would certainly make for a better fit in view of the fact that Merodach-baladan ceased to be king of Babylon in 710. But the biblical order is the logical one, since Hezekiah's illness can then be explained as the natural consequence of the stress and trauma caused by the invasion.

The objection is often raised that Tirhaka, the (Ethiopian) king of Egypt who opposed Sennacherib (2 Kings 19:9), would have been too young to lead an army much before 701 BC. This however is not the only or most likely interpretation of the relevant Stelae from Kawa.

Steven Robinson has shown that more probably he was 20 years old when he accompanied his uncle Shabaka to Memphis in Lower Egypt in about 712 BC.

Tirhaka (Taharka)

It has been said that Tirhaka would have been too young in 701 (let alone 709) to lead an Egyptian army. This was indeed the view of M.F. Laming Macadam who first published the Stelae from Kawa in 1949. But his interpretation has been challenged by more recent researchers, notably Leclant and Yoyotte (1952), W. Hamilton Barnes (1991) and Steven Robinson (1991/2). My own reading is limited to Barnes and Robinson where the various options are set out.

It is impossible to form any opinion on the subject without studying the relevant texts. So here are the relevant passages from Stela IV and Stela V as translated by Macadam.

(Stela IV) Now His Majesty had been in Nubia as a goodly youth, a king's brother, pleasant of love, and he came north to Thebes in the company of goodly youths whom His Majesty King Shebiktu had sent to fetch from Nubia, in order that he might be there with him, since he loved him more than all his brethren. He passed to the nome of Amun of Gempaten that he might make obeisance at the temple door, with the army of His Majesty which had travelled north together with him. He found that this temple had been built in brick, but that its sand-hill had reached to its roof, it having been covered over with earth at a time of year when one feared the occurrence of rainfall. And His Majesty's heart grew sad at it until His Majesty appeared as King, crowned as King of Upper and Lower Egypt, and when the Double Diadem was established upon his head and his name became Horus Lofty-of- Diadems, he called to mind this temple, which he had beheld as a youth in the first year of his reign.

(Stela V) I came from Nubia in the company of the King's brothers, whom His Majesty had summoned, that I might be there with him, since he loved me more than all his brethren and all his children, and I was preferred to them by His Majesty, for the hearts of the people turned toward me and the love of me was with all men. I received the crown in Memphis after the Hawk [presumably Shebiktu] had soared to heaven. . . . [Now she was] in Nubia, the King's mother, Abar, may she live. Now further I had departed from her as a youth of twenty years when I came with His Majesty to Lower Egypt. Thereupon she came north to see me after an interval of years.

Tirhaka says regarding his mother, Abar, "I had departed from her as a youth of twenty years when I came with His Majesty to Lower Egypt." By Steven Robinson this journey is identified with that made by Tirhaka's uncle, King Shabaka, in the second year of his reign when he left his native Nubia and established himself at Memphis, the capital of Lower Egypt. This was in about 712 BC. One needs to distinguish between the various "Majesties" in these extracts. Here it is understood to be Shabaka who reigned from about 713 to 699. Shabaka was succeeded by his nephew, Shebiktu, Tirhaka's brother, in about 699, and he was succeeded by Tirhaka himself in 689. If Tirhaka was 20 in 712 he was certainly old enough to command (at least nominally) an Egyptian army in 709/8.

Tirhaka records another journey which is often identified with the first. Speaking of himself he says in Stela IV, "Now His Majesty had been in Nubia as a goodly youth, a King's brother, pleasant of love, and he came north to Thebes, etc." And again in Stela V, "I came from Nubia in the company of the King's brothers, etc."

This time he goes to Thebes the capital city of Upper Egypt, and he is summoned by his brother Shebiktu who is now King. Robinson is surely right in differentiating this visit from the earlier one when he accompanied his uncle to Lower Egypt. Robinson says, "In view of the different destinations and different companions, and the fact that Stela V recalls and relates the two journeys as separate occasions, it is difficult to see how one can reach any other conclusion."

This second visit was either in 689, the year Tirhaka became king (so Robinson), or some years earlier (so Barnes, following Leclant and Yoyotte). It all depends on how Kawa IV,ii.12-13 should be punctuated. Macadam translated it, "he called to mind this temple [the temple of Amun of Gempaten], which he had beheld as a youth in the first year of his reign." But the concluding time-note should probably be construed with "he called to mind this temple" rather than "he beheld as a youth." In other words, "already in the first year of his reign Tirhaka called to mind the neglected state of the temple which he had originally beheld as a youth."

It was on the occasion of this second visit, when he was still a youth and his brother Shebiktu was on the throne, that his heart had grown sad at the dilapidated state of the temple of Amun. In the first year of his reign (689) he called this fact to mind. Then in his 6th year, as he goes on to narrate, he announced his decision to rebuild the Gematen temple.

If Tirhaka was 20 years old in 689, the first year of his reign (so Macadam), he would have been at most a babe in arms in 709. If he was 20 when he went to Thebes in the company of goodly youths (so Barnes), he still would not have been old enough, not at least if his brother was already king. Least objectionable is Robinson's suggestion that Tirhaka was 20 in about 712 when he accompanied his uncle Shabaka to Memphis, the capital of Lower Egypt.

At that time he was not even heir to the throne; his brother Shebiktu was next in line. He is called "king" proleptically in 2 Kings 19:9 since he did become king eventually. He reigned from 689 to 664, by which time he might have been 68 years old.

Menahem of Samaria

Menihimmu of Samerina is mentioned in a tribute list as having paid tribute to Tiglath-pileser III (743-728). Menahem is third in a list of 18 names and immediately follows Rasunnu (Rezin) of Aram. The text is little more than a list of names, but it raises an interesting problem in that Menahem died in 755 according to my dating, long before the accession of Tiglath-pileser (in 743) by any scheme derived from the Bible. The text is as follows:-

> I received the tribute of Kustspi, the kummuhite, Rezin, the Damascene, Menahem, the Samarian, Hiram, the Tyrian, Sibittibi'il, the Byblian, Urikki, The Quean, Pisiris, the Carchemishite, Eni-il, the Hamathite, Panammuwa, the Sam'alite, Tarhulara, the Gurgumite, Sulumal, the Melidite, Dadilu, the Kaskean, Uassurme, the Tabalian, Ushitti, the (A)Tunean, Urballa, the Tuhanean, Tuhamme, the Istundian, Uirime, the Hubisnean, Zabibe, queen of the land of Arabia: gold, silver, tin, iron, elephant hides, elephant tusks (ivory), multi-coloured garments, blue-purple wool, and red-purple wool, ebony, boxwood, all kinds of precious things from the royal treasure, live sheep whose wool is dyed red-purple, flying birds of the sky whose wings are dyed blue-purple, horses, mules, cattle and sheep, camels, she-camels together with their young. (*Context II*, 285f.)

This text is confirmed by the Iran Stela in which a tribute list almost identical to the one above is to be found. The only differences are (1) the absence of Eni-ilu of Hamath, (2) The name of the king of Tyre, Tubail in place of Hiram, (3) A somewhat different order of names. The section immediately preceding the tribute list is devoted to the events of Tiglath-pileser's ninth campaign, that of 737. This leads L.D. Levine, the publisher of this text, to conclude that:

"Menahem of Israel was still on the throne in the year 737 BC, and any scheme of Biblical chronology must take this firm synchronism into account"(1972: 40-42).

However, subsequent writers have seen fit to modify Levine's conclusion. M. Cogan for example concludes from the mention of Tubail in place of Hiram that this stele must precede the 738 annals list in which Hiram is noted. "Although the stele itself may date from 737 BC, its scribal author seems to have utilized an earlier listing in composing his text" (1973: 98).

Faulstich would go even further. The annals texts of Tiglath-pileser were originally engraved on slabs at his palace at Calah (Nimrud), but were subsequently removed by Esarhaddon to be used in his own south-west palace. In view of their fragmentary state resulting from their removal and retrimming, "it could even be possible that these texts which have been assigned to Tiglath-pileser are really annals of a previous king" (1986: 124). In Faulstich's view it was not Tiglath-pileser to whom Menahem paid tribute but Ashur-dan III (771-754), uncle of Tiglath-pileser and brother of Shalmaneser IV and Ashur-nirari V. 755, he says, is the only year in which Menahem could have paid tribute to Ashur-dan III judging from the annotations in the AEC. For that year (as for 765) the Canon has "to Hatarikka", that is Hazrak or Hadrach (Zech. 9:1), 25 km. south of Aleppo in northern Syria.

Dr Jones declares in no uncertain terms, "On the authority of the Hebrew text, the author positively asserts that the second 'slab' inscription has been wrongly assigned to Tiglath-pileser III whereas in truth it should be credited to an earlier Assyrian monarch whom the biblical text calls 'Pul' (Ashur-dan III)" (p.171).

It is true that Menahem gave "Pul king of Assyria" a thousand talents of silver in the hope of gaining his support and securing his own position (2 Kings 15:19-20). And the Assyrian king at that time was Ashur-dan III. It is possible that it is this payment which is mentioned in Tiglath-pileser's inscription.

But Millard finds it "very odd, if Faulstich is correct, that all the other kings in the list occur in Tiglath-pileser III's inscriptions, including Jehoahaz of Judah!" A less radical solution than Faulstich's is much to be desired.

Who was Pul?

But what are we to make of this reference to "Pul" in 2 Kings 15:19? Later in the same chapter, in connection with the reign of Pekah, we find a reference to "Tiglath-pileser king of Assyria" (15:29). Again it is Tiglath-pileser whom Ahaz called upon in his distress (16:7,10). There is nothing in the text of 2 Kings to suggest the identity of Pul and Tiglath-pileser. There are two possibilities here. Either Pul was an earlier king whose name is abbreviated to Pul, or (as is generally accepted these days) Pul was the pre-dynastic name of Tiglath-pileser himself. It is not impossible that Tiglath-pileser was already active in the service of his uncle Ashur-dan III more than twenty years before ascending the throne.

Pulu/ Poros is in fact the name by which Tiglath-pileser is called in King-list A and the Canon of Ptolemy (see Thiele, 1965: 92). J.A. Brinkman has confirmed that Pul is an authentic variant of Tiglath-pileser and not, as is often supposed, the king's official name in Babylonia (1968: 61f.). According to Thiele (p.93), "With such positive proof that Pul and Tiglath-pileser are one and the same king, it is clear that Menahem and Tiglath-pileser were contemporaneous and that, either the system of Biblical chronology which gives the date 761 (*sic*) for the termination of Menahem's reign is wrong, or Assyrian chronology is wrong when it provides the date 745 for Tiglath-pileser's accession."

It is far from certain however that Pul and Tiglath-pileser stand for one and the same king. I am far more in sympathy with George Smith who said, "The theory that Pul is Tiglath-pileser is supported by stronger evidence than any other which has been brought forward, but the difficulty of crowding all the events, from the accession of Menahem, king of Israel, down to that of

Hoshea, a period according to the Bible of three successive reigns, and forty-three years, into the seventeen years of Tiglath Pileser's annals, forms, I think, an insuperable objection to this view" (1875: 184 f.).

The text which might have decided the issue once and for all has been interpreted in more ways than one. That text is 1 Chronicles 5:26: "And the God of Israel stirred up the spirit of Pul king of Assyria, and the spirit of Tiglath-pileser king of Assyria, and he carried them away, even the Reubenites, and the Gadites, and the half tribe of Manasseh, and brought them to Halah and Habor and Hara, and the river Gozan unto this day" (*KJV*). The singular verb "and *he* carried" lends support to the *NIV* translation "Pul king of Assyria (that is, Tiglath-pileser king of Assyria)". That Tiglath-pileser and Pul designate a single ruler is generally taken for granted by scholars today.

Chronology apart, it is far from certain that the Hebrew of 1 Chronicles 5:26 permits their identification. The repetition of the accusative particle *'eth*, followed in each case by "the spirit of", seems expressly designed to *exclude* their identification. Even the *RSV* and *ESV* translation ("So the God of Israel stirred up the spirit of Pul king of Assyria, the spirit of Tilgath-pilneser king of Assyria ...") is inaccurate in so far as it leaves out the word "and" before "the spirit of Tilgath-pilneser". It never occurred to older commentators, who had only the Bible to guide them, to identify these two kings. Josephus, for example, speaks of them as two kings (*Ant.* IX.11.1).

It is natural to take the singular verb "and he carried them away" of the second king mentioned, Tiglath-pileser. Faulstich however refers it to Pul, the first of the two kings. It was, he says, Pul who deported the Transjordanian tribes of Reuben, Gad, and half Manasseh as recorded in 1 Chronicles 5:26. But of this there is no suggestion in the Bible. According to 2 Kings 15:20 Pul, having extracted his pound of flesh from Menahem, "withdrew and stayed in the land no longer". Menahem bought off the Assyrian predator for the time being. It was Tiglath-pileser who first deported Israel's inhabitants. This he did both from both sides of the Jordan (1 Chron. 5:26; 2 Kings 15:29).

Christine Tetley thinks that *two* kings are designated by Pul in the Bible. In 2 Kings 15:19 it is Shalmaneser IV to whom she thinks Menahem paid a thousand talents of silver, but in 1 Chronicles 5:26 it is Tiglath-pileser. "Pul of 2 Kgs 15:19 should not be identified as Pul of 1 Chr 5:26" (p.178). But it is far more probable that the same king is meant by Pul and that two kings are mentioned in 1 Chronicles: the earlier Pul to whom Menahem paid tribute and Tiglath-pileser who carried many of them into exile.

The name "Menahem" was well known to the Assyrians since Menahem had paid tribute to Pulu (namely, Assur-dan III, 771-754), Tiglath-pileser's predecessor but one. Menahem was the last king to provide stable government in Samaria. The throne of Israel was changing hands so rapidly by this time, it must have been difficult for a foreign power to keep track of them. It was in any case of little importance to the Assyrians who was reigning at any particular time so long as their tribute was paid promptly and in full.

There is something immediately suspicious about a tribute list in which Rezin of Aram is associated with Menahem of Samaria. In the Bible Rezin is constantly associated with "Pekah son of Remaliah" (2 Kings 15:37; 16:5; Isaiah 7:1 etc.). These two kings were contemporaries. Both died in the same year and their reigns coincided for at least eleven years (Rezin paid tribute in 743). Clearly Menahem is the odd man out so far as this tribute list is concerned. Though "Menahem" is the name given, the ruler intended was really Pekah.

O.T. Allis comments, "In view of the length of the list and the fact that it is simply a list of names, the nature of the tribute not being stated, the possibility is not to be rejected that either a tribute paid some thirty years previously to an earlier king is here listed by mistake, or that the Assyrian scribe was unaware that Menahem was not still king of Israel".

In any case, there is no cause to alter the whole of Israel's chronology just because an Assyrian scribe did not know (and probably did not care) who was currently reigning in Samaria.

Joash of Samaria

An inscription found in 1967 at Tell al-Rimah, some fifty miles west of Mosul, tells of a campaign in Syria in the reign of Adad-nirari III (presumed 810-783). It claims that the land of Amurru and all Hatti-land knelt at the king's feet, and in line eight Adad-nirari receives tribute from *Iu'asu mat-Samerina*, that is Joash of the land of Samaria.

Stephanie Page who published the inscription in 1968 describes its appearance as follows. "It was inscribed on the face with twenty-one lines, of which nine had been deliberately erased in antiquity; the writing ran across the skirt of the king, who was sculptured upon it slightly less than life-size, but not over the frame or sides of the stone. The stela is 1.30 m. high and measures 0.69 m. in width at the base; it is parabolic in shape. It is made of a single slab of hard grey, crystalline 'Mosul marble', in an excellent state of preservation."

The relevant part of the text reads as follows:-

Adad-nirari, mighty king, king of the universe, king of Assyria; son of Samsi-Adad, the king of the universe, king of Assyria; son of Shalmaneser, the king of the four quarters. I mustered (my) chariots, troops and camps; I ordered (them) to march to the land of Hatti. In a single year, I subdued the entire lands of Amurru (and) Hatti. I imposed upon them tax and tribute forever. I (text: "he") received 2,000 talents of silver, 1,000 talents of copper, 2,000 talents of iron, 3,000 linen garments with multi-coloured trim - the tribute of Mari' of the land of Damascus. I (text: "he") received the tribute of Joash (Iu'asu) the Samarian, of the Tyrian (ruler), and of the Sidonian (ruler). I marched to the great sea in the West. I erected a statue of my lordship in the city of Arvad which is in the midst of the sea. I climbed Mt. Lebanon; (and) I cut down timbers; 100 mature cedars, material needed for my palace and temples. (*Context II*, 276)

The expression "in a single year" is regarded by many as a literary convention in which several campaigns to Syria have been telescoped into one. But according to William H. Shea and others the campaign took place in Adad-nirari's fifth regnal year, 805 BC, for which the Eponym List has "to Arpad". The same campaign is ascribed to the king's fifth year in the Saba'a Stela, which records the submission of Mari' in Damascus and the tribute he paid.

Also on the Calah Orthostat Slab, a summary inscription, Adad-nirari includes "the land of Israel" among those on whom he imposed tax and tribute, along with Tyre, Sidon, Edom and Philistia. It does not seem likely that he actually invaded these lands. Jehoash and the other kings would have been quick to send their tribute rather than risk invasion from the Assyrian juggernaut. There is nevertheless a serious discrepancy between the date implied in the Tell al-Rimah Stela and mine for the reign of King Jehoash, 843-828.

According to Tadmor (1973), the ten-line inscription telescopes the entire western wars of 805-796 into what misleadingly appears as an account of an expedition of the fifth year. The most likely year in the view of many is 796, this being the only year, according to the Eponym Canon, that Adad-nirari reached southern Syria-Palestine. In this year he reached a place called Mansuate somewhere in the Lebanese Beka'a valley.

Either way a major dislocation is in view. If the date of Jehoash's submission was presumed 805, as seems most likely, we are faced with a stark discrepancy in the order of 25-35 years.

The temptation to lower the dates of the kings of Israel has proved irresistible to modern scholars. Their desire to reconcile the Israelite and Assyrian dates is a laudable one. This desire I cherish more strongly than most. The problem is how to do it without doing violence to either side. The discrepancy could possibly be explained on similar lines to the reference to "Menahem of Samaria" in the annals of Tiglath-pileser III. But in view of the widening divergence that we encounter in this earlier period, one cannot avoid the suspicion that the Assyrian record may not be as complete as it seems, some reign or period of unrest having been deliberately passed over for reasons of political expediency.

Ahabbu of Sir'alaia

The earliest synchronism between an Israelite king and a king of Assyria has been the subject of prolonged debate. It relates to Ahabbu of Sir'alaia (? Ahab of Israel) whose participation in the battle of Qarqar is recorded in Shalmaneser's Monolith Inscription and the Kurkh Stele. It was in the 6th year of Shalmaneser III (presumed 853 BC) that the twelve Western allies, under the leadership of Irhuleni of Hamath, came face to face with the Assyrian king at Qarqar on the Orontes. The relevant sections of the Kurkh Monolith reads as follows:-

> In the eponymy of Dayan Assur, in the month of Iyyar, the fourteenth day, I departed from Nineveh. I crossed the Tigris. I approached the cities of Giammu on the River Balih... I departed from the city of Aleppo (Halman). I approached the cities of Irhuleni, the Hamathite. I captured Adennu, Parga, (and) Argana, his royal cities. I carried off captives, his valuables, (and) his palace possessions. I set fire to his palaces. I departed from the city of Argana. I approached the city of Qarqar. I razed, destroyed and burned the city of Qarqar, his royal city. 1,200 chariots, 1,200 cavalry, (and) 20,000 troops of Hadad-ezer (Adad-idri) of Damascus; 700 chariots, 700 cavalry, (and) 10,000 troops of Irhuleni, the Hamathite; 2,000 chariots, (and) 10,000 troops of Ahab, the Israelite (Sir'alaia); 500 troops of Byblos; 1,000 troops of Egypt; 10 chariots (and) 10,000 troops of the land of Irqanatu (Irqata); 200 troops of Matinu-ba'al of the city of Arvad; 200 troops of the land of Usanatu (Usnu); 30 chariots (and) [ ],000 of Adon-ba'al of the land of Sianu (Siyannu); 1,000 camels of Gindibu' of Arabia; [ ] hundred troops of Ba'asa, (the man) of Bit-Ruhubi, the Ammonite - these 12 kings he took as his allies. They marched against me [to do] war and battle. With the supreme forces which Assur, my lord, had given me (and) with the mighty weapons which the divine standard, which goes before me, had granted me, I fought with them. I decisively defeated them from the city of Qarqar to the city of Gilzau. I felled with the sword 14,000 troops, their fighting men. Like Adad, I rained down upon them a devastating flood. I spread out their corpses (and) I filled the plain. <I felled> with the sword their extensive troops. I made their blood flow in the waddis (?) [ ]. The field was too small for laying flat their bodies (lit. "their lives"); the broad countryside had been consumed in burying them. I blocked the Orontes River with their corpses as with a cause way. In the midst of this battle I took away from them chariots, cavalry, (and) teams of horses. (*Context II*, 263 f.)

The identification of Ahab of Sir'alaia with Ahab of Israel has not been universally accepted. It was rejected by George Smith who first published the Eponym Canon back in 1875. "It does not seem likely", he said, "that the biblical Ahab, who was the foe of the king of Damascus, sent any troops to his aid, at least, such a circumstance is never hinted at in the Bible, and is contrary to the description of his conduct and reign" (pp.189-90). Likewise O.T. Allis states his opinion that "Such an undertaking by Ahab, king of Israel, seems highly improbable to say the least" (pp.414-15). Reasons for rejecting the identification include the following:

1) The name Sir'alaia, lacking the initial *yod*, is not indisputably Israel. But this, I understand, is explicable within the cuneiform script.

2) Jehu, in the inscriptions of the same king, is referred to as "Jehu, son of Omri", and in no subsequent inscription does Sir'alaia occur. "The Assyrians", we are told, "often denoted countries by the name of the founder of the ruling dynasty at the time of their first acquaintance with it (e.g. 'Bit Bahiani, Bit Agusi, Bit Humri'), regardless of which dynasty was currently in power" (*Context II*, 267). Why in that case is Ahab not so called by Shalmaneser? He was after all a true son of Omri, unlike his successors.

3) Ahab is credited with 2,000 chariots, the largest number among the allies and considerably more than Hadad-ezer of Damascus. Even Solomon had only 1,400 chariots (1 Kings 10:26) and Shishak king of Egypt even less, 1,200 according to 2 Chronicles 12:3. Assyria itself had only 2,000 chariots in (presumed) 843 BC.

The problem of Ahab's chariots is tackled by Na'aman (1976: 97-102). "Is it really feasible," he asks, "that the kingdom of Israel by itself had at its disposal a chariot force equal in strength to that of the Assyrian Empire at the height of its greatness under Shalmaneser III?" Chariots were an expensive commodity, and needed a large number of horses. These too were costly and had to be imported. According to 1 Kings 10:29, the price of a chariot was four times that of a horse. In view of the large number of scribal errors in this inscription (at least ten in the passage dealing specifically with the battle of Qarqar), Na'aman thinks two *hundred* to be far more appropriate. Ahab would have hesitated to send his entire chariot force to the assistance of his arch rival, the king of Damascus.

4) Ahab's recurring enemy was Syria, not Assyria. Is it likely that Ahab would have joined an alliance with his old enemy against such a distant foe? When however confronted by a common danger the smaller kingdoms would naturally sink their differences and unite. 1 Kings 20:32-34 and 22:1 allow for a period of alliance between Ahab and Ben-Hadad of Aram. Ahab, however, died fighting the king of Aram at Ramoth Gilead (1 Kings 22), so could hardly have joined an alliance with him in the year of his death as supposed by Thiele.

5) The Bible does not mention Assyria at all until the reign of Menahem, a hundred years later. Is there any evidence of contact between the two kingdoms at this early date? It would appear that subsequent to the reign of Shalmaneser III Assyria did not again reach so far to the south and west (except briefly under Adad-nirari III) until the reigns of Ashur-dan III and Tiglath-pileser. So its absence from the biblical record is not altogether surprising.

6) Ahab is not a typically Hebrew name, and might therefore refer to a non-Israelite ruler. In a work entitled *The Prosopography of the Neo-Assyrian Empire* (ed. Karen Radner, 1998,9), under *Ah-abi*, meaning "Father's brother", seven other Ahabs are mentioned besides Ahab of Israel, and under *Ah-abu* twenty-nine more, none of them Israelite.

Faulstich accepts the identification with Ahab of Israel, but thinks the battle took place in the reign of Shalmaneser's father, Ashur-nasir-pal II (884-859). He compares Shalmaneser's inscriptions with those of his predecessors and concludes that "Shalmaneser III was already quite adept at modifying records to assign the fame and glory of another monarch to himself" (p.143). With respect to the Monolith Inscription he says, "Shalmaneser has 'stolen' the Monolith Inscription from his father - Ashur-nasir-pal. Shalmaneser has removed his father's name and has removed the eponym years coinciding with his father's reign and has placed his own name there and has placed eponymous persons into the text to parallel his first six years" (p.153).

This, however, is a course of desperation! Insulting these kings is no substitute for rational argument!

Actually it makes good sense in the context of Shalmaneser's inscriptions to identify Ahab of Sir'alaia with Ahab of Israel. The same coalition of twelve kings, with or without Israel, came face to face with Shalmaneser, not only at Qarqar in his sixth year (presumed 853), but also in his tenth, eleventh and fourteenth years (presumed 849, 848 and 845). The composition of the alliance was basically the same each time, but Israel's continued participation is doubtful seeing that Ahab's son, Joram, spent so much of his reign fighting the Aramaeans (2 Kings 6-8). The coalition was strong enough to halt Shalmaneser's advance, it seems, but in his eighteenth year (presumed 841) the coalition broke up as a result of Hazael's coup in Damascus, and Shalmaneser was at last victorious. Jehu chose to submit rather than join Hazael in resisting the Assyrian menace. In that year Shalmaneser claims to have received tribute from Jehu son of Omri (*Iaua mat Humri*).

There are twelve years between 853 and 841, and there were also twelve years between the end of Ahab's reign and the beginning of Jehu's. This coincidence was used to good effect by E.R. Thiele to prove that Ahab's last year of reign was 853 and Jehu's first year 841. On these two pegs he hung the whole of his chronology of the Divided Kingdom. But Ahab died fighting the king of Aram, so could not have been in alliance with him in that year. An alliance might however have been forged the year before, when there was a window of peace between Aram and Israel (1 Kings 22:1). This would entail a dislocation of 44 years between the Israelite and Assyrian dating.

```
Ahab  21st    897 ---- 44 yrs ---- 853

          |                  |      12 yrs

Jehu   1st    885 ---- 44 yrs ---- 841
```

The identification of *Ahabbu* with Ahab of Israel is not beyond dispute. But, assuming it is correct, the coalition must have been hastily put together to meet the crisis. Only a year or two before Israel and Aram had been at each other's throats. Ben-hadad had been soundly defeated in two successive years, first in the hills and then in the plains (1 Kings 20). On the second occasion, in the plain south-west of Aphek in Transjordan, Ben-hadad lost a hundred thousand men and was forced to eat humble pie in order to save his life. Ahab treated him with unwise and undeserved leniency for which he was condemned by one of the prophets (20:31-43). The outcome was that a peace treaty was signed which lasted for three years (22:1).

It was during this break in hostilities that the coalition of western powers was forged in response to the mounting threat posed by the advancing Assyrian army. The Syrian, Palestinian and Phoenician kings, joined by contingents from Egypt and Arabia, lined up against Shalmaneser at Qarqar and succeeded, it seems, in halting his advance. At any rate, it was four years later before the Assyrian king returned to the West.

But as soon as the immediate crisis was over Israel and Aram resumed hostilities over the disputed frontier town of Ramoth-gilead. Ahab was joined by Jehoshaphat of Judah, and contrary to the advice of the prophet Micaiah they engaged Ben-hadad in battle at Ramoth-gilead. Ahab was badly wounded, and later died, from an arrow shot at random and the battle ended inconclusively. Eleven years later Ahab's son Joram was severely wounded fighting once more over Ramoth-gilead with Ben-hadad's successor, Hazael. It was then that Jehu slew both Joram and his ally, Ahaziah of Judah, and seized the throne for himself.

Jehu of Bit-Humri

The reference to Jehu comes in the Calah Bulls Annals, a reconstructed recension based on inscriptions on two monumental bulls found at Calah and supplemented by two small fragments of inscribed stones (*Context II*, 266 f.). In connection with the campaign of Shalmaneser's 18th year, when he crossed the Euphrates for the sixteenth time and defeated Hazael of Damascus, he says, "At that time, I received the tribute of the Tyrians and the Sidonians, and of *Ia-u-a bit-Humri* (Jehu son of Omri)."

In addition, on the Black Obelisk inscription there is a relief picturing Jehu (or his envoy) bowing down before the enthroned Shalmaneser. This is the earliest representation of a Hebrew dignitary. In the words of Alberto Green, "Iaua is portrayed as a prostrate figure at the king's feet; however, unlike Sua [the king of Gilzanu] his face is toward the ground. He is wearing a tasselled cap and clad only in his undergarment. All the Israelite tribute bearers, like their counterparts the Gilzanites, are fully clothed."

Green continues: "An important detail which is so evident is that only Sua and Jehu as vassal kings, are depicted on the obelisk. Both occupy the centre stage of registers and are portrayed in a prostrate position at the feet of the king. Hovering overhead is the *melammu* of the god Assur, whose divine and royal glory is conceptualized in the art motif of the winged sun disc ... The depiction of both kings in their undergarments, in contrast to the tribute bearers who are fully attired, is intended to emphasize their humility and complete submission to the Assyrian deity... in a real sense the scenes depicted in the first two rows of the obelisk, in all probability represent the actual and historical boundaries of the Assyrian Empire in the north-east and the west up to the death of Shalmaneser III" (1979: 38 f.). The text is as follows:

> I received the tribute of Jehu (Ia-u-a) (the man) of Bit-Humri: silver, gold, a golden bowl, a golden goblet, golden cups, golden buckets, tin, a staff of the king's hand, (and) javelins(?). (*Context II*, 270)

The identification with Jehu is not entirely beyond question. It has been suggested, by P. Kyle McCarter for example, that *Iaua* may be no more than a hypocoristicon (abbreviation or nickname) for any Israelite king whose name includes the theophorous element Yahu or Yau, in which case Jehoram and Jehoahaz have as much right to be considered as Jehu. It is pointed out that at least two kings of Tyre, whose full names are not known, are called simply "Ba'l" in the Assyrian records. O.T. Allis remarks, "If Shalmaneser knew so little about Jehu as to call him the son of Omri, he might easily have confused him with Jehoahaz or Jehoash" (p.418). Christine Tetley thinks that Jehoram is meant.

But these ideas have not been widely accepted. *Iaua* is far more likely to be Jehu than Joram or Jehoahaz. Even less acceptable is Faulstich's explanation, that Shalmaneser has appropriated an inscription belonging to his grandfather, substituting his own name for that of the true king! In his view, "The chronology of the Hebrew kings becomes historical nonsense when adjusted to fit such corruptions and forgeries" (p.154). But this is not an approach which is likely to commend itself to many people.

In the same inscriptions as mention Jehu, mentioned also are Hadad-ezer and Hazael, kings in Damascus. Hazael's seizure of the throne occurred in about 841 if Shalmaneser is to be believed (see below). In fact it took place shortly before the death of Joram in 885, some 44 years earlier (2 Kings 8:28-29). It was in this year apparently, 841/885, that Jehu paid tribute to Shalmaneser. John Bright describes what happened as follows:

> Shalmaneser III, who had not accepted the checkmate that he received at Qarqar in 853 as final, in succeeding years made repeated campaigns against the Syrian coalition, still

headed by Damascus and Hamath. The most serious of these came in 841, soon after Hazael had seized power. The Assyrian armies raged southward, defeated the Aramean forces and laid siege to Damascus, the gardens and groves of which they ravaged. Then, unable to make Hazael capitulate, Shalmanser pressed southward as far as the Hauran and west to the sea along the Phoenician coast, taking tribute from Tyre and Sidon, and Jehu, king of Israel, on the way (1980: 254).

Jehu, it seems, reversed the policy of his Omride predecessors. He refused to join an alliance headed by Hazael, the new king of Aram, and submitted willingly to the Assyrian king. Hazael for his part, deserted by his allies (which for the first time are not mentioned), was unable to resist the Assyrian advance.

Hazael and the Ben-Hadads of Damascus

The facts relating to these kings of Aram are recorded as follows in the pages of the Bible.

1) In 1 Kings 15:18 we read of "Ben-hadad son of Tabrimmon, the son of Hezion, the king of Aram, who was ruling in Damascus." This ruler came to the aid of Asa king of Judah when "Baasha king of Israel went up against Judah and fortified Ramah to prevent anyone from leaving or entering the territory of Asa king of Judah" (15:17). This was a shrewd act of diplomacy so far as Asa was concerned, but the Lord thought otherwise. To Him it was an act of unbelief which would reap its own bitter harvest in terms of unremitting warfare (2 Chron.16:7-9). The date is given in Chronicles as "the 36th year of Asa's reign", which we have found to be a textual error for Asa's 16th year, 939 BC, as explained in an earlier chapter.

2) Another Ben-hadad is mentioned in 1 Kings 20 as having besieged and attacked Samaria in the reign of Ahab (917-895). Ben-hadad made some extravagant demands, not only Ahab's silver and gold, wives and children, but also everything he fancied in Ahab's palace and the houses of his officials. Ahab baulked at such unreasonable demands and was encouraged to resist by a prophet who promised him in the Lord's name that Ben-hadad's vast army would be given into his hands. And so it happened. The arrogant Ben-hadad was completely routed and humiliated in two successive years. From verse 34 we learn that Ben-hadad's father had taken cities from Ahab's father, King Omri. This was probably the Ben-hadad of 1 Kings 15:18.

3) In 1 Kings 19:15-18 Elijah is told by the Lord to anoint three people: Hazael as king over Aram, Jehu as king over Israel, and Elisha as his own successor. Jehu seized the throne of Israel in 885, and it was during his reign that Hazael over-powered Israel throughout their territory east of the Jordan (2 Kings 10:32).

4) In 2 Kings 8:7-15 it is revealed to Elisha that Hazael would be the next king of Aram. The very next day Hazael smothered Ben-hadad with a thick cloth soaked in water, and reigned in his place. This was in the reign of Joram, son of Ahab (see 3:1), and near the end of his reign since Joram was fighting Hazael when he was killed by Jehu (2 Kings 8:28-29). Most probably it was in Joram's tenth year as a careful reading of 2 Kings 3-8 would suggest (so Tetley: 168). That was 887 BC (presumed 843). This agrees with the Assyrian evidence that Hazael seized the throne between Shalmaneser's 14th and 18th years, presumed 845 and 841.

5) We learn from 2 Kings 12:17-18 that Hazael, having captured Gath, moved in on Jerusalem. However Joash, king of Judah, persuaded him to withdraw with a massive bribe. This was in about the 23rd year of Joash (12:6), the year in which Jehoahaz, son of Jehu, became king in Samaria (13:1), 858 BC.

6) According to 2 Kings 13:22, Hazael king of Aram oppressed Israel throughout the reign of Jehoahaz (858-42). For a long time the Lord kept Israel under the heel of Hazael and Ben-hadad his son (2 Kings 13:3).

7) In 2 Kings 13:24-25 Hazael dies and is succeeded by Ben-hadad (III). Jehoash, son of Jehoahaz, recaptured from Ben-hadad the towns he had seized from his father Jehoahaz. This he did after defeating Ben-hadad on three separate occasions, answering to the three times he had struck the ground in response to Elisha's invitation (13:18-19).

From all this we learn that Hazael's reign coincided roughly with those of Jehu and Jehoahaz (885-842), and the reign of his son Ben-hadad with that of Jehoash (843-828).

Now for the Assyrian evidence. Shalmaneser claims to have defeated Hadad-ezer of Aram in his 6th year (presumed 853), his 10th year (849), his 11th year (848), and his 14th year (845). Then in his 18th year (841) he is fighting against Hazael. This is the year in which he received tribute from Jehu, (the man) of Bit-Humri. Another inscription on a statue of Shalmaneser (The Assur Basalt Statue, *Context II*, 270) says: "Hadad-ezer (Adad-idri) passed away. Hazael, son of a nobody, took his throne. He mustered his numerous troops; (and) he moved against me to do war and battle...."

The campaign described is that against Hazael of Damascus in (presumed) 841. It has been deduced from this that Hazael, a commoner, usurped the throne in 841 or shortly before. The Assyrian expression for "passed away", *shadashu emid*, means "to die an unnatural death" or "be forcibly removed, murdered", according to E.F. Weidner (1939: 233f.). But in the *Chicago Assyrian Dictionary* (1958) and W. von Soden's *Akkadische Handworterbuch* (1965) the more colourless meaning "disappeared for ever" is preferred. The death of Hadad-ezer, violent or otherwise, and the seizure of the throne by the commoner Hazael, are strongly reminiscent of 2 Kings 8:13-15 where Hazael ("a mere dog") murders Ben-hadad and reigns in his place. If this took place in 887/6, King Joram's 10th or 11th year, we have once more a dislocation of 44 years. While this discrepancy is embarrassing and difficult to explain, there is at least a consistent displacement between the two accounts, biblical and Assyrian, for this period.

The fallacy of the 'Objective' approach

George Smith made a bold attempt at reconciling the two accounts on the assumption that both sources are trustworthy, following the Objective Approach which he adopts throughout (1875: 191). The result is a duplication of Ben-hadads and Hazaels, the events of the tenth century BC being more or less duplicated in the ninth. Nowhere does the objective theory break down more completely than over these kings of Aram. The confusion created by this theory is self-evident if it is followed through consistently. The following is a tabulation of what we are landed with when the biblical and Assyrian evidence is combined on the principle that the dating of both is correct:

Benhadad besieges Samaria in the reign of Ahab (1 Kings 20)....	917-895
Hazael smothers Ben-hadad near the end of Joram's reign (2 Kings 8:15)	c.886
Joram of I. and Ahaziah of J. fight Hazael (2 Kings 8:28; 9:15)....	885
Hazael takes Gath in about the 23rd year of Joash of Judah (= 1st year of Jehoahaz of Israel, 2 Ki.12:17; 13:1)....	c.858
Hazael oppresses Israel during the reign of Jehoahaz (2 Kings 13:22)..	858-842

But Hadad-idri (= Ben-hadad) is already fighting Shalmaneser in	853
Ben-hadad, son of Hazael I, continues to oppress Israel (2 Kings 13:3)	
Hazael II "son of nobody" succeeds Hadad-idri	842/1
Jehoash defeats another Ben-hadad, son of Hazael, thrice (13:25) ...	c.840-830

This is more or less what George Smith himself proposed (p.191). On this showing there was a Ben-hadad ruling in Damascus during the reign of Jehoahaz, though the Bible requires Hazael to be reigning at this time. The Ben-hadad of 2 Kings 13:3 has to be distinguished from his namesake of 13:25, though in the Bible they are clearly the same person. And between these two Ben-hadads there is squeezed a second Hazael who is not only son of a nobody, but no-one at all who could have lived at that time!

If I have laboured this point it is only to show the confusion which this approach gives rise to. The Objective Approach proposed by Smith ("of taking the Assyrian records to be correct as to Assyrian dates, and the Hebrew records as to Hebrew dates") and adopted by Allis and others, is the one we should all like to be correct. But faced with the parallel references to Ben-hadad and Hazael, not to mention Joash, Jehu and Ahab, this approach can no longer be seriously entertained. I am compelled to the view that a more radical revision of Assyrian chronology is demanded.

Proposed breaks in the Eponym Canon

One writer (P.J. James) remarks:

> Apart from synchronisms with Egypt, controls on the accuracy of the AKL (Assyrian King List) tradition are limited. Even so, the available material, including contemporary royal inscriptions and the internal evidence of the lists and their variants, provides clear evidence that the surviving recension of the Kinglist has been deliberately 'smoothed out' to give the impression of an unbroken succession of rulers from the earliest times to the 8th century BC. For example, the names of several rulers who were usurpers, or for some reason considered illegitimate by later kings, have been completely omitted from the canonical AKL (1987: 68-78).

One such missing ruler, he thinks, is "Assur-danin-apli (son of Shalmaneser III) who may have taken the throne during the six year rebellion he led at the end of his father's reign, 826-821 BC." "It is highly likely", says James, "that there were other rulers whose inscriptional evidence (if any) has been lost or was deliberately destroyed by subsequent kings." There is also evidence of adjustment in genealogical relationships to give the impression of continuity in the kingship, with the result that subterfuges of this kind are almost undetectable. At any rate, "We can no longer afford the naivety of late 19th to early 20th century scholarship, eager to accept the statements of the Assyrians regarding genealogy and chronology."

The phenomenon known as 'telescoping' is discussed by David Henige. He says: "The accidental or structural forgetting of the past, called telescoping, is a feature of historical thought that is unusually difficult to identify. Telescoping can usually be detected only with the aid of external data, and often not even then. Although there are few attested examples of *damnatio memoriae* for the ancient Near East, there is little reason to doubt that there were more, perhaps many more" (1986: 63f.).

For the period in question the Bible provides the external evidence required, for those who will accept it. We are possibly thinking of several short periods of telescoping, rather than one long one which could not be so easily concealed. Henige says, "The loss of independence has frequently provided the occasion for deliberate attempts at telescoping", and sometimes "individual rulers are simply 'genealogized' out of the historical record by being succeeded by nondirect heirs, perhaps brothers or cousins."

Historians are naturally reluctant to face up to this possibility, since it inevitably casts doubt on their pursuit. Henige says, "The notion that immeasurable and possibly rather large chunks of the past are irretrievably lost is distressing to historians. As a result, the question of memory is almost never addressed..."

In view of the increasing divergence between Bible dates and their Assyrian counterparts, there is cause for suspicion that the Assyrian royal succession may not be as regular as it looks. I am in agreement with Christine Tetley that prior to the eclipse of 763 BC such gaps do occur, and that this consideration explains the widening discrepancy between the Assyrian and Israelite dates.

Breaks in the Canon proposed by Tetley

Christine Tetley's chronology, though different from mine, suffers from the same embarrassment of being 44 years longer than its Assyrian counterpart. She solves this problem by proposing two places where names appear to have dropped out of the eponym sequence. Into each of these she inserts 22 additional years, thereby filling up the deficiency on the Assyrian side.

The more recent of these breaks she would place in the reign of Adad-nirari III prior to the *limmu*-ship of Nabu-sharru-usur and Balatu who seem to have shared the post of eponym in 786 BC. There is considerable confusion between the rival lists for this period. Tetley says, "Instead of assigning Nabu-sharru-usur and Balatu to the same year or omitting Balatu, the positioning of the names may be explained by proposing a disruption in the lists" (see Tetley: 97-99). She would insert 22 forgotten eponyms at this juncture involving a gap of 22 years.

She goes on to say, "The very possibility of names missing from one area of the collated AEC means that the years afforded to the AEC prior to 763 BCE cannot be confirmed as correct ... If eponyms have dropped from the list between Nabu-sharru-usur and Balatu at a presumed year 786, any number of years could be missing in this section of eponyms" (p.99).

For Christine Tetley 22 years is sufficient to align Jehoash's reign with the fifth year of Adad-nirari III when Jehoash paid tribute to the Assyrian king. For me at least one more year is required and probably a few more.

The second place where Tetley divines a hole in the eponym sequence is in the reign of Adad-nirari's predecessor, Shamshi-Adad V (presumed 822-810). Shamshi-Adad claims to have conquered Babylon in the 11th and 12th years of a presumed 13-year reign. He claimed the title of "King of Sumer and Akkad", implying effective control over Babylon. The Babylonian Chronicle at this point indicates an interregnum: "for x years there was no king in Babylon." The number is no longer legible, though it could be 2,12,22 or even longer. Tetley asks, "Was Shamshi-Adad king over Babylon for only one year?" (see pp.102-104) It is highly probable, she thinks, that he was king over Babylon for much longer than that. To meet this requirement she would insert a further 22 years at this point, thereby raising the reign of Shalmaneser III to the level required by her chronology.

There is no proof that these are the correct places in which to insert additional eponyms. Assyriologists are unlikely to be impressed. But breaks there must have been and their total length, 44 years, is what is required. A dislocation of at least 24 years is revealed if Jehoash of Israel paid tribute to Adad-nirari III and a further displacement of 20 years if Hazael became king in Damascus near the end of Joram's reign.

Another suggestion, made by Dr Jones, is that the king who repented at Jonah's preaching, along with his immediate successor(s) of the same obedient outlook, may have been expunged from the record. These kings would have been regarded by their successors as sacrilegious apostates, blasphemers all, and might well have been removed from the record in an attempt to obliterate their memory. If that is what happened their plot was all too successful! (see Jones: 157)

Concluding remarks

Alan Millard comments, "It is easy to assume a lacuna, but what evidence is there? Why should Assyrian scribes create an apparently continuous list of eponyms if there was a gap? The royal inscriptions name fathers and grandfathers and make a complete sequence, with no sign of an hiatus."

It all depends, I suppose, on the relative importance one attaches to the Assyrian Eponym Canon over against the chronology of the Bible. It is clearly impossible to reconcile the two without the assumption of gaps on the Assyrian side, and those who take the Bible seriously have been forced to make this assumption. Earlier attempts at locating possible gaps in the AEC were given short shrift by Assyriologists. Jules Oppert was an early casualty in this arena. Although most of his ideas were found wanting, I nevertheless share his conviction that (ultimately) "the pretended cuneiform chronology must bow to the mathematical correctness of the Holy Scriptures" (1898: 24).

Scholars treat the Assyrian Eponym Canon as providing the 'master' chronology for the period in question and the Bible as providing a secondary alternative. But in fact they are wrong: that honour belongs to the Bible! The Bible dates hold supreme down to the first year of Nebuchadnezzar, 605/4 BC. Only then did the "times of the Gentiles" commence and dates are given in terms of Gentile reigns. But down to 605/4 the Bible reigns supreme; other sources must bow to its superiority!

Summary

It was found, dating back from the death of Josiah assuming regular successions in each case, that the first year of King Ahaz worked out at 735 BC, the year which agrees best with the Eponym Canon. The Assyrian Canon has "to Philistia" for 734 and "to Damascus" for 733 and 732, which is what we would expect if Ahaz came to the throne in 735. All the subtleties and manipulations of scholars are made superfluous by the discovery that Ahaz' reign falls in exactly the right place without any gerrymandering at all.

At the same time the dates of the fall of Samaria and Sennacherib's invasion are fixed at 716 and 708 respectively. These dates are not the ones we have been led to expect, but instead of prejudging the issue and forcing the Bible into line, is it not better to look for ways to reconcile them? In fact the problems are not insuperable at all. Once it is recognized that the name Shalmaneser in 2 Kings 18:9 could be a scribal addition to the text, the way is opened up for lowering the dates of the siege and fall of Samaria to their natural place in the reign of Sargon.

As for Sennacherib's invasion in Hezekiah's fourteenth year, only eight years after the fall of Samaria, the solution was found in the two-invasion theory which, in one form or another, has been around for a long time. The most satisfactory solution is to place the biblical story in 708 and the Assyrian story in 701, and to assume that Sennacherib, when writing up his campaign of 701 in which Judah was not involved, incorporated by way of compensation the defeat and submission of Hezekiah which he had achieved (initially) in his campaign of 708. We have therefore in Sennacherib's account a mishmash of both invasions, incorporating the more creditable elements of both.

The mention of Menahem as paying tribute to Tiglath-pileser III in two inscriptions of about 740 BC has caused a flurry of speculation in scholarly circles. Reigns have been torn apart and telescoped in the effort to bring the two sides together. But why so much surprise and concern over a situation where an Assyrian king was evidently unaware of who precisely was reigning in

Samaria? Menahem had been the last king to provide stable government in Samaria and had himself paid tribute to "Pul" king of Assyria. In the circumstances it is not altogether surprising that they still thought of Menahem as king of Israel half way through the reign of Pekah.

A little imagination and commonsense are sufficient to reconcile the two divergent accounts back to Menahem. But, prior to that, another problem arises. We find a close agreement between the two sources, but a chronological disparity which seems to increase. From some 25 years in the reign of Jehoash, it has grown to 44 years by the time of Jehu and Ahab. This discrepancy is in need of further elucidation, but the conclusion is unavoidable that the Assyrian record is missing some years. Unfortunately, those who are best qualified to solve this problem are least disposed to do so. So this is a problem for which only tentative solutions are currently available.

Chapter Seven

After the Exile

So Zedekiah and the majority of the citizens remaining in Jerusalem and Judea were carried off to Babylon in the summer of 586 BC. There they joined their fellow countrymen who had been taken captive with King Jehoiachin in 598/7 and subsequent years. The burden of prophetic denunciation, pronounced against them, had come down on their heads with terrifying force. They had drunk to the last dregs the cup of divine wrath. In misery and shame they had hung up their harps by the waters of Babylon.

But what of the future? The magnificent city and empire established by Nebuchadnezzar soon began to crumble. As we know, Babylon fell to the Medes and Persians on 16 Tishri (about 12 October), 539. Belshazzar, their last king, was holding a banquet for his nobles when the writing appeared on the wall, Mene, Mene, Tekel, Parsin (Numbered, Numbered, Weighed, Divided). That very night, we are told, Belshazzar was slain and Darius the Mede took over the kingdom, being 62 years of age (Dan. 5:30-31).

Darius the Mede

But who was this Darius the Mede? Secular history knows nothing of this king, but from the book of Daniel we know that he was the first king of the Medo-Persian Empire after the fall of Babylon in 539. In Daniel 5:30-31 we read of his rise to power, while the next chapter, the heroic story of Daniel and the Lions' Den, shows Darius to be a man of high moral principles but easily led astray by flattery and deception. The next two chapters of Daniel describe visions which he had already seen in the first and third years of Belshazzar. Then in Daniel 9 he is back in the first year of Darius, followed in chapters 10 and 11 with visions he received in the third year of Cyrus king of Persia.

Traditionally the Medes had been the senior partner in the Medo-Persian alliance. This is shown by the order Medes and Persians as found invariably in the book of Daniel. But Daniel saw a vision of a Ram with two horns (Dan. 8). To begin with the two horns were of equal height, but as he watched one of the horns shot up above the other one. That was the Persian horn which eclipsed the Median horn as Cyrus the Persian rose rapidly to prominence. This is reflected in the book of Esther where the order is reversed. Instead of Medes and Persians, there we find Persians and Medes (1:3,14,18,19). Only in Esther 10:2, where the records of former years are referred to is the more ancient style employed. There we read of "the books of the Chronicles of the kings of Media and Persia".

Darius cannot have reigned very long. He was 62 when he came to the throne and we hear only of his first year of reign in Daniel. There is evidence that Cyrus was not in fact "King of Babylon" during the fourteen months following the fall of Babylon. William H. Shea (1971-72) has established this fact in great detail. With but one exception Cyrus is called "King of Lands" rather than "King of Babylon" until the tenth month of his first year, after which he is regularly called "King of Babylon, King of Lands".

William Shea wrote articles more specifically on Darius the Mede in 1982 and 1991. One fact which appears to be established is that Cyrus appointed his son Cambyses as co-regent with the title "king of Babylon" during the first nine or ten months of his first year of rule. Shea refers to six tablets which are dated to the reigns of both kings, "Cyrus king of Lands", and "Cambyses king of Babylon". One of them reads "... the 18th day of the month Iyyar, 1st year of Cyrus, king of Lands, Cambyses, king of Babylon." Even more telling are two tablets which mention also the concluding years of Nabonidus, the last King of Babylon. One refers in a broken passage to the

17th year (of Nabonidus) and to the first year of "Cambyses, king of Babylon, son of Cyrus, king of Lands."

We have therefore a situation in which Cyrus is "King of Lands" and Cambyses his deputy king in Babylon. Where, then, does Darius fit into this triangle? Darius cannot be identified with Cambyses (contra Charles Boutflower), since Cambyses was still a young man and Darius 62 years old (Dan. 5:31). So is it possible to identify him with Cyrus? This is in fact the identification made by Shea, following a suggestion by D.J. Wiseman. Shea does his level best to justify this equation. The crucial reference, Daniel 6:28, was translated by Wiseman "during the reign of Darius, even the reign of Cyrus the Persian." But Shea thinks it may refer to successive stages of the reign of Darius/Cyrus under the names by which his authority was exercised.

My own reservations are best expressed by Shea himself in his earlier article on Darius the Mede (1982), when he still held to the view that Darius should be identified with Gubaru, the general who captured Babylon for Cyrus on 12 October 539. Granted that Cyrus had a Median ancestry on his mother's side, "it would seem strange to refer to Cyrus the Persian, who was the son of Cambyses, as Darius, who was the son of Ahasuerus. Beyond that, this theory makes the dated references to these two kings in Daniel appear to be quite haphazard in arrangement." (1982: 232) He refers in particular to the third year of Cyrus in Daniel 10:1 in connection with the back-reference to the first year of Darius in 11:1.

The traditional view, explained and defended by C.F. Keil amongst others, is that Darius the Mede is none other than Cyaxares II, son and successor of Astyages king of the Medes, according to Xenophon's *Cyropaedia*. This identification, in the words of G.F. Hasel, "fits admirably well with Darius' age (62 years in 539 B.C., Dan. 5:31), parentage (Dan. 9:1), and nationality (a Mede)." (1981: 47) But we have already two kings for the year 538, Cyrus and his son Cambyses. On the face of it, yet another is something of an embarrassment.

One thing is certain: Darius appears in Daniel as undisputed ruler of the Medo-Persian empire. Like Nebuchadnezzar (Dan. 4:1), he addresses his decree to "all the peoples, nations, and languages that dwell in all the earth" (6:25); and he appoints 120 satraps throughout the whole kingdom, which compares favourably with the 127 provinces "from India to Ethiopia" ruled over by Xerxes (Esther 1:1). In Daniel 8 the Median and Persian kingdoms are represented as two horns on the head of a ram. Both horns are high but one of them (the Persian), though less high to begin with, rises rapidly to prominence. This is well served if the Median king under Darius the Mede held power to begin with, but soon after was eclipsed by the Persian horn under Cyrus the Persian. Perhaps we should think of Darius as supreme king at this time, and Cyrus and Cambyses as subordinate kings in the vast domains which now constituted the Medo-Persian empire.

We are told that Darius received (*qabbel*) the kingdom (5:31). He received the kingdom in the same sense as the saints of the Most High will receive (*yeqabbelun*) the kingdom of God in 7:18, and Daniel was given to understand he would receive gifts and rewards if he revealed and interpreted the king's dream (2:6). It seems that the kingdom was conferred on Darius as the venerable incumbent of the Median throne, the last of an illustrious line. According to Daniel 9:1 Darius was "made king" over the realm of the Chaldeans. Cyrus was himself the king-maker, the man who held in his power the fate and destiny of kings.

If Darius and Cyrus were two names for the same king, we would expect this fact to have been made abundantly clear. In the case of Daniel and Belteshazzar there is no room for doubt: "Daniel, whose name was Belteshazzar" (2:26; 4:19), "Daniel, whom the king named Belteshazzar" (5:12). Apart from 6:28 there is no passage where Cyrus and Darius are mentioned together, and that reference speaks against their identification rather than for it. If the two names stand here for the same person, we must assume (with Shea) that this king in his capacity as Darius the Mede ruled for about nine months, and then continued to rule in the capacity of Cyrus the Persian - not in my view a convincing explanation of Daniel 6:28. It is more natural to think of two kings: Darius, whose first year alone is mentioned in the book of Daniel, followed by Cyrus. If in fact Darius reigned for two years, Cyrus' first year as king of the Chaldeans would be 536, so fulfilling as far as the Jewish exiles were concerned Jeremiah's prophecy of seventy years (605-536).

This is also the view of Keil: "From the nine years of the reign of Cyrus, according to our exposition (p.198), two years are to be deducted for Darius the Mede, so that the reign of Cyrus by himself over the kingdom which he founded begins in the year 536, in which year the seventy years of the Babylonish exile of the Jews were completed" (*Daniel*: 320).

I have the impression that Cyrus and Darius were very different characters. Darius comes across as an insecure person, on the one hand vain and impressionable, on the other sensitive and loyal. Would Cyrus, the victorious general and capable ruler, have been taken in so easily by his devious officials? Would Cyrus, I wonder, have relied so heavily on one minister, or allowed himself to become so emotionally attached to one man? Darius was not, I think, a strong king; he was king by reason of ancestry and royal succession. Cyrus however was justly called "the Great" on account of his own personal achievements. Two such very different characters are difficult to identify as one and the same person.

Cyrus' decree and Jeremiah's 70 years

The text of Cyrus' decree, issued in the first year of his reign, is given three times in Scripture, 2 Chronicles 36:23; Ezra 1:2-4; and 6:3-5. The last is rather different from the other two and gives instructions on how the temple should be built. These are only summaries of what must have been a much longer document. The salient points are to be found in Ezra 1:2-4:

> This is what Cyrus king of Persia says: 'The Lord, the God of heaven, has given me all the kingdoms of the earth and he has appointed me to build a temple for him at Jerusalem in Judah. Anyone of his people among you - may his God be with him, and let him go up to Jerusalem in Judah and build the temple of the Lord, the God of Israel, the God who is in Jerusalem. And the people of any place where survivors may now be living are to provide him with silver and gold, with goods and livestock, and with freewill offerings for the temple of God in Jerusalem. (*NIV*)

This decree was issued "in order to fulfil the word of the Lord spoken by Jeremiah" (Ezra 1:1). But to which of Jeremiah's prophecies does Ezra refer? Daniel also was profoundly exercised over Jeremiah's prophecy that seventy years would elapse before the end of the desolations of Jerusalem (Dan. 9:2). He was very much aware that this period had all but finished in the first year of Darius the Mede, and of the urgent need consequently to seek the Lord in repentance and faith. These seventy years need careful examination. The following are the different texts that speak of this period.

Jeremiah 25:8-12

Jeremiah 25 is dated in the fourth year of Jehoiakim which was the first year of Nebuchadnezzar king of Babylon. This was the regnal year beginning Tishri 605. Already two or three months previously, before the end of Jehoiakim's third year (Dan. 1:1; 2 Kings 24:1), Nebuchadnezzar had besieged and captured Jerusalem, and had taken captive Daniel and his companions. Jeremiah now predicts that even worse is yet to come:

Therefore thus saith the Lord of hosts: Because ye have not heard my words, Behold, I will send and take all the families of the north, saith the Lord, and Nebuchadrezzar the king of Babylon, my servant, and will bring them against this land, and against the inhabitants thereof, and against all these nations round about, and will utterly destroy them, and make them an astonishment, and an hissing, and perpetual desolations .... And this whole land shall be a desolation, and an astonishment; and these nations shall serve the king of Babylon seventy years. And it shall come to pass when seventy years are accomplished, that I will punish the king of Babylon, and that nation, saith the Lord, for their iniquity, and the land of the Chaldeans, will make it perpetual desolations. (25:8-9,11-12 *KJV*)

There are three things that are predicted here:-

1) Nebuchadnezzar would return to the land. Whereas previously he had been content with having the nations as his vassals, in a servant-master relationship, next time he would devote them to systematic destruction. Not only would Judah suffer in this way, but all the surrounding nations as well would become "an object of horror and scorn, and an everlasting ruin".
2) All these nations would serve the King of Babylon for seventy years. Note, it was the period of servitude, or vassalage, which was to last seventy years, not the period of desolation which at this stage was only a threat.
3) At the end of the seventy-year period punishment would be meted out to "the king of Babylon and his nation", and they in turn would become a perpetual ruin.

It was after the battle of Carchemish in the early summer of 605 BC when Nebuchadnezzar, the Crown Prince of Babylon, routed the Egyptians, that Syria-Palestine was opened up to the victorious Babylonian army. In his accession year (605, Elul to Adar) and first year of reign (604) Nebuchadnezzar marched across the whole area demanding submission and collecting tribute. It is clear from the Babylonian Chronicle (BM 21946) that the conquest of this whole land, called Hatti in the Chronicle, was accomplished during Nebuchadnezzar's accession year and first year of reign.

In the accession year Nebuchadrezzar went back again to Hatti-land and marched victoriously through it until the month of Sebat. In the month of Sebat he took the heavy tribute of the Hatti-land back to Babylon ... In the first year of Nebuchadrezzar he mustered his army in the month of Sivan and went to the Hatti-land. He marched about victoriously in the Hatti-land until the month of Kislev. All the kings of Hatti-land came before him and he received their heavy tribute. He marched to the city of Ashkelon and captured it in the month of Kislev.

It was therefore in his accession year and first year of reign (605-604) that this whole land was conquered. By Kislev (Nov/Dec) 604 the conquest was completed and Nebuchadnezzar returned to Babylon laden with the tribute of conquered nations.

Jeremiah 29:10

The reference comes in a letter which Jeremiah wrote to the exiles in Babylon soon after the capture and exile of King Jehoiachin in 598/97 BC. It is a message of hope and encouragement to the displaced citizens of Judah and Jerusalem. They are advised to "marry and have sons and daughters: find wives for your sons and give your daughters in marriage, so that they may have sons and daughters. Increase in numbers there; do not decrease." But what are the grounds for this advice?

This is what the Lord says: "When seventy years are completed for Babylon, I will come to you and fulfil my gracious promise to bring you back to this place. For I know the plans I have for you," declares the Lord, "plans to prosper you and not to harm you, plans to give you hope and a future." (29:10-11 *NIV*)

The translation "*for* Babylon", as opposed to "*at* Babylon" as in the *KJV*, is recognised as being correct. The seventy years are not primarily those of the exile (still less those of the desolation); they are the years of Babylonian rule over the nations, the years *for* Babylon. They are the years allocated to Babylon to exercise suzerainty over the nations. They begin with the conquest of the nations in 605 and following, and they conclude with the overthrow of Babylon itself. It seems that the return of the exiles was expected to synchronise with the fall of Babylon, or at least to follow it soon after, according to the terms of this prophecy.

Carl Olof Jonsson correctly says, "Clearly, the nations in the Hattu area became vassals to Babylon very soon after the battle at Carchemish. The seventy years of servitude had evidently begun to run their course" (1998: 204).

It needs to be emphasised that the judgment of desolations did not begin until considerably later. In the early years of Zedekiah's reign Jeremiah was still saying, "Serve the king of Babylon and you will live" (27:12,17). The same applied to all the nations: "if any nation will bow its neck under the yoke of the king of Babylon and serve him, I will let that nation remain in its own land to till it and to live there" (27:11). "If, however, any nation or kingdom will not serve Nebuchadnezzar king of Babylon or bow its neck under his yoke, I will punish that nation with the sword, famine and plague, declares the Lord, until I destroy it by his hand" (27:8).

Nothing could be clearer. The period of servitude began in 605 with the submission to Nebuchadnezzar of Judah and the other nations in that region, but the actual desolation of the land began much later on. In the case of Judah it began in 598/97 when Nebuchadnezzar carried away the greater part of the nation, and was completed in 589-86 with the siege and destruction of Jerusalem.

2 Chronicles 36:20-21

The sense of this passage is clarified by its structure, as Ross E. Winkle has shown (1987: 210):

He (Nebuchadnezzar) carried into exile to Babylon the remnant who escaped
from the sword, and they were servants to him and his sons,
   until (*'ad*) the reign of the kingdom of Persia
      in order to fulfil (*lemall'ot*) the word of the Lord by the mouth of
      Jeremiah,
   until (*'ad*) the land enjoyed its sabbath: all the days of its desolation
   it kept sabbath,
      in order to fulfil (*lemall'ot*) seventy years.

The two clauses beginning with "until" reach forward to the same point in time. Likewise the two clauses beginning "in order to fulfil" refer to the same word of the Lord, namely Jeremiah's prophecy of the seventy years. The second "until" clause, however, is an intrusion since Jeremiah never said anything about the land enjoying its Sabbaths. This clause is lifted from Leviticus 26:34-35 which it repeats almost word for word:

Then shall the land enjoy her sabbaths, all the days of its desolation, and you are in the land of your enemies; then shall the land rest and enjoy her sabbaths. All the days of its desolation it shall rest (or keep sabbath), because it did not rest in in your sabbaths, when you dwelt upon it. (Lev.26:34-35)

The Chronicler has inserted this section from Leviticus to show how this prophecy also was fulfilled at that time. This however has no connection with the seventy years or with the word of the Lord through Jeremiah, since Jeremiah never mentions the subject of Sabbath-enjoyment, nor does Leviticus mention the seventy years. This would suggest that the second "until" clause is parenthetical to the verse as a whole. Carl Olof Jonsson agrees: "By inserting the two clauses from Leviticus 26, the Chronicler did not mean to say that the land enjoyed a Sabbath rest of *seventy years*, as this was not predicted, either by Moses or by Jeremiah" (p.222).

The period of Babylonian rule came to an end when "the kingdom of Persia came to power." Likewise Cyrus' decree allowing the exiles to return to their land to rebuild their Temple was also "to fulfil the word of the Lord by Jeremiah" (2 Chron. 36:22). There is no suggestion that any appreciable interval would separate the two events. In Jeremiah 50 they are placed together. The return and restoration of Israel immediately follows the fall of Babylon, "in those days and at that time" (50:4,20), not a few years later.

Interestingly, a different word for "fulfil" is used in verses 21 and 22 of 2 Chronicles 36. In the first verse it is *male'* (as we have seen), the usual word for fill or fulfil, but in the second verse it is *kalah*, to complete. "Thus, while the overthrow of Babylon fulfilled (*male'*) Jeremiah's prophecy of the seventy years, Cyrus' decree completed or accomplished (*kalah*) this prophecy by allowing for the return of the exiles" (Winkle: 209). But Jeremiah does not indicate any interval between the fall of Babylon and the release of the exiles: the two events should have followed one another in quick succession according to his foresight of future events.

In Furuli's view, Winkle's arguments, while "not completely impossible", "are forced and unnecessary if the *context* does not suggest such an understanding." The "unnatural parenthetical sense of Winkle" has for its basis nothing more than "faith in the traditional chronology" (pp.90-1). Only a person with "a particular agenda, namely, to try to harmonize the Bible with the traditional New Babylonian Chronology" could interpret Daniel 9:2 and 2 Chronicles 36:21 otherwise than that "Jerusalem should be a desolate waste for a full 70 years" (p.80).

But Furuli also has his particular agenda, namely to defend and uphold the Watch Tower insistence that Jerusalem lay desolate for a full 70 years beginning in 607 BC. In this year Jerusalem was destroyed according to their chronology, but in fact, as Jonsson has conclusively proved, it was not for another twenty years that Jerusalem finally fell.

Daniel 9:2

In the first year of his reign [Darius the Mede's] I, Daniel understood from the scriptures the number of years, whereof the word of the Lord came to Jeremiah the prophet, to fulfil for the desolations of Jerusalem, seventy years.

Versions which equate the seventy years with the desolations of Jerusalem have misunderstood the text. Daniel does not go beyond what Jeremiah had said. The period of desolations would end at the same time as the period of servitude, and the ending of both was dependent on the downfall of Babylon at the end of the seventy years.

Seeing that Babylon had now fallen, Daniel "discerned from the books" that the desolations of Jerusalem were due to conclude. But Israel's restoration was not an automatic consequence of Babylon's demise, for Jeremiah had said in the name of the Lord, "You will seek me and find me *when you seek me with all your heart*. I will be found by you (declares the Lord) and will bring you back from captivity ..."(29:13-14). This is what Daniel now does. He seeks the Lord with all his heart in the wonderful prayer of Daniel 9:4-19. His great fear is that the Lord will "delay" the fulfilment of His promise because of Israel's continued impenitence (v.19).

Predictably, Rolf Furuli strongly disagrees with this interpretation. In his opinion, "The words of Daniel and the Chronicler are unambiguous. They show definitely that Daniel and the Chronicler understood Jeremiah to prophecy about a 70-year period for the Jewish people *when the land was desolate*" (p.76).

He paraphrases Daniel 9:2 as saying, "God gave Jerusalem as a devastated city 70 years to fill." But what it really says is: "to fill up *for* (as to, with reference to) the desolations of Jerusalem 70 years." The words "as to the desolations of Jerusalem" could be placed in brackets since the 70 years are not applied to the desolations of Jerusalem in Jeremiah. They had reference to the period of desolation only in so far as both the desolation and the servitude were due to end at the same time. "It is only the *expiration* of the seventy-year period – not the period as a whole – that he relates to the 'fulfilling of the desolations of Jerusalem" (Jonsson: 219).

Furuli says that Daniel and the Chronicler, with the benefit of hindsight, knew better than Jeremiah how the prophecy was to be fulfilled. But that is to put the cart before the horse. As Jonsson points out, the interpretation "must *proceed from the prophecy*, not from the references to it."

The problem

The problem which confronts every interpreter of this prophecy is how it was fulfilled. There can be no doubt that Babylon fell to the Medes and Persians in October 539. There is also no question that the battle of Carchemish occurred in the summer of 605. But the difference between these dates is 66 years, not exactly seventy. There was of course no way of knowing, humanly speaking, how long the Babylonian Empire would continue. 66 is a remarkably close approximation, exceeding all expectations humanly speaking. Uninspired prophets like Hananiah were predicting an imminent return within two years (Jer. 28:11) or even less (27:16), and doubtless there were pessimists who were saying they would never return at all. Jeremiah alone came up with a number which came close to the truth. Should we therefore agree with Avigdor Orr that, "The period 605-539 is sufficiently close to seventy years to be so labelled, especially when the power of the 'mystical seven' and its derivatives is borne in mind."(1956: 304-6)

Logically there are only two ways of making up the shortfall of three or four years: it can either be added on at the beginning or tagged on at the end. The usual method has been to tag it on at the end, assuming a two or three year reign for Darius the Mede (so e.g. Anstey). But the seventy year time-limit was primarily "for Babylon", and Babylon fell in 539 as everyone agrees.

If the seventy years cannot be drawn out beyond 539 when Babylon fell to the Medo-Persians, could they possibly be drawn back before 605 when Nebuchadnezzar came to the throne? That is the view of Ross E. Winkle and Carl Olof Jonsson. They point out that the Assyrian empire came finally to an end early in 609 with the capture of Harran by Nabopolassar and the flight of Ashur-uballit, the last king of Assyria. Says Jonsson, "From that year the Babylonian king regarded himself as the legitimate successor of the king of Assyria, and in the following years he gradually took over the control of the latter's territories" (p.233). From 609 to 539 was exactly seventy years.

It was not simply Judah and nations in that neighbourhood which were required to submit to Nebuchadnezzar. According to Jeremiah 27:7 "all the nations must serve him and his son and his grandson." Among the nations singled out for conquest in Jeremiah 25:17-26 are "Elam and Media, and all the kings of the north, near and far." The conquest of these nations began before 605. So why not begin the seventy years in 609 rather than 605?

This is certainly an attractive proposition, not least because it offers an exact fulfilment of the seventy years for Babylon. But opposed to it are the following considerations.

1) Jeremiah 25 is dated in the fourth year of Jehoiakim which was the first of Nebuchadnezzar, that is 605. There is no record of the years preceding 605.

2) Dominion is given to Nebuchadnezzar in these chapters, not to his predecessors (25:9; 27:7).

3) It is contrary to the plain sense of Jeremiah 25:9-11: "I will summon all the peoples of the north (declares the Lord), and I will bring them against this land and its inhabitants and against all the surrounding nations.... This whole country (the one just mentioned regarded as a single unit) will serve the king of Babylon (Nebuchadnezzar) for seventy years." It was those specific nations, Judah and the other nations of that area, which would serve the king of Babylon (Nebuchadnezzar) for seventy years, not all the others mentioned in Jeremiah 25:17-26.

4) Lastly, Jeremiah nowhere shows any knowledge of, or interest in, Nabopolassar or the downfall of Ashur-uballit. If the events of 609 had been important to the understanding of his prophecies, he would surely have made this fact abundantly clear.

One has only to read Jeremiah 25-29 to see that Nebuchadnezzar was the one to whom dominion was given. His father Nabopolassar does not come into the picture at all. It was moreover Nebuchadnezzar who conquered the land of Hatti according to both the Bible and his own inscriptions.

Avigdor Orr rightly says, "It follows from (Jer. 25) v.11b that the seventy years begin from the imposition of the Babylonian yoke on Judah and its neighbours. This took place as a result of the battle of Carchemish in 605, and is therefore in accord with the (genuine or attributed) date of the prophecy" (1956: 305). There is no good reason to doubt the genuineness of the date, nor that the seventy years are reckoned from that epoch - the world-changing annihilation of the Egyptian army at Carchemish on the Euphrates, and the beginning of Nebuchadnezzar's reign.

This much is clear, but the problem remains unsolved, namely the shortfall of three years (on inclusive reckoning) in the fulfilment of Jeremiah's prophecy. Could it be a round number? The number 70 is not always used in the Bible with undoubted precision. In Isaiah 23:15 for example ("Tyre shall be forgotten 70 years, according to the days of one king "), if this refers to the normal lifespan of a king, it can hardly be understood as an exact length of time, any more than in Psalm 90:10. In Jeremiah however, in a prophecy of this importance, there must be a good reason why the period of years was not accurately fulfilled.

A possible solution

There is no escape, it would seem, from the conclusion that these seventy years were not accurately fulfilled. But how do we explain this apparent failure in a prophecy of such importance? A possible answer is to be found in the nature of prophecy itself. Prophecy is not the straightforward phenomenon that most people imagine, a matter simply of matching a prediction with its historical fulfilment. Many prophecies were uttered with the express intention that they should *not* be fulfilled (e.g. Jonah 3:4), while others were clearly conditional on repentance and faith. These principles are laid down by Jeremiah himself in ch. 18:7-10:-

If at any time I (the Lord) announce that a nation or kingdom is to be uprooted, torn down and destroyed, and if that nation I warned repents of its evil, then I will relent and not inflict on it the disaster I had planned. And if at another time I announce that a nation or kingdom is to be built up and planted, and if it does evil in my sight and does not obey me, then I will reconsider the good I had intended to do for it. (*NIV*)

Jeremiah in the later chapters of his book lays down a programme for the future which could have been fulfilled if only it had met with the right response, a contrite attitude of repentance and faith. Daniel, when he came to understand what Jeremiah was saying, responded in the right way, but how many of his countrymen, one wonders, joined him in fasting and prayer, in sackcloth and supplication? Their failure to do so may well be the reason why so much prophecy was not fulfilled at that time. There was, it is true, a partial fulfilment, but the complete and satisfying fulfilment was not realised at that time. It was postponed (as so often) to a time still future.

Expositors go wrong in their study of prophecy because they look at it from the wrong end. They will look at prophetic forecasts retrospectively from the viewpoint of their supposed fulfilment instead of prospectively from the viewpoint of the prophet himself. The first thing to do is to ascertain what the prophet himself expected to happen, what his prophecy actually predicts. In this case, Jeremiah predicts a period of seventy years, and he indicates two specific events which would transpire at the close of this period. These are the destruction of Babylon and the release of the Jewish captives.

What Jeremiah predicts is not simply the capture of Babylon and the transfer of power to another overlord (as happened in 539 BC). He clearly predicts that both the city Babylon and the land of the Chaldeans would be made "desolate for ever" (25:12). That he means what he says is underscored in Jeremiah 50-51 where the fate of the doomed city is described in detail. This however is not what happened in 539 when Babylon was captured by the Medes and Persians. Not at least according to the Cyrus Cylinder:

Marduk the great lord, compassionate to his people, looked with gladness on (his) good deeds and his upright intentions. He gave orders that he go against his city Babylon. He made him take the road to Babylon and he went at his side like a friend and comrade. His vast army, whose number like the waters of a river cannot be determined, with their armour held close, moved forward beside him. He got him into his city Babylon *without fighting or battle*. He averted hardship to Babylon. He put an end to the power of Nabonidus the king who did not show him reverence. The entire population of Babylon, the whole of Sumer and Akkad, princes and governors, bowed to him (Cyrus) and kissed his feet. They were glad that he was king. Their faces lighted up. The master by whose aid the mortally sick had been made alive all had been preserved from ruin.. [For this] they praised him and honoured his name.

Nor according to the Nabonidus Chronicle: "On the 16th day (of Teshrit), Ugbaru, the district-governor of Gutium, and the troops of Cyrus entered Babylon without battle... On the 3rd of Marcheswan Cyrus entered Babylon and they waved branches before him. Peace settled on the city (and) Cyrus proclaimed peace to Babylon."

Nor for that matter was the return of the exiles, two or three years later, fulfilled in the comprehensive manner anticipated by Jeremiah. That would have included Ephraim as well as Judah and the institution of the new covenant in a nation restored to favour, in a land and city also restored and renewed (Jer. 31). There was only an unfinished and partial fulfilment in the return from exile in the first year of Cyrus' reign as reckoned in Daniel and Ezra - 537 or 536. If the latter date is assumed to be correct, the seventy years of Jeremiah 29:10 were exactly fulfilled between 605 and 536, inclusively reckoned.

The Edict of Cyrus to rebuild the Temple

The first thing the returning exiles did was to build an altar to the God of Israel and to reinstitute the regular morning and evening sacrifices and other offerings. This was done even before the foundation of the second temple had been laid. Work on the temple itself was not delayed for long. It was begun in the second month of the second year after their return, cedar wood having been transported by ship from Lebanon and Joppa.

When the foundation of the temple was laid there was a pageant of priests and Levites giving praise and thanksgiving on cymbals and trumpets. But at the same time there was loud lamentation from some of the older folk who remembered the former temple in all its glory. A start had been made on the second Temple, but it was not destined to continue for long. Their ever-present adversaries began immediately to harass them and frustrate their efforts in every way possible. The result was that work on the temple was discontinued "during the entire reign of Cyrus king of Persia and down to the reign of Darius king of Persia" (Ezra 4:5). It was not until the second year of Darius (520 BC) that work was resumed, urged on by the prophets Haggai and Zechariah.

Once again their enemies raised objections asking on what authority they acted. So a delegation was sent to Darius to find out whether Cyrus had really granted them permission to rebuild the temple as they were claiming. Darius mounted a search, and sure enough the document was discovered in the citadel of Ecbatana in the province of Media. Thereupon Darius issued another decree granting the Jews unrestricted freedom to rebuild their temple, fully paid for out of the royal exchequer. Even animals for sacrifice and other provisions were to be supplied on a daily basis.

According to Haggai 2:18, the temple was founded on the 24th day of the ninth month in Darius' second year. "Consider, I pray you, from today and onwards: (yea) from the four and twentieth day of the ninth month, from the day on which the foundation of the Lord's temple has been laid, consider! ... from this day I will bless you!"

The regnal years of Persian kings are reckoned in Ezra from Nisan, as was the practice in Persia. This is also the case in Haggai as has been explained in an earlier chapter. If this were not the case it would be necessary to deduct one year from the received date, 520, for the second year of Darius, since it was in the *ninth month* that the temple was founded. Not only would this date need to be antedated, so also would the date of the temple's completion in the *twelfth month* of Darius' sixth year (Ezra 6:15).

Soon after the completion of the temple in 516, the ceremony of dedication took place. We assume it was celebrated in the same month though this is not specifically stated. This was followed, on the fourteenth of the first month, by a joyful celebration of the Passover and the Feast of Unleavened Bread.

The seventy years of Indignation

The foundation of the Second Temple saw the end of another period of 70 years. In Zechariah 1 the prophet sees a vision on 24 Shebat in the second year of Darius, two months after the foundation of the temple. In course of this vision the question is asked by the revealing angel, "O Lord of hosts, how long wilt thou not have mercy on Jerusalem and on the cities of Judah against which thou hast had indignation these threescore and ten years" (1:12). To this the answer is given, "I am returned to Jerusalem with mercies: my house shall be built in it, saith the Lord of hosts."

This period of 70 years began in 589 with the siege of Jerusalem in the ninth year of Zedekiah (2 Kings 25:1). This date was revealed to Ezekiel on the banks of the Euphrates, and he is told expressly to record the name of the day, this very day on which the king of Babylon set himself against Jerusalem (Ezek. 24:1,2). There can be no doubt that this was the day on which indignation commenced against Jerusalem and the cities of Judah. From the date of the siege to the foundation of the Temple was 69 years to the month, or 70 years on inclusive reckoning.

Yet another period of 70 years is mentioned in Zechariah 7:5. At the Lord's direction the prophet pointedly asks both priests and people, "When you fasted and mourned in the fifth month and in the seventh, for these seventy years, was it for me that you fasted?" This occurred on 4 Kislev (the ninth month), in Darius' fourth year, that is 518 BC, two years after the foundation of the temple.

The fasts of the fifth and seventh months commemorated the month Jerusalem was burnt (2 Kings 25:8,9) and the month Gedaliah the governor was assassinated (2 Kings 25:25), both in 586. From 586 to 518 is 68 years, or 69 on inclusive reckoning. In point of fact their fasting did not begin in 586, since two more fasts are mentioned in Zechariah 8:19, namely the fasts of the fourth and tenth months. These commemorate the month the city wall was breached (Jer. 39:2) and the beginning of the siege in 589. In either case it was about 70 years. This is not a divinely ordained measure of time, but a statement in human terms of how long they had fasted.

The decree of Artaxerxes' 7th year (Ezra 7)

Ezra the scribe came up from Babylon in the seventh year of Artaxerxes, 458 BC. He arrived in Jerusalem on the first day of the fifth month after a journey of exactly four months. He was accompanied by a large retinue of returning exiles, priests and Levites. He came to Jerusalem armed with a letter from Artaxerxes, which contained the following provisions.

First, with the silver and gold freely given by the king and his advisers, along with the money collected from the province of Babylon and freewill offerings from the people and priests, he was to purchase all the animals and offerings required for the temple services. Secondly, he could spend the rest of the money in whatever way seemed best to him and his brother Jews. From this source the temple should be provided with everything it needed. Thirdly, the king himself specifically commanded that the treasurers of Trans-Euphrates, that is the region Beyond the River, should provide whatever Ezra requested up to the prescribed amount, a hundred talents of silver, etc. This was to be done with diligence for the benefit of the temple of the God of heaven. And fourthly, Ezra was to appoint magistrates and judges to administer justice to all the people of Trans-Euphrates.

The decree of Artaxerxes' 20th year (Nehemiah 2)

It will have been noticed that all the decrees so far have exclusive reference to the Temple. No permission or provision had been granted to rebuild the city of Jerusalem. No-one doubts of course that the returning exiles lived in houses, even fine houses with panelled woodwork (Haggai 1:4). It is one thing, however, to live in makeshift houses and encampments, quite another to live in a city with walls and moat. The situation at Jerusalem even after the walls had been rebuilt is plainly stated in Nehemiah 7:4, "Now the city was large and spacious, but there were few people in it, and the houses had not yet been rebuilt."

Although permission had not been forthcoming to rebuild the city, there is good evidence that an attempt had been made, albeit unauthorised, to restore the walls and repair the foundations in the early years of Artaxerxes' reign. This wall is referred to in Ezra 4:7-16 where there is a letter dated "in the days of Artaxerxes", in which their adversaries complain to the king that "the Jews which came up from thee to us are come unto Jerusalem, building the rebellious and the bad city, and have set up the walls thereof, and joined the foundations." For this unauthorised attempt to rebuild the city walls Ezra himself cannot be blamed. In his capacity as Secretary of State for

Jewish Affairs (as he has been called) he probably returned to Babylon when his business was accomplished, as did Nehemiah on a later occasion (Neh. 13:6).

It may seem strange to find this letter in that part of the narrative which relates to the reigns of Cyrus and Darius. Since however the date was included, no confusion was intended. Between Ezra 4:6 and 23 the writer has grouped together the various efforts to oppose the work of God prior to Nehemiah's arrival. The last verse of the chapter, 4:24, resumes the narrative from verse 5. The intervening material deals with two letters of complaint in the reigns of Darius' successors, the first in the reign of Xerxes (485-465) and the second in the reign of Artaxerxes (464-424). The outcome of this second letter was a decree from Artaxerxes authorising the Jews' adversaries to put an end to the rebuilding of the city, "so that this city will not be rebuilt until I so order." And this they immediately did "by force and power" (4:23).

This is the point at which Nehemiah takes up the story. It is reported to Nehemiah, "The remnant that are left of the captivity there in the province are in great affliction and reproach; the wall of Jerusalem also is broken down, and the gates thereof are burned with fire" (Neh. 1:3). On hearing this sad news, Nehemiah "sat down and wept, and mourned certain days, and fasted, and prayed before the God of heaven." It was not the destruction of Jerusalem by Nebuchadnezzar 140 years before which caused this paroxysm of grief. It was the forceful cessation of building described in Ezra 4:23. Evidently the adversaries interpreted their mandate to include the destruction of what had already been built.

Nehemiah's royal master for whom he acted as cupbearer noticed how sad his servant was looking, and asked him the reason for this sadness of heart. At this Nehemiah, afraid at what might be the response (after all Artaxerxes had himself authorised it!), told him the cause of his sadness. The king replied sympathetically, "What is it you want?" After a silent prayer Nehemiah made his request, "If it pleases the king and if your servant has found favour in his sight, let him send me to the city in Judah, where my fathers are buried so that I can rebuild it." His request was granted. He also asked for letters to the governors of Trans-Euphrates to provide him with safe conduct, and a letter to Asaph, keeper of the king's forest, to give him timber to make beams for the citadel, for the city wall, and for his own residence. All this was granted as well.

This took place in Nisan of Artaxerxes' twentieth year. This was the first month of a new regnal year in Persia and the date was 445 BC. From the fact that the previous Kislev (the ninth month) is also reckoned to the king's twentieth year (Neh. 1:1), we have concluded that Artaxerxes' reign is here brought into line with the Jewish Tishri-to-Tishri calendar. His regnal years have been antedated by six months like those of the kings of Judah, and like those of Nebuchadnezzar whose first year was made to agree with the fourth year of Jehoiakim (Jer. 25:1). There may have been earlier attempts to rebuild the city, but never before had the word of command from a Persian king gone forth to authorise this project. This is the only recorded word "to restore and rebuild Jerusalem" and must therefore be the starting-point of Daniel's famous prophecy of the Seventy Weeks (Dan. 9:25).

Or could it be 444?

It is frequently stated (or assumed) that Artaxerxes' twentieth year as reckoned in Nehemiah was 444 rather than 445. Many writers have a vested interest in 444 because it seems to provide the desired end-result (that is, the result which they would like to be correct) respecting Daniel's prophecy of the Seventy Weeks. If Christ was crucified in AD 33 (as seems most likely), then the 70 weeks of years should have begun in 444 rather than 445.

It has however already been established that the reigns of Nebuchadnezzar and Artaxerxes were antedated by the Jews, not postdated as would have to be the case if 444 were the correct date. The interpretation of Daniel's prophecy will be discussed in a moment.

The earliest account of the circumstances attending Artaxerxes' accession to the throne is given by Ctesias, a Greek physician at the court of Artaxerxes II (grandson of Artaxerxes I) about 65 years after Xerxes' death. Ctesias' story is summarised as follows by Julia Neuffer (1968: 64):-

Artabanus, a very powerful courtier, with the aid of an influential palace chamberlain, assassinated Xerxes, then procured the death of Darius, the older son and heir, by accusing him to Artaxerxes, the younger son. Thus Artaxerxes reigned with the support of Artabanus. But later the powerful Artabanus decided to put his young protege out of the way and take the throne. He made the mistake of enlisting the help of Megabyzus, a brother-in-law of Artaxerxes. When Megabyzus told the king everything - the plot against him, the murder of Xerxes, and the false accusation against Darius - Artaxerxes asserted himself, and Artabanus was put to death. There followed a battle with the partisans of Artabanus in which three of his sons were killed. Then the Bactrians revolted under their satrap, another Artabanus, but after two battles they submitted.

Ctesias does not give the date of Xerxes' death, but the date is given as 14 Ab (approx. 4-8 July 465) on a clay tablet from Babylonia of the Hellenistic period - late fourth century or possibly later. Artaxerxes' first year is reckoned from Nisan 464 in Persia, and antedated to Tishri 465 by Nehemiah. Hence his twentieth year, as reckoned in Nehemiah, ran from Tishri 446 to Tishri 445. The circumstances are very similar to those of Nebuchadnezzar's accession. Nebuchadnezzar's father died on 8 Ab 605. His first year is reckoned in Babylon from Nisan 604, but in Judah from Tishri 605.

Rolf Furuli's "Oslo" Chronology

A new chronology for the Persian Empire has recently been constructed by Rolf Furuli. Instead of relying rather heavily on the Canon of Ptolemy as chronologists have done in the past, Furuli bases his chronology on dated business tablets and so-called astronomical diaries, the recordings of eclipses and planetary movements from actual observation rather than calculation long after the event as Ptolemy is suspected of doing. This is certainly a sound approach since it cannot be taken for granted that Ptolemy's Canon (more correctly the Royal Canon) is one hundred percent correct. It is important to test it in every way possible. Scholars have not been remiss in this respect but have tended to bring contrary evidence into line with the received dating and to assume copyist's errors.

According to Furuli, the usurper Bardiya (Gaumata), who followed Cambyses and preceded Darius I, reigned for 18 months judging from the evidence of dated business tablets, instead of the accepted eight months. This means that Darius began his reign in 521 rather than 522, and that his second year when the Second Temple was founded was 519 rather than 520.

He further proposes a coregency between Darius and his successor Xerxes of no less than eleven years. If this is true, Xerxes began to reign in 496 rather than 486. He was succeeded by Artaxerxes I in 475 rather than 465, and Artaxerxes himself reigned for 51 years instead of the traditional 41. This means that his twentieth year when he gave Nehemiah permission to rebuild Jerusalem was 455 rather than 445.

If all this could be established it would level a serious blow at our chronology. The most serious casualty would be Daniel's prophecy of the Seventy Weeks. If these began in 455 instead of 445 the arithmetic is in total disarray (see below). The first 69 weeks, if reckoned in solar years, would have expired in AD 29. If reckoned in luni-solar years as the evidence would suggest, they would have expired in AD 22. But in neither of these years was Messiah "cut off" as the prophecy states.

Furuli's Oslo chronology is unlikely to win many converts. The evidence is not all in his favour as he candidly admits. Ancient authors, Ptolemy, Herodotus, Ctesias, Diodorus Siculus, Manetho and others, all ascribe to Artaxerxes a reign of 41, 40 or 42 years, as shown in Table 31 (p.181) of Furuli's work. There are also four double-dated tablets which include the words "accession year of Darius, king of lands" alongside "year 41". This is usually taken to mean that Darius' accession year coincided with Artaxerxes' 41st year – not his 51st year as maintained by Furuli.

In Furuli's view, the most likely explanation of these tablets is that they belong to the reign of Artaxerxes *II* who, when fifty years old, chose his son Darius as his successor. There may, he thinks, have been a coregency between Artaxerxes and his son before the latter was executed for conspiring against his father. This however is only a guess since there is no actual evidence for such a coregency.

With respect to the traditional view, Furuli says, "The strength of this view is that a natural explanation of the double-dated tablets is used, namely that the '41st year' refers to the predecessor of Darius II, who reigned 41 years. It is also close to the regnal years (40, 41 or 42) given by ancient historians. Its weakness is that it must postulate that the tablets referring to Artaxerxes' 50th and 51st years contain errors" (p.187).

That in fact is probably true in this instance, especially since there are no dated tablets at all for the years 42 to 49 of Artaxerxes' protracted reign. The evidence is inconclusive for a radical revision of Artaxerxes' dates along these lines. The traditional chronology may well need modification in the future in the light of business tablets and astronomical diaries, but the time has not yet come to accept the modifications proposed by Furuli. The current chronology agrees well with the Bible and should not be abandoned in a hurry.

A detailed critique and refutation of Furuli's chronology is given by Jonsson on the internet. He concludes with the remarks:

The amount of evidence against Furuli's revised chronology provided by the Cuneiform documents – in particular the astronomical tablets – is enormous. Furuli's attempts to explain away this evidence are of no avail. His idea that most, if not all, of the astronomical data recorded on the tablets might have been retrocalculated in a later period is demonstrably false. Furuli's final, desperate theory that the Seleucid astronomers – and there were many – systematically redated almost the whole astronomical archive inherited from earlier generations of scholars is divorced from reality.

Be that as it may, Furuli is right to call attention to texts and tablets which do not fit the established pattern. These texts should be allowed to speak for themselves, not forced into a preconceived mould.

The Seventy Weeks

The prophecy of the Seventy Weeks in Daniel 9:24-27 may be rendered as follows:-

Seventy weeks (of years) are decreed concerning your people and your holy city, to finish the transgression, to seal up sins, to atone for iniquity, to bring in everlasting righteousness, to seal up vision and prophet, to anoint the most holy (place). Know therefore and understand that from the going forth of the word to restore and build Jerusalem until Messiah the prince shall be seven weeks and sixty-two weeks. It shall be built again with squares and moat, but in troubled times. And after the sixty-two weeks shall Messiah be cut off, having neither the city nor the sanctuary. The coming prince will destroy the people, and their end will be with a flood, and unto the end of the war desolations are determined. And he will make a covenant with many for one week, and for half the week he will cause sacrifice and offering to cease, and upon a wing (of the Temple) there will be desolating abominations, even until the determined end is poured out on the desolator. (See my *Empires of the End-Time*: 111ff.)

Daniel had every reason for thinking that Cyrus would be the one to send forth the word to restore and build Jerusalem. Had not Isaiah actually prophesied concerning Cyrus, "He is my shepherd, and he shall fulfil all my purpose, saying of Jerusalem, She shall be built, and of the temple, Your foundations shall be laid" (Isaiah 44:28)? And again in 45:13, "he shall build my city and set my exiles free." Besides, if the body of the great image (of Daniel 2) was not to be severed from the head, it was natural for the Seventy Weeks to follow on without a break after the completion of the seventy years of Babylonian rule.

But, as we have already seen, the prophecies relating to Cyrus and the close of the seventy years were not fulfilled as punctually as might be expected. Babylon was not significantly destroyed, the exiles were not completely restored, and even the seventy years were not literally fulfilled. Furthermore, in spite of Isaiah's prediction, Cyrus gave no permission to rebuild Jerusalem, and even the Temple, which he did command to be rebuilt, was not begun for another sixteen or seventeen years. As Sir Robert Anderson once said, "a few refractory Samaritans were allowed to thwart the execution of this the most solemn edict ever issued by an Eastern despot, an edict in respect of which a Divine sanction seemed to confirm the unalterable will of a Medo-Persian king" (1895: 56).

As we have seen, the predictions of the Old Testament (and of the New) are subject to a process of postponement. Prophecies which should have been fulfilled in the foreseeable future, according to the plain sense of the words, are manifestly postponed to a far more distant future, and this process is repeated over and over again. The reason of course is the absence of genuine repentance, belief and obedience on the part of the people involved (Jer. 18:9). Without those ingredients it is impossible for God to save and restore with outstretched arm in power and compassion as He longs to do. If the nation as a whole had responded in the way that Daniel responded (Dan. 9:3-19), the outcome might have been very different.

It is not only the beginning of the period which was subject to delay, so also was its end. It should have been wound up and finished in 490 years, but of course it was not. Because the Jews rejected their Messiah when He came, the last week of years was severed from the previous sixty-nine, and still to this day has not been completed. Indeed, His judgments are unsearchable, His ways past finding out!

According to Sir Robert Anderson and all right-minded expositors (in my view), the Seventy Weeks are reckoned in terms of luni-solar year of 360 days. "The only data (he says) which would warrant our deciding unreservedly that the prophetic year consists of 360 days, would be to find some portion of the era subdivided into the days of which it is composed. No other proof can be wholly satisfactory, but if this is forthcoming, it must be absolute and conclusive. And this is precisely what the book of Revelation gives us" (1895: 72).

This subdivision is found in Revelation 11:2,3; 12:6 and 13:5 where the last half-week of years is given as 1260 days or 42 months. What is said of the Beast in Revelation 13:5 corresponds exactly with the description of the little horn in Daniel 7:8 and the wilful king in Daniel 11:36. Forty-two months of thirty days is equivalent to 1260 days, and this corresponds to three and a half years on the luni-solar scale of 360 days to a year. In terms of solar years, the 70 weeks work out at 483 years, and the 69 weeks at 476 years.

The prophecy says, "From the going forth of the word to restore and build Jerusalem unto Messiah the prince shall be 7 weeks and 62 weeks. It shall be built again with squares and moat, but in troubled times. And after the 62 weeks shall Messiah be cut off." The only word to restore and build Jerusalem we read about in Ezra and Nehemiah is that which was uttered by

Artaxerxes in the twentieth year of his reign, 445 BC (Neh.2:1-8). The first seven weeks (49 years) were spent in rebuilding the city, squares and moat. The reason it took so long was due to the "troubled times" they were living in, concerning which Nehemiah leaves us in no doubt. As for the 69 weeks (7+62), Anderson pointed out that from Nisan 445 BC (the date of Artaxerxes' decree) to Nisan AD 32 (the presumed date of the Crucifixion) was exactly 483 luni-solar years (or 476 solar years). He even attempted to prove that the prophecy worked out to the precise day, expiring on Palm Sunday when Jesus was haled as Israel's King and Messiah.

But the Old Testament prophecies are not all cast in iron. Rather, they are cast in gold, and gold being a pliable metal can be moulded or modified as circumstances demand. This prophecy is an excellent example. It did not begin on schedule and it did not end on schedule. Nor, it seems, did the sixty-nine 'sevens' expire in the year of the Crucifixion. The sixty-ninth 'seven' ended in AD 32, as Anderson proved, but the Messiah was not cut off until AD 33, as will be shown in the next chapter. How do we explain this discrepancy?

It was in AD 32 that the divine Owner of the fig-tree, symbolic of Israel, declared, "For three years now I've been coming to look for fruit on this fig-tree and haven't found any. Cut it down! Why should it use up the soil?" (Luke 13:7). But the Vinedresser replied, "Sir, leave it alone for one more year, and I'll dig round it and fertilise it." It would seem that this extra year, graciously added, was not foreseen by Daniel. According to his prophecy Messiah would be cut off and the fig-tree cut down in AD 32, but as it turned out Messiah was cut off in AD 33 and even then the fig-tree was not cut down. That did not happen until AD 70 after a further reprieve of 37 years. I shall have more to say on this subject when considering the year of the Crucifixion and the length of our Lord's ministry.

Conclusion

We have then a period of 483 luni-solar years or 476 solar years leading up to an offer of Messianic rest. Actually the chronology indicates five other periods of 476 years, and in each case the significance would seem to be the same - a period of preparation leading up to an offer of Messianic rest, but which in each case was forfeited through unbelief. The history of Israel from the call of Abraham (2090) to the death of King Solomon (3036) consists of two periods of 476 years, the six years during which the land was conquered being shared by both periods:-

```
2090                        2560  2566                        3036
|_____470_____|_ 6_|_____470_____|
```

But both periods of 470 years conclude with three periods of 40 years. These were: the life of Moses which was divided into three forties, and the reigns of Saul, David, and Solomon, each of which lasted forty years. The result is five periods of 476 years:-

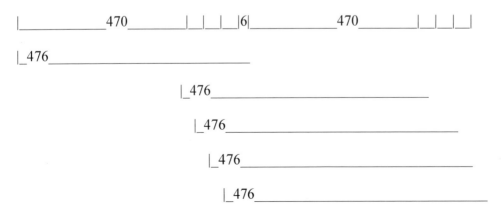

According to Hebrews 4:6, "those who formerly received the good news failed to enter because of unbelief." The writer is saying that they could have entered God's Sabbath rest in the time of Joshua but failed to do so through unbelief. This is clearly stated in verses 8-9, "if Joshua had given them rest, God would not have spoken of another day later on. So then, there remains a Sabbath rest for the people of God."

They had another opportunity in the time of David, as verse 7 makes plain: "again he appoints a certain day, 'Today', saying through David so long afterwards ..." They could, it seems, have entered God's rest on quite a number of occasions, but on each occasion they failed through unbelief. For this reason (v.9), "there (still) remains a Sabbath rest for the people of God."

This they will eventually receive at the second coming of Christ. Already six periods of 476 years have been allowed to come and go (counting the true fulfilment of Daniel's prophecy). Each of these awaits the last seven years which will cap them all. This is the period we know as Daniel's seventieth week.

Summary

Babylon fell to the Medes and Persians on 16 Tishri (12 October) 539. That very night Belshazzar the Chaldean king was killed and Darius the Mede received the kingdom (Dan. 5:30-31). But who was this Darius the Mede?

He cannot be identified with Cambyses or Cyrus, though both have had their supporters. He was possibly Cyaxares, son and successor of Astyages king of the Medes. Traditionally the Medes had been the senior partner in the Medo-Persian alliance and Darius was probably the last king of Median descent.

Cyrus' decree was issued "that the word of the Lord by the mouth of Jeremiah might be fulfilled" (Ezra 1:1). The reference is especially to Jeremiah's predictions of seventy years. The texts which speak of these 70 years are as follows.

1) Jeremiah 25:11-12, where it is predicted that "these nations" would serve the king of Babylon for 70 years, and that on their conclusion the king and nation of Babylon would themselves be punished. It was in fact during his accession year and first year of reign (605-604 BC) that Nebuchadnezzar conquered the whole land of Hatti (Syria-Palestine).

2) Jeremiah 29:10. The 70 years were primarily "for Babylon". They set a limit to the duration of the Neo-Babylonian kingdom, but they also set a limit to the duration of the Jewish exile.

3) 2 Chronicles 36:20-21. The 70 years would continue until (a) the establishment of the kingdom of Persia when the Jewish exiles would be allowed to return, and (b) the land had enjoyed its Sabbaths: "all the days that it lay desolate it kept Sabbath, to fulfil 70 years."

4) Daniel 9:2. "The desolation of Jerusalem" is not synonymous with the period of Exile, but both were due to end at the same time, on the completion of the 70 years prophesied by Jeremiah.

These periods came to an end with Cyrus' decree in 536 BC.

A start was made on the Temple in 536, but the work was opposed by the Jews' adversaries and was consequently discontinued throughout the reigns of Cyrus and Cambyses. In the second year of Darius (520) a delegation was sent to the king to inquire whether Cyrus had really made such a decree. After much searching, the document was found at Ecbabtana and Darius accordingly issued another decree confirming that of Cyrus.

According to Haggai 2:18 the Temple's foundation was laid on the 24th day of the ninth month in Darius' 2nd year. The years of Persian kings commence in Nisan in Ezra and Haggai, so the Temple was founded in 520 and completed in 516, in the twelfth month.

Another period of 70 years is mentioned in Zechariah 1:12. This is the period of "indignation". It began in 589 with the start of the siege and ended in 520. Yet another comes up in Zechariah 7:5. From the fasts of the fifth and seventh months (both in 586) to the year of the prophecy (518) was only approximately 70 years, actually 69 on inclusive reckoning.

In the seventh year of Artaxerxes, 458 BC, Ezra came up from Babylon. He arrived in Jerusalem on the first day of the fifth month after a journey of four months, and he carried with him letters from Artaxerxes in which ample provision was made for the Temple.

An unauthorized attempt to rebuild the city was made in the reign of Artaxerxes. But the Jews' adversaries, Rehum the commander and Shimshai the scribe, complained to the king in the letter of Ezra 4:11-16. In response the king commanded the work to cease *"until a decree is made by me"* (17-22). Rehum and Shimshai wasted no time in forcefully bringing the work to a halt (23).

This is where Nehemiah takes up the story. Nehemiah was distraught on hearing that the wall of Jerusalem had been broken down and its gates destroyed by fire. The king, whose cupbearer Nehemiah was, noticed Nehemiah's sadness of face and asked him the reason. Fearfully Nehemiah told him all. Then the king said, "What are you requesting?" Nehemiah boldly replied, "If it pleases the king and if your servant has found favour in your sight, that you send me to Judah, to the city of my fathers' graves, that I may rebuild it" (2:5). His request was granted in full. So Nehemiah returned to Jerusalem and work was begun without delay on the city wall. It was in Nisan 445 that Artaxerxes had made the decree.

Daniel's prophecy of the Seventy Weeks starts from "the going forth of the word to restore and rebuild Jerusalem" (Dan.9:25). This has to be the decree of 445 BC since this is the only one to authorise the rebuilding of the city. The "weeks" are really sevens of years computed in terms of luni-solar years of 360 days. The first 7+62 weeks ended in AD 32 when Messiah should have been cut off in fulfilment of Daniel 9:26. But the Crucifixion was postponed for one year in response to the Vinedresser's request, "Sir, let it alone this year also..." (Luke 13:8). It was therefore in AD 33 that Christ was cut off as astronomy confirms.

69 weeks of luni-solar years come to 483 years, which works out as 476 solar years. It was noticed that Israel's chronology demonstrates five other periods of 476 years, each carrying the possibility of Sabbatical rest.

Chapter Eight

The Days of the Messiah

In this chapter we move into the New Testament area and will try to establish the dates of the Birth, Baptism, and Death of the Lord Jesus Christ. Other topics will also be discussed but only as they relate to the pivotal events just mentioned. Obviously all three hang together both in the unfolding drama of God's redeeming purpose and in their chronological relationship.

In the New Testament we shall look for the same clear pointers to the truth as we have found in the Old Testament. Initially, it is true, we find ourselves in a seemingly no-win situation. So many different interpretations are on offer, so many conflicting views and values, it seems almost impossible to arrive at a firm solution. A variety of plausible dates and determinations are thrown at us, but we shall be looking for something more than plausible dates. The truth has that intangible ring about it, the assurance that we are on the right track and not pursuing a mirage.

For me the most helpful work on *New Testament Chronology* is that by Kenneth F. Doig (1991). Doig is particularly good on the chronology of Herod the Great and the birth of Christ. On other matters he is less convincing but always informative. In view of his unrivalled mastery of the subject it is surprising that recent writers have not paid more attention to his work. Jack Finegan for example does not seem to have heard of him.

In this chapter I shall proceed step by step in search of the best solution to each problem as it arises. I shall avoid ingenious and over-subtle interpretations based on speculation and surmise rather than clear pointers in the text of Scripture. I shall move forward circumspectly avoiding as far as possible the pitfalls that litter the road.

The fifteenth year of Tiberius

The ministry of John the Baptist is dated with a fulness unrivalled by any other. Luke has done his level best to print this event in the chronicle of time by means of a sixfold reference to contemporary rulers. We may be sure that he fulfilled his purpose admirably so far as his first readers were concerned, but for us it is not so simple. Many different opinions have been expressed as we shall see in a moment. But here at the outset is the reference in question.

In the fifteenth year of the reign of Tiberius Caesar, Pontius Pilate being governor of Judea, and Herod being tetrarch of Galilee, and his brother Philip tetrarch of the region of Ituraea and Trachonitus, and Lysanias tetrarch of Abilene, in the high-priesthood of Annas and Caiaphas, the word of God came to John the son of Zechariah in the wilderness; and he went into all the region about Jordan, preaching a baptism of repentance for the forgiveness of sins (Luke 3:1-3).

Of the six time-notes given only the first is of any assistance in the dating of John's ministry. The other five indicate only the broad limits within which this epoch-making initiative must be located. Pilate was prefect of Judea from AD 26 to 36 (or 27 to 37); Herod Antipas was deposed in AD 39; Philip died in 34; Lysanias has defied attempts to date him; Caiaphas was high priest from AD 18 until no later than 37. We are left therefore with the fifteenth year of the reign of Tiberius. Surely no question can exist as to the dates of the Roman emperors and the method employed in reckoning their reigns. Regrettably that is not the case! A disconcerting array of possibilities confronts us with no consensus as to which is most probably correct.

The point chosen by most writers has been predetermined, one suspects, by their preferred date for the Crucifixion. Those who would place the Crucifixion in AD 33 usually prefer AD 29 (rather than 28) as the year when John's ministry began, whereas those who opt for an AD 30 Crucifixion prefer AD 27. Clearly objectivity is essential if one's conclusion is to carry any weight at all. Finegan in his authoritative Handbook lists no less than sixteen ways in which Tiberius' reign might have been reckoned by Luke. Most of these can be discounted, but a substantial number remain. The problem arises from the fact that Tiberius's reign was reckoned in different ways in different parts of the Empire. A brief look at the various possibilities will prove instructive and hopefully decisive.

1) In the past it was thought that Tiberius' reign should be reckoned from his co-regency with Caesar Augustus. The decree which made Tiberius coregent was in AD 11 according to Ramsay, three years before his sole reign began. On this view Tiberius' fifteenth year would be AD 25/26. Those who think the Crucifixion took place in 29 or 30 (and the Nativity in 5 BC) have found this date to agree well with their chronology. By scholars today, however, it finds little support. In the words of George Ogg, "Not only are there no traces of this epoch on coins or in inscriptions, but the ancient historians – Roman and Jewish, secular and ecclesiastical alike – nowhere indicate any acquaintance with it" (1940: 187f.). Doig agrees: "There is a total lack of hard evidence from either historical documents or coins of the period which date the reign of Tiberius from a co-regency" (1991: 184).

This interpretation was adopted by Sir William Ramsay. But even Ramsay admitted that this method "is never employed elsewhere in reckoning the reign of that emperor. When his tribunician years are not stated, his reign is always counted from the death of his predecessor, Augustus; and it is beyond dispute that he was not in any proper and strict sense emperor until that time" (1998: 201f.).

2) Using the accession-year system some would reckon Tiberius' first year from 1st January, AD 15 and his fifteenth year from 1st January, 29. This is the view of Jack Finegan in his Handbook. He writes, "Since Roman historians of the time (Tacitus, Suetonius, our para 580) generally date the first regnal year of a ruler from Jan. 1 of the year following the date of accession (i.e. follow the accession-year system), we judge that Luke would do likewise" (1998: para 583).

It is not certain however that Tacitus and Suetonius used this method at all. According to Doig their reckoning was dynastic measured from the actual date of Tiberius' accession, 19 August, 14. In any case, there is general agreement that this was not the method used in the East. Ormond Edwards quotes from a letter which J.K. Fotheringham wrote to *The Times* on 31 December, 1932. He said there, "Technical chronology proves just as decisively that the fifteenth year of Tiberius was the year AD 28-29. Regnal years were always reckoned from the New Years's Day of the local calendar and the January New Year was not in use in the eastern Roman Empire" (1986: 146).

3) If the method is dynastic, Tiberius' years are reckoned factually from the precise date of Tiberius' accession, 19 August, AD 14. His fifteenth year would then be 19 August 28 to 18 August 29. According to Doig, "This was the usual Roman method for reckoning Tiberius' reign. It is the only reckoning, besides use of the Syro-Macedonian calendar, that makes sense in the historical context of Scripture" (p.186). The Roman coins of Tiberius, including those of the prefects of Judea, were dated by this means.

Thomas Lewin was doubtless overstating the case when he said, "The reign of Tiberius, as beginning from 19th Aug. A.D.14, was as well-known a date in the time of Luke as the reign of Queen Victoria in our own day, and no single case has ever been or can be produced in which the years of Tiberius were reckoned in any other way" (1865: liii).

But Ramsay is not convinced. "That mode of reckoning," he says, "seems to have been always used by the emperors of the first century … But that method was rarely, if ever, used by the general public or by historians in the East" (1998: 221). How many people, I wonder, can remember the day that Queen Victoria came to the throne, or our present Queen for that matter?

4) Our options are narrowing down. Ramsay is in agreement with Fotheringham that Luke would have used a local calendar. "It seems improbable", he says, "that he used any kind of year other than the Macedonian, Anatolian, and North Syrian, beginning at or near the autumn equinox" (1904: 481). Doig is in agreement that Luke is using the Syro-Macedonian calendar beginning at 1st Dios, the month roughly corresponding to Tishri.

George Ogg argues along the same lines, "In early days in Egypt and in the Orient, where monarchical regime had long obtained, it had been customary to date according to the years of the current reign. That method survived in those regions even after they became part of the Roman Empire and at the time of which we speak was confined almost entirely to them. Luke's 15th year of the reign of Tiberius Caesar is, therefore, neither Roman nor imperial, rather it is Oriental and provincial; its affinities are with methods in vogue in Egypt, Palestine, Syria, and neighbouring regions, and it is through a study of them that a true understanding of it is most likely to be reached" (1940: 188).

5) Was it therefore a Jewish calendar that Luke invoked? Ogg at least thought it was, as does G.B. Caird in *The Interpreter's Dictionary of the Bible.* Ogg concludes:

Now it is known how the Jews reckoned the regnal years of their own princes, but how they reckoned those of the Roman emperors is not known. There is evidence, however, that the Egyptians reckoned the regnal years of the Roman emperors as they had done those of the Ptolemies, the Syrians as they had done those of their native rulers. Reasoning from analogy we conclude that the Jews reckoned them as they did those of their own native princes. (200)

That for Ogg was 1st Nisan to 1st Nisan. But in fact the kings of Judah counted their regnal years from 1st Tishri, not from 1st Nisan. Hence the same result is achieved whether the calendar was Syro-Macedonian or Jewish: Tiberius' years are reckoned from Tishri. This was the Jews' new year for secular matters, whereas Nisan was their new year for ecclesiastical matters. Edwards finds confirmation of this usage in a coin dated Q. Caecilius Metellus, governor of Syria AD 12-17. The coin is numbered 45 (of the Actian era, corresponding to AD 14), and bears the letter A (meaning Tiberius 1). Hence Tiberius' year 15 began in autumn 28 (1986: 146). This mode of reckoning would have been recognised by both Theophilus, the Gentile official to whom Luke's Gospel is addressed, and the Jewish audience who might be expected to read it.

6) There is one other possibility that deserves a mention. It is that Tiberius' years are reckoned from 1st Nisan preceding his accession. By this method Tiberius' fifteenth year would run from 16 March 28 to 3 April 29. This was the method used by the Jewish historian Josephus for his Roman patrons and might therefore have been used by Luke as well.

In Doig's opinion, "The Nisan interpretation is an expected usage by a Jewish writer such as Josephus, and it is in accord with the later Mishna. However, neither Luke nor Theophilus were Jews, and they are unlikely to have used the Jewish Second Temple calendar" (p.186).

But this raises the delicate question whether Luke was really a Gentile? This is generally regarded as an established fact on the strength of the fourth chapter of Colossians where Luke is evidently distinguished from "those of the circumcision". But in Romans 3:2 we are told that the oracles of God were entrusted to the Jews, and that surely must include the New Testament oracles as well as the Old. Luke was responsible for more of the New Testament than any other writer (marginally more than Paul). Is it likely in view of Romans 3:2 that so much of the New Testament would have been committed to a Gentile writer?

There are some who think "those of the circumcision" were a sub-section of the Jews, not the people as a whole, those namely who maintained a strict observance of the law and circumcision in particular. They were "the circumcision party" as the phrase is often translated. The Jews were divided into two well-defined sections, the Hebrews and the Hellenists (Acts 6:1). Those of the circumcision (mentioned in Acts 10:45; 11:2; Gal. 2:12; Col. 4:11 and Titus 1:10) would line up with the Hebrews. Some of them insisted on imposing the law and circumcision on Gentile believers, but they were not all of this opinion. Others were more flexible in their attitude. They were happy to work alongside Paul and were recognised as fellow workers by Paul. Luke is distinguished from the circumcision party, not from the Jews as a whole. He was therefore a Hellenist, a Greek speaking Jew of liberal persuasion, like Stephen, Apollos and many others.

It is possible therefore that Luke would have used the Jewish Nisan calendar along with Josephus. But in my view he is more likely to have used the Jewish Tishri calendar as in the Old Testament. But one question remains.

7) If Luke was using the Jewish Tishri calendar (or the Syro-Macedonian Dios calendar) would he have antedated Tiberius' reign to Tishri AD 13 or reckoned it from Tishri AD 14? Many writers, including Doig, Caird and E.L. Martin, prefer the first alternative. According to them our Lord's ministry was only two years in length, AD 28 to 30. For this to work Tiberius' fifteenth year must have included the autumn of 27 with Jesus Himself baptised early in 28.

If this is allowed, Tiberius' first year would have been only a few weeks in length, from 19 August AD 14 when Augustus died to 15 September, 1st Tishri; and his fifteenth year from 1st Tishri 27 (21 September) to 1st Tishri 28 (9 September). Augustus died very near the end of the civil year. Tiberius, his designated successor, was voted by the Senate the new head of State on 17 September (Finegan: para 570). This was two days *after* 1st Tishri in that year. In the circumstances is it not more probable that Tiberius' first year was reckoned from Tishri 14 than antedated to Tishri 13?

It will be remembered that Nebuchadnezzar came to the throne on 8 Ab, 605 BC. His first year was reckoned in Babylon from 1st Nisan 604, but was antedated by the Jews to Tishri 605. This was seven weeks after the death of Nabopolassar, the previous king of Babylon. Likewise Xerxes, father of Artaxerxes, died probably on 14 Ab, 465 BC. By the Persians Artaxerxes' first year was postdated to 1st Nisan 464, but was antedated by Nehemiah to Tishri 465. This again was six weeks after the death of Xerxes. It was also in Ab that Tiberius succeeded to the throne. If his first year was reckoned in the East from 1st Dios (15 October in AD 14) or 1st January AD 15, Luke would doubtless have reckoned it from 1st Tishri, 15 September, AD 14.

I conclude therefore that Tiberius' fifteenth year as reckoned by Luke was AD 28-29. The same result is arrived at with four of the above possibilities. Hence the balance of probability is strongly in favour of this time-slot.

John's Baptism

It is surprising to find an event so elaborately dated to be that of the ministry of John, and not, say, the baptism of Jesus Himself. It is a fact however that John's ministry is mentioned both here and elsewhere as a turning point in sacred history. This is plainly stated in Luke 16:16, "The law and the prophets were until John; since that time the kingdom of God is preached," and it is implied in many other passages, e.g. Matthew 11:12, Acts 1:22; 10:37 and 13:24. The good news of the Kingdom was first preached by John. Jesus repeated the same message and His whole ministry was an elaboration on the same theme. In this connection many have quoted Alfred Plummer's significant words:

A nation, which from Samuel to Malachi had scarcely ever been without a living oracle of God, had for three or four centuries never heard the voice of a Prophet. It seemed as if Jehovah had withdrawn from His people. The breaking of this oppressive silence by the voice of the Baptist caused a thrill through the whole Jewish population throughout the world. Luke shows his appreciation of the magnitude of the crisis by the sixfold attempt to give it an exact date (1922: 80).

Assuming that Tiberius' fifteenth year, as reckoned by Luke, began in September or October AD 28, it may be inferred that John's clarion call for national repentance was first heard in the autumn of that year. Finegan's statement must surely be correct: "Climatically, the great summertime heat in the sub-sea level and semitropical Jordan valley makes it unlikely that it was in the summer, or even in the spring with summer coming on, and allows us to think of the fall the most likely" (para 584).

According to Josephus, the climate in the Jordan valley in the winter months "is so mild that the inhabitants wear linen when snow is falling throughout the rest of Judea" (*Wars* IV.8.3 (473)). Herod had every reason for making Jericho his winter capital and residing there during the cold winter months. John also would have chosen that region because the congenial climate would have attracted large crowds of people. Later, when the heat in the Jordan valley became oppressive, we find him baptising at Aenon in Samaria "because water was plentiful there" (John 3:23).

An abundance of water was a prime consideration of course. That would have been provided by the autumn rain swelling the Jordan river to maximum capacity. The autumn was also the time when the people's thoughts turned to repentance and atonement. The Day of Atonement fell on 17/18 September in AD 28. Jesus Himself came to be baptised a while later, probably in January AD 29.

The Temple 46 years in building.

In John 2:20 we are provided with a precise statement which ought to give an exact date for the first Passover of our Lord's ministry. But once again we are confronted with a number of possible interpretations which can be accommodated to any year in the range AD 27 to 30. On the occasion of His first Passover Jesus parried the Jews' demand for a sign with the words, "Destroy this temple, and I will raise it again in three days." In surprise and unbelief the Jews exclaimed, "It has taken forty-six years to build this temple, and you are going to raise it in three days?"

Assuming the usual translation to be correct, the next thing to do is to inquire when Herod's Temple began to be built. According to Josephus (*Ant.* XV.11.1 (380)), "in the eighteenth year of his reign … Herod undertook an extraordinary work, (namely) the reconstruction of the temple of God at his own expense, enlarging its precincts and raising it to a more imposing height." See Finegan, para 592. Herod's eighteenth year was 20/19 BC, but work on the Temple may not have begun until 18 BC.

It all depends on what Josephus meant by "undertook … to build". Does it mean that work actually commenced in that year, or only that preparations to that end were set in motion? Josephus explains what was done by way of preparation and it must have taken a considerable time. Herod had first to convince the people of his good intentions, since they were understandably afraid that the Temple having been pulled down would not be rebuilt. So he gave them assurance that the work would not commence until all the necessary preparations had been made. He accordingly "prepared a thousand wagons to carry the stones, selected ten thousand of the most skilled workmen, purchased priestly robes for a thousand priests, and trained some as masons, others as carpenters, and began the construction only after these preparations had diligently been made by him."

In the opinion of Lewin and Ogg, Herod spent at least two years in preparation and that the building was not actually begun until 18 BC. Forty-six years from 18 BC bring us to AD 29, which is also my date for the Lord's first Passover. Others would agree with Doig that the building itself began in Herod's eighteenth year. That produces the result which suits his chronology, but it cannot be assumed that such extensive preparations were accomplished in less than a year. The Jews of our Lord's day had exact knowledge when the rebuilding had commenced without access to the writings of Josephus. *They* knew whether it was 20, 19 or 18 BC, but we do not.

In pursuit of a more definite solution some writers have found fault with the standard translation of John 2:20. Their reservations are almost certainly unfounded, but their alternative solution does have some plausibility. The correct translation, it is argued, should be as follows: "For forty-six years has this shrine been built, and will you in three days raise it up?" In other words, "How can you possibly raise up in three days a temple (or sanctuary) that has stood for forty-six years?" So Finegan, para 595. Josephus tells us that the sanctuary (the *naos*) was completed in eighteen months (*Ant.* XV.11.6(421)). From 18/17 BC, when the sanctuary was built, forty-six years bring us to AD 29/30. This produces a definite result which some people have found more agreeable to their chronology.

There are two words in particular which call for comment. The first of these is *naos*. The *naos* is properly the inner sanctuary or Holy of Holies, not the Temple as a whole which is *hieron*. Elsewhere in John (eleven times, including John 2:14,15 in the same context) the word is *hieron*, and the Temple courts are indicated. John, it is claimed, always distinguishes between these two words, and consequently his use of *naos* in John 2:20 points to the sanctuary to the exclusion of the rest of the Temple.

Jesus, however, was not in the *naos* when He said, "Destroy this *naos*, and in three days I will raise it up." He was in the Court of the Gentiles facing the Temple. The Jews would have thought He was speaking of the Temple buildings, especially since the distinction between the two words was not always observed. They used the same word as Jesus had used and said it had taken forty-six years to build.

The second word is *oikodomethe*. Strictly speaking this word should be translated "has been built" (rather than "has taken to build"), in accord with the correct sense of the aorist passive tense. But it was not always used in this strict way. Our attention is drawn to the use of this word in the Greek text of Ezra 5:16: "From then (that is, from the time Sheshbazzar laid the foundation of the Temple) until now it has been built (*oikodomethe*, meaning "under construction") and has not been finished." This provides an excellent parallel with the Temple of our Lord's day, which had been in process of building for forty-six years and was still unfinished.

Lewin notes that the very words *oikodomethe* (*de*) *ho naos*, found in John 2:20, are used by Josephus in *Ant.* XV.11.3 with reference to the building of the Temple itself: "Now *the temple was built* of stones that were white and strong ..." Here, as Finegan himself admits (para 594), "Josephus evidently used the word [*naos*] in its general sense in saying that Herod built the temple."

The interpretation defended by Finegan does full justice to both *naos* and *oikodomethe*. But the matter in dispute was not how long the Temple had already been built, but how long it had taken to build it. The contrast is between the forty-six years it had taken so far to build the Temple and the three days that Jesus said, according to their understanding of His words, He could build it all over again. Hence the standard translation makes far better sense in the present context.

On which day was the Crucifixion: Was it Wednesday?

The view that Christ died on Wednesday still has its supporters today. I have before me this moment two works defending this view. Advocates of this idea base their case on Matthew 12:40 which, taken quite literally, suggests that the Son of Man was three 24-hour periods in the tomb, assuming that is what is meant by "the heart of the earth."

The coup de grace to this theory (as it seems to me) is the statement of the two travellers to Emmaus, "Today is the third day since these things were done" (Luke 24:21). By no mode of reckoning, ancient or modern, can Sunday afternoon be counted as the third day from Wednesday. The events referred to are the trial and crucifixion of Jesus of Nazareth (vv.19-20). Peter John-Charles, however, tries to extend it by including the sealing of the tomb and the posting of the guard on the following day. But these events are irrelevant in this connection, and they do not even help with the chronology, since three 24-hour periods from Thursday morning would only reach to Sunday morning, not Sunday afternoon.

It was moreover common knowledge that Jesus had said that He would rise on the third day. Even the Pharisees remembered this saying, Matthew 27:63-64. Evidently the two from Emmaus had this prophecy in mind, hoping against hope that it was not all a terrible mistake. It was already late afternoon; in a short time the third day would have ended and, so far as they were aware, their Lord had not risen!

It was early on Sunday morning that the women converged on the tomb with their spices and ointment. This was evidently the earliest opportunity they had to anoint the Lord's body. Yet, on the Wednesday theory, there was the whole of Friday (between the Passover Sabbath and the weekly Sabbath) on which to perform this office. In the words of Adam Rutherford, "To put off all that time and then in the end to get up suddenly one morning at an abnormally early hour before dawn to anoint Christ four days after he was dead just does not make sense. The more fully and carefully this Wednesday-Crucifixion theory is investigated, the more does the fallacy of it become evident" (1957: 479). They would not have contemplated opening the tomb on the fourth day (John 11:39).

Was it Thursday?

If Wednesday is found wanting, how about Thursday? Is it possible that Christ died on Thursday? This theory, though rarely discussed, has far more to commend it. Once again the main argument derives from Matthew 12:40, for even if Christ died on Thursday there were still three days and three nights, in whole or in part, before His resurrection on the Sunday morning. Supporting arguments include the following:

1) It is fundamental to the Thursday (as to the Wednesday) idea that the Sabbath day following the Crucifixion was the Feast of Passover, the day the Passover meal was eaten, not the weekly Sabbath which was the day after that. Jesus died on the day of Preparation, which is explained in Mark 15:42 as "the day before the Sabbath" (*prosabbaton*), but in John 19:14 as "the Preparation of the Passover". This Sabbath, therefore, was the day of Passover, the day the Passover was eaten (John 18:28), 15 Nisan (beginning in the evening of 14 Nisan). It was a day of sacred assembly on which no work was to be done (Exod. 12:16; Lev. 23:5-7; Num. 28:18), and was reckoned as a Sabbath.

In John 19:31 we are told that this Sabbath (the day of Preparation) was a high or special day. It was not a regular weekly Sabbath but a day of special importance. This could mean that the two Sabbaths coincided that week, as the Friday view maintains, but it could also mean that this day was not the weekly Sabbath at all, but a day of solemn convocation. The first and last days of Unleavened Bread, 15 and 21 Nisan, were both rest-days (*shabbaton*), according to Leviticus

23:39. And 15 Nisan was a true Sabbath (*shabbat*) according to the Pharisaic interpretation of the phrase "the morrow after the Sabbath" in Leviticus 23:11.

2) The most distinguished defender of a Thursday Crucifixion was Bishop Westcott. He drew attention to the roundabout way in which the day after the Crucifixion is described in Matthew 27:62: "On the morrow, which is (the day) after the Preparation, the chief priests and the Pharisees gathered before Pilate." But why this circumlocution for "the Sabbath day"? Westcott found the answer in the supposition that not the weekly Sabbath, but the First Day of Unleavened Bread was intended. "Such a circumlocution", he says, "seems most unnatural if the weekly Sabbath were intended; but if it were the first day of unleavened bread, then, as the proper title of that day had already been used to describe the commencement of the Preparation day (Matt. 26:17, *te de prote ton azumon*) no characteristic term remained for it"(1895: 343f.).

It should be explained that by the first century AD the first day of Unleavened Bread had been brought forward one day in order to include the sweeping of the houses and the preparing of the feast. Whereas originally it had begun with the arrival of 15 Nisan (in the evening of 14 Nisan by our reckoning), it now began 24 hours earlier, in the evening of 13 Nisan. Hence, when the disciples came to Jesus "on the first day of Unleavened Bread" with their question "Where will you have us prepare for you to eat the Passover?" (Matt. 26:17; Mark 14:12), this was the evening of 13 Nisan, twenty-four hours before the meal was scheduled to take place. Preparations for the meal could not be left to the last minute. At least 24 hours were needed to find a suitable location and to make provision for the meal.

Matthew's circumlocution is obviously deliberate, but his reason for using it is not immediately obvious. This day was both the Sabbath and the Passover, so why does Matthew avoid these terms. He may have done so out of contempt for the Jewish leaders who that very moment were about to profane this holy day by entering Pilate's palace ("an astonishing breach of Sabbath law", Michael Green). For Matthew the Crucixion overshadowed both the Sabbath and the Passover. He therefore calls it "the day after the Preparation" since everyone knew that Jesus had died on the day of Preparation (e.g. Mark 15:42).

3) If the Thursday theory is followed, it is necessary to distinguish carefully between the two Sabbaths, the Passover Sabbath and the weekly Sabbath which immediately followed. In Luke 23:54 we read, "It was the Preparation day, and the Sabbath was about to begin." This would have to be the Passover Sabbath, the day the Passover was eaten. The women who had come from Galilee, having seen the tomb and how the body of Jesus was laid in it, returned home and prepared spices. It then says, "And on the Sabbath day they rested according to the commandment." They must have rested on both Sabbath days, but the fourth commandment spoke of the weekly Sabbath, so this must be the Sabbath intended here. Likewise Mark 16:1, "And when the Sabbath was past, Mary Magdalene, Mary the mother of James, and Salome bought spices..." This would have been the close of the weekly Sabbath, their first opportunity to buy spices.

4) According to Luke 23:54 Jesus was laid in the tomb as the Sabbath was about to begin (*epephosken*, dawning, coming on), that is about six pm. The three night-days during which the Son of Man was to remain in the heart of the earth, according to Matthew 12:40, would then be: Thursday night-Friday; Friday night-Saturday; Saturday night-Sunday. Jesus rose from the dead early on Sunday morning, and it was still "the third day" on the Sunday afternoon when He revealed Himself to the two disciples from Emmaus.

5) If Jesus died on Thursday, 14 Nisan, He would have risen on Sunday, 17 Nisan. It has been pointed out that there are several Old Testament events which probably or certainly took place on 17 Nisan. The most certain of these is the resting of Noah's ark on the mountains of Ararat. This took place on the seventeenth of the seventh month according to Genesis 8:4, but prior to the Exodus the year began in Tishri and consequently the seventh month was Abib or Nisan. Noah's ark is a type of Christ crucified, He who weathered the storms of death and emerged victorious on the resurrection morning. The wood of the ark is a type of the cross daubed with the blood of Christ, while the pitch itself (Hebrew, *kopher*) signifies ransom (Exodus 30:12) or atonement (Job 33:24; 36:18). *Kapporeth*, from the same root, was the covering of the mercy seat, the propitiatory sprinkled with blood where atonement was made. 17 Nisan would certainly have been an appropriate day for Christ to have risen from the dead. But is it correct?

The evidence points to Friday

In many ways the Thursday distribution of events produces a satisfactory result. But does it really suit a straightforward reading of the Gospel narrative? Most people would say it does not. The following objections make it difficult to accept it.

1) The Gospels, whether taken separately or together, give no indication that more than one day elapsed between the burial of the Lord and His resurrection. Luke, who gives the fullest account, records first the entombment as the Sabbath day was coming on (23:54-55); second the women's preparation of spices (56a); third their resting on the Sabbath (56b); and fourth their going to the tomb early on the first day of the week (24:1). Likewise Mark records the entombment in the evening of the Preparation day "which is the day before the Sabbath *(prosabbaton)*"(15:42-47); the purchase of spices "when the Sabbath was past" (16:1); and their going to the tomb early on the first day of the week (16:2). There is no indication in either Gospel that more than one day intervened, and that day was Saturday, the weekly Sabbath. Evidently the women from Galilee (Luke 23:55) already had all the spices they needed, but the two Mary's and Salome had insufficient or none at all. They bought their spices on the Saturday evening "when the Sabbath was over" (Mark 16:1).

2) It is true that the word "Sabbath" is used in the *Old* Testament to denote other occasions besides the weekly Sabbath. It is so used of the Sabbatical year (Lev. 25), and the Day of Atonement (Lev. 16:31; 23:32), as we have seen. In the New Testament, however, it is never used of any other occasion than the weekly Sabbath. Hence it does not seem reasonable to interpret it differently in Mark 15:42, Luke 23:54 and John 19:31. Christ died therefore on the day before the weekly Sabbath, the day we call Friday.

3) In the vast majority of places the Resurrection is said to have occurred "on the third day" after the Crucifixion. See Matthew 16:21; 17:23; 20:19; Luke 9:22; 18:33; 24:7,21,46; Acts 10:40; 1 Corinthians 15:4. The meaning of this expression is "the next day but one", as the Lord Himself makes crystal clear in Luke 13:32, "Go and tell that fox, Behold I cast out demons and perform cures today and tomorrow, and *the third day* I finish my course." This is also the meaning throughout the Bible wherever the days are defined. So Exodus 19:10-11; Leviticus 7:16-17; 19:6; 1 Samuel 20:12; Acts 27:18-19.

In four places, Mark 8:31; 9:31; 10:34, and Matthew 27:63, the alternative wording "after three days" is found. That the Pharisees understood these words to hold the same meaning as "on the third day" is clear from their request to Pilate in Matthew 27:63-64: "Sir, we remember how that impostor said, while he was still alive, After three days I will rise again. Therefore order the sepulchre to be made secure until *the third day*." The same is true of the other three references, for Mark 8:31 is paralleled by Luke 9:22 where "on the third day" is found. Likewise Mark 9:31

is paralleled by Matthew 17:23, and Mark 10:34 by Luke 18:33, where again "on the third day" is given. Evidently, of the two synonymous expressions, Matthew and Luke preferred the one and Mark the other. Old Testament references which may be consulted are Genesis 40:18-20; 42:17-18; 1 Kings 12:5,12 (= 2 Chron. 10:5,12), and Esther 4:16-5:1 where periods of "three days" are completed on the third day.

Three days and three nights

Apart from Matthew 12:40 and Jonah 1:17, the only other instance of "three days and three nights" comes in 1 Samuel 30:12. It is said there concerning the Egyptian found in the open country, "he had eaten no bread, nor drunk any water, *three days and three nights*." This is equivalent to "the third day" in verse 1 and to "three days ago" in verse 13 (lit. "today, three (days)"). If "after three days" means "the next day but one", it is reasonable to conclude that "three days ago" means "the previous day but one". This finds support in the common Hebrew idiom for "in former times", namely *ethmol shilshom*, which means literally "yesterday, the third day." Compare also Esther 4:16, "Do not eat or drink for three days, night or day." This period was completed on the third day (5:1).

While there are only three occurrences of "three days and three nights" in the Bible, there are ten occurrences of "forty days and forty nights" and one of "seven days and seven nights". These include the days of continuous rain at the time of the Flood (Gen. 7:4,12); the days that Moses stayed on the Mount while receiving the Ten Commandments (Exod. 24:18; 34:28; Deut. 9:9,11); the days he lay prostrate on the ground after Israel had sinned (Deut. 9:18,25); the days he spent on the Mount for the second time (Deut. 10:10); the time it took Elijah to travel to Mount Horeb after the Lord had fed him (1 Kings 19:8); and the days Job's three friends sat in silence on the ground (Job 2:13). The emphasis is not on the precise number of nights involved (40 as opposed to 39), but on the continuous unbroken nature of the period mentioned, coupled with the hardship or deprivation involved. According to Adam Rutherford, "The introduction of the word 'night', as in 'day and night' in place of just the term 'day', was done when it was desired to express continuity, as a process, activity or condition continuing without interruption for the said period."

It is possible, therefore, that "three days and three nights" is simply an idiom for three days of uninterrupted privation without any emphasis on the specific number of nights. Scholars draw attention to a statement attributed to Rabbi Eleazar ben Azariah (c. AD 100): "A day and night are an *Onah* (a portion of time) and the portion of an *Onah* is as the whole of it" (Jerusalem Talmud: *Shabbat* IX.3).

The heart of the earth

But let's have a closer look at the wording of Matthew 12:40. What precisely is the meaning of "in the heart of the earth"? The literal meaning is simply "in the midst (or depth) of the earth", as in the expression "the heart of the sea" (Jonah 2:3, "You have cast me into the deep, into the heart of the sea", and Exodus 15:8, "the deep waters congealed in the heart of the sea"). The precise phrase "the heart of the earth" does not occur anywhere else, but the meaning must be "in the midst of the earth".

If the allusion is to *Sheol*, the grave or state of death, our Lord is referring to the period of death before His rising "on the third day". This agrees with the Old Testament parallels in 1 Samuel 30:12 and Esther 4:16; 5:1, where "three days and three nights" are completed on the third day.

But our Lord may have intended His words to be taken more literally. Similar expressions in the Old Testament indicate a state of extreme danger and distress. Psalm 71:20 for example,

"Though you have made me see troubles, many and bitter, you will restore my life again; from the depths (lit. *abysses*) of the earth you will again bring me up." Jonah was cast into the heart of the sea, our Lord into the heart of the earth, as if into a deep pit. The reference is not to the time He spent in the tomb, nor even to the period of death; the reference is to the duration of His deep affliction, when He was handed over to the powers of darkness (Luke 22:53). Consider for example Psalm 69, a messianic psalm:

> Save me, O God, for the waters have come up to my neck. I sink in the miry depths, where there is no foothold. I have come into the deep waters; the floods engulf me... Rescue me from the mire, do not let me sink; deliver me from those who hate me, from the deep waters. Do not let the floodwaters engulf me or the depths swallow me up or the pit close its mouth over me (vv.1-2,14-15).

See also Psalm 42:7 and Lamentations 3:54. The same meaning is conveyed by the use of "pit" instead of "deep", as in Psalm 40:2 "He lifted me out of slimy pit, out of the mud and mire"; Psalm 88:6 "You have put me in the lowest pit, in the darkest depths"; Zechariah 9:11 "I will free your prisoners from the waterless pit."

In this connection we think of the patriarch Joseph. Joseph was thrown into a waterless pit by his brothers (Gen. 37:23-24). This for him was "the heart of the earth", the beginning of his intense ordeal. It was only after this that he was sold to Midianite merchants for twenty pieces of silver, and later still that he died a symbolic death when a goat was slaughtered and his multi-coloured coat dipped in its blood. As with Christ, Joseph's ordeal began some while before his betrayal and symbolic death. It began very literally in the heart or depth of the earth.

In the Garden of Gethsemane the soul of the Lord Jesus was overwhelmed with sorrow to the point of death (Matt. 26:38), and His sweat was like drops of blood falling to the ground (Luke 22:44). This is when He was handed over to the powers of darkness, when He was thrown into the great deep. If the three night-days are reckoned from then, they are the same as on the Thursday theory: Thursday night-Friday, Friday night-Saturday, Saturday night-Sunday. This, surely, is a better solution than that of injecting an additional day into the Passion story, a day which the narrative neither requires nor permits.

I have tried to state the arguments fully and fairly both for and against the Thursday point of view. In spite of the many advantages which Thursday seems to offer, the weight of evidence is decisively against it. We are left therefore with the traditional view that our Lord died on Good Friday and rose "on the third day", early on the Sunday morning.

Was the Crucifixion on 14 Nisan or 15?

In view of the huge amount written on this subject and the large number of views expressed it is unwise to be too dogmatic. All too often it is affirmed that John and the Synoptic Gospels (Matthew, Mark and Luke) disagree over the date of the crucifixion. According to the Synoptic Gospels it was on 15 Nisan, the day after the Passover meal, that the Lord was crucified, but according to John it took place the previous day, 14 Nisan. From our standpoint there are only two possibilities: either the 15th is right and John has been misinterpreted, or the 14th is right and the Synoptic Gospels have been misinterpreted.

The position adopted here is that of George Ogg and the majority of expositors, that Christ died on 14 Nisan at about the time the lambs were being slain in the Temple. The opposing view has been vigorously defended by C.C. Torrey and others. Crucial to the whole question is the precise meaning of certain texts in John's Gospel. To these we now turn our attention.

John 13:1: "Now before the feast of the Passover, Jesus knowing that his hour was come that he should depart out of this world unto the Father, having loved his own which were in the world, he loved them unto the end."

This verse is in continuation of John 12:1 where we find the time-note "Six days before the Passover", and it is the preface to the next five chapters, John 13-17. Some would connect the words "before the feast of the Passover" with "Jesus knowing that his hour was come." That is, already before the feast He knew that the hour of His departure had come. More naturally they refer the principal verb, "he loved them unto the end." This He did at the Last Supper about to be related. "John here indicates clearly that that supper with all that Jesus did and said during and immediately after it took place before Passover," says George Ogg (1965: 76).

It is however open to question whether Ogg's confidence is fully justified. In Torrey's view this is "a tangled and awkward passage, which may be 'interpreted' in various ways ... the Greek text of 13:1 does not represent what the evangelist wrote ... The verse is absolutely useless as a support for the theory of his earlier dating" (1931: 229f.).

John 13:1 does say that the last supper, about to be described, took place "before the Passover", *unless* "before the Passover" simply anticipates the Passover meal about to take place. This is the view of Torrey: "The mention of the passover feast must have been made in mental anticipation of the 'supper' which is described in the next verses." In view of this ambiguity it would be unwise to place too much emphasis on this particular verse.

John 13:29: "Some supposed that, because Judas had the money-bag, Jesus was telling him, 'Buy what we need for the feast', or that he should give something to the poor."

When the disciples made this supposition, they did not imagine that Judas would go off immediately, in the middle of the night, but thought he would do what he had to the following day. "This shows that according to John the Last Supper was not the Passover meal" (Ogg: 88).

But again, it is begging the question to insist that "the feast" can only mean the Passover meal. It could equally well signify the Feast of Unleavened Bread which went on for another seven days. This is the position of Torrey who asks, "Does anyone suppose that the provision required to last thirteen able-bodied men through the festal meals of seven days were all purchased in advance?" Not unreasonably he finds the idea "a bit ridiculous". Once more, no far-reaching conclusion can be based on this verse.

John 18:28: "It was early, and they themselves did not enter the praetorium lest they should be defiled but might eat the Passover."

It is true that in Luke 22:1 the feast of Unleavened Bread is comprehensively termed "the Passover". Nevertheless, the expression "*eat* the Passover", without qualification, can only mean "eat the Passover meal", and the paschal lamb in particular. According to C.K. Barrett, "to eat the pascha is not an 'odd' phrase (if this means strange, or unusual), but a common one; that whenever it is used it means not 'to celebrate the feast or rite of Passover', but 'to eat the Passover lamb'"(1958: 305-7). He then proceeds to give the Old Testament evidence though, as he explains, "In many cases the verb 'to eat' has not 'the Passover' but a pronoun (directly referring, however, to the Passover) as its object."

Exodus 12:11, "eat it in haste: it is the Lord's Passover."
Exodus 12:43, "These are the regulations of the Passover: No foreigner is to eat it."
Exodus 12:46, "In one house it shall be eaten."
Numbers 9:11, "The fourteenth day of the second month at even they shall keep it .

With unleavened bread and bitter herbs they shall eat it."
Deuteronomy 16:6,7, "You will sacrifice the passover at even ... and you will roast and eat it."
2 Chronicles 30:18, "They did eat the passover contrary to what was written."
Ezra 6:20,21, "they killed the passover ... and the children of Israel did eat."

There are also numerous references in the book of Jubilees and the Mishnah, as well as the New Testament (Matt. 26:17; Mark 14:12,14; Luke 22:11,15), all with the same meaning. Hence, on the morning of the Crucifixion, the Jewish leaders had not eaten the Passover meal. Even if there should be the occasional passage in the Old Testament (as there are in the New) where "Passover" is used broadly of the feast as a whole, that does not alter the fact that *eating* the Passover is used exclusively of the Passover meal itself.

Some have tried to avoid the clear implication of John 18:28 by suggesting that the Jewish leaders had missed out on the Passover meal through pressure of business - the business of arresting and convicting the Lord Jesus Christ! According to Dr. H. Mulder, quoted by Hendriksen, "the text simply means that the members of the Sanhedrin had been so thoroughly pre-occupied with the arrest and trial of Jesus that they had not had time for their Passover meal." (Hendriksen: 403) If that were the case, one might have expected an explanation. It is certainly not the meaning which first springs to mind.

Others (Hoehner, Doig) have conjectured that the Passover night, 14 Nisan, was differently reckoned by different sections of the populace. The Galileans and Pharisees, reckoning the day from sunrise, ate the Passover a day before the Judeans and Sadducees who reckoned the day from sunset-to-sunset.

This is Hoehner's theory; Doig has a more sophisticated version. In the first century AD the Sadducees were firmly in control of the Temple and priesthood, and the day they recognised began at sunrise. Among the Diaspora however, and by the Pharisees, the day was reckoned to begin at sunset. There were therefore two calendars in use: the Temple calendar in which 14 Nisan began at sunrise and the Diaspora calendar by which it began at sunset. Following the Temple calendar, Jesus observed the Passover meal with His disciples in the evening of 14 Nisan and was crucified on the 15th. John however follows the Diaspora calendar used by the Pharisees. Their Passover took place the following evening, but because they were not permitted to slay the lambs on two consecutive days they observed a *Seder* instead, that is a surrogate Passover meal without a lamb. This is what is meant by "eat the Passover" in John 18:28. This was the situation in AD 30 when the Crucifixion took place according to Doig. In 33 however it could not have happened at all because in that year the new moon of Nisan 1 was first observed during the day before sunset, and Passover would have been on the same evening by both morning and evening reckoning (see Doig: 285-89).

While an explanation along these lines would solve the apparent contradiction between John's Gospel and the Synoptics, it is not a solution which I find convincing. It is ingenious and over-subtle. There is no firm proof that it ever occurred and, as Hoehner admits, "there is no explicit statement to support the view." The Jewish leaders had still to "eat the Passover", but this has no meaning if there was no paschal lamb to eat (see above), and these leaders included the Sadducees as well as the Pharisees.

According to Torrey, "It would be perfectly natural and idiomatic, in either Hebrew or Aramaic, to speak of 'eating the Passover festival,' meaning the sacrificial meals (*shelamim*) of the successive days." He refers to 2 Chronicles 30:22, "So they ate the feast, the seven days." But this is not a true parallel since the word for feast is *mo'ed* rather than *pesach*. On the face of it John 18:28 is strong evidence that the Passover meal had not been eaten on the morning of the Crucifixion.

John 19:14: "And it was the (day of) preparation (*paraskeue*) of the Passover."

Here also we should give precedence to the natural meaning, and undoubtedly that meaning is that this was the day before the Passover, the day on which preparation was made for the Paschal meal. The rival interpretation is that this was "the preparation-day in Passover week". This however is dismissed by George Ogg (p.77). He quotes C.K. Barrett who says, "The meaning of this phrase in Jewish literature is quite clear. It does not mean Friday ('eve of Sabbath') in Passover week, but 'eve of Passover', Nisan 14."

According to Leon Morris, "The fact must be faced that no example of the use of *paraskeue* is cited for any other day than Friday ... The evidence that the term was used for Friday must be accepted" (1971: 777n). Certainly it was used of the day before the Sabbath in Matthew 27:62, Luke 23:54, and Mark 15:42. It is also the day before the Sabbath in John (19:14,31,42) if it was on Friday that Jesus was crucified.

The fact that Josephus uses this word of the day before the Sabbath does not preclude its use in other connections. I am in agreement with Finegan that "the day of Preparation for the Passover must have been the day of getting ready for it, namely, the day on which the Passover lamb was slain, Nisan 14. This was the day on which Jesus also was put to death" (para 607).

John 19:31: "for great was the day of that Sabbath".

If Christ died on 14 Nisan, as we believe, then the day following was the first day of the Feast of Unleavened Bread, one of the highest days of the year. The best the rival interpretation can offer is that 16 Nisan was the day on which the *omer*, or first sheaf of barley, was waved before the Lord. But 16 Nisan was not itself a Sabbath or a day of supreme significance, but an ordinary working day. Once more it makes much better sense if the Crucifixion took place on 14 Nisan.

John 19:36: "these things took place that the scripture might be fulfilled, 'Not a bone of him shall be broken'".

There was a clear ruling that no bone of the paschal lamb should be broken (Exod. 12:46; Num. 9:12). Hence Jesus must have died on Nisan 14 as Israel's paschal lamb and no bone of His was broken in fulfilment of these scriptures.

But not so, says Torrey, an allusion to these verses cannot be proved. Even closer in its wording is Psalm 34:20, "He keeps all his bones; not one of them is broken", where the righteous are referred to and their deliverance from affliction. Here in the Septuagint version the words "shall not be broken" are exactly the same as in John 19:36. Hence an allusion to Psalm 34:20 is more probable. There can however be no evasion of 1 Corinthians 5:7 where the plain statement is found, "Christ, our paschal lamb, has been sacrificed."

What Matthew, Mark and Luke say

It is widely believed that Matthew, Mark and Luke are unanimous in teaching that the Last Supper was a Passover meal, and that no amount of hermeneutical ingenuity can avoid this conclusion. Leon Morris quotes with approval George Ogg's statement, "According to all three Synoptics it was for a Paschal Supper that Jesus ordered preparation to be made, and that the meal to which he subsequently sat down with his disciples was such a supper is what all three of them plainly intend their readers to understand" (Morris: 781f.) Ogg remained of this opinion, even though he regarded the Johannine chronology to be correct, and the Synoptics in error.

Likewise Howard Marshall, having reviewed the twelve arguments adduced by Jeremias for identifying the Last Supper with the Passover meal, concludes, "In our opinion points (3), (7), (9), (10) and (12) offer the evidence on which most weight can be placed, and it should be observed that point (12) belongs to the central core of the tradition about the meal ... The prima facie impression which we get from the Synoptic Gospels is thus confirmed when we dig below the surface of the narrative" (1980: 62).

The main points he adduces are as follows along with the answers I would give: (3) The meal was held in the evening, whereas the normal mealtimes for the Jews were in the morning and the afternoon. *Answer*: this was not a normal meal on an ordinary day; it could therefore have commenced in the evening. (7) Both Mark and Luke place the eating of the bread in the middle of the meal, rather than the beginning. This was unusual and corresponds with the order of the Passover meal. *Answer*: it is precarious to base too much on the order of events. In Luke (22:15-23) the words about who would betray Him and the institution of the Eucharist are reversed. (9) When Judas went out, the disciples thought he was going to buy what was needed for the feast or give to the poor (John 13:29). *Answer*: giving to the poor was not a one-off on Passover night, but an ever-present necessity funds permitting. (10) The fact that the meal ended with singing corresponds to the second part of the Passover *Hallel*. *Answer*: after such an important meal, "Jesus and his disciples may fittingly have joined in praise" (Ogg). (12) To interpret the significance of the bread and wine was the normal practice at the Passover meal. *Answer*: bread and wine were elements of every normal meal. The significance Jesus attached to them was very different from that of the Passover meal.

Having surveyed all Jeremias' arguments Ogg concludes, "Examination thus shows that the indications adduced by Jeremias are indications, not that the Last Supper was a Passover, but only that in some respects it resembled one. Taken in their totality they do not outweigh the united testimony of John 13:1; 18:28 and 19:14 that the Last Supper anticipated the Passover by twenty-four hours"(1965: 85f.).

In addition to these points, there is our Lord's statement, "My time is at hand; I will keep the Passover at your house with my disciples" (Matt. 26:18; Mark and Luke: "Where is the guest room, where I am to eat the Passover with my disciples?"). There can be no doubt that Jesus, on the Thursday evening when the Feast of Unleavened Bread commenced, instructed His disciples to make preparations for the Passover meal (Mark 14:12; Luke 22:7). He knew that He would never eat this meal in this life, but His disciples were not privy to this secret. It was essential that they should remain in ignorance of what was about to happen. So they prepared for the meal as if for the following evening. When Jesus utilised the room that same evening for the purpose of the Last Supper, their suspicions were still not aroused. They imagined it would be used again the following evening for the Passover proper.

But what of Luke 22:15-16?

Having sat down at the table Jesus said, "With desire I have desired to eat this passover with you before I suffer; for I tell you I shall not eat it (again) until it is fulfilled in the kingdom of God." The meaning of this saying depends on whether the word "again" (*ouketi*) is correctly omitted in some of the most ancient codices (Vaticanus, Sinaiticus, Alexandrinus). Finegan says, "The first and less well attested form of the saying supposes that he was actually then eating the real Passover meal. The second and much better attested form of the saying supposes that he wanted to do so but was unable. If the latter form of the saying represents the actual situation at the time, we may think that the Johannine record is literally correct in picturing the last supper as a meal held one evening prior to the real Passover meal" (para 613).

F.C. Burkitt paraphrased this saying: "Near as this Passover is and much as I have longed to celebrate it with you, it is not so to be, for I shall not eat it; within the next twenty-four hours the enemy will have done his worst and the next Passover that I shall eat with you will be the Messianic Feast" (1908: 569-72).

But many have thought it more probable that Jesus observed a genuine Passover, but that He did so a day early. Godet, an able defender of this view, paraphrases Matthew 26:18, "My death is near; tomorrow it will be too late for me to keep the Passover; let me celebrate it at thy house [this evening] with my disciples." Most recently this view is defended by R. T. France in his impressive commentary on Matthew's Gospel (2007: 982 ff.)

This idea was thoroughly canvassed by James Macnight back in 1809 and has had many followers since. According to Macnight, "in celebrating his last passover, Jesus did not observe the national day, but ate it the day before. Wherefore, as he was crucified the day after he solemnized the passover, his giving up the ghost about three o' clock in the afternoon of that day, happened just at the time when the passover was killed. By this means he who was the true passover, and who was sacrificed for us, as the apostle speaks, 1 Cor. 5:7, most exactly answered the type, as in every other particular, so in the very time also of its oblation"(1809: 102).

With most of this I am in agreement. However, there is a general consensus that it would not have been possible or permissible to observe the Passover a day before the national celebration. If the Last Supper was indeed an anticipated Passover meal, how is it that none of the apostles was aware of anything unusual? Their curiosity and suspicion would have been unavoidably aroused. Yet not one of them asked the Lord why He was acting in this way, what He was doing in observing the Passover meal a day early.

In the evening of 13 Nisan, as the first day of Unleavened Bread was beginning, Jesus sent Peter and John with instructions to prepare a room for the Passover meal, ostensibly for the following evening. This was perfectly in order, since to have left it till the following day would have left it too late. The disciples did as they were told without the least suspicion or alarm. This was what their Lord intended, since had they realised that He was in immediate danger of His life they would have done their level best to prevent Him from being arrested, Judas would have shied off from his clandestine plot, and the redemption of the world would have been complicated if not delayed. Even at the supper they were completely unaware that any mischief was afoot. If however their Lord had celebrated the Passover a day ahead of schedule, their suspicions would have been aroused, a profound unease would have come over the disciples, and many questions would have been asked.

Not a Passover meal

Contrary to what many scholars assert, it is far from obvious that the Last Supper was a Passover meal. In addition to the points already raised, we would draw attention to the following features.

The bread is called *artos*, the usual word for bread, not *azuma*, unleavened bread. There is no mention of a lamb or bitter herbs. The Passover was essentially a family occasion, but at the Last Supper there is no mention of women or children. The chief priests had resolved not to arrest Him during the feast (Matt. 26:5; Mark 14:2), but this is exactly what they did if this was Passover night. The carrying of arms was forbidden on the feast day, likewise the purchase of linen by Joseph of Aramathea (Mark 15:46). Simon of Cyrene had probably been working in the fields (Mark 15:21), which would not have been allowed at Passover. The burial of Jesus on the feast day would have been prohibited, but here all haste is applied to bury Him before sundown (Luke 23:54). There is, moreover, a Jewish tradition that Jesus was executed "on the eve of the Passover" (*Sanh*. 43a). And the apostle Paul describes the previous evening simply as "the night in which he was betrayed" (1 Cor. 11:23), not as "the night of the Passover", as might be expected if such it was.

With reference to John's record of the Last Supper J.B. Segal remarks:

In spite of his obvious knowledge of complex details of ritual, he (John) makes no mention of the preparation for the Passover or of the peculiar food eaten at the Passover or the order of service or the special prayers that distinguished the Pesah meal. The one detail that he does give – the washing of feet - is not in fact a feature of the Pesah meal, according to later Jewish practice; the other details of the Last Supper in John – reclining and dipping into a common bowl - would have occurred at any communal meal. On the other hand, alms are said by John to have been donated at the Last Supper; this might have taken place at any time before the Passover - but it could not have taken place at the Pesah meal itself, when money could no longer be employed for the festival requirements (1963: 37).

Segal is disposed to think that the Synoptics have transformed the Last Supper into a Pesah meal, but that they have not done it thoroughly. "The very fact that the most important component of the Pesah meal is not mentioned in the Synoptic Gospels is a clear indication that the identification of the Last Supper as a Pesah meal is an artificial device ... A Pesah meal at Jerusalem without the Pesah victim was meaningless - as long as the Temple stood" (245-46).

Finally, 15 Nisan was a holy convocation on which no manner of work was permitted except for the preparation of food (Exod. 12:16). "In it therefore", says George Ogg, "the carrying of arms by the arresting party (Mk. 14:43), the trial, condemnation and crucifixion of Jesus, and Joseph's purchase of linen (Mk. 15:46) are most unlikely occurrences. The bearing of arms on a day of Sabbath rest was forbidden by law (Shab. 6.24) which appears to have been already valid in the Maccabean period. The law (Bez. 5.2) also prohibited judicial procedure on the Sabbath and on feast days ..." (1965: 86).

Later he says, "The most telling objection to the Synoptic dating [that dating associated with the Synoptic Gospels] is the fact that it involves the desecration of a sabbatical feast day by actions compared with which, in the words of B. Weiss, 'all the violations of the Sabbath of which Jesus was accused would have appeared as trifles'" (89).

What was it then?

But if it was not a Passover meal, what in fact was it? One answer that has frequently been given is that it was a Passover *kiddush*. Ogg however will have none of this. "The Sabbath-*kiddush* ceremony", he says, "goes back only to the late Tannaite or perhaps the early Amorean period [second or third century]. Further the *kiddush* ceremony took place at the beginning of each Sabbath and religious festival, not twenty-four hours earlier. There cannot have been a Sabbath-*kiddush* on a Thursday evening, and a Passover-*kiddush* twenty-four hours before the feast began is 'a product of fancy for which there is no evidence'" (77).

There is no need to label the Last Supper with a technical name. All that needs to be said is said by Jack Finegan: "The Last Supper was not a Passover or other ritual meal of Judaism but a farewell meal of Jesus with his disciples, deliberately arranged by Jesus in view of the ominous developments of those days" (para 613).

The Hour of the Crucifixion

An interesting problem is presented by the respective time-notes in Mark and John as to the hour of the Crucifixion. According to Mark 15:25, "it was the third hour when they crucified him" (that is 9 am). But according to John 19:14, "it was about the sixth hour" when Pilate gave his verdict. It will help at this point to have a list of the time-notes in Mark's Gospel for the day of the Crucifixion.

> Mark 14:72 .. "cockcrow" - Peter's denial
> 15:1 ....   "early" - Jesus is taken to Pilate
> 15:25 ....   "the third hour" - they crucify Him

15:33 ....   ."the sixth hour" - beginning of darkness
15:33,34 ...   "the ninth hour" - end of darkness
15:42 ...   "evening" - Joseph asked for the body of Jesus

Since all these time-notes are approximately three hours apart it has been suggested that Mark may have thought in terms of quarters of a day and consequently that "the third hour" might mean any time between 9 am and noon. It is true that the ancients were nothing like so time-conscious as we are; there is nevertheless no documentary evidence for measuring time in quarters of a day by the naming of a single hour. Josef Blinzler significantly comments, "It is quite obvious that in 15:33 he is reckoning, not in quarters of a day, but in real hours. It is surely clear that he does not mean that the darkness began between twelve and three, and ended between three and six. No, what is meant is this: the darkness began at the hour when the sun stood at its zenith (cf. Amos 8:9) and ended three hours later, therefore it lasted from about midday until three o'clock" (1959: 266).

Turning now to John, we find the following indications of time:

John 18:27 ..   "cockcrow" - Peter's denial
18:28 ...   "early" - Jesus is taken to Pilate
19.14 ....   "about the sixth hour" - Pilate gives his verdict

The first two are in exact agreement with Mark; only the third is apparently out of line. The following proposals have been made.

1) John's time-note is only approximate: "about the sixth hour". Leon Morris comments, "People in antiquity did not have clocks or watches, and the reckoning of time was always very approximate. The 'third hour' may denote nothing more firm than a time about the middle of the morning, while 'about the sixth hour' can well signify getting on toward noon. Late morning would suit both expressions unless there were some reason for thinking that either was being given with more than usual accuracy" (801).

I would have thought the importance of the event itself, no less an event than the crucifixion of Christ, was sufficient reason for "more than usual accuracy", not to mention John's careful timing of other events which we shall be looking at in a moment.

2) On the strength of a variant reading it has been suggested that in John also the original reading was "the third hour", and that it was changed to the sixth hour by a writing error (a confusion of similar letters). But this is most improbable. The few manuscripts which show the third hour in John have obviously been "corrected" to bring them into line with Mark.

3) The third possibility is that John is employing modern or Roman time-reckoning, that is he is reckoning his hours from midnight as we do ourselves. The best known advocate of this solution among recent writers is Norman Walker (1960: 69-73). Walker draws attention to something that Pliny said in his *Natural History* (II,79, para 188): "The Babylonians reckoned from sunrise to sunset, the Athenians from sunset to sunset, the Umbrians from noon to noon, the common people everywhere from dawn to dark, the Roman priests and those by whom the civil day has been defined, as also the Egyptians and Hipparchus, from midnight to midnight."

It is, we believe, this Egyptian or Roman time that John is using in John 19:14, and in the other passages where he mentions the hour of the day. The other passages are as follows:

John 1:39: The two disciples who followed Jesus "stayed with him that day, for it was about the tenth hour." By Jewish hour-reckoning this would be 4 pm, too late surely for a day's stay. It was on the same day that Andrew found his brother Simon Peter and brought him to Jesus. 10 am allows time for these events whereas 4 pm does not.

John 4:6: It was "about the sixth hour" when the woman of Samaria came to draw water at Jacob's well. Noon was not a normal time for drawing water, the evening was. The best commentary on this is Genesis 24:11, where we read that Abraham's servant rested his camels by a well of water in the evening, *even the time that women go out to draw water.* Probably, therefore, it was six in the evening that the woman of Samaria came to draw water. She may have come rather earlier (or later) than the other women in order to avoid their unwelcome attention, but most unlikely that she would have come at noon.

It cannot very well have been 6 pm in the winter since by that time it would have been dark. In December and January sunset occurs at about 5 pm and darkness ensues almost immediately. We are thinking therefore of the summer months. But many have concluded from John 4:35 ("There are yet four months and then comes the harvest") that it was in fact December or January. We have therefore to decide: either it was not six o'clock in the evening or the saying just quoted is a proverb which Jesus quoted, not an indication of the time of year.

There are in fact clear indications in the text that it was not winter, but soon after Passover as implied in John 4:45. The Galileans welcomed him because they had seen all that He had done in Jerusalem at the (Passover) Feast, for they also had been there. Passover, therefore, was still fresh in their memory.

Leon Morris comments, "Jesus' request for water points to a time of heat. Moreover, four months before harvest there would have been plenty of surface water. A weary traveller would not depend on the charity of a chance acquaintance. A proverbial saying is rendered the more likely in that the introduction 'Say not ye' is not suited to a casual remark about the state of the crops" (Morris: 278).

There is no need to omit the word "yet" in John 4:35 (as does J.A.T. Robinson, 1985:133). What our Lord is saying is this: "You have a proverb to the effect that 'There are yet four months, then comes the harvest.' But I tell you, raise your eyes and look around, the fields are already white for harvest."

He then (v.37) quotes another proverb, "One sows and another reaps", referring probably to John the Baptist who had already done the sowing. By the month of May the barley harvest in the plain of Sychar would have been ready for reaping. So also was the harvest of souls around Samaria.

By this time John had changed his location. He was now baptising at Aenon near Salim in the region of Samaria (John 3:24). John had moved to a more congenial spot where water was plentiful, because of the unbearable heat in the wilderness of Judea as summer drew on. He could there expect many more people to come to him for baptism.

John 4:52: The nobleman asked at what hour his son began to recover, and the answer he received was "Yesterday at the seventh hour the fever left him." Seeing that Cana was about sixteen miles from Capernaum over hilly country, the nobleman is more likely to have arrived at seven in the evening than at one in the afternoon. It was moreover the following day that he returned to Capernaum. If it had been only one in the afternoon he would surely have returned the same day in his eagerness to find out whether his son had been healed.

John 19:14: It was about the sixth hour when Pilate said "Behold, your King!" But according to Mark He was crucified at the third hour! If it was 6 am when Pilate handed Jesus over, this leaves plenty of time for all the cruel preliminaries before the crucifixion itself (Mark 15:15-23; Luke 23:25-33).

This is the only solution which does justice to John as well as Mark. The only logical alternative is that of Jack Finegan who agrees with Josef Blinzler that "Mark 15:25 and John 19:14 are 'plainly unreconcilable' and Mark 15:25 can even be thought to be an 'interpolation'" (para 614). It is a mystery to me why anyone should prefer a situation where two verses of Scripture are "plainly unreconcilable" to one which provides an easy reconciliation to both of them and several others in addition!

It must be admitted however that scholarly opinion is generally against the midnight/noon mode of reckoning. Westcott, Wordsworth and Hendriksen are among those in favour of it, but Alford, Ramsay and most moderns support a sunrise reckoning as in the other Gospels. Making full allowance for imprecision, John's sixth hour cannot surely be *earlier* than Mark's third hour by the same mode of reckoning! But such it is on their interpretation. Finegan's verdict that the texts are "plainly unreconcilable" when interpreted in this way is fully justified. All this tends to confirm the midnight/noon interpretation. Here at least is an easy reconciliation of the two references that requires no forcing or emendation. And this is confirmed by the other time-notes in John's Gospel as Hendriksen has convincingly explained in his commentary on John's Gospel
Norman Walker mentions F.C. Cook and B.F. Westcott as having thoroughly discussed this idea back in the 1880s. He does not mention that it was also thoroughly discussed by James Macnight in 1809, and it would surprise me if he was the first. Macnight has this to say:

> It seems the Romans used both the civil and the natural form of the day. Pliny, in the passage quoted above, says, *"Omne vulgus a luce ad tenebras*: all the vulgar counted the hours from morning to night." This implies that the better sort did not do so. For he adds, that the priests, and those who spake of the civil day, reckoned from midnight to midnight, and by consequence computed their hours accordingly. To this agrees the account given by Varro. Nevertheless, it is reasonable to suppose, that in common conversation and familiar epistles, the language of the vulgar may have been adopted even by people of fashion, especially when they spake or wrote of labour, bathing, eating, and the like ordinary affairs of life. This accounts for the passages quoted above from Cicero and Martial, and for others not mentioned, particularly the letter of the younger Pliny to Calvisius, in which he gives an account of how Spurinna spent the day. Historians, however, and others who wrote with precision, in reckoning the hours of the day, would for the most part make use of the civil form: because the hours of the natural day were altogether uncertain, varying according to the seasons of the year (1809: 43).

But why should John resort to this mode of reckoning the hours of the day? Walker, I believe, is right in saying that "The Fourth Gospel differs from the other three in its purpose. For whereas the latter were written primarily for the edification of the faithful, the former was written primarily for the conversion of the Greek-speaking Jews of the Diaspora." That the Fourth Gospel was written with the Jews of the Diaspora in mind has been ably argued by J.A.T. Robinson in his various works on John's Gospel. Walker goes on to say that the use of 'modern' or 'Egyptian' hour-reckoning suggests either Alexandria or Ephesus as the area addressed. John wrote the seven letters of the Apocalypse to Diaspora Jews in Asia Minor (Rev. 2-3), and it is probably to them also that he addressed the Fourth Gospel.

The Year of the Crucifixion

AD 29 is a well established date for the first Passover of our Lord's ministry. Thereafter we have two alternatives. Either His ministry was a little over three years and He died in 32, or His ministry was a little over four years and He died in 33. In my youth I read Sir Robert Anderson's classic work *The Coming Prince*. In this work Anderson provides evidence from Daniel's prophecy of the Seventy Weeks that Israel's Messiah was cut off in AD 32, and from then on I was fully convinced that this year had to be correct. As we have seen, the first 7 + 62 weeks (483 luni-solar years) expired in AD 32, and the prophecy says "After the 62 'sevens', the Anointed One will be cut off." I reasoned therefore, as Anderson had done, that Christ, the Anointed One, was cut off in AD 32.

Daniel gives two terminal events for the 69 'sevens': in verse 25 "unto the Messiah the Prince" (*NIV*: "the Anointed one, the ruler"), and verse 26 "shall Messiah be cut off" (*NIV*: "the Anointed One will be cut off"). Anderson argued that "until Messiah the Prince" was fulfilled on Palm Sunday when the crowd cried out, "Blessed is the King who comes in the name of the Lord! ... Hosanna to the Son of David!" And six days after that He was cut off on the cross of Calvary. The fulfilment did not seem to admit of any doubt.

More recently it came to my notice that Anderson's calculations were not entirely correct. He does state the facts correctly to begin with: "in A.D.32, the date of the true new moon, by which the Passover was regulated, was the night (10h 57m) of the 29th March. The ostensible date of the 1st Nisan, therefore, according to the phasis, was the 31st March. It may have been delayed, however, till the 1st April; and in that case the 15th Nisan should apparently have fallen on Tuesday the 15th April" (pp.102 f.). Parker and Dubberstein agree that 1st Nisan in this year fell on 1st April.

However Anderson continues: "But the calendar may have been further disturbed by intercalation.... As, therefore, the difference between the solar year and the lunar is 11 1/4 days, it would amount in three years to 33 3/4 days, and the intercalation of a thirteenth month (Ve-adar) of thirty days would leave an epact still remaining of 3 3/4 days; and the 'ecclesiastical moon' being that much before the real moon, the feast day would have fallen on the Friday (11th April), exactly as the narrative of the Gospels requires" (p.103).

Anderson assumes that the "ecclesiastical moon" was four day ahead of the real moon, and accordingly that 15 Nisan fell that year on Friday 11 April instead of Tuesday 15 April. But this is not how it worked at all. In a leap year the first month, Nisan, was simply postponed by one lunar month. There is no question of it beginning before the phasis (appearance) of the new moon. The fiction of an ecclesiastical moon is simply an invention on Anderson's part. J.K. Fotheringham is certainly correct: "In 32 Nisan 14 should have fallen on Sunday April 13, or Monday April 14. It is absolutely impossible to shift this to a Thursday or Friday"(1943: 160). Anderson also erred in thinking the Crucifixion took place on 15 Nisan instead of 14 Nisan. If 14 Nisan is to fall on a Friday, the first of the month has to be a Saturday. But in AD 32 that was not the case, and accordingly 14 Nisan was not a Friday either.

In any given year there is no absolute certainty which month was reckoned as the first month in Judea. Could it be that these authorities have isolated the wrong month and that Nisan was really the month preceding? For that month Parker and Dubberstein give 2 March, a Sunday, as the first of the month. In that month the new moon did not rise in Jerusalem until about 9:30 pm on 29 February, and by that time 1st March would have already begun in Judea. The first of the new month might have been Sunday 2 March or Monday 3 March, but it cannot have been Saturday 1st March. Barring some very exceptional circumstance, 32 is the one year which astronomy appears to exclude completely as the year of the Crucifixion.

When however we turn our attention to AD 33 there is no problem at all. In that year 1st Nisan could well have been Saturday 21 March, and 14 Nisan, Friday 3 April. This month is given as Second Adar 32 by Parker and Dubberstein, but there is absolutely no reason why it should not have been counted as Nisan 33 by the Jews. It is therefore with good reason that many modern expositors have accepted 33 as the most probable year of the Crucifixion.

This is confirmed by Colin Humphreys and W.G. Waddington in their essay "Astronomy and the Date of the Crucifixion" (Vardaman: 169). According to them Friday, 7 April 30 and Friday,

3 April 33 are the only possible dates if it was on Nisan 14 that Jesus died. Since AD 30 is too early we are left with 3 April AD 33 as the only date which astronomy supports.

What therefore do we make of Daniel's prophecy that there would be sixty-nine 'sevens' "until Messiah the Prince" and that after that period Messiah would be cut off? This number of "sevens" totals 483 luni-solar years (=476 solar years) and they expired in Nisan AD 32, as Anderson has shown (p.128). It was then, we submit, that the nation was given a final opportunity to accept the Lord Jesus as their Messiah and Prince. Only after that year was finished was Messiah cut off in fulfilment of Daniel's prophecy: "After the 62 'sevens', the Anointed One will be cut off."

In that last year of ministry our Lord travelled up and down the country calling on the people to accept Him as their promised Messiah. Simon Peter accepted Him without reservation, "You are the Christ, the Son of the living God", and there were many others who did the same. But the response of the majority was that of the delegation in the parable, "We don't want this man to be our king" (Luke 19:14). This year was AD 32, the last year of the 69 'sevens', and Christ was cut off fourteen days after it had expired, on 3 April 33.

A Four-year ministry

That our Lord's earthly ministry was in fact four years long is more than hinted at in the parable of the Fig-tree in Luke 13:6-9. A man planted a fig-tree in his vineyard; he came seeking fruit on it and found none. He said to the vinedresser, "For three years now I've been coming to look for fruit on this fig-tree and haven't found any. Cut it down! Why should it use up the soil?"

The meaning is clear: it is God the Father speaking to His Son. The fig-tree symbolises Israel as elsewhere in the Bible, and the three years are those of Christ's ministry down to this juncture. The vinedresser replies, "Leave it alone for one more year, and I'll dig it round and fertilise it. If it bears fruit next year (lit: in the future), fine! If not, then cut it down."

Commentators have been reluctant to draw any chronological deductions from this passage. Many would agree with Archbishop Trench "that if the three years are chronological, the one year more, presently granted, must be chronological also; whereas not one, but forty years of grace were allowed to the Jews, before the Romans came and took away their name and place"(*Notes on the Parables*: 355).

My answer to that is the stay of execution suggested by this parable did not come to an end after only one year. The vinedresser said, "If it bears fruit *in the future*, fine. Otherwise cut it down." The reprieve is open-ended, not restricted to a single year. The future time referred to was in fact drawn out for nearly forty years. It was not until AD 70 that the fig tree was felled.

According to J.A.T. Robinson (1985:146f), the three years of the parable implies only two years on inclusive reckoning. "A further year of grace is requested as a last chance for repentance. But it was not taken." He thus finds confirmed his own predilection for a two-year ministry.

But the three years are clearly three successive seasons when the fig tree might have been expected to bear fruit. We should think therefore of three calendar years. As for the suggestion that the vinedresser's request for an additional year was *refused* (!), that requires no refutation. When did the Father ever refuse a petition by His Son? See John 11:22,42.

This parable of the Fig-tree cannot be considered apart from the cursing of the fig-tree in Matthew 21:18-19 and Mark 11:12-14. Here also we see a fig-tree on which our Lord "found nothing" but leaves only. By the month of April there should have been early figs, growing from the sprouts of the previous year. The absence of this fruit proved that the tree was moribund. The fruitless tree is straightway cursed and "withered at once". The occasion was after the triumphal entry into Jerusalem and within a few days of the Crucifixion. By this time the initial year of grace granted to the nation had expired. They were ripe for judgment, though in the Lord's forbearance the judgment itself was again postponed for a further 37 years.

A four year ministry is accepted by Thomas Lewin in his *Fasti Sacri* and by Johnston M. Cheney in *The Life of Christ in Stereo*. Lewin explains the parable of the Fig-tree in much the same way as I would explain it myself. These are his words.

Does not our Lord here plainly intimate that his ministry had already lasted three years without producing repentance, and that his labours would continue for one year more, and then that Jerusalem would be abandoned to its fate? The facts correspond with the parable. Our Lord opened his public ministry at Jerusalem at the Passover of A.D. 29. For the next three years he exercised his ministry in Judea and Galilee. Then, in the fourth year, he made his longest and most laborious circuit, and thus dug about the ground and dressed it in the hope of eliciting fertility; and at the end of the fourth year, that is, at the Passover of A.D. 33, he expired on the cross, and then closed his ministry with the dying words which might be applied to the fate of Jerusalem, 'it is finished!' (p.lxi)

The Four years

1) I assume that John the Baptist began his ministry in the autumn of 28 with the arrival of the rainy season. It was probably in January following that Jesus was Himself baptised. John's Gospel allows about two and a half months between His baptism and attending the Passover of John 2:13 (on 18 April, 29). Immediately after His baptism He was tempted in the desert for the space of forty days. After that He returned to the river Jordan and was seen by John the Baptist (John 1:29). Two days later (1:43) He resolved to go to Galilee. The journey to Galilee would have taken four to five days. The "third day" of John 2:1 would be the third day after His arrival, or the third day after the recruitment of Philip and Nathaniel.

This third day was the occasion of the wedding in Cana of Galilee. After the wedding, which may have gone on for seven days, He went to Capernaum where He stayed "not many days" (2:12, *ESV* "a few days"). The Passover was then at hand and Jesus went up to Jerusalem. That was the first Passover of His ministry.

2) Jesus' ministry in Judea is mentioned in John 3:22-36. This was before John the Baptist was imprisoned (3:24). How long He stayed there is not recorded, but it must have been long enough for Jesus to have made more disciples than John (4:1).

3) He then left Judea and set out for Galilee, passing through Samaria on the way (4:3-42). It was while in Samaria that He said to His disciples, "Do you not say, 'There are yet four months, then comes the harvest'?" (4:35). By quoting a familiar proverb He indicated that the fields were already white for harvest and the time of reaping had arrived (35-38). It was a time of year when it was still daylight at 6 pm (4:6), and the Passover was still fresh in the minds of the Galileans (4:45). It was probably June or July, 29.

4) By the time He arrived in Galilee John was already in prison. It is at this point that Matthew, Mark and Luke take up the story (Matt.4:12; Mark 1:14; Luke 4:14).

5) Beginning at Capernaum He made a series of tours, teaching and preaching in the towns and hamlets of Galilee, returning each time to "his own city" of Capernaum (Matt.8:5; 9:1). On one such tour, while going through the grain fields on the Sabbath day, His disciples ate some ears of corn, rubbing them in their hands (Matt.12:1; Mark 2:23; Luke 6:1). The time of year is early summer, the season of the grain harvest (wheat or barley), May or June, 30. The Passover in this year is not mentioned in John's Gospel, the first of two which he overlooks.

6) The Galilean ministry is recorded in John in only a few verses (4:43-54). It is recorded here that He healed an official's son residing in Capernaum. "After this" (*meta tauta*, an indefinite indication of time meaning "some time later"), He went up to Jerusalem for "a feast of the Jews" (5:1). This feast is unlikely to have been Passover since elsewhere Passover is called by its name. It could be Pentecost or Tabernacles. Either way, we are still in AD 30, whether it be spring or autumn.

7) In the next chapter it is Passover time again, the Passover of 31 (John 6:4). At this time occurred the Feeding of the Five Thousand, one of the few events recorded in all four Gospels (Matt.4:13-21; Mark 6:30-44; Luke 9:10-17; John 6:5-14.). There was "much grass" (John 6:10) and it was still green (Mark 6:39). After April it would have been scorched brown.

In the interests of a two-year ministry, so attractive to scholars, Doig considers the grain-plucking episode to have occurred about three weeks before "the second Passover" when Jesus fed the five thousand. It was however during this interval that Jesus summoned the Twelve and gave them authority over demons and to cure diseases (Luke 9:1; Mark 6:7). They had already returned from this mission before the feeding of the five thousand (Luke 9:10; Mark 6:30). A considerable period of time is implied. Besides, the grain-plucking episode was later in the year (May or June) than the feeding of the five thousand in March or April. Hence it must have been in the year following that Jesus fed the five thousand.

8) The events of April to October (Passover to Tabernacles) are summarised in only one verse in John, namely 7:1. During this time transpired the Galilean ministry as recorded in Matthew 15-18 and Mark 7-9. Jesus then went up to Jerusalem for the Feast of Tabernacles (John 7). After His brothers had left for the feast, Jesus also went up, not publicly but in secret. It is twice mentioned that His time had not yet come (7:8,30). Some have placed this journey during His last visit to Jerusalem (Luke 9:51 ff.), but the two journeys could not be more different, one hurried and secret, the other prolonged and public. It does not say that He returned to Galilee after the feast; He may have stayed in the vicinity of Jerusalem until the Feast of Dedication (10:22).

9) Jesus was still in or near Jerusalem the following December, since it was "at that time" that He attended the Feast of Dedication in the winter (on 25 Kislev, John 10:22). It was the winter of disbelief as well the season of winter. The Jews took up stones to stone Him and tried to arrest Him, but were unable to do so. He then withdrew across the Jordan to the place where John had first baptised (10:40). Jerusalem would not see Him again until His final visit fifteen months later.

10) Jesus' last visit to Jerusalem must surely have followed (rather than included) His previous visit. It must therefore have followed the Feast of Dedication in December, AD 31. If John was our only source of information, it would seem that Jesus stayed in the wilderness of Judea until going to Bethany to raise Lazarus. But we believe He returned to Galilee in the meantime, and from there set out on His last protracted journey to Jerusalem. In Matthew and Mark the journey does not seem very long (Matt.19:1-20; Mark 10:1-52). In Luke however the same journey occupies considerably more than a third of the Gospel (9:51-19:27). It is represented as one and continuous though punctuated by many diversions and delays. If His ministry was only three years, as most people would say, all this has to be fitted into the winter months, January to

March. A four-year ministry, on the other hand, allows plenty of time for this leisured, roundabout journey.

There is however a question whether the raising of Lazarus followed soon after the Feast of Dedication in AD 31 or took place over a year later, shortly before the last Passover in 33. An argument in favour of the first alternative has been found in John 11:8. The disciples here call in question Jesus' decision to return to Judea with the words, "Rabbi, the Jews were *just now* seeking to stone you, and are you going there again? (*ESV*). This verse looks back to 10:31-33 where, at the Feast of Dedication, the Jews had picked up stones to stone Him then and there.

The word "now" might seem to imply only a brief interval since the Feast, but it could also imply a rather longer interval as for example in Acts 7:52 where Stephen says, "And they (your fathers) killed those who announced beforehand the coming of the Righteous One, whom you have *now* betrayed and murdered." In John 11 the attempt to stone Jesus the previous year was still fresh in the disciples' memory and that is why they said, "Rabbi, *just now* the Jews were seeking to stone you."

Thomas Lewin believed that a year or more transpired between verses 54 and 55 of John 11. The words "Now the feast of the Jews was at hand", he says, "should have commenced a new chapter, as opening an entirely new subject and one separated by an interval of more than a year" (p.218). More naturally they follow on without a break. Jesus retired to the town called Ephraim, and there He stayed until the Passover. Six days before the Passover He went to Bethany "where Lazarus was, whom Jesus had raised from the dead" (12:1). There a dinner was held in His honour by Martha and Mary. It was not long before a crowd assembled, "not only on account of him but also to see Lazarus, whom he had raised from the dead" (12:19). This moreover was the same "crowd that had been with him when he called Lazarus out of the tomb and raised him from the dead." The reason they came was "that they had heard he had done this sign" (12:17-18).

All this proves that the feast at Bethany and the following Passover followed the raising of Lazarus after only a short interval. The break in the narrative occurs at the end of John 10 (not chapter 11). At this point the narrative moves forward to the last phase of Jesus' life and ministry, beginning with the raising of Lazarus. This, from the Jews' point of view, was the last straw; it triggered off the chain of events which lead inescapably to the Crucifixion. In the meantime Jesus returned to Galilee before setting out on His last extended journey to Jerusalem.

11) One of the first things He did was to send out the seventy (or seventy-two). He sent them on ahead of Him, two by two, into every town and district where He Himself was about to go (Luke 10:1). We are not to suppose that only 35 or 36 places were visited. Probably there were many more, all of which Jesus Himself visited later on. The mission of the Seventy, and the subsequent tour by our Lord, must have occupied many months. This was no whistle-stop tour, but one of reaping and gathering. The harvest was plentiful but the workers were few (10:2). In our view the entire journey took the best part of a year, the "one year more" during which the fig tree was dug around and fertilised (13:8).

According to Ramsay, "the historian is describing a general movement southwards, accompanied and complicated by many short journeys to and fro, up and down, 'through towns and villages teaching'. If he is Bethany in x., and at Jericho in xviii., and in Samaria in xvii., zigzag wanderings are clearly implied" (1898: 211). This was a leisured roundabout journey taking many months and ending with His passion.

12) John takes up the narrative again near the end of this journey. After raising Lazarus, Jesus went to a town called Ephraim and stayed there with His disciples (11:54). Ephraim was probably situated north-east of Bethel and about twenty miles from Bethany.

Six days before the Passover Jesus went to Bethany where Lazarus and his sisters laid on a dinner in His honour (12:1-8). Six days before Friday is Sunday, not Saturday. It was on the next day that Jesus made His triumphal entry into Jerusalem (12:12). It follows that the triumphal entry took place on Monday, not the traditional Palm Sunday. The Gospels nowhere say it was the first day of the week. This in Robinson's view, "is almost certainly correct. Otherwise Jesus and his disciples would have made the journey of over twenty miles [from Ephraim to Bethany] on the Sabbath, and there is no good reason for supposing that he would have breached the Sabbath law for this reason" (1985: 145f.). If the traditional Palm Sunday is to hold, Jesus must have died on Thursday rather than Friday.

Other arguments

Besides the parable of the Fig-tree, Thomas Lewin finds two other references which seem to him to indicate a four-year ministry. In Matthew 17:24 Jesus was asked to pay the didrachma, the Temple tax called the *korban*. This, according to the Mishnah tractate *Shekalim*, was due between 15 and 25 Adar. But in practice there was often considerable delay in collecting the tax, arising from the absence of some rate-payers and the inability of others. In consequence the tax was collected as opportunity arose, and especially before one of the great feasts when the arrears could be conveniently conveyed to Jerusalem.

Lewin thinks that Jesus must have already paid the tax for the year 30/31 since He had been in Capernaum both before the Feeding of the 5000 (Luke 7:1) and after it (John 6:24,59). It must refer therefore to the payment due for 31/32. It cannot have been the Adar immediately preceding the Crucifixion since, in Matthew 17, the long journey to Jerusalem had not yet begun. Hence it must have been the Adar of 31/32, before the journey began.

Lewin's second reference is Luke 13:1. Jesus is informed by some present at that time concerning the Galileans whose blood Pilate had mingled with their sacrifices. There is no external confirmation of this event, but it must have happened during one of Israel's great feasts since only then would the Galileans have been present in Jerusalem. It cannot have been Pentecost, argues Lewin, since Pentecost was too long before Luke 13, and the information was presented as news. Nor can it have been Tabernacles since Jesus was present at that feast and would have known about the outrage. It must therefore have occurred in the following year, at Passover or Pentecost, feasts which Jesus did not attend during His journey to Jerusalem. Ogg thinks it was Passover since only at Passover were the lambs slain by the persons who brought them (1971: 44). It could have happened therefore at Passover AD 32.

These arguments are too uncertain to carry much weight. I mention them only in passing.

Luke 3:23, "about thirty years of age"

We are told in Luke 3:23 *KJV* that "Jesus himself began to be about thirty years of age" at the time of His baptism. This has been taken to mean that Jesus was nearing His thirtieth birthday at the time in question. This is how it was understood by Irenaeus and Epiphanius in ancient times, and is allowed by Finegan (para 587). Plummer however pronounces this "impossible". Tyndale was right in translating, "Jesus was about thirty yere of age when He beganne", that is, when He began His ministry. But these words are uttered in connection with His baptism. It is therefore from the time of His baptism that His ministry is measured (cp. Acts 1:22), and it was then that He was about thirty years old.

It is assumed by most commentators that "about thirty years" allows for some leeway, though generally speaking the extent of this leeway has been left to presupposition and guesswork without any serious examination of biblical usage. In Lewin's view the meaning is "nearer thirty than forty or twenty" (1865: xv), and Paul M. Maier agrees: "Luke's 'about thirty' could well serve for any actual age ranging from 26 - 34 ... an age of 32 or 33 easily falls within the flexible parameter of *hosei*" (Vardaman: 22). Likewise H.W. Hoehner: "no more than two or three years on either side of thirty is feasible" (p.25). By and large the amount of leeway allowed has been determined by considerations outside this passage, such as the dates preferred for the Nativity and the beginning of our Lord's ministry.

Maier, however, in support of his view draws attention to other references of a similar nature: "about 5000 men" (Luke 9:14), "about 120" (Acts 1:15), "about 3000 converts" (Acts 2:41), "about 100 years old" (Romans 4:19), "about three months" (Luke 1:56). But all these, except for the last, are relatively high numbers. Exact enumeration is not expected in such cases, and the same applies to "about three months" where about 90 days is implied.

According to Dean Alford, "about 30" allows latitude in only one direction, *viz*. over 30, thirty being the appointed age for the commencement of public service, Numbers 4:3,23,43,47. But A.T. Robertson disagrees: "The Levites entered upon full service at that age, but that proves nothing about Jesus. God's prophets enter upon their task when the word of God comes to them" (*Word Pictures*: II, 45). While this is true, Jesus is unlikely to have begun His ministry before the age of thirty, especially if that was the appointed age for rabbis as well as priests. I agree with Doig that "Luke's statement fits best if Jesus was baptized while He was still thirty, earlier or later dates being less likely" (Doig: 162). It is possibly significant that Joseph and David were both thirty years old before entering public life.

The principles which determined Luke's employment of the word "about" may not be fully understood, but there is plenty of evidence that he often qualifies exact numbers by *hos* or *hosei*. He says of Jairus' daughter that she was "about twelve years old" (8:42), but Mark that she was "twelve years old" (5:42). He says that darkness came over the whole land at "about the sixth hour" (23:44), but Matthew that it was "the sixth hour" (27:45). He says that the Israelites wandered in the wilderness for "about forty years" (Acts 13:18), though in point of fact it was forty years almost to the day. If about forty years means precisely forty years, or as near as makes no difference, we cannot be far wrong in concluding that "about thirty years" means thirty years within at most a few months. In addition we find "about eight days" in Luke 9:28 and "about twelve men" in Acts 19:7, in neither of which is there room for uncertainty. This was also the view of Sir William Ramsay who wrote as follows:-

> Luke 3:23 tells us that Jesus appeared before the world as the teacher, when he was about thirty years of age. Now it is a characteristic usage in Greek to employ this vague expression, when there is no intention to imply doubt as to the age; it lies in the genius of the language to avoid positiveness in assertion, and to prefer less definite and pronounced and harsh forms of statement. It is unnecessary to think that Luke was really doubtful what was the age of Jesus, whether twenty-eight or thirty-two. His elaborately careful and precise dating, 3:1,2, may be taken as an indication that he had good and accurate information on the subject; that he 'had investigated all the circumstances accurately in their origin.' But, like a true Greek, he says 'about thirty', where the less sensitive barbarian of our northern island would use a rudely positive and definite number (1898: 197f.).

Luke, who claims to know the exact date of the Nativity (2:2) and the exact date of the public appearance of John the Baptist (3:1), was certainly in a position to know the exact difference between them!

If Christ was thirty years old in AD 28/29, one would assume he was born in 3/2 BC (3+28-1). This is the time approved by many of the early Fathers. Clement of Alexandria for example gives a very precise date, 18 November 3 BC (Finegan: para 488), or more probably 5/6 January 2 BC (Beckwith: 73). 3/2 BC is also indicated by Irenaeus, Tertullian, Julius Africanus,

Hippolytus, Origen, Eusebius, and Hippolytus of Thebes (Finegan: paras 487-495). Epiphanius prefers 2 BC when the consuls were Octavian for the thirteenth time and Silvanus. Finegan (para 500) concludes: "There is a remarkable consensus of the nine most important authorities for the year 3/2 B.C. So, from this evidence, the date of the nativity of Jesus is to be sought within the period of 3/2 B.C."

According to Josephus the death of Herod the Great (which in Matthew and Luke follows the birth of Jesus by less than 40 days as explained below) occurred some months after an eclipse of the moon and shortly before a Passover. There are only two eclipses which come within our frame of reference: 12/13 March 4 BC and 9/10 January 1 BC. The traditional view is that Herod died after the eclipse of 12 March and before the Passover on 11 April in the same year. The view taken in this work is that Herod died some considerable time after the eclipse of 4 BC and before the Passover of 3 BC. If that is correct, Jesus would have turned thirty in February 28 and would have been still thirty when His ministry began with His baptism shortly before His thirty-first birthday. If however He was born after the eclipse of 1 BC, as would have to be the case if that eclipse is chosen, He would have been only 28 or 29 at most.

Quirinius

Luke is well known for his accurate dating of historical events. But regrettably, what was intended as a concise and conclusive time-note for the Saviour's birth has become in process of time the topic for argument and disagreement!

In Luke 2:2 he tells us that the census, or enrolment, which took Joseph and Mary to Bethlehem was "the first enrolment", and that it took place "when Quirinius was governor of Syria" or "when Quirinius was governing Syria". This is a precise piece of information, but the only governorship of Syria known to history, exercised by Quirinius, was much later on, in AD 6.

It is known that Quirinius was governor of Syria in AD 6-7, and it was probably at that time that the uprising led by Judas the Galilean "in the days of the census" occurred, to which reference is made in Acts 5:37. Some have even surmised that Luke has confused this census with the earlier one when Jesus was born.

The situation is complicated by the fact that the governors of Syria for the period in question are now known and Quirinius was not one of them. They are listed as follows by Jack Finegan (para 522, Table 147):

Prior to 7 BC	M. Titius
7 or 6 - 2 BC	P. Quintilius Varus
4 BC - 2 BC	C. Sentius Saturninus
2 BC - AD 1	P. Quintilius Varus (a second term)
AD 1 - 4	G. Caesar

This is confirmed by Tertullian (Against Marcion 4:19) who says that the enrolment when Jesus was born was "taken in Judea by Sentius Saturninus", and for Tertullian that meant 3/2 BC. G.B. Caird observes, "Since Tertullian did not get this name from Luke, he must have had access to an independent, perhaps official, record."

Older commentators make reference to a slab of marble found near Tibur (Tivoli) in 1764, which bears a mutilated inscription concerning a Roman official who (among other things) "twice governed Syria as legatus of the divine Augustus." Though the name of the official is missing, it was thought by Sir William Ramsay, along with "all the highest authorities" of his day, that the indications were "sufficient to show with practical certainty" that this distinguished officer was none other than Publius Sulpicius Quirinius (1898: 228). But this identification has now been discredited. A far more likely candidate is Quintilius Varus. Varus was certainly governor of Syria in 1 BC, and Josephus says he had succeeded Saturninus in the previous summer (*Ant.* XV11.5.2(89)). Furthermore, the inscription was found about a quarter of a mile from Varus' villa at Tibur. Ernest Martin explains the situation at length (1998: 181-199), and Finegan is in agreement (para 522).

How then should we explain Luke 2:2 which says that Quirinius was governor (or governing) Syria at the time of the first enrolment? The most reasonable explanation is that Quirinius was the administrator for Syria (which included Palestine) with special responsibilities for this particular enrolment. Justin Martyr (Apol.1.34) says Quirinius was the Roman Emperor's "first procurator in Judea". And Martin, quoting *The Cambridge Ancient History* (Vol. X, p.216), says that "Each province had its equestrian procurator who in the eyes of the provincials was almost as important as the governor himself."

The words translated "governor of Syria" could just as well be translated "was governing Syria". In fact the same word is used of Pilate in Luke 3:1, "while Pontius Pilate *was governing* Judea." Quirinius and Pilate were both *Hegemon* in the sense of procurator. Martin says, "The word *hegemoneuontos* could refer to any type of rulership from that of an exalted President or a military commander on down through various lesser officers to that of the local dog catcher for the city. The word could very well refer to the fact that Quirinius was a procurator as Justin Martyr attests" (p.196).

Ramsay was prepared to admit the legitimacy of this interpretation. This word, he says, "might be applied to any Roman official holding a leading and authoritative position in the province of Syria. It might quite naturally denote some special mission of a high and authoritative nature; and many excellent authorities have argued that Quirinius was despatched to Syria on some such mission, and that Luke, in assigning the date, mentions him in preference to the regular governor" (1898: 229).

Lower down he mentions the idea "that Quirinius was one of a number of commissioners, appointed by Augustus to hold the enrolment throughout the Roman world, Quirinius being the commissioner for Syria and Palestine." "This theory", he says, "is possible; - it offends against no principle of Roman procedure or of language. It may be the truth" (p.248).

The occasion of this particular census may have been connected with the bestowal on Augustus of the prestigious title of Pater Patriae, Father of the Fatherland, which he received on 5 February 2 BC. E.L. Martin says, "For the totality of the citizenry to approve the bestowal of the Pater Patriae must have involved an Empire-wide accounting. Since Augustus was officially given the award in early 2 BC, the registering of the citizens must have been decreed and begun to be carried out sometime in 3 BC" (Martin: 189). Alternatively it may have been a tax in aid of the military might of Rome (so Doig), or for the maintenance of public works and services throughout the empire. According to Dio Cassius the decree of 6 AD was the second attempt at such a tax. The first may have been that of 3 BC (Doig: 100-103).

One other possibility deserves a mention since it has the support of experts in Greek idiom such as Nigel Turner (*Grammatical Insights into the New Testament*: 23-24) and F.F. Bruce (*New Testament History*: 30 n.1). It has also the support of Doig and Hoehner. Bruce translates Luke 2:2, "This enrolment was before that made when Quirinius was governing Syria." The census under Quirinius in AD 6-7 was the one which everyone remembered. Luke here informs us that there was a census before that one and that this earlier census was the occasion of Joseph and Mary going to Bethlehem.

That this translation is grammatically possible cannot be denied, but to say it is contextually appropriate is another matter entirely. The identical construction recurs in Luke 3:1, "Pontius Pilate being governor of Judea." The meaning in 2:2 must surely be the same: "Quirinius being governor of Syria." These are the only two places where *hegemoneuontos* occurs in the Greek New Testament. A reference to a census or governor nine years later is clearly out of the question. Compare also Acts 18:12 where the same genitival construction appears: "Gallio being proconsul of Achaia."

The time of year

Ramsay also discusses the time of year when the census is most likely to have taken place. The winter months, he says, had to be avoided. "As the day had to be fixed a long time beforehand, it must have been fixed in the season when good weather could be calculated on. In winter, weather might be good or it might be bad, and at the best it would be cold and trying." Furthermore, "it was urgently necessary that the time which was fixed should not interfere with agricultural operations - that it should not come between the earliest date for the first harvest and the latest date for finishing the threshing, and getting in the grain and the fine cut straw from the threshing floors." He concludes "with considerable confidence" that August to October is the period to be considered (1898: 192f.).

On most matters I am in close agreement with Ramsay, but in this instance I must beg to differ. There is evidence in Matthew and Luke that Jesus was born about thirty days before the death of Herod, while Herod himself according to Josephus died a short time before a Passover. This points to February as the most likely month in which Jesus was born. This might also have been a suitable time to hold the census. The barley harvest would not have begun and the weather would have been cool for travelling if a little wet.

Lance Lambert has written, "It is this rainy season which makes Israel a paradise of flowers in the months of February and March. For a few weeks the whole land becomes a riot of colour and scent, the air filled with the song of birds and the hum of insects. This annual miracle of resurrection never fails to capture the imagination of all who witness it." And again: "The wilderness also turns to green and is covered with many kinds of flowers; and even the desert blossoms. It is an unforgettable experience to smell its scent-laden air in February and March" (*The Uniqueness of Israel*, 25-26).

More to the point, the fields would have been teeming with new-born lambs, most of them destined to be sacrificed in the Temple. This surely is the most appropriate and welcoming time of year for the Lamb of God to be born, far more so than the hot summer months when the weary traveller is faint with thirst and dehydration as Jesus was by Jacob's well in Samaria (John 4:6). No pregnant woman would have wanted to travel in the summer heat, least of all one soon to give birth. The suitability of February will be explained more fully in connection with Herod's death and the coming of the Magi.

The course of Abijah

Luke informs us that Zachariah, father of John the Baptist, belonged to the priestly course of Abijah, and that his course was on duty when the angel of the Lord appeared to him (Luke 1:5-11). The angel told him that his wife Elizabeth would bear him a son whose name was to be John. What he heard seemed incredible to Zachariah in view of his age and that of his wife, and for this lapse of faith his voice was taken away and he remained dumb until the fulfilment of the promise. We are further informed by Luke that it was in the sixth month of Elizabeth's pregnancy that the angel Gabriel appeared to the virgin Mary (1:26).

Five months had elapsed (1:24) and the sixth month had begun. Jesus therefore was about five months younger than John the Baptist, and about 14 months would have elapsed between Zachariah's term of duty and the birth of the Saviour. This prompts the inquiry whether it is possible to work out the approximate time of Jesus' birth from the time that the course of Abijah was on duty in the Temple. Though nothing very conclusive can be expected, the inquiry is nevertheless worth pursuing.

The twenty-four priestly courses are enumerated in 1 Chronicles 24. We there learn that the courses were chosen by lot from the descendants of Eleazar and Ithamar, Aaron's two surviving sons. Since a larger number of leaders were found among the descendants of Eleazar, sixteen were chosen from Eleazar's family and eight from Ithamar's. From the list of names provided it can be seen that the first lot fell to Jehoiarib and the eighth to Abijah, to whose course Zachariah belonged. From 2 Chronicles 23:8 it is evident that the courses officiated in orderly succession, a week at a time, from one Sabbath to the next.

After the return from exile only four of the original families were accounted for: Jedaiah (the ninth), Immer (the sixteenth), Pashur (the fifth), and Harim (the third), Ezra 2:36-39. But by the time of the high priest Joiakim, Jeshua's successor, the number had risen to twenty priestly families, of which eight, including Joiarib and Abijah, correspond to names in 1 Chronicles 24. From these a new set of 24 courses was instated, called by their original names, and the cycle of weekly duties was resumed as before.

Unfortunately the specifics of how the courses operated and in which month the cycle began are not mentioned in the Bible, and even the Jews themselves seem to have forgotten these details within a hundred years of the fall of Jerusalem in AD 70. As a result scholarly opinion is divided and a number of conflicting assumptions have been made to explain how it worked. There are three in particular which are confidently asserted by scholars today.

1) A saying of Rabbi Abbahu (c. AD 300) recorded in the Jerusalem Talmud seems to imply an unbroken succession of courses continuing year after year without interruption. This was adopted by Thomas Lewin, Henry Browne, Alfred Edersheim, and most recently by Kenneth Doig.

Doig draws attention to Ezra 6:15,18 where we learn that "the priests in their divisions and the Levites in their divisions" were set in motion after the dedication of the Second Temple in Adar 616 BC (=12 March 515). Thereafter he thinks they ran without a break except during the disruption caused by Antiochus Epiphanes, 167-164 BC, and probably twice again during the rule of the Pharisees. There was however no interruption from at least 67 BC to AD 70.

There is a saying attributed to Rabbi Jose ben Halafta (c. AD 150) which says, "Fortunate things happen on a fortunate day, and evil things on an evil day. For as the First Temple was destroyed on a Sunday, the year after a sabbatical year, when the course of Jehoiarib was on duty, on Ab 9, so it was with the Second Temple."

Working back from Saturday, 4 August AD 70, when Jehoiarib (the first course) was on duty, Doig calculates that the course of Abijah, the eighth course, would have served from 3-10 September 5 BC. If Elizabeth conceived on 10 September, Jesus might have been born 63 weeks (14.5 months) later, on 25 November 4 BC (see Doig: 125). The course of Abijah would also have served from 18-25 February 4 BC. If 63 weeks are added to 25 February, we arrive at 3 May 3 BC. Neither of these dates is of any help to us.

2) A Midrashic saying attributed to Rabbi Hiyya (c. AD 200) seems to imply that the cycle began anew each Nisan, the ecclesiastical new year when the Temple services commenced (Exodus 40). Working on this evidence, it is assumed by Ernest Martin and Floyd Jones that two full cycles were completed each year, beginning respectively in Nisan and Tishri. This would account for 48 weeks in an average Jewish year of 51 weeks. However, during the three major festivals, Passover, Pentecost and Tabernacles, "all the priests that were present did not then wait by course" (2 Chron. 5:11), or, as the *NIV* makes clear, "All the priests … consecrated themselves, regardless of their divisions." During these three weeks the sequence of courses was suspended while all the priests worked together.

According to Martin the first course came on duty on the Sabbath day before 1st Nisan, but Jones thinks it was the first Sabbath after 1st Nisan. This however need not delay us since, according to Jones (p.212), 1st Nisan in 5 BC was in fact a Sabbath. Assuming that to be the case, the course of Abijah would have served during the tenth and thirty-fifth weeks of the year, making allowance for the three festival weeks when they all served together.

In 5 BC the tenth week was 4-11 Sivan (= 10-17 June) and the thirty-fifth week 2-9 Kislev (= 3-10 December). In view of his dumbness Zachariah would have been disqualified from further service in the Temple (Lev. 21:16-23). John Lightfoot, commenting on this passage, says, "in the Jews' Canons, *harash* is one of five sorts of persons, that they commonly exclude from all employments and matters of honour, trust, or import; and it means, 'one that can neither hear nor speak'"(Vol.III,22). Zachariah was deaf as well as dumb (Luke 1:62). In view of his impediment he would have been sent home immediately and Elizabeth may have conceived soon after. If she conceived in June, John would have been born nine months later, in March 4 BC, and Jesus five months after that, in August 4 BC. If she conceived in December, Jesus might have been born in February 3 BC.

3) A third scenario is offered by Roger T. Beckwith with the support of Jack Finegan. Beckwith thinks he has found proof that the cycle began in Tishri, the civil New Year, rather than Nisan, the ecclesiastical New Year. It is the saying of Rabbi Jose ben Halafta, already quoted, which provides the evidence. He finds in that saying proof that Jehoiarib, the first of the 24 courses, came on duty on Saturday 8 Ab in AD 70. Working back from this date through two complete cycles of 24 priests, assuming that AD 69 was a leap year (it does not work if 69 was not a leap year), it turns out that the first course began on 27 Elul, the Sabbath before 1st Tishri AD 69. For Beckwith this creates a strong presumption that the cycle began on the Sabbath day preceding 1st Tishri, this being the month when the Temple services were resumed in the time of Ezra (Ezra 3:1-6) and the month when Solomon's Temple was dedicated (1 Kings 8:2; 2 Chron. 5:3). See Beckwith: 79-87.

The courses he reckons continued without a break for two complete cycles and a little more, and then began again with the first course on the Sabbath before the next 1st Tishri. The courses did indeed minister all together during the three great festivals, but the regular sequence was not interrupted. The course on regular duty would have served as usual while the remaining 23 priests would have performed all the additional duties required of them during the feast.

Beckwith reckoned that the course of Abijah came on duty each year on the Sabbaths falling on or about 17 Heshvan and 8 Iyyar (Finegan, para 471). Its term of service would have ended a week later, on about 24 Heshvan and 15 Iyyar, which correspond in 5 BC to 25 November and 22 May. If to these are added on 14 months we arrive at January/February and July/August 3 BC. Again, the January/February slot would agree well with our chronology.

Beckwith criticises the first possibility, that of Lewin and Doig, on the grounds that it "gave them no yardstick for checking which course ought to be on duty at a particular time, should doubt or disagreement arise." It is difficult to see how this system could have operated without confusion. In the event of a dispute there would be no resolution by reference to the calendar. But Beckwith's theory is also open to criticism, since it breaks down if AD 69 was not a leap year. 1st Nisan in AD 70 fell on 1st April according to Parker and Dubberstein. A leap year in 70 or 71 would have been imperative, but barely possible in 68 or 69, on the information provided by Parker and Dubberstein.

I conclude therefore that the second possibility, that of Martin and Jones, is the most probable. This interpretation was defended by John Lightfoot in the seventeenth century and has had many supporters since. It does not explain, however, how Jehoiarib, the first course, could have been on duty in Ab, AD 70. It must be assumed that Rabbi Jose's saying is a pious tradition with no basis in fact. Nor does it explain what happened in a leap year. Maybe four priests were chosen by lot to fill in the interval.

Nothing is proved by this exercise; there are far too many areas of doubt. But at least the available evidence is compatible with a February nativity which is the month required by other lines of inquiry.

His star in the East

The Magi were wise men from the east, but there is no agreement as to what their function precisely was or where exactly they came from. It is assumed that they were astrologers who had preserved a correct understanding of the primitive gospel contained in the signs of the Zodiac. The star itself may have been a unique and miraculous event or it may have been a rare celestial marvel whose profound significance only the Magi were permitted to understand. There was, it seems, a great abundance of stellar activity around this time. Martin devotes a large part of his book to describing these astral displays in 3 and 2 BC. But from our point of view they are all too late. If Jesus was born in March 3 BC, the star ("*His* star", Matt.2:2) would have had to appear in the autumn of 4 BC to allow time for the Magi to make their way to Jerusalem, assuming they came from Babylon or Persia.

Moreover, the widely-held notion that Jesus was at least a year old and possibly fifteen months when the Magi arrived is contradicted by Matthew and Luke, as Floyd Jones has shown (pp.214-17). The sequence of events is there clearly set out when the record is taken at its face value.

1) News of the Saviour's birth was conveyed to the Shepherds on the same day that Jesus was born (Luke 2:11). They went immediately to Bethlehem while Jesus was still "lying in a manger."

2) The Magi arrived a few days later. This is implied in Matthew 2:1, and is confirmed by their question, "Where is he that is born king of the Jews?" By this time Joseph and Mary were in a house (Matt.2:11), but this need not imply that many days had passed. They would have moved to more salubrious accommodation at the earliest possible opportunity, even the very next day. They may have moved only from the animal quarters to the living quarters in the same building. As soon as the census was over most people would have left, leaving plenty of room in the inn.

Another argument which is frequently invoked is that in Matthew Jesus is called *paidion*, a child, whereas in Luke He is called *brephos*, an infant. Jesus therefore had ceased to be an infant by the time the wise men arrived. *Paidion*, however, can mean a child of any age like its English equivalent. In Luke 1:59 it is applied to John the Baptist when eight days old, and again in verses 66 and 76. It is used of Jesus by the Shepherds in Luke 2:17 and when He was forty days old in 2:27. It is also used of Moses when still a baby in Hebrews 11:23 and of a child just delivered in John 16:21. It is true Jesus *could* have been older, but no proof of this is provided by Matthew's use of *paidion*.

3) As soon as the Magi had departed Joseph was told by the angel to flee to Egypt because of Herod's intention to murder the infant King. Jesus was probably circumcised in Bethlehem before the family left for Egypt. It was at least 150 miles to the nearest point in Egypt (France: 79), so this journey might have taken ten or twelve days or even longer depending on their mode of transport.

4) Not many days later Herod "sent and killed all the male children in Bethlehem and in all that region who were two years old or under" (Matt.2:16). But why did he include the children of two years if Jesus was only a few days old? He did so, Matthew tells us, "according to the time he had ascertained (carefully inquired) from the wise men." The information he had thus ascertained related to the time of the star's appearing (Matt. 2:7). He seems to have thought that the infant King was born at the time of the star's first appearing, and that might have been six months to a year before the arrival of the wise men. If Herod raised the age to two, it was to provide a safe margin and to ensure that no child slipped through the net because of doubt concerning his age. It was after all an irrelevance to him how many children he killed, so long as the one he wanted dead was among them. There is no need to assume Jesus Himself was approaching two.

5) Herod died about a month later, probably less (Matt.2:19).

6) When the time came for their purification, Joseph and Mary brought Jesus to Jerusalem to present Him before the Lord (Luke 2:22). The time appointed for a male child was forty-one days after birth (Lev.12:1-4). They must have returned from Egypt in time for this ceremony, Herod having died in the meantime. These forty-one days are crucial.

7) After the ceremony they returned to Galilee, to their home town of Nazareth (Luke 2:4,39; Matt.2:19-23). The view is often expressed that the family returned to Bethlehem after the ceremony and that the Magi arrived soon after that, but this flies in the face of Luke 2:39. According to Luke "they returned into Galilee, to their own town of Nazareth", *not* to Bethlehem. Alfred Plummer says, "There is no improbability in Joseph's going back to Bethlehem for a while before returning to Nazareth." Humanly speaking perhaps not, but the Bible does not speak of a return to Bethlehem. According to Matthew 2:22 Joseph was afraid to go to Judea out of fear of Archelaus, Herod's son, and being warned in a dream he withdrew to the district of Galilee.

In order to get to Galilee they would have had to pass through Judea, and we know they stopped off at Jerusalem on the way for the ceremony of purification. But they did not stay or linger in Judea, but travelled as quickly as possible to Nazareth.

According to Kenneth Doig, the holy family revisited Bethlehem when they returned to Jerusalem for the feast of Passover (Luke 2:41), and it was then that the Magi made their appearance. But this again is pure speculation. What reason had they to return to Bethlehem after the census was finished with? I prefer to believe that the One who directed the star knew what He was doing, and that the Magi arrived at the right place at the right time, exactly when Jesus was born!

The visit of the Magi is most unlikely to have occurred when Jesus was a year old. At most He can have been only a few days. The star which prompted the Magi's departure, and showed them the way, may have been a miraculous event. Alternatively, it may have been one of the many planetary conjunctions which lit up the sky around that time. Martin mentions many such conjunctions but they are all too late. Every chronologist seems to have his own comet or supernova to agree with his own Nativity date. If an explanation along these lines is to be sought, someone who knows about these matters must provide the answer. It was in any case *His* star, one uniquely associated with Him and recognised as such by the Wise Men.

The death of Herod

For us the importance of Herod's death consists in the fact that he died within only a few weeks of the birth of the Lord Jesus. In fact he cannot have outlived the Nativity by more than about thirty days if Joseph and Mary were to travel from Egypt to Jerusalem in time for the ceremony of purification only forty-one days after the birth.

There are two fixed points which are crucial for determining the date of Herod's death, the first being an eclipse of the moon which occurred on the very night that the high priest Matthias was burnt to death on the orders of Herod. Josephus (*Ant.* XVII.6.4(167)) relates how certain young men at the instigation of two eminent rabbis, Judas and Matthias, pulled down in broad daylight (thinking that Herod was dead) a large golden eagle which the king had erected over the great gate of the Temple. Herod however was not dead, and being furious at the effrontery of these men had Matthias and his companions burnt alive. "And that night there was an eclipse of the moon."

This eclipse has been identified with the lunar eclipse in the night of 12/13 March, 4 BC. After this there was not another eclipse until that on 10 January, 1 BC. The eclipse of 10 January, 1 BC has gained popularity through the writings of E.L. Martin and its acceptance by Jack Finegan, but it is difficult to reconcile with the chronology of Herod's reign and that of his successors. The evidence still points to Herod having died in 4/3 BC as persuasively argued by Kenneth Doig.

The eclipse of 12/13 March, 4 BC is confirmed by the fast which Josephus mentions as having occurred the day before Matthias was burnt. This fast can be identified with the Fast of Esther on 13 Adar, which immediately preceded the festival of Purim on 14 and 15 Adar. 13 Adar was the day decreed for the destruction of the Jews by the wicked Haman (Esther 3:13) and was observed as a fast by the Jews. In 5/4 BC, 13 Adar fell on 11 March, the day before the eclipse. The correctness of this eclipse is thereby confirmed.

The second fixed point is the Passover which followed Herod's death by only a few weeks. If this Passover was that of 4 BC, as is generally assumed, there were only thirty days between the eclipse on 12 March and the Passover on 11 April. Furthermore, Herod's last year of reign did not begin until 1st Nisan 4 BC (28 March). Hence Herod cannot have died before 2 or 3 Nisan, nor indeed any later if the events subsequent to his death are to be squeezed in before the Passover. This allows only two and a half weeks for the events following the eclipse down to the death of Herod, and a mere nine or ten days between his death and the Passover. It is not difficult to appreciate that this schedule is impossibly tight.

Immediately after the eclipse Herod's condition became noticeably worse. His physicians tried "one remedy after another." They then suggested that he should try the mineral baths at Callirrhoe on the Dead Sea. But this therapy also proved ineffective and Herod was conveyed back to Jericho. Having no longer any hope of recovery Herod summoned all the provincial Jewish elders, "principal men of the entire nation, wheresoever they lived", to Jericho without stating any reason for their presence being required. When they arrived he locked them up in the hippodrome intending to have them executed as soon as he had died. He did not want the nation to rejoice at his death (as he knew they would), so he would give them cause to mourn and lament! Such was his state of mind. After this letters came from Augustus permitting Herod to kill Antipater, his seditious son and heir. This news revived him for a while, but he relapsed soon after and attempted suicide. He died himself five days after Antipater's demise.

Most of the action takes place at Jericho and Callirrhoe which would suggest the winter months. However, it is almost impossible to fit all these events into the sixteen days between 13 and 29 March, 4 BC. They "make a very tight schedule", as Doig remarks (p.81).

If this schedule is tight, the schedule following Herod's death is tighter still, tight to bursting point. Herod's funeral was to be the grandest ever bestowed on a king, his final resting place being the Herodium, a fortress-palace about eight miles south of Jerusalem. The elaborate preparations must have taken some days. The funeral procession travelled on foot at the rate of eight stadia (one Roman mile) on the first day and then on to the Herodium at a normal pace. Herod's burial was followed by seven days of mourning by Herod's family. This was called *shivah* and was normally reckoned from the day of burial.

When this was over Archelaus, Herod's successor, addressed the people in a conciliatory manner. But this only encouraged the people to press for their demands all the more forcefully. These Archelaus granted in order to gain their goodwill. One of their most persistent demands was that the high priest appointed by Herod should be replaced by one more agreeable to the law and of greater purity. Archelaus again complied with their wishes although "mightily offended at their importunity." This however failed to appease the crowd who now clamoured for revenge on the murder of Matthias.

The Feast of Unleavened Bread was now approaching, when the people came up from the provinces in great numbers to worship God. This invasion began "on the eighth day of the month Xanthicus [Nisan]" (*Wars* VI.5.3). Doig remarks, "If Nisan 8 here follows the prior events that began the earliest on Nisan 9, then this cannot have been the same Passover." Moreover, the high priest had to be replaced before 8 Nisan to allow for the mandatory seven days of purification before he could officiate at the Passover. His replacement cannot have been later than 7 Nisan, but Archelaus was still in mourning on that day. Again, "this Passover cannot have been that of 4 BCE."

Doig's conclusion must surely be accepted. "All of the above events could have extended from the eclipse over a year to the following Passover of 3 BCE. There is no requirement that worsening illness, trips to Callirrhoe and Jericho, and subsequent death be compressed into sixteen days. A period of months is an acceptable and preferable interpretation" (p.83).

The same conclusion was arrived at more than a century ago by Sir Robert Anderson. Writing in *The Coming Prince* he said, "The history establishes conclusively that Herod's death was more than fourteen days before the Passover, and therefore *at the close and not at the beginning of the Jewish year.*" And again, "The natural inference from the history is that the death was not weeks but months after the eclipse, and therefore, again, at the *close* of the year" (1895: 261f.). Like Doig he concluded that Herod died before the close of the Jewish year 4 BC, that is before 17 March 3 BC.

This conclusion is significantly confirmed if Doig's analysis of contemporary coins is correct. On the basis of this evidence he says, "according to contemporary coins, year 1 of Herod Antipas and Philip [Herod's sons] was measured from Tishri (or Dios) of 4 BCE. When this dating is lined up with Josephus' reckoning from Nisan 4 BCE, then Herod the Great must have died after Tishri of 4 BCE, but before Nisan of 3 BCE. Herod died between September 22, 4 BCE and March 17, 3 BCE." (p.92). If Doig is right here, Herod cannot have died in Nisan 4 BC but at some point later than 1st Tishri.

For the exact date of Herod's death there is no reliable record. There is however a marginal note in the Jewish tractate *Megillat Ta'anit* (Scroll of Fasting) which Doig is prepared to accept. Here there are listed days when fasting is appropriate, but it also includes two days when no mourning is permitted, namely 7 Kislev and 2 Shebat. Against 7 Kislev a Jewish commentator, of the seventh century it is thought, has appended the note "on that day Herod died." This notation has not been generally accepted, but it is nevertheless the only date on record for Herod's death. It corresponds to 27 November in 4 BC. If Herod died on 27 November, Jesus would have been born about a month earlier. By AD 28/29 He would have been 31 years old. This is a possibility worth bearing in mind, but rather sooner than I would deem desirable. Jesus' age of "about thirty" is best taken to mean that He was still thirty years old.

Others, notably E.L. Martin, have assumed that the marginal note has been wrongly placed and that it was in fact on 2 Shebat that Herod died. In 4/3 BC, 2 Shebat fell on 20 January. This is nearer the time I would find acceptable, but if Herod died on 20 January, 3 BC, Jesus would still have turned 31 before He was baptised by John.

While accepting 27 November as possibly the correct date, Doig admits that "the events listed in Josephus fit somewhat better" if Herod's death is placed "before a Passover in the prior month of Adar, in early 4 BCE or 3 BCE, depending on the chronology" (p.94). This is what I would assume myself. Herod died in Adar 4/3 BC, about four weeks before the Passover in 3 BC.

Provisionally, therefore, I accept the view that the eclipse was that of 12 March, 4 BC, and that Jesus was born nearly a year later in February 3 BC.

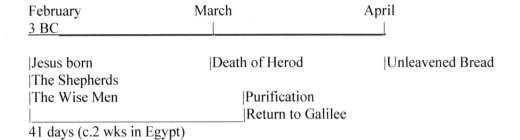

February	March	April
3 BC		

|Jesus born |Death of Herod |Unleavened Bread
|The Shepherds
|The Wise Men |Purification
|_____|Return to Galilee

41 days (c.2 wks in Egypt)

Herod's reign: its beginning and end

Herod's reign had two beginnings: a *de jure* beginning when he received the kingship from Antony and Octavian in Rome, and a *de facto* beginning when he captured Jerusalem three years later.

According to Josephus he received the kingdom from Antony and Octavian "in the 184th Olympiad, the consuls being Gnaeus Domitius Calvinus, for the second time, and Gaius Asinius Pollio" (*Ant.* XIV.14.5(389)). The consuls mentioned were not in office when the fourth year of Olympiad 184 ended on 30 June, 40 BC, but the consuls were officially listed for the entire year beginning 1st January (Doig: 75). It was therefore in 40 BC that Herod received the kingdom in Rome.

It was three years later that Herod actually captured Jerusalem with the help of the Roman general Sossius. This was "when Marcus Agrippa and Caninus Gallus were consuls at Rome, on the 185th Olympiad, on the third month, on the solemnity of the fast, as if a periodical revolution of calamities had returned since that which befell the Jews under Pompey; for the Jews were taken by him on the same day, and this after twenty-seven years' time" (*Ant.* XIV.16.4(487)).

Herod captured Jerusalem in Sivan, the third month, June 37 BC. Pompey's capture of Jerusalem was in Sivan, 63 BC (*Ant.* XIV.4.3. see Doig: 76f.), a difference of twenty-seven years by inclusive reckoning. The fast mentioned for both years is not the Day of Atonement on 10 Tishri since that was not the third month. More probably it was 22 Sivan when (tradition has it) a fast was observed in memory of Jeroboam's defection and idolatry. Soon after beginning to reign Herod prevailed on Mark Antony to have Antigonus, the last Hasmonean ruler, beheaded.

Josephus also tells us (*Wars* I.33.8(665) and *Ant.* XVII.8.1(191)) that Herod died "after a reign of 34 years, reckoned from the date when, after putting Antigonus to death, he assumed control of the state; of 37 years, from the date when he was proclaimed king by the Romans." His years are reckoned from Nisan 37 and 40 respectively. The year of Herod's death, therefore, was 4/3 BC, that is, between 28 March 4 and 17 March 3 (Doig: 78).

Antedated to 1st Nisan, Herod's second years of reign would have begun in Nisan 39 and 36, and his last years (the 37th and 34th) in Nisan 4 BC. It is usually said that he died during the first two or three days of Nisan and that these two or three days are counted as a full year to make up the required totals. It is very doubtful however whether two or three days would ever be counted as a full year. This anomaly is removed if Herod died near the end of the year instead of the beginning.

It may be questioned whether Herod's years are really antedated to Nisan in Josephus' reckoning. This however is confirmed by his dating of the battle of Actium (when Octavian defeated Mark Antony), as G.B. Caird observes. This battle is dated by Josephus to Herod's seventh year (*Ant.* XV.5.2). In fact it was fought on 2 September, 31 BC, but this was Herod's seventh year only if Herod's reign is reckoned to have begun in Nisan 37.

That Herod died in 4/3 BC is confirmed by the reign of his son Philip. Josephus tells us that Philip died in the twentieth year of Tiberius after a reign of 37 years (*Ant.* XVIII.4.6 (106)). If

Tiberius' reign is reckoned here from 1st Nisan, AD 14, his twentieth year would have begun on 1st Nisan, 33. Deduct 37 years from AD 33 and we arrive at 4 BC.

There is however a variant reading in Josephus' *Antiquities* to the effect that Philip died in the *twenty-second* year of Tiberius. This would suggest that Philip did not begin his reign until 2 BC. Those who believe that Herod died in 1 BC after the eclipse of 10 January in that year, have found a welcome confirmation of their theory in this variant reading. See for example Finegan, para 518. Most other lines of evidence, however, confirm the correctness of 4/3 BC as the year of Herod's death. Besides, if Jesus was in born in 2 or 1 BC, He would have been only 28 or 29 in AD 28/29, not fully 30. 2/1 BC is too late; 4/3 BC the only feasible alternative.

There are many other questions which might be discussed, and have been discussed by Doig and others, but *our* concern is the date of the birth of Christ and related events, not those of Herod himself and Josephus. For our purposes therefore enough has been said.

Summary

The year in which John the Baptist called upon the nation to repent and be baptised is given as the fifteenth year of Tiberius Caesar. This date has been subjected to many different interpretations, but a broad consensus points to the summer or autumn of AD 28. John's ministry most probably began in the autumn of that year with the onset of the rainy season, and our Lord was Himself baptised in January of AD 29.

The next subject to come under scrutiny was the length of our Lord's ministry. Was it two years, three years or four? The Gospel evidence points to four years or a little more. Two years is far too short and even three allows too short a time for our Lord's final journey to Jerusalem. Arguments in favour of four years by Lewin and Cheney were found convincing.

The building of the Temple in 46 years (John 2:20) is another disputed datum. But whichever view one takes, there is no conflict with our Lord's ministry beginning in AD 29.

Moving forward to the Crucifixion, an array of disputed points confronted us. To begin with, did it occur on Wednesday, Thursday or Friday? It was concluded that Wednesday is impossible (in view of Luke 24:21), Thursday improbable, and Friday correct after all. This day alone agrees with all the evidence.

The expression "the third day" and its equivalent "after three days" both point to Friday. As for Matthew 12:40 "three days and three nights", these are to be reckoned from Gethsemane the previous evening. Old Testament references similar to "the heart of the earth" indicate that what is meant is not death itself, but a life-threatening situation, a condition of overwhelming sorrow and distress. It was in the Garden of Gethsemane that the powers of darkness took control of events.

Another disputed point is the date of the Crucifixion. Was it 14 Nisan or 15 Nisan? Verses in John's Gospel point decisively to 14 Nisan, and the Synoptics, rightly understood, point in the same direction. The last Supper was not a Passover meal though it did resemble one in some respects. It took place the evening before and was simply a farewell meal of Jesus with His disciples.

The Crucifixion itself was at the third hour according to Mark 15:25, that is nine o'clock in the morning, but in John 19:14 "it was about the sixth hour" when Pilate gave his verdict. How are these time-notes to be reconciled? The answer is that John is here using Egyptian or Roman time, counting the hours from midnight. This is confirmed by the other time-notes in John's Gospel.

The year of the Crucifixion is best located in AD 33 (3 April) in line with the requirements of astronomy and the implied length of our Lord's ministry. His last journey to Jerusalem, which occupies nearly half of Luke's Gospel, must have taken many months, not the brief winter period allowed by the three-year ministry.

Our Lord's age at His baptism was "about thirty years". There is no reason to doubt that this denotes His exact age, not an approximation as is usually supposed. This would indicate that He was born in 4/3 BC, near the end of the Jewish year (February 3 BC).

According to Luke 2:2 Quirinius was "governor of Syria" or "governing Syria" at the time of the enrolment which took Joseph and Mary to Bethlehem. Quirinius was not the designated Governor at that time, but he could well have been the administrator for Syria (which included Palestine) in charge of this important enrolment. If this enrolment was in connection with the bestowal on Caesar Augustus of the prestigious title of Pater Patriae, Father of the Fatherland, the registration for this would have been carried out in 3 BC.

Attempts have been made to pin down the date more precisely by reference to the course of Abijah, the course to which Zachariah belonged and was on duty when the angel of the Lord appeared to him. There is however a difference of opinion as to how the courses were conducted and in which month the cycle began. The three prevailing opinions were tested, and two were found to be compatible with the Nativity of our Lord in February 3 BC. But the precise purpose of the census is not recorded.

It is commonly believed that the infant Jesus was at least a year old when the Wise Men made their appearance, and that the ceremony of purification had already transpired before their arrival. This however is contrary to the plain sense of the narrative in Matthew and Luke. They are far more likely to have come within two or three days as Matthew 2:1 would suggest , "Now when Jesus was born in Bethlehem," and their inquiry in 2:2, "Where is he who has been born King of the Jews?"

The star in the east may have been a unique and miraculous event, or it may have been a sign in the sky of such a remarkable nature that the Magi knew exactly what it signified. There was an abundance of stellar activity around this time. Something must have occurred which these expectant and perceptive men had been long awaiting, something which they recognised as *His* star.

The year of Herod's death is another disputed subject. The eclipse of the moon which preceded his death by some months has been identified with that of 12/13 March 4 BC. There was another eclipse on 9/10 January 1 BC which has been defended with great learning as the one which preceded Herod's death. It has not however been widely accepted and from our point of view is too late for comfort. Josephus also tells us that Herod's death occurred shortly before a Passover. Traditionally this has been assumed to be the Passover of 4 BC, but that Passover allows too short a time for the intervening events. It was, we believe, the Passover of 3 BC which followed Herod's death by three or four weeks. The importance of Herod's death is that the Nativity of Jesus preceded it by only about a month according to the requirements of Matthew and Luke.

Chapter Nine

Acts and After

One would have thought that having rejected and crucified their Messiah, the Jews would have felt God's displeasure in no uncertain terms. It might be expected that their candlestick would be removed (Rev.2:5), their fig-tree cut down (Luke 13:7), and their city destroyed (Luke 19:41-44) without further delay. But this is not what we find. So far from an outpouring of wrath on the guilty nation, we are surprised to find an outpouring of the Holy Spirit in fulfilment of Joel's prophecy of future blessing. When Peter stood up on the day of Pentecost he held out an olive branch, not a stick to beat them with. He addressed them in positive, almost irenic tones with a renewed appeal to repent and the promise that if they did so they would receive the Holy Spirit.

The concept of ignorance

Is this just another example of God's amazing forbearance, or is there another explanation suggested by the scriptural context? For me the clue to what we find in Acts is summed up in the word *ignorance*. Our Lord had prayed on the cross, "Father, forgive them, for *they do not know what they are doing*" (Luke 23:34). And Peter repeats the same sentiment after healing the crippled beggar: "Now, brothers, I know that you acted in *ignorance*, as did your leaders." This is followed by another call to repent accompanied by the promise that their sins would be wiped away, that times of refreshing would come from the Lord, and that He would send (back) the Christ, even Jesus who was appointed for them (Acts 3:17-20).

Under the law there was forgiveness for the man who acted in ignorance if he was truly sorry for what he had done (Lev.4; Num. 15:22-29). The apostle Paul testified, "Even though I was once a blasphemer and a persecutor and a violent man, I was shown mercy (why?), because I acted in ignorance and unbelief" (1 Timothy 1:13). And he says to the Athenian idolaters, "In the past God overlooked such ignorance, but now he commands all people everywhere to repent" (Acts 17:30). Paul's experience of repentance and forgiveness could have been that of the Athenians and of Israel itself. The prescribed Offering had already been made; they had only to repent and believe.

This helps to explain the unique character of the book of Acts. Israel was given a second chance in which to repent on the grounds that they had acted in ignorance when they crucified the Lord of glory. In the prophecy of the Seventy Weeks it is assumed that the last week of years would follow on immediately after the close of the sixty-ninth. But in Acts the seventieth week is seen as already severed from the weeks that preceded it. The tribulation and the desecration of the Temple - events associated with the seventieth week - are spoken of as still future though, at this stage, their fulfilment is still presumed to be reasonably near (2 Thess. 2:4; Rev. 11-13; cp. Matt. 24:15,34). These events were postponed initially for only a short period, but when the nation failed to repent in response to the concerted appeals of apostles and evangelists, they were postponed yet again for a much longer period at about the end of Acts. The net result is that the last seven years of Daniel's prophecy have still not been fulfilled. They contain the most significant cluster of events still to occur before the second coming of Christ.

I have not felt it necessary to discuss in such great detail the chronology of the book of Acts. This has already been done by experts in the field, though it has to be said that no two of them are in total agreement. All I aim to do is to set up a few signposts pointing the reader in the right direction.

Paul's conversion and Peter's dissimulation

If it is true that the Crucifixion of Christ and the Pentecost which followed took place in AD 33, it is obvious that Paul's conversion cannot have happened in the same year. It could however have occurred in the winter of 34, about eighteen months after Pentecost. The true date, whether 34 or 36, depends entirely on the identification of Paul's second visit to Jerusalem which took place in the fourteenth year after his conversion (Gal.2:1-10).

Paul tells us that after his conversion he went to Arabia for three years (Gal.1:17-18). Luke does not mention this stay in Arabia, but it should probably be placed between verses 22 and 23 of Acts 9, where it says "After many days had gone by..." There followed Paul's first visit to Jerusalem mentioned in Galatians 1:18-19.

In Galatians 2 Paul describes his second visit to Jerusalem, which took place "fourteen years after". If the visit intended is the second visit mentioned in Acts, the famine-relief visit of Acts 11:29,30; 12:25, and if the fourteen years are reckoned inclusively from Paul's conversion, this visit could have occurred in AD 47 at the time of the great famine in Judea. Traditionally, however, it has been assumed that the visit intended is not that of Acts 11-12 but that of Acts 15, the occasion of the Jerusalem conference. This conference is thought to have occurred in AD 49. Paul's conversion, thirteen years previous, could then have happened in 36, allowing plenty of time for the events of Acts 3-8 culminating in the martyrdom of Stephen and the consequent dispersion of all except the apostles throughout Judea and Samaria.

This sequence of events has the support of big names like J.B. Lightfoot and is still very popular today, partly no doubt because the resultant chronology is less tight and compressed. But in our view it cannot be correct. The two visits, those of Galatians 2 and Acts 15, could not be more different: the one private in response to a revelation, the other a public conference convened to sort out once and for all the dissension caused by the Judaizers, the legalists in the Jewish Christian community, those who insisted that the Gentiles should be circumcised and keep the law. By this time Paul's mission to Gentile lands was well under way (Acts 13-14). The missionary strategy agreed to in Galatians 2, that Peter, James and John should go to places of Jewish concentration and Paul and Barnabas to places of Gentile concentration, must surely have preceded Paul's second missionary journey, not followed it.

That may be disputed, but it cannot be denied that Paul's purpose in Galatians 1-2 is to provide proof of his complete independence of the apostles in Jerusalem. His gospel, he insists, was not received from them, nor had he been taught it. Rather, he had received it by direct revelation from Jesus Christ. To this end he declares that when he first went to Jerusalem, three years after his conversion, he only stayed there a fortnight and saw none of the apostles except for Peter and James the Lord's brother. On his second visit, fourteen years after his conversion, he went up by revelation with the express purpose of setting before the apostles the gospel which he was already preaching to the Gentiles. It was, he insists, a private visit, with no intention of supplementing his message ("those men added nothing to my message"), but simply to explain what he was doing and to establish an informed and amicable relationship with the pillar apostles in Jerusalem.

The three *epeita* (Gal. 1:18,21; 2:1) imply that Paul is omitting nothing germane to his argument. As F.F. Bruce comments, "Had he been suspected of leaving out (however innocently) any such visit or contact, the question would have been asked: 'But what happened on that occasion which you have suppressed?' The conference which he is about to describe was his first meeting with the Jerusalem leaders after the end of the fifteen days of 1:18f."

This view is accepted by Bruce in his Commentary on the Greek Text, *The Epistle to the Galatians* (1982). It is ably defended by Sir William Ramsay in *St. Paul the Traveller and the Roman Citizen* (1942: 55-64, 152ff.). It has far more to commend it than the traditional view that

Paul's second visit in Galatians was in fact his third visit mentioned in Acts, the occasion of the Jerusalem conference.

There can be little doubt that the occasion when "certain men came from James" (Gal. 2:12) is identical with that described in Acts 15:1, where we read that "certain men came down from Judea to Antioch", and with Acts 15:24 where James says, "We have heard that certain men went out from us without our authorisation and disturbed you, troubling your minds by what they said." James here denies that these men held any mandate from him. They may have come from him but their divisive message was entirely their own. Their disruptive visit to Antioch seems to have preceded the Jerusalem conference by only a brief period. In fact the council was convened as a matter of urgency to deal with this very issue.

But by far the strongest reason for maintaining this order of events is the moral impossibility that Peter's dissimulation in Galatians 2:11ff. could have happened after the Jerusalem council as argued by the rival point of view. Before that meeting the Gentile issue was still an open question. At that time Peter's lapse is perfectly understandable. As Ramsay says, "Only rare and exceptional natures could have risen unaided above the prejudices and the pride of generations, and have sacrificed the Law to their advancing experience" (p.157).

Paul's nature had this rare and exceptional quality, but the rest had yet to be fully persuaded. The Jerusalem conference was convened to deal with this very problem, not so much the doctrinal issue as its social implications. The Judaizers were then put firmly in their place by none other than Peter himself (Acts 15:7-11). After that the Judaizers can have had no further influence over him, and any such lapse on his part would be as inexplicable as it would be inexcusable.

If that were the case, says Ramsay, "Peter abandoned his publicly expressed conviction, which in a formal letter was declared with his approval to be the word of the Holy Spirit. We are asked to accept as a credible narrative this recital of meaningless tergiversation, which attributes to Peter and to Barnabas, not ordinary human weakness and inability to answer a grave issue at the first moment when it is presented to them, but conduct devoid of reason or sanity... That is not the faith, that is not the conduct, which conquered the world! The only possible supposition would be that the Apostles were men unusually weak, ignorant, and inconstant, who continually went wrong, except where the Divine guidance interposed to keep them right" (pp. 164f.).

I conclude therefore that Paul's second visit to Jerusalem according to Galatians 2 is best identified with the famine-relief visit of Acts 11-12. The next point to ascertain is the date of this famine so far as that can be determined.

The year of the Famine

In Ramsay's view, "Our identification, if proved, would make it certain that the Death of Christ cannot be dated so late as 33" (p.363). That however is only true if Paul's famine visit to Jerusalem was in AD 46. If it was in 47, there is still time for the Crucifixion to have happened in 33 and Paul to have been converted in 34. This much Colin Hemer concedes though he himself takes a different view: "Even 33 for the crucifixion with a lapse of fourteen years all told would give a very possible 47 for the famine visit" (1980:14). George Ogg is of the same opinion. Assuming the Crucifixion took place in 33, "Paul's conversion can hardly have taken place later than AD 35 and must be dated either in that year or, less probably, in AD 34" (1968: 30). Most probably the fourteen years are reckoned inclusively and were really thirteen or a little more. What therefore are the facts?

According to Josephus (*Ant*.XX.5.2(100f.)), it was under the procurator Tiberius Alexander "that great famine happened in Judea, in which Helena bought corn in Egypt at a great expense, and distributed it to those that were in want." Cuspius Fadus, Tiberius Alexander's predecessor, was still in office in June 45, and it seems likely, thinks Ogg, that his successor may have arrived in 46. This would narrow the great famine to 46-48. Due to famine conditions in Egypt, Helena is unlikely to have been able to help before 47, by which time many in Jerusalem were dying of hunger. Paul and Barnabas on the other hand, having collected supplies in the months or years following Agabus' prophecy (Acts 11:27-28), would have distributed their aid as soon as they received word of the famine. "That word," says Ogg, "must have reached them in the fall of AD 45-6 or in the fall of AD 46-7" (1968: 53). Ogg considered the earlier date to be more likely, but for reasons already stated it must in fact have been 47.

A different view is taken by Jeremias. He notes that autumn 47-48 was a Sabbatical year. From this fact he deduces the following course of events: "Summer 47, the harvest failed; the Sabbatical year 47-48 aggravated the famine, and prolonged it until the next harvest of spring 49" (1969: 143). But, as Ogg points out, Josephus nowhere mentions any Sabbatical year in this connection, and the Christians of Antioch would have offered their assistance earlier rather than later.

Herod Agrippa

Paul's famine visit to Jerusalem is first mentioned at the end of Acts 11 and again at the end of Acts 12. In between is the record of the scandalous career of Herod Agrippa I, who first beheaded James the brother of John and then, when he saw that the Jews approved of his action, imprisoned Peter as well. It was his intention to make a public spectacle of Peter after Passover, but the Lord intervened to rescue him by means of a notable miracle that took even the church by surprise. The chapter concludes with the record of Agrippa's miserable death when the angel of the Lord struck him down for ascribing to himself the glory due to God alone.

Herod Agrippa I, called just Herod in Acts 12, became king over all Judea in AD 41. Agrippa had helped Claudius secure the throne after the death of Caligula, and Claudius now rewarded him with the territories of Judea and Samaria. Agrippa now ruled over the entire kingdom of his grandfather Herod the Great, as Josephus explains (*Ant*. XIX.5.1(274)). This may have been the occasion of the execution of James and the imprisonment of Peter. Finegan says, "The events involving Peter took place near Passover (Acts 12:4), and in the spring of A.D. 41 the Passover date (Nisan 14) fell on April 21. This may therefore be accepted as a well-established approximate date for Peter's 'departure'" (para 640).

Ogg however prefers a date much closer to Herod's death. In his view Agrippa's persecution was in 43 "at the latest" (p.42). Bruce agrees: "The year 42 or 43 is most probable for this attack" (1986: 276). Agrippa reached Jerusalem not long before Passover in 42, but at that time he had more pressing matters to see to than attacking the apostles. "As for AD 44, he died in that year five days after taking ill at Caesarea while presiding at games in honour of the emperor which are usually identified with those celebrated quadrennially on the *dies natalis* of the city – that is, on 5 March" (Bruce: 277). Agrippa was dead by Passover in this year, so 43 is the most likely date for his attack on the apostles.

Agrippa died, having reigned four years under Caius Caesar and three years under Claudius (*Ant*. XIX.8.2(351)). Finegan says, "Agrippa died in A.D. 43/44 during the fourteenth celebration of the games at Caesarea, between Tishri (Sept/Oct) A.D. 43 and Shebat (Jan/Feb) 44, probably at the very beginning of the period" (para 636). But according to Ogg, he died in early 44 (p.39f.). The games were instituted by Herod the Great in 9 BC in honour of the emperor and the founding of Caesarea. The fourteenth celebration would have been in 44.

Josephus describes Agrippa's death with many morbid embellishments. He describes how Agrippa "saw an owl sitting on a certain rope over his head, and immediately understood that this bird was the messenger of ill tidings." Soon after a severe pain arose in his belly. The pain became so violent that he was carried to his palace where he died five days later.

Acts 12 concludes with the statement that Barnabas and Saul, when they had finished their mission in Jerusalem, returned to Antioch. This mission is the famine relief visit of Acts 11:30. As we have seen, it must have been in 47 if Paul's conversion was in 34. Agabus' prophecy of a famine engulfing the Roman world must have preceded Herod Agrippa's persecution of James and Peter. It even preceded the reign of Claudius (11:28). In the intervening years Paul and Barnabas were busy collecting supplies and these were distributed to those in need when the famine began to bite.

Paul's first missionary journey (Acts 13-14)

It was soon after their return to Antioch, in AD 47, that Paul and Barnabas set out on their first missionary journey. From the port of Seleucia they sailed to Cyprus which was Barnabas' home country. They began by preaching the word of God in the synagogues at Salamis, and then travelled the whole length of the island (about 90 miles) to Paphos at the other end. From Paphos they sailed to Perga in Pamphylia. They probably landed at Attalia (modern Antalya) and walked the twelve miles or so to Perga.

It was there that John Mark left them, for reasons not recorded. They went on to Pisidian Antioch, more than 100 miles north of the Taurus range. It may have been the prospect of this gruelling trek which prompted John Mark to turn back. Paul and Barnabas went next to Iconium (modern Konya). The apostles stayed there for a considerable time. Discovering, however, a plot to apprehend and stone them, they fled to the neighbourhood of Lystra and Derbe. At Lystra Paul was stoned and left for dead. Miraculously "he got up and went back into the city." After that, the two missionaries retraced their steps back to Attalia, strengthening and encouraging the disciples in each place they had been to. They then sailed back to Syrian Antioch and reported to the church all that God had done.

Estimates of how long this journey took vary from six months to two years four months, which Ramsay considered the least possible time. Taking all things into consideration Ogg concludes that eighteen months is all that is required (pp. 65-71). On our reckoning this would have occupied the years 47 and 48.

Having returned to Antioch, they stayed there "no little time" (14:28, *NIV* "a long time"). It was probably during this rest period in Antioch that "certain men came from James" as recorded in Galatians 2:11-14. If this was the same visit as that of Acts 15:1-2, it immediately preceded the conference of Acts 15, which was convened with the express purpose of sorting out the problems caused by these trouble-makers. This conference must have occurred in AD 49, as maintained e.g. by Finegan (para 682).

Paul's second missionary journey (Acts 15:40-18:22)

Paul and Barnabas were keen to revisit the places they had been to on their first missionary venture, but they disagreed sharply on whether to take John Mark with them. The dispute was resolved when Barnabas took John Mark to Cyprus while Paul chose Silas to accompany him. The result was two missionary outreaches instead of one.

Paul and Silas first went through Syria and Cilicia strengthening the churches, and then on to Derbe and Lystra. It was at Lystra that they were joined by a young disciple called Timothy. They found themselves unable to proceed in the direction they had chosen. The Holy Spirit would not allow them to preach in the provinces of either Asia or Bithynia. At Troas, however, Paul had a vision of a man from Macedonia begging him to "come over to Macedonia to help us" (16:9).

Having received his marching orders, Paul prepared at once to leave for Macedonia. Accompanied by Luke (the first "we" section begins at 16:10), they sailed from Troas to the mountainous Aegean island of Samothrace, and on to Neapolis. Evidently the wind (as well as the Holy Spirit) was with them since they covered the 150 miles from Troas to Neapolis in only two days. A further ten mile walk along the Egnatian Way brought them to Philippi.

After humiliation and imprisonment at Philippi the irrepressible pair proceeded to Thessalonica which was a hundred miles further down the Egnatian Way in a south-westerly direction. A large number of God-fearing Greeks joined them there, but the Jews as usual became jealous and started a riot. Paul and Silas slipped away at nightfall and went on to Berea, another fifty miles down the Egnatian Way. There also the Jews from Thessalonica stirred up trouble, so Paul departed to the coast, leaving instructions to Silas and Timothy to join him in Athens as soon as possible. At Athens Paul addressed a meeting of the Areopagus where his speech was cut short at his mention of the resurrection.

Paul went next to Corinth where he was at last joined by Silas and Timothy. He stayed there for eighteen months (18:11) before returning to Antioch stopping off at Ephesus on the way. There are two events relevant to Paul's second missionary journey which confirm that our dates are still on course. The first is the expulsion of the Jews from Rome by the emperor Claudius, and the second is the year in which Gallio became proconsul of Achaia.

The Jews expelled from Rome

On arriving at Corinth Paul met a Jew named Aquila, "who had recently come from Italy with his wife Priscilla, because Claudius had ordered all the Jews to leave Rome" (Acts 18:2). There is evidence from Orosius (c. 418) that Claudius expelled the Jews from Rome in the ninth year of his reign. That was AD 49. If Paul arrived in Corinth in the autumn of 50 (see below), his arrival would have come soon after that of Aquila and Priscilla.

Orosius' exact words are: "Josephus relates that the Jews were expelled from the city by Claudius in the ninth year of his reign, but I am influenced more by Suetonius, who speaks in this way: 'The Jews, who by the instigation of one Chrestus were evermore tumultuous, Claudius banished from Rome" (*Historia ad paganos*, VII.6,15).

There is however no reference to this event in the extant writings of Josephus, nor does Suetonius indicate when the edict of expulsion was issued. It cannot be proved that Orosius' date is correct, but as Ogg observes, "The fact that the date given by Orosius thus harmonizes so satisfactorily with Acts cannot be taken without more ado as proof of its soundness; but it is certainly remarkable" (p.103). Finegan concurs that Orosius' date "agrees well" with Paul's arrival in Corinth "probably in Dec. A.D.49." Bruce however is less sanguine: "Orosius may have quoted from an interpolated text of Josephus, or he may have simply made a mistake; either way, the error robs him of all title to be cited as an authority on this incident" (p.282).

Gallio's proconsulship

It was during his stay in Corinth that Paul was arraigned by hostile Jews before Gallio, the proconsul of Achaia. The charge against him was that of propagating a religion not sanctioned by Roman law. Gallio, however, was in no mind to get involved. So far as he was concerned Paul's version of Judaism was simply a variation on the same theme, a matter for the Jews to decide for themselves. There is some evidence that Gallio became consul of Achaia in May/ June AD 51.

This is based on a fragmentary inscription, a copy of a letter from the emperor Claudius (41-54) to the city of Delphi. The matter is discussed at some length by Finegan, paras 674-677, and especially by Ogg (pp.104-111). Since consuls held office for only one year (save in exceptional cases), this inscription is thought to provide a fairly precise date for the incident recorded in Acts

18:12-17. The inscription (replete with conjectural supplements) is given as follows by C.K. Barrett:

Tiberius [Claudius] Caesar Augustus Gemanicus, [Pontifex Maximus, in his his tribunician] power
[year 12, aclaimed Emperor for] the 26th time, father of the country,[consul for the 5th time, censor, sends greetings to the city of Delphi.]
I have for long been zealous for the city of Delphi [and favourable to it from the] beginning, and I have always observed the cult of the [Pythian] Apollo, [but with regard to]
the present stories, and those quarrels of the citizens of which [a report has been made by Lucius]
Junius Gallio my friend, and [pro]consul [of Achaea] ...

The first line of the inscription mentions the name of Claudius Caesar, giving his names in full. The second line has been reliably restored to state that Claudius had received the imperial acclamation for the twenty-sixth time. The number 26 is above suspicion. Lines 5 and 6 mention a report made by Lucius Junius Gallio "my friend and proconsul of Achaia." The twenty-sixth acclamation of Claudius as imperator was in the year 52. This, as we know from another inscription, corresponded to Claudius' twelfth tribunician power, and that again was in 52. Claudius, however, was already in his twenty-seventh imperial acclamation by August 52. We are thinking therefore of January-July, 52.

The year of Gallio's proconsulship was 52. But governors were required to leave Rome before the middle of April, so Gallio must have entered upon this office in May/June 51. Bruce says, "The narrative of Acts implies that Paul was accused before him shortly after his arrival as proconsul and stayed on in Corinth a good while after the case against him was dismissed. It is a near certainty, then, that Paul's eighteenth months in Corinth lasted from the fall of A.D.50 to the spring or early summer of 52" (p.283).

Finegan however thinks that Paul was arraigned before Gallio near the end of his stay in Corinth which he dates accordingly from the winter of 49 to 51, a year earlier than Bruce (para 679). Seeing however that "Paul stayed many days longer" after the Gallio incident (Acts 18:18), he is more likely to have moved on in 52. His arraignment before Gallio would then fall about half way through his stay at Corinth.

Colin Hemer has this to say, "If Paul's residence extended from the close of a summer journey through a full year to the spring of the next, he faced only one change of governor, in the summer of the middle year. Opposition grew over several months, and came to a head when Gallio arrived. Then Gallio's decision secured Paul's position for almost a year, and perhaps he moved before the advent of another proconsul put this facility at risk. If then Gallio came in summer 51, Paul was in Corinth from autumn 50 to early summer 52" (1980: 8).

Aquila whom Paul found in Corinth had "recently come from Italy with his wife Priscilla, because Claudius had commanded all the Jews to leave Rome" (Acts 18:2). This agrees well with the presumed date of Claudius' decree, namely 49.

Paul's third missionary journey (Acts 18:23-20:38)

Paul's third missionary journey is summarised in Acts 18:23. He began by revisiting the churches of Pisidian Antioch, Iconium, Lystra and Derbe, which he had founded during his first missionary journey (Acts 13-14) and consolidated during his second (16:6). His travels are passed over with lightning speed. From his departure from Ephesus in 18:21 to his return there in 19:1 is reckoned to have been all of 1500 miles. But Luke was not with him, and there was nothing much he felt constrained to record. Paul may have set out in the summer of 52 arriving at Ephesus later in the year.

He stayed in Ephesus for some three years (20:31), during which time he warned them night and day concerning the "savage wolves" which would ravage the flock after his departure. This period was made up as follows: three months in the synagogue (19:8), two years in the lecture hall of Tyrannus (19:10), and the "little longer" (lit. "a time") of 19:22. This brings him to the early summer of 55, which agrees with 1 Corinthians 16:8: "I will stay on at Ephesus until Pentecost."

It is here that the problem begins. The situation is complicated and the following reconstruction only tentative. According to Acts 20:1-5 Paul went next to Macedonia, and having travelled through that region arrived in Greece, where he stayed three months. He intended to sail from there for Syria, but he changed his plans in order to avoid a Jewish plot to kill him. Instead he went back through Macedonia and set sail from Philippi "after the Feast of Unleavened Bread". Five days later he arrived at Troas, where he was joined by his companions who had gone on ahead. If we had only Acts to go by, the date would have to be April 56.

But in 2 Corinthians we find a rather different travel-plan. In 1:16 Paul states his intentions: "I planned to visit you on my way to Macedonia and to come back to you from Macedonia, and then to have you send me on my way to Judea." The order here - Corinth - Macedonia - Corinth - is the opposite of that in Acts 20 (Macedonia - Greece - Macedonia). This intended journey was not fully carried out, it seems. He implemented the first two stages, Corinth and Macedonia, but in order to spare the Corinthians additional grief, he decided against the return journey to Corinth. In 1:23 he says, "I call God as my witness that it was in order to spare you that I did not return to Corinth"; and in 2:1-2, "So I made up my mind that I would not make another painful visit to you. For if I grieve you, who is left to make me glad but you whom I have grieved?"

Instead he wrote them a letter which was evidently sent by means of Titus. At any rate Titus was sent to Corinth as Paul's representative to find out the situation there (12:18: "I urged Titus to go to you"). Paul was expecting Titus to rejoin him in Troas, but in Troas he says, "I still had no peace of mind, because I did not find my brother Titus there" (2:13). For this reason, in spite of an open door of opportunity in Troas, he "said good-bye to them and went on to Macedonia" (2:12-13). In Macedonia, though harassed at every turn ("conflicts on the outside, fears within"), Paul was both comforted and overjoyed by the coming of Titus who brought very encouraging news from Corinth. Paul's letter, which he feared might have been too severe, had in fact been extremely effective. "He (Titus) told us about your longing for me, your deep sorrow, your ardent concern for me, so that my joy was greater than ever" (7:2-16).

In response to all this Paul wrote another letter to the Corinthian church, the letter we know as 2 Corinthians, written from Macedonia. This letter was conveyed by Titus who was accompanied by another unnamed brother who, he says, "is praised by all the churches for his service to the gospel" (8:16-24). In this letter he refers twice to the generosity of the Corinthians "last year" (8:10; 9:2), an eagerness on their part which gave Paul much cause for boasting to the Macedonians. It was Titus' mission "to visit you in advance and finish the arrangements for the generous gift you had promised" (9:5). Then, when Paul himself arrived, he would find all things prepared. His own confidence would be confirmed and the Macedonians would be suitably impressed.

He also says in this letter, "Now I am ready to visit you for the third time" (12:14; 13:1-2). His first visit was that of Acts 18:1-18; his second that of 2 Corinthians 1:16,23; the third that of Acts 20:2-3. It was during this third visit to Corinth that he spent the winter with Gaius and wrote the epistle to the Romans (1 Cor. 16:6; Rom. 16:23).

All this has led scholars to conclude that the account in Acts has been compressed, Paul's second and third visits to Corinth being telescoped into one. So what appears in Acts to be a visit to Corinth in 55 and a return journey to Troas in the spring of 56, was in reality two visits to Corinth in 55 and 56, returning to Troas in the spring of 57.

One week in Troas

Luke says, "we sailed away from Philippi after the days of Unleavened Bread, and in five days we came to them [Paul's companions] at Troas, where we stayed for seven days" (Acts 20:6). According to Ramsay, it was on 22 Nisan, immediately after the days of Unleavened Bread, that Paul left Philippi, and on 26 Nisan that he arrived at Troas where he stayed until 3 Iyyar. The previous day, the day before he left Troas, was a Sunday (Acts 20:7). In which year, then, did 3 Iyyar fall on a Sunday? That year was AD 57, and so (Ramsay confidently concluded) 57 is the year in question.

This may well be correct, but it cannot be taken for granted that Paul left Troas punctually on 22 Nisan. As Bruce observes, "they would have had to wait until they could embark on a convenient ship. Further, Paul preached at Troas on the evening of the first day of the week, and 'prolonged his speech until midnight' (Acts 20:7); but did Luke reckon that day as having started at sunset or at midnight? We cannot be sure, but again it could make a difference to the calculation. Ramsay may be right in making Paul leave Philippi on Friday, 15 April, and preach at Troas on Sunday, 24 April, in A.D.57; but the evidence is not firm enough to prove beyond question that the year was in fact 57" (288 f.). He nevertheless believed that "A.D.57 was indeed the year in question."

It was at Troas that a young man called Eutychus, overcome by the fumes from the "many lamps in the upper room" and the excessive length of Paul's preaching, fell from the third storey to an untimely death. Paul however by God's power restored him to life, much to the relief of everyone present.

On to Jerusalem and Caesarea

It was Paul's aim to reach Jerusalem, if possible, by the day of Pentecost (Acts 20:16), and there is no reason to suppose that his aim was not fulfilled. In 57 Pentecost fell on 28/29 May. He had been repeatedly forewarned that he would suffer bonds and imprisonment in Judea (21:4, 10-11), and this of course is what happened. Within days there was a riot because of him and he was taken into custody. He was then transferred to Caesarea, and five days later (only twelve days since his arrival in Jerusalem, 24:11) he was arraigned before Felix. Felix interviewed Paul on a number of occasions, hoping that Paul would offer him a bribe. It was two years later that Felix was succeeded by Porcius Festus, and Paul was still in prison (24:27).

There has been some considerable discussion over the date of Festus' appointment as procurator of Judea. Eusebius gives the date as the 14th year of Claudius and the tenth of Agrippa II, namely 54. Realising that this cannot be right, Jerome corrects it in his version of the Chronicle of Eusebius to AD 56, and this is accepted by Finegan (paras 691-92). Eusebius has made a simple mistake as Ramsay (and G.B. Caird) have observed. He has reckoned the reign of Agrippa II from AD 45, the year after the death of his father, whereas it should have been reckoned from AD 50, when he received the kingdom of his uncle, Herod of Chalcis. Reckoned from AD 50, his tenth year was 59, not 54. See Ramsay's essay on *The Pauline Chronology* (1906: 350).

Ramsay had such confidence in the year 59 that he regarded Paul's two-year captivity in Caesarea as the central point of the Pauline chronology. Others have not been so sure. J.A.T. Robinson comments, "From the external evidence the conclusion must be that no firm date can be given. 59 seems as likely as any other, putting Paul's arrival in Jerusalem at 57. But the actual date must be decided, if we can, from what the New Testament story itself requires"

(1976: 46). F.F. Bruce says, "The date of his Felix's recall is debatable, but a change in the Judaean provincial coinage attested for Nero's fifth year (A.D.58/9) may be a pointer: this coin issue, says Professor E. Mary Smallwood, 'is more likely to be the work of a new procurator than of an outgoing one who had already minted a large issue'" (p.286).

Tempest and shipwreck en route to Rome

It was probably in the late summer of 59 that Paul was finally put on board ship for Italy. The first ship they boarded was a coasting ship sailing to Myra in Lycia. Paul was accompanied by Luke and Aristarchus (from Thessalonica, 20:4). At Myra they changed ship for one carrying grain from Alexandria to Italy. They began to experience difficulties soon after leaving Myra. Making slow progress they got as far as Crete and put in at Fair Havens near the town of Lasea. Much time had already been lost and it was now after the Fast - that is the Day of Atonement.

In the year 59 the Day of Atonement fell on 5th October, and this was after the equinox (23 or 24 September). The dangerous season for sailing began about 14 September and navigation ceased altogether on 11 November. J.A.T. Robinson observes, "there would have been no point in this further time-reference if the Day of Atonement was not late that year or at any rate later than the equinox. Of the years in question only 59 really fits, when it fell on October 5" (p.52). This is another indication that 59 is likely to be the correct date.

Paul had already completed eleven voyages on the Mediterranean before setting sail for Rome. It has been estimated that his travels thus far amounted to 3,500 miles by sea. He had also suffered shipwreck on three previous occasions (2 Cor. 11:25). He was by far the most experienced mariner on that ship, and he now warned them that to go any further would be to court disaster. It was decided, however, to press on to Phoenix which was a more suitable place to spend the winter. Deceived by a gentle south wind they began to sail along the coast in the direction of Phoenix. But the wind suddenly blew up into a typhonic hurricane-force gale called Euraquilo (or Euroclydon, meaning north-easter). They passed by the island of Cauda (or Clauda) and then frapped the ship by passing heavy ropes round the hull to prevent it from breaking up. Fearing they might run aground on the sandbars of Syrtis (off the north coast of Africa), they lowered the sea anchor and let the ship be driven.

For many days (eleven according to some) the storm raged, blotting out the sun by day and the stars by night. Luke says, "we finally gave up all hope of being saved." Paul however had received assurance from an angel the night before that he would stand trial before Caesar. Not only would his life be saved, but those also of all who sailed with him. When daylight came (to cut a long story short), they saw a bay with a sandy beach. They tried to run the ship aground, but it stuck on a sandbar and was pounded to pieces. But one way or another everyone got to shore safely, some swimming, some on planks or pieces of the ship.

They spent three months in Malta, the winter months, November to January (28:11). In probably the second week of February they boarded another grain ship from Alexandria and continued their journey. Their first port of call was Syracuse on the east coast of Sicily, rather less than a hundred miles from Malta. There they stayed three days before proceeding to Rhegium on the toe of Italy. They did not have to wait long for a favourable wind to take them through the Straights of Messina, past the famous Scylla and Charybdis, and then on to Puteoli in the Bay of Naples, 180 miles in only two days. From Puteoli to Rome was a further 140 miles along the Appian Way, one of the best Roman roads in southern Italy.

News of Paul's impending arrival had already reached the brethren in Rome. Some of them travelled as far as the market town of Appii Forum, 43 miles from Rome, and others to the Three Taverns, about 33 miles. Their welcome was a source of enormous encouragement to Paul. Luke also stayed with him ("When we got to Rome", 28:16). This is the last "we" in Acts, but

Luke did not abandon his friend, no not for a moment, as Colossians, Philemon and 2 Timothy bear witness.

So Paul arrived in Rome in the spring of AD 60. He allowed himself three days to recuperate before setting a day to meet with the Jewish leaders who were eager to hear what he had to say. A large number turned up and Paul talked and debated with them for the entire day. Some of those present were convinced, but others (the majority, alas) refused to believe. They could not even agree among themselves and began to leave (or "were dismissed"). They were not only dismissed by Paul, but as a nation they were dismissed by God as well (vv. 25-28). This dismissal has continued to the present day *but will not continue for ever*. Paul was now under house arrest in Rome where he stayed for two whole years, AD 60-62.

Later years

The Book of Acts ends in 62 with the conclusion of Paul's imprisonment in Rome. It is reasonable to assume that he was then released, and this is confirmed by 1 Timothy and Titus where he is evidently free again to travel. However, by the time he wrote 2 Timothy he is back in prison again and seems to hold out little hope of any further reprieve. "I am already being poured out like a drink offering," he says, "and the time has come for my departure. I have fought the good fight, I have finished the race, I have kept the faith" (4:6-7).

His martyrdom may have followed shortly after, possibly in AD 67. According to Jerome, Seneca the famous philosopher "was put to death by Nero two years before Peter and Paul were crowned with martyrdom" (Finegan: para 671). If this statement carries any weight, it would suggest that Peter and Paul were martyred in 67, two years after the death of Seneca.

The martyrdom of James the Lord's brother

An event which happened in Jerusalem about a year before Paul's release from prison in Rome was the stoning of James, the Lord's brother. Josephus relates how the high priest Ananus the younger, when "Festus was now dead, and Albinus was yet upon the road"... "convened a council (*synedrion*) of judges and brought before it the brother of Jesus the so-called Christ, a man called James, together with certain others, and handed them over to be stoned on a charge of having broken the law" (*Ant.* XX.9.1(200)). According to Eusebius he was thrown from the roof of the temple and then bludgeoned to death by a laundryman.

F.F. Bruce says, "The sober account of Josephus may be accepted without question" (1977: 354 f.). James, it seems, had compromised himself in the eyes of the Sanhedrin by receiving Paul when he came to Jerusalem. Paul had slipped through their fingers by appealing to Caesar, but James and his companions had no such recourse. This crime took place during the three-month interregnum between the death of the procurator Festus and the arrival of his successor in 62. A crime it was since the high priest had no jurisdiction to impose the death penalty, and to avoid any offence to the Romans Ananus was in fact removed from office by Agrippa without delay.

Bruce explains, "The procuratorships of Albinus and, after him, Gessius Florus were the last before the Jewish revolt of September, A.D.66. Four years would not be too much to allow to these two procuratorships, so that the generally accepted date of A.D.62 for the death of James the Just (and therefore for the death of Festus a few weeks previously) cannot be wide of the mark" (285).

Others however, Ramsay included, prefer a date one year earlier, AD 61. The Hieronymian Martyrology, an excellent authority according to Ramsay, gives 25 March as the day of James' martyrdom, and Hegesippus, another excellent authority, says it occurred at Passover time. In

AD 61 Passover may well have occurred on 24 or 25 March, whereas in 62, it fell on 12 or 13 April. See Ramsay (1906: 358).

Hierosolyma est perdita

The plea of ignorance which had given the Jews a stay of execution from Pentecost onward could no longer be invoked after AD 60. By that time the gospel of Christ had been preached "from Jerusalem all the way round to Illyricum", and all the way to Rome itself (Rom. 15:19). Not only Paul, but the other apostles as well, though their labours are not recorded, had carried the gospel to the furthest bounds of the Roman Empire, wherever Jews were to be found. As the writer to the Hebrews says, "If we deliberately keep on sinning after we have received the knowledge of the truth, no sacrifice for sins is left, but only a fearful expectation of judgment and of raging fire that will consume the enemies of God" (Heb. 10:26f.). That expectation overtook them in AD 70 when Jerusalem was destroyed and the surviving population scattered over the face of the earth.

The destruction of Jerusalem in AD 70 was a judgment of the same order and magnitude as that of 586 BC, with this difference, that in 586 they went into exile for only fifty years while in AD 70 they were banished from their land for nearly 1900 years. The events of 589-86 BC were indeed a painful lesson, but they did not rob the Jews of their favoured status as God's chosen people, the custodians of His revealed truth and ultimately of the Truth Himself in human guise. In AD 70 however they lost their favoured position and became *Lo-Ammi* (Not God's people) and *Lo-Ruhamah* (No longer beloved), as had the Northern Kingdom of Israel in the eighth century BC (Hosea 1:6-9).

If that was not enough, an even more severe destruction overcame the unhappy city a few years later. In AD 135 at the time of the Bar-Cochba revolt, on the dreaded Ninth Ab it seems, the anniversary of the destruction of the Temple in both 586 BC and AD 70, its very soil was torn up with a plough, and so was fulfilled Micah's prophecy that Zion would be ploughed like a field (Micah 3:12). The Jews had now drunk to the last drop the cup of Divine retribution.

E.B. Pusey has written, "At this time there appears to have been a formal act, whereby the Romans marked the legal annihilation of cities, an act esteemed, at that time, one of the most extreme severity. When a city was to be built, its compass was marked with a plough; the Romans, when they willed to unmake a city, did, on rare occasions, turn up its soil with a plough. Hence the saying, 'A city with a plough is built, with a plough overthrown.' The city so ploughed forfeited all civil rights; it was counted to have ceased to be" (*The Minor Prophets*: at Micah 3:12). Thus was Jerusalem ploughed as a field in AD 135 at the orders of the emperor Aelius Hadrianus. When, shortly after, the city was rebuilt, it was given, like Samaria before it, a pagan name. It was called Aelia after the emperor Hadrian.

All this, however, comes as no surprise, for the Jews had been repeatedly forewarned of the consequences of unfaithfulness and disobedience. The unimaginable suffering of the Jewish people during the sieges and destruction of Jerusalem and during the long years of their dispersion had all been predicted in frightening detail way back in Deuteronomy 28. See especially verses 47-52 and 64-68.

A few comments on the dates of Paul's epistles may be in order.

The date of Galatians

The date of the epistle to the Galatians depends on the occasion of Paul's visit to Jerusalem recorded in Galatians 2:1-10. If that visit is identified with the conference visit of Acts 15, Galatians must have been written a while after that conference. If however it is identified with the famine visit of Acts 11:30; 12:25, as we have found reason to believe, Galatians could have been written even before the Jerusalem conference.

If it was in AD 47 that Paul set before the apostles in Jerusalem the gospel that he preached among the Gentiles, the men from James who came to Antioch in Galatians 2:12 may be identified with those of Acts 15:1. This took place immediately before the conference which was convened to sort out the problem caused by these men. Paul's epistle to the Galatians may have been written before the conference which would explain why no mention is made there of the decisions reached at that meeting. Conversely, having stressed his independence of the Jerusalem apostles, Paul may have preferred to reason from theological principles arising from his own gospel. These were far more significant than the apostolic 'decrees' which offered little more than practical guidelines on points of social relations.

We may conclude that Galatians was written in 49, either before or soon after the conference of Acts 15.

1 and 2 Thessalonians

1 Thessalonians was written soon after Timothy's return from Thessalonica with good news of the faith and love of the Thessalonian saints (1 Thess. 3:6). Having been prevented by Satan from making the visit himself, Paul, unable to wait any longer, sent Timothy while he himself remained at Athens (2:17-3:2).

According to Acts 17:14 Silas and Timothy stayed on at Berea when Paul went to Athens. Paul waited for them at Athens (17:6), but it was not until he had left Athens for Corinth that Silas and Timothy rejoined him from Macedonia (18:1-5).

Putting the two accounts together, it would seem that Timothy did in fact return to Athens where Paul was waiting for him. He was then sent on another mission to the Thessalonians. It is his return from that mission which is mentioned in 1 Thessalonians 3:6. Hence 1 Thessalonians was written from Corinth soon after the beginning of Paul's eighteen-month stay in that city, probably in early AD 50.

Though only Timothy is mentioned in 1 Thessalonians 3:6, we know from Acts that Silas was with him. This is confirmed by the salutations at the beginning of both Thessalonian epistles where Silas as well as Timothy is mentioned. Only on his second missionary journey was Paul accompanied by Silas. After Acts 18:5 we do not hear of him again.

Paul also mentions that he had suffered many insults at Philippi (2:2). This agrees with Acts 16:22-23 where he and Silas are flogged and imprisoned on the orders of the Philippian magistrates. This occurred immediately before their going to Thessalonica.

2 Thessalonians, like the first epistle, includes Silas and Timothy along with Paul (1:1). It was also written from Corinth, not long after the first probably, in 50 or 51.

1 and 2 Corinthians

In 2 Corinthians 1:19 Paul speaks of the gospel which he had preached to the Corinthians in the company of Silas and Timothy. This agrees with Acts 18:5 where Silas and Timothy join Paul in Corinth in preaching to the Jews that Jesus was the Christ.

In 1 Corinthians 16:5-11 Paul states his intention to revisit Corinth via Macedonia, having sent Timothy on ahead to prepare the way. This fits in with Acts 19:22 where Timothy and Erastus are sent on to Macedonia, while Paul himself remained in the province of Asia a little longer. He intends, he says, to stay on at Ephesus until Pentecost, because of the many opportunities for effective work which had opened up in that city. This confirms what he had already said in 4:17-19, "I am sending you Timothy, my son whom I love ... But I will come to you very soon, if the Lord is willing."

There seems to have been a change of plan, as has already been explained. It was nevertheless in 55, around early summer, that Paul went to Corinth. He must have written I Corinthians from Ephesus earlier the same year.

2 Corinthians was written from Macedonia after he had received from Titus encouraging news of the Macedonians' enthusiasm and generosity. Titus was then sent back to Corinth, in advance of Paul's visit, to make final arrangements about their generous gift (2 Cor. 8:16-9:5). This would have been early in 56 and he carried with him Paul's second letter to the Corinthians.

Romans

Paul clearly states in Romans 15:25 that, at the time of writing the epistle, he was on his way to Jerusalem in the service of the saints there. He speaks with reference to the contribution made by the saints of Macedonia and Achaia for the poor among the saints in Jerusalem. He is writing therefore during the three months he stayed in Greece before returning to Macedonia on his way back to Jerusalem (Acts 20:2-3). He subsequently sailed from Philippi after the Feast of Unleavened Bread determined, if possible, to reach Jerusalem by the day of Pentecost (20:6). Hence he must have written Romans early in AD 57.

There are several pointers which confirm this dating. His host at the time was Gaius (Rom. 16:23), who is doubtless the same person as the Gaius whom Paul baptised at Corinth (1 Cor. 1:14). He commends Phoebe, a servant of the church in Cenchrea (Rom. 16:1), Cenchrea being the port of Corinth. Erastus, who sends greetings in 16:23, was sent with Timothy to Macedonia and Corinth (Acts 19:22; 1 Cor. 4:17). According to 2 Timothy 4:20 Erastus stayed in Corinth. Last but not least, Timothy and Sosipater, mentioned in Romans 16:21, were among Paul's travel-companions as he journeyed from Greece to Jerusalem (Acts 20:4-6).

The Captivity Epistles

Under this heading we include Ephesians, Philippians, Colossians and Philemon, all written from prison. 2 Timothy is also a prison epistle, but is included more conveniently with the Pastoral Epistles.

Ephesians and Colossians are of course very similar in content and were almost certainly written from Rome, during Paul's period of house arrest mentioned at the end of Acts. Philippians stands apart from the other two. It too was probably written from Rome as maintained by the majority of conservative scholars. But Ephesus and Caesarea also have able defenders. A serious, if not insuperable, objection to the Ephesus theory is the complete silence in Acts of any mention of an imprisonment there. In Caesarea, however, he was in prison for two years (Acts 24:27), the same length of time as later in Rome. The possibility that Philippians was written from prison in Caesarea has much to commend it. But for me the contents of the epistle place it among Paul's latest correspondence.

There have been many who have felt that Philippians is doctrinally closer to Romans than to Ephesians and Colossians. J.B. Lightfoot is one who felt the force of this argument. He said, "The inference from such a comparison, if I mistake not, is twofold; we are led to place the Epistle to the Philippians as early as possible, and the Epistles to the Colossians and Ephesians as late as possible, consistent with other known facts and probabilities" (*Philippians*: 41).

This however is more than offset by Paul's altered attitude towards his Jewish ancestry. Whereas in Romans 11:1 he speaks with pride of his Israelite descent and membership of the tribe of Benjamin, in Philippians 3:4-7 he counts them all loss. These things, which were previously gain to him, have now no more value than his persecution of the church! (v.6). They all belong equally to the realm of the flesh. This repudiation of his Jewish heritage places Philippians among Paul's very latest epistles, not somewhere midway between Romans and

Ephesians. In Philippians Paul's situation seems far less secure than in Ephesians and Colossians. He here fears for his life (1:19-24), which is not expressed in the other epistles. It must therefore have been written from Rome, probably a year later than Ephesians and Colossians.

The Pastoral Epistles

Strenuous efforts have been made to squeeze the Pastoral Epistles, 1 Timothy, Titus and 2 Timothy, into the narrative of Acts. But it is generally admitted that it cannot be done without unacceptable forcing. When Romans was written Titus was evidently no longer with him or he would have featured, like Timothy, in the greetings of Romans 16:21-23. According to Robinson, it was at that time that Titus was left in Crete as stated in Titus 1:5. But to leave someone in Crete implies that Paul had been there himself. Paul however never visited Crete on any of his missionary journeys described in Acts.

Furthermore, Timothy was not left behind in Ephesus when Paul went to Macedonia as stated in 1 Timothy 1:3. From the information we have, he was sent to Macedonia and Corinth (Acts 19:21-22; 1 Cor. 4:17; 16:10), and was soon back with Paul in Macedonia (2 Cor. 1:1). He then went with Paul to Corinth, returned with him to Macedonia, awaited him at Troas, and was probably with him in Jerusalem (Rom. 16:21; Acts 20:3-5; 1 Cor. 16:3).

We know that 2 Timothy was written from Rome (2 Tim. 1:17), or at any rate after Paul had been to Rome. Since all three epistles seem to belong together, it is natural to place them in chronological proximity. Hence I concur with the traditional view that 1 Timothy and Titus were written after Paul's release from house arrest in Rome and 2 Timothy after his re-arrest, when he was again in prison in Rome.

The Times of the Gentiles

For every prophecy of judgment and doom there must be at least one predicting Israel's return and restoration in the latter days. I shall finish therefore with a brief look at the recent past and the situation today. What evidence is there of God's renewed interest in His ancient people? The first event which draws our attention is the capture of Jerusalem by General Allenby on 9 December 1917, the climax of a brilliant offensive against the Turks. This followed the famous Balfour Declaration, which was a letter from Arthur James Balfour to Lord Rothschild, Chairman of the British Zionist Federation, dated 2 November 1917. In this declaration he assured Lord Rothschild that "HM government view with favour the establishment in Palestine of a national home for the Jewish people."

Many have seen in this turn of events the fulfilment of the prophetic time-period known as the Times of the Gentiles. There were in fact exactly 2,520 years between the first year of Nebuchadnezzar (604 BC) and 1917. This is the number in days of the last week of years of Daniel's Seventy Weeks, and there is reason to believe that it has one or more applications in terms of years as well. It is highly probable, as explained in the first chapter, that there were 2,520 years from Adam to the Exodus, during which time the world (and the Promised Land in particular) were dominated by Gentile nations before Israel was constituted a nation in covenant with God at the Exodus.

This year 1917 was foreseen by Dr. Grattan Guinness more than thirty years before the event. Writing in 1886 he said, "There can be no question that those who live to see this year 1917 will have reached one of the most important, perhaps the most momentous, of these terminal years of crisis" (*Light for the Last Days*: 342-46).

Commenting on the number 2,520 he said, "Arithmetically, this is a very notable number, one peculiarly fit to be the basis of chronologic prophecy. It is altogether unique - a king among numbers. It is the least common multiple of the first ten numbers - the first in the entire series of numbers, which is exactly divisible without remainder by all the first ten numerals. Thus it is adapted to harmonise several series of periods of different orders and magnitudes in a way that no other conceivable number could do. Is it by chance that this number has been chosen to be the vertebral column of prophetic chronology?" (Revised edition, 1917: 35)   There are few today who would agree with Guinness' Historicist approach to the time-periods in Daniel and Revelation, but his forecast of 1917 is nevertheless impressive. Actually he was not the first. The same prediction was made by John Aquila Brown in 1823.

We have found however in our study of prophecy that prophesied events and periods are rarely fulfilled as soon as the prediction might lead one to expect. All too often they are fulfilled in stages separated sometimes by hundreds of years. Doubtless the times of the Gentiles could have been fulfilled in 1917 if the circumstances had been correct and the Jewish people in the right frame of mind. Our Lord had predicted that Jerusalem would be trodden down by the Gentiles *until* the times of the Gentiles were fulfilled (Luke 21:24). But in 1917 the old city of Jerusalem of which our Lord spoke was still in Arab hands, and remained so until its capture by the Israeli army in 1967 during the Six Day War.

Lance Lambert is one of many who think that the Times of the Gentiles ended in 1967. In his book *Till the Day Dawns* he wrote, "Since the year A.D.70, with the one exception of a few months in A.D.135, Jerusalem has never been under sovereign Jewish government until 7th June 1967. Then the Israel Defence Forces recaptured the Old City and reunited Jerusalem to become 'the eternal and indivisible capital of Israel and the Jewish people' as it was later proclaimed by an act of Knesset on 30th July, 1980. The times of the Gentiles have been fulfilled" (1982: 89).

One wonders however whether even now the times of the Gentiles have been really fulfilled. The most important part of Jerusalem, the Temple Mount, is still trampled by Gentile Arabs and the Temple site itself defiled by a heathen shrine, the Dome of the Rock. Jerusalem today is not unlike it was in the days of the Judges when the Benjaminites were living there cheek to jowl with the Jebusites (Judges 1:21). The situation is unlikely to change before the return of David's all-powerful Son who will liberate Jerusalem and claim it for Himself. Hence it is my belief that the times of the Gentiles began to be fulfilled in 1917 with the close of the significant 2,520 year period, that after a delay of fifty years they received another significant nudge in 1967 with the capture of the Old City, but that the complete and satisfying fulfilment must now await the Second Coming of Christ.

The Second Coming

There is of course no knowing when the second coming will occur. There is an ancient theory dating back to the early church (if not before) that the history of the world would consist of seven thousand years, a week of millennial days, on the principle of a thousand years to a day (see 2 Peter 3:8). The millennial reign of Christ on this theory is the Sabbath rest of this great millennial week (see Hebrews 4:9). If this is a valid inference we are now living on borrowed time, since on any reckoning the first six thousand years have already expired.

In my view the Second Coming cannot happen for some considerable time yet, since there is still much pre-millennial prophecy to be fulfilled. Besides, the world is not yet ready to receive Him. The Lord will return when the world is on the point of self-destruction, when "nations will be in anguish and perplexity at the roaring and tossing of the sea" and "men will faint from terror, apprehensive of what is coming on the world" (Luke 21:25,26). Mankind has not yet reached this pitch of despair, and it will require all the horror of the great tribulation to bring Israel to repentance.

But even now the Lord's arm is outstretched to all who will receive Him! His coming to them is a matter of urgency which should not be delayed.

Summary

At Pentecost we are surprised to find an outpouring of the Holy Spirit instead of an outpouring of wrath on the guilty nation. The reason for this clemency was found in the concept of *ignorance*. The Jews were given a second chance to repent and receive their Messiah because they had acted in ignorance when they crucified the Lord of glory (Luke 23:34; Acts 3:17-20).

This explains the purpose of the book of Acts. Daniel's seventieth week had by now been severed from the preceding sixty-nine, but was still anticipated in the not-too-distant future along with the return of Christ Himself (Acts 3:19-20).

Whether Paul was converted in AD 34 or 36 depends on the occasion of Paul's second visit to Jerusalem in the fourteenth year after his conversion (Gal. 2:1-10). If this visit was the famine-relief visit of Acts 11:29-30; 12:25, the date would be 47, the year of the great famine in Judea, and Paul was converted in 34. Traditionally, however, it has been identified with the Conference visit in Acts 15 which took place in AD 49. In that event Paul would have been converted in 36. But the evidence is strongly against this scenario. It is morally inconceivable that Peter's dissimulation in Galatians 2:11-14 could have happened *after* the Jerusalem conference when the Judaizing party was firmly put in its place by none other than Peter! The conclusion is unavoidable that Paul was converted in 34.

The year in which Herod Agrippa had James executed and Peter imprisoned (Acts 12) was probably 43. Agrippa reached Jerusalem not long before the Passover in 42, but on arrival he had more pressing business than persecuting the apostles. He was dead before the Passover of 44, so we are left with 43.

"That great famine happened in Judea", according to Josephus, when Tiberius Alexander was procurator. This narrows the great famine to the years 46-48. The year must have been 47 if Paul was converted in 34.

It was soon after their return to Antioch in 47 that Paul and Barnabas embarked on their first missionary journey. Assuming the whole thing took no more than eighteen months, it would have taken place in 47-48.

On their return they stayed in Antioch "no little time" (Acts 14:28). It was then that "certain men came from James" and Peter compromised himself out of fear for the circumcision party (Gal.2:11-14). The Jerusalem Conference was convened in 49 to deal with this problem.

Soon after, Paul and Silas set out on the second missionary journey. They went to Philippi where Lydia was converted and the apostles were flogged and imprisoned. They went to Athens where Paul addressed the Areopagus, and on to Corinth where they stayed with Aquila and Priscilla who had recently come from Italy "because Claudius had commanded all the Jews to leave Rome" (18:2).

There is evidence from Orosius that the Jews were expelled from Rome in the ninth year of Claudius, which was 49. Orosius is not considered reliable, but the date may nevertheless be correct. During his eighteen months in Corinth Paul was arraigned before Gallio, proconsul of Achaia (18:12). There is evidence that Gallio became proconsul of Achaia in May/June 51, based on a fragmentary inscription. Paul's brush with the proconsul was probably in 52, making Paul's stay at Corinth from the autumn of 50 to early summer 52.

It may have been in the summer of 52 that Paul hit the road again, arriving at Ephesus later in the year. He stayed around there for three years in all (20:31), until the early summer of 55.

Paul's second and third visits to Corinth seem to be telescoped in Acts. What appears in Acts to be a visit to Corinth in 55 and a return journey to Troas in the spring of 56, was in reality two visits to Corinth in 55 and 56, returning to Troas in the spring of 57. It was in Troas that Eutychus fell from the third storey and was taken up for dead (20:7-12).

It was Paul's intention, if possible, to reach Jerusalem by Pentecost (20:16). In 57 Pentecost fell on 28/29 May. Two years later Felix was succeeded by Porcius Festus and Paul was still in prison (24:27). Festus was appointed in 59 probably, in the tenth year of Agrippa II, reckoned from AD 50 when he received the kingdom from his uncle, Herod of Chalcis.

It was probably in the summer of 59 that Paul finally set sail for Italy (27:1-2). By the time they got to Fair Havens in Crete it was already after the Fast, that is the Day of Atonement (27:9). In 59 this fell on 5 October, after the equinox on 23/24 September. Only in 59 do the conditions agree.

In spite of Paul's protestations they decided to press on to Phoenix, but their progress was stalled by a hurricane-force gale which left them stranded on the island of Malta where they stayed for the winter months, November to January. The following February they boarded another grain ship from Alexandria, in which they sailed to Puteoli in the Bay of Naples. From there it was a journey of 140 miles along the Appian Way to Rome where they arrived in the spring of AD 60.

The book of Acts ends in 62 with the conclusion of Paul's first imprisonment in Rome. During this period, in 61 or 62, James the Lord's brother was stoned to death. This crime was committed during the three month interregnum between the death of Festus and the arrival of his successor.

The end of the road for the Jews (for a very long time) was the destruction of Jerusalem by the Romans in AD 70, and again in 135. On the second occasion the city was ploughed as a field in fulfilment of Micah 3:12.

A glance at more recent times indicates the expiry of another period of 2,520 years in 1917, and the deliverance of Old Jerusalem in 1967. It may however be quite a while yet before the Lord returns as we know He will.

A provisional chronology of the Acts period

Pentecost	AD	33 (24 May)	Acts 2:1-41
Martyrdom of Stephen		34	7:54-58
Paul's conversion		34 (autumn)	9:1-19
Paul's first visit to Jerusalem		37	9:26-30
			(Gal. 1:18-20)
Martyrdom of James		43	Acts 12:2
Death of Herod Agrippa I		44	12:20-23
Paul's famine visit to Jerusalem		47	11:30; 12:25
			(Gal. 2:1-10)
Paul's first missionary journey		47-48	Acts 13-14
Certain men came from James		49	15:1 (Gal.2:12)
Paul wrote Galatians		49	
The Jerusalem Conference		49	15:6-29
Paul's second missionary journey		49-51	15:40-18:22
The Jews expelled from Rome		49	18:2
Eighteen months in Corinth		50-52	18:11
1 Thessalonians		50	
2 Thessalonians		51	
Gallio's proconsulship		51-52	18:12-17
Paul's third missionary journey		52-57	18:23-21:16
Three years in Ephesus		52-55	19:8,10; 20:31
1 Corinthians		55	
Second visit to Corinth		55	2 Cor.1:16,23
2 Corinthians		56	

Third visit to Corinth	56	Acts 20:1 (2Cor.12:14)
Romans	57	
Arrived at Jerusalem (Pentecost)	57	Acts 20:16
In prison in Caesarea	57-59	24:27
They set sail for Rome	59	27:1
Spent three months in Malta	59-60	28:11
Arrived in Rome	60	28:14-16
In prison in Rome	60-62	28:30
Stoning of James, the Lord's brother	61	*Ant.* XX.200
Ephesians, Colossians & Philemon	61	
Philippians	61/62	
Released from prison	62	Acts 28:30
1 Timothy and Titus		
2 Timothy		

Appendix 1

The Reigns of the Divided Kingdom

Israel			A.H.	B.C.		Judah
Jeroboam (22)		1	3036	972		
					1	Rehoboam (17)
		2	3037	971		
					2	
		3	3038	970		
					3	
		4	3039	969		
					4	
		5	3040	968		
					5	
		6	3041	967		
					6	
		7	3042	966		
					7	
		8	3043	965		
					8	
		9	3044	964		
					9	
		10	3045	963		
					10	
		11	3046	962		
					11	
		12	3047	961		
					12	
		13	3048	960		
					13	
		14	3049	959		
					14	
		15	3050	958		
					15	
		16	3051	957		
					16	
		17	3052	956		
					17	
		18	3053	955	1	Abijam (3) 1Ki.15:1f.
					2	
		19	3054	954		
					3	
		20	3055	953	1	Asa (41) 1Ki.15.9f
					2	
Nadab (1) 1Ki.15:25	1	21	3056	952		
					3	
Baasha (24) 1Ki.15:33	1	22	3057	951		
					4	

	2		3058	950
					5
	3		3059	949
					6
	4		3060	948
					7
	5		3061	947
					8
	6		3062	946
					9
	7		3063	945
					10
	8		3064	944
					11
	9		3065	943
					12
	10		3066	942
					13
	11		3067	941
					14
	12		3068	940
					15
	13		3069	939
					16
	14		3070	938
					17
	15		3071	937
					18
	16		3072	936
					19
	17		3073	935
					20
	18		3074	934
					21
	19		3075	933
					22
	20		3076	932
					23
	21		3077	931
					24
	22		3078	930
					25
	23		3079	929
					26
Elah (2) 1Ki.16:8	24	1	3080	928
					27
Zimri (7 days) 2 Ki. 16:15		2	3081	927
					28
			3082	926
					29

Kings of Israel	Omri yr	Ahab yr	AM	BC	Asa yr	Jehoshaphat yr	Kings of Judah
			3083	925			
					30		
Omri (12) 1Ki.16:23	1		3084	924			
					31		
	2		3085	923			
					32		
	3		3086	922			
					33		
	4		3087	921			
					34		
	5		3088	920			
					35		
	6		3089	919			
					36		
	7		3090	918			
					37		
	8		3091	917			
Ahab (22) 1Ki.6:29		1			38		
	9	2	3092	916			
					39		
	10	3	3093	915			
					40		
	11	4	3094	914			
	12	5	3095	913	41	1	Jehoshaphat(25) 1Ki.22:41
		6	3096	912		2	
		7	3097	911		3	
		8	3098	910		4	
		9	3099	909		5	
		10	3100	908		6	
		11	3101	907		7	
		12	3102	906		8	
		13	3103	905		9	
		14	3104	904		10	
		15	3105	903		11	
		16	3106	902		12	
		17	3107	901		13	
						14	

Israel King				AM	BC			Judah King
			18	3108	900		15	
			19	3109	899		16	
			20	3110	898		17	
Ahaziah (2) 1Ki.22:51	1	21		3111	897		18	
Joram (12) 2KI.3:1	2	22	1	3112	896		19	
			2	3113	895		20	
			3	3114	894		21	
			4	3115	893		22	
			5	3116	892	1 2	23	Jehoram (8) 2 Ki.8:16f.
			6	3117	891	3	24	
			7	3118	890	4	25	
			8	3119	889	5		
			9	3120	888	6		
			10	3121	887	7		
			11	3122	886	8		
Jehu (28)	1	12		3123	885	1		Ahaziah (1) 2Ki.8:25f. (Athaliah 6) 2Ki.11:3
	2			3124	884			
	3			3125	883			
	4			3126	882			
	5			3127	881			
	6			3128	880			
	7			3129	879	1 2		Joash (40) 2Ki.12:1
	8			3130	878	3		
	9			3131	877	4		
	10			3132	876	5		

	11	3133	875	
				6
	12	3134	874	
				7
	13	3135	873	
				8
	14	3136	872	
				9
	15	3137	871	
				10
	16	3138	870	
				11
	17	3139	869	
				12
	18	3140	868	
				13
	19	3141	867	
				14
	20	3142	866	
				15
	21	3143	865	
				16
	22	3144	864	
				17
	23	3145	863	
				18
	24	3146	862	
				19
	25	3147	861	
				20
	26	3148	860	
				21
	27	3149	859	
				22
	28	3150	852	
Jehoahaz (17)	1			23
2Ki.13:1	2	3151	857	
				24
	3	3152	856	
				25
	4	3153	855	
				26
	5	3154	854	
				27
	6	3155	853	
				28
	7	3156	852	
				29
	8	3157	851	
				30

			AM	BC		
		9	3158	850		
					31	
		10	3159	849		
					32	
		11	3160	848		
					33	
		12	3161	847		
					34	
		13	3162	846		
					35	
		14	3163	845		
					36	
		15	3164	844		
					37	
Jehoash (16) 2Ki.13:10	1	16	3165	843		
					38	
	2	17	3166	842		
					39	1 Amaziah (29) 2Ki.14:1f
	3		3167	841		
					40	2
	4		3168	840		
						3
	5		3169	839		
						4
	6		3170	838		
						5
	7		3171	837		
						6
	8		3172	836		
						7
	9		3173	835		
						8
	10		3174	834		
						9
	11		3175	833		
						10
	12		3176	832		
						11
	13		3177	831		
						12
	14		3178	830		
						13
	15		3179	829		
						14
	16		3180	828		
Jeroboam (41) 2Ki.14:23	1				15	
	2		3181	827		
					16	
	3		3182	826		
						17

4	3183	825	
5	3184	824	18
6	3185	823	19
7	3186	822	20
8	3187	821	21
9	3188	820	22
10	3189	819	23
11	3190	818	24
12	3191	817	25
13	3192	816	26
14	3193	815	27
15	3194	814	28
16	3195	813	29
17	3196	812	
18	3197	811	
19	3198	810	
20	3199	809	
21	3200	808	
22	3201	807	
23	3202	806	
24	3203	805	
25	3204	804	
26	3205	803	
27	3206	802	
28	3207	801	

1   Azariah (52) 2Ki.15:1f.

2

29	3208	800	
			3
30	3209	799	
			4
31	3210	798	
			5
32	3211	797	
			6
33	3212	796	
			7
34	3213	795	
			8
35	3214	794	
			9
36	3215	793	
			10
37	3216	792	
			11
38	3217	791	
			12
39	3218	790	
			13
40	3219	789	
			14
41	3220	788	
			15
	3221	787	
			16
	3222	786	
			17
	3223	785	
			18
	3224	784	
			19
	3225	783	
			20
	3226	782	
			21
	3227	781	
			22
	3228	780	
			23
	3229	779	
			24
	3230	778	
			25
	3231	777	
			26
	3232	776	
			27

		3233	775
			28
		3234	774
			29
		3235	773
			30
		3236	772
			31
		3237	771
			32
		3238	770
			33
		3239	769
			34
		3240	768
			35
		3241	767
			36
		3242	766
			37
		3243	765
			38
Zechariah (6 ms)		3244	764
Shallum (1 m)			39
Menahem (10)	1	3245	763
2Ki.15:8,13,17			40
	2	3246	762
			41
	3	3247	761
			42
	4	3248	760
			43
	5	3249	759
			44
	6	3250	758
			45
	7	3251	757
			46
	8	3252	756
			47
	9	3253	755
			48
	10	3254	754
			49
		3255	753
			50
Pekahiah (2)	1	3256	752
2Ki.15:23			51
	2	3257	751
Pekah (20)	1		52

2Ki.15:27	2	3258	750	1	Jotham (16) 2Ki.15:32f.
				2	
	3	3259	749		
				3	
	4	3260	748		
				4	
	5	3261	747		
				5	
	6	3262	746		
				6	
	7	3263	745		
				7	
	8	3264	744		
				8	
	9	3265	743		
				9	
	10	3266	742		
				10	
	11	3267	741		
				11	
	12	3268	740		
				12	
	13	3269	739		
				13	
	14	3270	738		
				14	
	15	3271	737		
				15	
	16	3272	736		
				16	
	17	3273	735	1	Ahaz(16) 2Ki.16:1f.
	(17)			2	
	18	3274	734		
	(18)			3	
	19	3275	733		
	(19)			4	
	20	3276	732		
	(20)			5	
		3277	731		
				6	
		3278	730		
				7	
		3279	729		
				8	
		3280	728		
				9	
		3281	727		
				10	
		3282	726		
				11	

		3283	725		
Hoshea (9) 2Ki.17:1	1	3284	724	12	
	2	3285	723	13	
	3	3286	722	14	
	4	3287	721	15	1 Hezekiah (29) 2Ki.18:1f.
	5	3288	720	16	2
	6	3289	719		3
	7	3290	718		4
	8	3291	717		5
	9	3292	716		6

Jeroboam	972-951 BC	Rehoboam	972-955 BC
Nadab	952-951	Abijam	955-953
Baasha	951-928	Asa	953-914
Elah	928-927	Jehoshaphat	914-890
Zimri	927	Jehoram	892-885
Omri	924-913	Ahaziah	885
Ahab	917-895	(Athaliah)	884-879
Ahaziah	897-896	Joash	879-841
Joram	896-885	Amaziah	842-814
Jehu	885-858	Azariah	801-750
Jehoahaz	858-842	Jotham	750-735
Jehoash	843-828	Ahaz	735-721
Jeroboam II	828-788	Hezekiah	722-694
Zechariah	764	Manasseh	694-640
Shallum	764	Amon	640-639
Menahem	763-754	Josiah	639-608
Pekahiah	752-751	Jehoahaz	608
Pekah	751-732	Jehoiakim	608-598
Hoshea	724-716	Jehoiachin	598
		Zedekiah	597-586

Appendix 2

Dated Events in the Bible

Included here are most of the significant dated events in the Bible. It should be noted that the *Anno Hominis* years are here completed years after the creation of Adam, not current years.

Reference		AH date	BC/AD date
Gen.1:26;2:7	Creation of Man	0	4008
5:3	Birth of Seth	130	3878
5:24	Translation of Enoch	987	3021
11:10	Birth of Shem	1558	2450
5:27	Death of Methuselah at 969	1656	2352
7:6-12	Noah 600: The Flood	1656	2352
8:13,14	Noah 601: The earth dry	1657	2351
11:14	Birth of Eber	1723	2285
9:29	Death of Noah at 950	2006	2002
11:26	Birth of Abraham	2015	1993
11:32	Death of Terah in Haran	2083	1925
12:4	Abraham 75: leaves Haran	2090	1918
16:16	Abraham 86: Ishmael born	2101	1907
17:1-14	Abraham 99: Covenant of Circumcision	2114	1894
19:1-29	Destruction of Sodom and Gomorrah	2114	1894
21:5	Abraham 100: Isaac born	2115	1893
21:8-19	Isaac weaned and Ishmael cast out	2120	1888
23:1 (17:17)	Death of Sarah at 127	2152	1856
23:3-20	Abraham buys the cave of Machpelah	2152	1856
25:20	Isaac 40: marries Rebekah	2155	1853
11:11	Death of Shem at 600	2158	1850
25:24-26	Isaac 60: Esau and Jacob born	2175	1833
11:17	Death of Eber at 464	2187	1821
25:7,8	Death of Abraham at 175	2190	1818
26:34	Esau 40: marries Hittite women	2215	1793
25:17	Ishmael dies at 137	2238	1770
29:1-14	Jacob goes to Paddam Aram at 77	2252	1756
29:21-30	Jacob marries Leah and Rachel at 83	2259	1749
29:35	Birth of Judah	2263	1745
30:23,24	Jacob 91: Joseph born	2266	1742
31:41,55	Jacob leaves Laban	2272	1736
32	Jacob and Esau are reconciled	2272	1736
35:18	Rachel dies giving birth to Benjamin		
37:2,28	Joseph sold to merchants at 17	2283	1725
39:20	Joseph sent to prison	2294	1714
41:39-46	Joseph in charge of all Egypt at 30	2296	1712
35:28,29	Isaac dies at 180	2295	1713
41:53,54	The seven years of famine begin	2303	1705

45	Joseph makes himself known to his bros	2305	1703
47:1-12	Jacob goes down to Egypt at 130	2305	1703
47:28; 49:33	Jacob dies at 147	2322	1686
50:26	Joseph dies at 110	2376	1632
Exod. 2:1,2	Birth of Moses	2439	1569
Acts 7:23	Moses flees to Midian	2479	1529
Exod. 7:7	Moses and Aaron speak to Pharaoh	2519	1489
12:31-42	The Exodus from Egypt, 15 Nisan	2520	1488
16:1	They come to the Desert of Sin	2520	1488
19:1	They reach the Desert of Sinai	2520	1488
19:16; 20	The Ten Commandments, 17 Sivan	2520	1488
40:17	The Tabernacle set up, 1st Nisan	2521	1487
Num. 9:1-4	Passover celebrated, 14 Nisan	2521	1487
Num. 1	Census taken, 1 Iyyar	2521	1487
10:11	They set out for the Desert of Paran	2521	1487
13:21-25	The spies explore the Land	2521	1487
20:1	Miriam dies in Nisan, 40th year	2559	1449
33:38-39 (20:28)	Aaron dies at 123, 1 Ab	2559	1449
Deut. 1:3	Moses addresses the people, 1 Shebat	2559	1449
34:5-7	Moses dies in plains of Moab at 120	2559	1449
Josh. 4:19	Jordan crossed they camp at Gilgal	2560	1448
5:10	They celebrate Passover, 14 Nisan	2560	1448
5:11,12	Manna stops		
	They eat food from the Land, 15 Nisan	2560	1448
14:6-10	The Land is divided by lot	2566	1442
Judg. 3:11	Othniel: the Land had rest 40 years	2595	1413
3:30	Ehud: the Land had rest 80 years	2653	1355
4:4-24	Barak	2753	1255
8:28	Gideon: the Land had rest for 40 years	2753	1255
16:31	Samson judges for 20 years	2859	1149
12:7	Jephthah judges for six years	2859	1149
1Sam.7:15	Samuel judges all his life	2881	1127
Acts 13:21	Accession of Saul	2916	1092
2Sam.5:4	Birth of David	2926	1082
2Sam.5:5	David reigns for 40 years	2956	1052
1Ki.2:10,11	Solomon begins to reign	2996	1012
6:1	Foundation of the Temple	3000	1008
6.37	Temple finished	3006/7	1002/1
8:2	Dedication of the Temple	3007	1001
9:10	The royal palace finished	3019/20	989/8
11:42,43	Solomon dies	3036	972
12	Jeroboam/ Rehoboam	3036	972
2Chron.12	Judah attacked by Shishak of Egypt	3041	967
1Ki.15:9	Asa becomes king: 41 years	3055	953
15:27-30	Jeroboam's family wiped out by Baasha	3057	951
2Chr.15:10	Asa's covenant to seek the Lord	3069	939

1Ki.16:16	Omri proclaimed king in Israel	3081	927
16:23	Omri's reign begins: he builds Samaria	3084	924
22:41,42	Jehoshaphat becomes king: 25 years	3094	914
22:29-38	Ahab killed at Ramoth Gilead	3112	896
2Ki.9-10	Jehu kills both Joram and Ahaziah	3123	885
11:1	Athaliah destroys Judah's royal family	3123	885
11:12;12:1	Joash proclaimed king	3129	879
14:1	Amaziah becomes king: 29 years	3166	842
14:23	Jeroboam II king in Israel	3180	828
14:19	Amaziah assassinated at Lachish	3194	814
15:1,2	Azariah reigns after interregnum: 52yrs	3206	802
14:29	Jeroboam dies; civil war takes over	3220	788
15:8	Zechariah reigns briefly in Israel	3244	764
15:27	Pekah becomes king in Israel	3257	751
Isaiah 6:1	The year that King Uzziah died	3257	751
2Ki.16:1	Ahaz becomes king: 16 years	3273	735
17:1	Hoshea becomes king, last in Israel	3284	724
18:1,2	Hezekiah becomes king: 29 years	3286	722
Isaiah 14:28	Ahaz dies	3287	721
2Chr.29:3	Hezekiah repairs the Temple	3288	720
30:2	Passover kept in 2nd month	3288	720
2Ki.18:9	King of Assyria lays siege to Samaria	3290	718
18:10,11	Samaria captured and Israel deported	3292	716
18:13;19:35	Sennacherib invades Judah	3300	708
21:1	Manasseh becomes king: 55 years	3314	694
21:19	Amon becomes king: 2 years	3368	640
22:1	Josiah becomes king: 31 years	3369	639
Jer.1:2	13th Josiah: Jeremiah prophesies	3381	627
2Chr.34:8	18th Josiah: Josiah starts reform	3386	622
34:14	They find the Book of the Law		
35:20-24	Josiah dies at Megiddo	3400	608
Jer.46:2	Pharaoh Necho defeated at Carchemish	3403	605
Dan.1:1	3rd Jehoiakim: Jerusalem besieged	3403	605
Jer.25:1-11	4th Jehoiakim: Servitude to Babylon	3403	605
36:1-26	4th/5th Jehoiakim: Jeremiah and scroll		
	Jehoiakim burns it in the fire	3404	604
Dan.2:1	2nd Nebuchadnezzar: the king's dream	3405	603
2Ki.24:10-17	Exile of King Jehoiachin	3410/11	598/7
Ezekiel	Era of the Exile	411	597
Ezek.1:2	5th Exile: Ezekiel began to prophesy	3415	593
8:1	6th Exile: Ezekiel sees detestable		
	things in Jerusalem	3416	592
20:1	7th Exile:Ezekiel confronts the elders	3417	591
24:1,2	9th Exile,10 Tebeth:Jerusalem besieged	3419	589
Jer.32	Jeremiah buys the field at Anathoth	3420	588
39:2	9 Tammuz: the city wall broken through	3422	586
52:6-9	9 Tammuz: Zedekiah captured	3422	586
52:12-14	10 Ab: the City and Temple are burnt	3422	586
41:1-3	Tishri: Ishmael kills Gedaliah	3422	586

Ezek.40:1	25th Exile, 10 Nisan: Ezekiel's vision	3435	573
29:17	27th Exile, 1 Nisan: "I am going to give Egypt to Nebuchadnezzar"	3437	571
52:31	37th Exile, 25 Adar: Jehoiachin released	3446/7	562/1
Dan.7:1	1st Belshazzar: the Four Beasts	3455	550
8:1	3rd Belshazzar: the Ram and the Goat	3457	548
5:30	Belshazzar slain: Darius the Mede	3469	539
6:1	Daniel in the Lions' Den	3469/70	539/8
9:1	1st Darius: the Seventy Weeks prophecy	3470	538
Ezra 1:1-4	Cyrus' decree to rebuild the Temple	3472	536
3:8-13	Work on the Second Temple begun	3473	535
Hag.1:1	2nd Darius, 1 Elul: Haggai speaks	3488	520
Zech.1:1	2nd Darius: Zechariah prophesies	3488	520
Hag.2:18	24 Kislev: foundation of 2nd Temple	3488	520
Ezra 6:15	6th Darius, 3 Adar: Temple completed	3492	516
6:19	The Passover celebrated	3493	515
Est.1:3	3rd Xerxes: the king holds a banquet	3525	483
3:7	12th Xerxes, 1 Nisan: Haman's request	3534	474
3:12,13	Decree to destroy the Jews on 13 Adar	3534	474
6-7	16/17 Nisan: Mordecai honoured	3534	474
7:8,9	7th Artaxerxes,1 Ab: Ezra in Jerusalem	3550	458
Neh.1:1-3	Nehemiah told "The wall broken down"	3562	446
2:1-9	20th Artaxerxes, Nisan: permission to rebuild Jerusalem granted	3563	445
6:15	25 Elul: the wall completed in 52 days	3563	445
8:2,3	1 Tishri: Ezra reads Book of the Law	3563	445
13:6	32nd Artaxerxes: Nehemiah returns	3575	433
Luke 1:24	Elizabeth conceives, in December	4003	5
1:57	John (the Baptist) is born, in Oct.	4004	4
2:6,7	Jesus is born, in February	4005	3
Matt.2:19	Herod died, in March	4005	3
Luke 2:41-50	Jesus 12: they go to Jerusalem	4017	AD 10
3:23	Jesus is 30 years old, in February	4035	28
3:1-3	15th Tiberius: John's baptism	4035	28
3:21,22	Jesus is baptised, in January	4035/6	29
John 2	Jesus turns water into wine at Cana	4036	29
Luke 6	Pick ears of corn: spring time again	4037	30
John 6 &c	Feeding of the 5000. Passover near	4038	31
Jn.19 &c	14 Nisan (3 April): Jesus is crucified	4040	33
Jn.20 &c	16 Nisan (5 April): He is resurrected	4040	33
Acts 2	Pentecost	4040	33
7:54-58	Martyrdom of Stephen	4041	34
9:1-19	Paul's conversion	4041	34
12:2	Execution of James	4048/9	41/2
12:20-3	Death of Herod Agrippa I	4051	44
11:30	Paul's famine visit to Jerusalem	4054	47
13-14	Paul's first missionary journey	4054-5	47-8
15:6-29	The Jerusalem Conference	4056	49

15:40-18:22	Paul's second missionary journey	4056-8	49-51
18:2	The Jews expelled from Rome	4056	49
18:12	Gallio proconsul of Achaia	4058-9	51-2
18:23-21:16	Third missionary journey	4059-64	52-7
19-20	Paul stayed in Ephesus	4059-62	52-5
20:16	Pentecost in Jerusalem	4064	57
24:27	Imprisonment in Caesarea	4064-6	57-9
27:1	They set sail for Rome	4066	59
28:11	They spend three months in Malta	4066-7	59-60
28:14	Paul arrived in Rome	4067	60
28:30	Two years under house arrest	4067-9	60-2
	Martyrdom of James the Lord's brother	4068	61
	Fall of Jerusalem	4077	70

Bibliography

Books: Old Testament (chiefly)

Allis, Oswald T., *The Old Testament: Its Claims and its Critics* (Chapter Six: Chronology), Phillipsburg, N.J., 1972.

Anderson, Robert, *The Coming Prince*, Fifth ed., London 1895; Twelfth ed. no date.

Anstey, Martin, *The Romance of Bible Chronology*, London 1913.

Barnes, William Hamilton, *Studies in the Chronology of the Divided Monarchy of Israel*, Harvard Semitic Monographs 48, Harvard University 1991.

Becking, Bob, *The Fall of Samaria: An Historical and Archaeology Study,* Leiden, Brill, 1992.

Bright, John, *A History of Israel*, 3rd ed. London, SCM, 1981.

Brinkman, J.A., *A Political History of Post-Kassite Babylonia, 1158-722 B.C.*, Rome 1968.

Browne, Henry, *Ordo Saeclorum: A Treatise on the Chronology of the Holy Scriptures*, London 1844.

Faulstich, E.W., *History, Harmony & The Hebrew Kings*, Spencer, Iowa, 1986.

Furuli, Rolf, *Assyrian, Babylonian, Egyptian and Persian Chronology Compared with the Chronology of the Bible.* Vol.1: *Persian Chronology and the Length of the Babylonian Exile of the Jews*, Oslo 2003. Vol.2: *Assyrian, Babylonian and Egyptian Chronology*, Oslo 2007.

Galil, Gershon, *The Chronology of the Kings of Israel and Judah*, Leiden, Brill, 1996.

Grayson, A.K., *Assyrian and Babylonian Chronicles*, New York 1975.

Hallo, William W. (Editor) and Younger, K. Lawson (Ass. Editor), *The Context of Scripture*; Vol.II *Monumental Inscriptions from the Biblical World*, Leiden, Brill, 2000.

Hayes, John H. and Hooker, Paul K., *A New Chronology for the Kings of Israel and Judah*, Atlanta 1988.

Henry, Roger, *Synchronized Chronology: Rethinking Middle East Antiquity*, Algora Publishing, 2003.

Hobbs, T.R., *Word Biblical Commentary*; Vol.13: *2 Kings*, Waco, Texas, 1985.

Humphreys, Colin J., *The Miracles of Exodus*, London, New York, 2003.

Jones, Floyd Nolen, *The Chronology of the Old Testament*, New Leaf Press Edition, Master Books, Arizona 2005.

Jonsson, Carl Olof, *The Gentile Times Reconsidered*, Third ed., Atlanta 1998.
Supplement: *Refutation of Criticism and Additional Evidence*, Odeon Books, Danville, 1989.

Keil, C.F. and Delitzsch, F, *Biblical Commentary on the Old Testament: ThePentateuch;Joshua, Judge and Ruth; Daniel*, Eerdmans reprint.

Kitchen, Kenneth A. *On the Reliability of the Old Testament*, Michigan/Cambridge, 2003.

Larrson, Gerhard, *The Secret System*, Leiden 1973.

Lightfoot, John, *The Whole Works of the Late Rev. John Lightfoot, D.D.*, 13 Vols, Pitman edition, London 1825.

Millard, Alan, *The Eponyms of the Assyrian Empire 910-612 BC*, State Archives of Assyria Studies, Vol. II, Helsinki, 1994.

Miller, J. and Hayes, John H., *A History of Ancient Israel and Judah*, London, SCM, 1986.

Moeller, Lennart, *The Exodus Case*, Scandinavia Publishing House, 2002.

Morris, Henry M. *The Genesis Record*, Grand Rapids 1976.

Olmstead, A.T., *Assyrian Historiography*, Columbia 1916.

Ozanne, C.G., *Empires of the End-Time*, Open Bible Trust, 2007.

Parker, R.A. and Dubberstein, W.H., *Babylonian Chronology 626 B.C.-A.D.75*, 2nd ed. Providence 1956.

Radner, Karen (ed), *The Prosopography of the Neo-Assyrian Empire*, Neo-Assyrian Text Corpus Project, Vol.1/1 and 1/2, Helsinki 1998/9.

Rohl, David M., *A Test of Time: The Bible-From Myth to History*, London 1995.

Rowley, H.H., *From Joseph to Joshua*, Schweich Lectures for 1948, London 1950.

Shenkel, J.D., *Chronology and Recensional Development in the Greek Text of Kings*, Harvard 1968.

Smith, George, *The Assyrian Eponym Canon*, London 1875.

Tetley, M. Christine, *The Reconstructed Chronology of the Divided Kingdom*, Eisenbraun 2005.

Thiele, Edwin R, *The Mysterious Numbers of the Hebrew Kings*, Exeter 1965; Grand Rapids 1983.

Unger, Merrill F., *Israel and the Aramaeans of Damascus*, London 1957.

Ussher, James, *The Annals of the World*, 1658. Revised and updated by Larry and Marion Pierce, Master Books, Inc., AR. First paperback edition, 2006.

Wilson-Haffendon, D.J., *Operation Exodus*, Marshall, Morgan & Scott 1957.

Wiseman, Donald J., *Chronicles of Chaldaean Kings (626-556 B.C.) in the British Museum*, London 1956.
Nebuchadrezzar and Babylon, Schweich Lectures for 1983, Oxford 1985.

Wood, Leon J., *A Survey of Israel's History*, Grand Rapids 1970.
Distressing Days of the Judges, Grand Rapids 1975.
Israel's United Monarchy, Grand Rapids 1979.

Young, Edward J., *The Prophecy of Daniel*, Grand Rapids 1949.

Books: New Testament (chiefly)

Barrett, C.K., *The New Testament Background: Selected Documents*, London, SPCK, 1958.

Beckwith, Roger T., *Calendar and Chronology, Jewish and Christian*, Leiden, Brill, 2001.

Blinzler, Josef, *The Trial of Jesus*, Second ed., Westminster, MD, 1959.

Bruce, F.F., *New Testament History*, Marshall, Morgan & Scott, 1977.
    The Epistle to the Galatians, A Commentary on the Greek Text, Exeter 1982.

Cheney, Johnston M., *The Life of Christ in Stereo*, Portland, Oregon, 1969.

Doig, Kenneth F., *New Testament Chronology*, San Francisco 1991.

Eedle, Arthur, *Seven Steps to Bethlehem*, Lulu 2007.

Edwards, Ormond, *The Time of Christ: A Chronology of the Incarnation*, Floris Books, Edinburgh 1986.

Finegan, Jack, *Handbook of Biblical Chronology*, Revised ed., Princeton 1998.

France, R.T., *The Gospel of Matthew*, Eerdmans 2007.

Godet, F., *A Commentary on the Gospel of St. Luke*, 2 Vols, Edinburgh 1878.
    Commentary on the Gospel of St. John, 3 Vols, Edinburgh 1895.

Hoehner, Harold W., *Chronological Aspects of the Life of Christ*, Grand Rapids 1977

Jeremias, Joachim, *The Eucharistic Words of Jesus*, Third ed., London 1966.

Lewin, Thomas, *Fasti Sacri, Or a Key to the Chronology of the New Testament*, London 1865. Reprinted
    by Kessinger Publishing.

Macnight, James, *Harmony of the Four Gospels*, London 1809.

Marshall, I. Howard, *Last Supper and Lord's Supper*, Exeter 1980.

Martin, Ernest L., *The Birth of Christ Recalculated*, Second ed., Pasadena & Newcastle-upon-Tyne, 1980.
    The Star that Astonished the World, Portland, OR, 1998.

Morris, Leon L., *The Gospel according to St. John*, Grand Rapids 1971.

Ogg, George, *Chronology of the Public Ministry of Jesus*, Cambridge 1940.
    The Chronology of the Life of Paul, London, Epworth, 1968.

Plummer, Alfred, *The Gospel according to St. Luke*, ICC, Fifth ed., Edinburgh 1922.

Ramsay, William M., *Was Christ Born at Bethlehem*, London 1898.
    Pauline and other Studies in early Christian History (XIV "The Pauline Chronology"), London 1906.
    St. Paul the Traveller and the Roman Citizen, 19th ed., London 1942.

Robinson, J.A.T., *Redating the New Testament*, London, SCM, 1976.
    The Priority of John, SCM, 1985.

Rutherford, Adam, *Bible Chronology*, London 1957.

Segal, J.B., *The Hebrew Passover*, London 1963.

Vardaman, Jerry and Yamauchi, Edwin M. (editors), *Chronos, Kairos, Christos*, Eisenbrauns, Winona Lake, 1989.

Westcott, B.F., *An Introduction to the Study of the Gospels*, Cambridge and London 1881.

Articles and Essays: Old Testament

Auerbach, Elias, "Der Wechsel des Jahres-Anfangs in Juda im Lichte der Neugefundenen Chronik", *Vetus Testamentum* 9(1959), 113-121; 10(1960),69-70.

Clines, D.J.A., "Regnal Year Reckoning in the Last Years of the Kingdom of Judah", *Australian Journal of Biblical Literature* 2(1972), 9-34.
"The Evidence of an Autumnal New Year in Pre-exilic Israel Reconsidered", *Journal of Biblical Literature* 93(1974), 22-40.

Cogan, M., "Tyre and Tiglath-pileser III", *Journal of Cuneiform Studies* 25(1973), 96-99.

Depuydt, Leo, "'More valuable than Gold', Ptolemy's Royal Canon and Babylonian Chronology", *Journal of Cuneiform Studies* 47(1995), 97-117.

Elat, M., "The Campaigns of Shalmaneser III against Aram and Israel", *Israel Exploration Society* 25(1975), 25-35.

Ford, N., "The Contradictory Records of Sargon II of Assyria and the Meaning of *palu*", *Journal of Cuneiform Studies* 22(1969), 83-84.

Gelb, I.J., "Two Assyrian King-lists", *Journal of Near Eastern Studies*", 13(1954), 209-230.

Grayson, A.K., "Assyria and Babylonia", *Orientalia* 49(1980), 271-274.

Green, Alberto R., "The Chronology of the Last Days of Judah: Two Apparent Discrepancies", *Journal of Biblical Literature* 101(1982), 57-73.
"Sua and Jehu: The Boundaries of Shalmaneser's Conquest", *Palestinian Exploration Quarterly* 111(1979),35-39.

Hallo, W.W. "From Qarqar to Carchemish: Assyria and Israel in the Light of New Discoveries", *The Biblical Archaeologist*, 23(1960), 34-61.

Hasel, Gerhard F., "The Book of Daniel: Evidences Relating to Persons and Chronology", *Andrews University Seminary Studies* 19(1981), 37-49.
"The First and Third Years of Belshazzar (Dan 7:1; 8:1)", *AUSS 15*(1977), 153-168.

Hayes, J.H. and Kuan J.K., "The Final Years of Samaria (730-720 BC)", *Biblica* 72(1991), 153-181.

Henige, D., "Comparative Chronology and the Ancient Near East: A Case for Symbiosis", *Bulletin of the American Schools of Oriental Research* 261(1986), 57-68.

Horn, Siegfried H., "The Babylonian Chronicle and the Ancient Calendar of the Kingdom of Judah", *Andrews University Seminary Studies* 5(1967), 12-27.

Humphreys, Colin J. "The Number of People in the Exodus from Egypt: Decoding mathematically the very large numbers in Numbers I and XXVI", *Vetus Testamentum* 48(1998), 196-213.

James, P.J., "Mesopotamian Chronology: An Independent Control?", *Journal of the Ancient Chronology Forum* 1(1987), 68-78.

Jepsen A., "Zur Chronologie der Konige von Israel and Juda: Eine Uberprufung" *Zeitschrift fur Alttestamentliche Wissenschaft*, Beihefte 88(1964), 1-48.

Larrson, Gerhard, "The Chronology of the Pentateuch: A comparison of the MT and LXX", *Journal of Biblical Literature* 102(1983), 401-409.

Levine, L.D., "Menahem and Tiglath-pileser: A New Synchronism", *Bulletin of the American Schools of Oriental Research*, 206(1972), 40-42.

Malamat A., "The Last Kings of Judah and the Fall of Samaria: An Historical-Chronological Study" *Israel Exploration Journal*, 18(1968), 137-155.
"Josiah's Bid for Armageddon", *Journal of the Ancient Near Eastern Society*, 5(1973), 267-279.
"The Twilight of Judah: In the Egyptian-Babylonian Maelstrom", *VetusTestamentum*, (Suppl.) 28(1975), 123-145.

McCarter, P. Kyle, "Yaw, Son of 'Omri'", *Bulletin of the American Schools of Oriental Research*, 216(1974), 5-7.

Mendenhall, George E., "The Census Lists of Numbers 1 and 26", *Journal of Biblical Literature* 77(1958), 52-56.

Millard, Alan, "Sennacherib's Attack on Hezekiah", *Tyndale Bulletin* 36(1985), 61-77.

Morgenstern, Julian, "The New Year for Kings", *Occident and Orient*, 439-456. Gaster Memorial Volume, edited by Bruno Schindler, London 1936.

Na'aman, Nadav, "Historical and Chronological Notes on the Kingdoms of Israel and Judah", *Vetus Testamentum* 36(1986), 71-92.
"The Historical Background to the Conquest of Samaria (720 BC)",*Journal of Biblical Literature* 71(1990), 206-225.
"Tiglath-pileser III's Campaigns against Tyre and Israel (734-732 B.C.E.", *Tel Aviv* 22(1995), 268-278
"Jehu Son of Omri: Legitimizing a Loyal Vassal by his Overlord", *Israel Exploration Journal* 48(1998), 236-238.

Neuffer, Julia, "The Accession of Artaxerxes I", *Andrews University Seminary Studies* 6(1968), 60-87.

Oppert, Jules, "Noli me tangere", *Proceedings of the Society for Biblical Archaeology* 20(1898), 24-47.

Orr, Avigdor, "The Seventy Years of Babylon", *Vetus Testamentum* 6(1956), 304-6.

Page, Stephanie, "A Stela of Adad-nirari III and Nergal-eres from Tell al-Rimah", *Iraq* 30(1968), 139-153.

Poebel, Arno, "The Assyrian King List from Khorsabad", Part 3, *Journal of Near Eastern Studies* 2(1943), 56-90.

Robinson, Steven J., "The Chronology of Israel Re-examined: The First Millennium BC", *Journal of the Ancient Chronology Forum* 5(1991/2), 89-98.

Shea, William H., "An Unrecognised Vassal King of Babylon in the Early Achaemenid Period", *Andrews University Seminary Studies* 9(1971), 51-67; 99-128; 10(1972), 88-117;147-178.
"Darius the Mede: An update", *AUSS* 20(1982), 229-247.
"Darius the Mede in his Persian-Babylonian Setting", *AUSS* 29(1991), 235-257.
"Adad-nirari III and Jehoash of Israel", *Journal of Cuneiform Studies* 30(1970), 101-113.
"Sennacherib's Second Palestinian Campaign", *Journal of Biblical Literature* 104(1985), 401-418.

Tadmor, H., "The Campaigns of Sargon II of Asshur: A Chronological Study", *Journal of Cuneiform Studies* 12(1958), 22-40, 77-100.
"Philistia under Assyrian Rule", *The Biblical Archaeologist* 29(1966), 86-102.

Talmon, S., "The Judaean *'am ha'arets* in Historical Perspective", *Fourth World Congress of Jewish Studies* 1(1967), 71-76.

Thiele, E.R., "New Evidence on the Chronology of the Last Kings of Judah", *Bulletin of the American Schools of Oriental Research* 143(1956),22-27.
"Coregencies and Overlapping Reigns among the Hebrew Kings", *Journal of Biblical Literature* 93(1974), 174-200.

Weidner, E.F. On *shadashu emid:* er starb eines unnaturlichen Todes, *Archiv fur Orientforschung* 13(1939), 233f.

Winkle, Ross E., "Jeremiah's Seventy Years for Babylon, a Reassessment: Part 1: The Scriptural Data", *AUSS* 25(1987), 201-214.Part II: "The Historical Data", pp.289-299.

Younger, K. Lawson, "The Deportation of the Israelites", *Journal of Biblical Literature* 117(1998), 201-227.
"The Fall of Samaria in the Light of Recent Research", *Catholic Biblical Quarterly* 61(1999), 461-82.

Articles and Essays: New Testament

Barnes, T.D., "The Date of Herod's Death", *Journal of Theological Studies* 17(1966), 283-298.

Barrett, C.K., "Luke XXII.15: 'To eat the Passover'", *Journal of Theological Studies* 9(1958), 305-307.

Bernegger, P.M., "Affirmation of Herod's Death", *Journal of Theological Studies* 34(1983), 526-531.

Brindle, W. "The Census and Quirinius, Lk.2:2", *Journal of the Evangelical Theological Society* 27(1984), 43-52.

Bruce, F.F., "Chronological Questions in the Acts of the Apostles", *Bulletin of the John Rylands University Library* 68(1986), 173-195.

Burkitt, F.C., On Luke 22:15-16, *Journal of Theological Studies* 9(1908), 569-572.

Caird, G.B., "The Chronology of the New Testament", *The Interpreter's Dictionary of the Bible*, Nashville 1962, Vol.I, pp. 599-607.

Edwards, Ormond, "Herodian Chronology", *Palestinian Exploration Quarterly* 114(1982), 29-42.

Filmer, W.E., "The Chronology of the Reign of Herod the Great", *Journal of Theological Studies* 17(1966), 283-298.

Fotheringham, J.K., "The Evidence of Astronomy and Technical Chronology for the Date of the Crucifixion", *Journal of Theological Studies* 35(1934), 142-162.

Hemer, Colin J., "Observations on Pauline Chronology", *Pauline Studies: Essays presented to F.F. Bruce on his 70th birthday*, Paternoster, Exeter, 1980, pp.3-18.

Humphreys, Colin J. and Waddington, W.G., "Dating the Crucifixion", *Nature* 30(1983), 743-746.

Miller, Johnny V. "The Time of the Crucifixion", *Journal of the Evangelical Theological Society* 26(1983), 157-166.

Ogg, George, "The Chronology of the Last Supper", *Theological Collections VI: Historicity and Chronology in the New Testament*, London 1965, pp.75-96.
"The Quirinius Question To-day", *The Expository Times* 79(1968), 231-236.

Torrey, C.C., "The Date of the Crucifixion according to the Fourth Gospel", *Journal of Biblical Literature* 50(1931), 227-241.

Turner, H.E.W., "The Chronological Framework of the Ministry", *Historicity and Chronology in the New Testament*, London 1965, pp.59-74.

Walker, Norman, "The Reckoning of Hours in the Fourth Gospel", *Novum Testamentum* 4(1960), 69-73.

Index of Authors

Alford, H., 187
Allis, O.T., 108, 126, 131, 133, 136
Anderson, R., 96, 157, 180-1, 196
Anstey, M., 45, 78
Ashton, J.F., 10
Auerbach, E., 60

Barnes, W.H., 128-9
Barrett, C.K., 172, 173, 206
Becking, B., 116-19, 121, 127
Beckwith, R.T., 192
Blinzler, J. 178, 180
Blum, H., 43
Bright, J., 126, 136
Brinkman, J.A., 112, 130
Browne, H., 23, 71
Bruce, F.F., 45, 189, 201, 203, 205-10
Burkitt, F.C., 175

Caird, G.B., 163-4, 188, 197
Carey, C.P., 25

Cassuto, U., 20
Clark, R.E.D., 37
Clines, D.J.A., 55, 58, 61-2
Cogan, M., 130

Depuydt, L., 101, 112
Doig, K.F., 161-64, 173, 184-87, 191,
    194-97
Driver, G.R. 53

Edwards, O., 162-63
Eichrodt, W., 63, 105

Faulstich, E.W., 57, 82-3, 92, 115, 123-25
    130-1, 130-131, 134, 136
Finegan, J., 103-4, 162, 164-66, 174-7, 180
    188, 195, 202, 203-6, 210
Fotheringham, J.K., 162, 181
France, R.T., 176, 193
Furuli, R., 110, 148-49, 155-56

Galil, G., 17, 65, 71-4, 79, 81, 85, 94, 101,
    117, 119,
Godet, F., 176
Gray, J., 43
Grayson, A.K., 112, 126
Green, A., 97-8, 136
Green, M., 168
Guinness, G., 214-5

Hasel, G.F, 144
Hayes, J.H. and Hooker, P.K., 105
Hayes, J.H. and Kuan, J.K., 119
Henry, R., 42, 72
Hemer, C., 202, 206
Hendriksen, W., 173, 180
Henige, D., 139
Hobbs, T.R., 82, 101
Horn, S.H., 62, 64, 99
Hoehner, H., 173, 187
Hoffmeier, J.K., 28, 33, 36, 42
Horn, S.H., 63, 99
Hughes, J., 87
Humphreys, C.J., 34-6, 42, 181

James, P.J., 139
Jepsen, A., 115
Jeremias, J., 174, 203
Jones, F.N., 17, 29-33, 59, 86, 97, 103, 106,
    126, 130, 140, 191
Jonnson, C.O., 92-3, 103, 147-9, 156
Josephus, F., 23, 94, 102, 131, 165-6, 188, 194,
    197-8, 202-3

Keil, C.F., 32, 37, 47-50, 73, 80, 99, 144-5
Kitchen, K.A., 17, 33, 41, 50
Kosmala, H., 57

Lambert, L., 190, 215
Larsson, G., 17
Levine, L.D., 129
Lewin, T., 162, 166, 182, 185-6
Lightfoot, J., 69-70, 73, 87, 192
Lightfoot, J.B., 201, 213

Macadam, M.F.L., 128-29
Macnight, J., 176, 180
Maier, P.M., 186
Malamat, A., 82, 98, 102
Marshall, H., 174
Martin, E.L., 164, 189, 191, 195-6
McCarter, P.K.,
Mendenall, G.E., 34
Millard, A.R., 109, 125, 127, 130, 141
Miller, J and Hayes, J.H., 85, 98
Moeller, L., 21, 43
Morgenstern, J., 59
Morris, H.M., 10, 17
Morris, L.L., 173-4, 178-9

Na'aman, N., 116, 118, 134
Neuffer, J., 155

Subject Index

Aaron, 43,44
Abijam, 70
Abijah, Course of, 190
Abraham, 21, 22, 38
Accession year, 65, 98-9
Adad-nirari III, 132
Admin, 16
Agabus, 204
Ahab, 74-76, 133-34
Ahaz, 86-88, 113-14
Ahaziah, 77
Amaziah, 78-80, 82, 90
Amel Marduk, 101-2
Amon, 91, 106, 122
Ammonite oppression, 48
Amram, 26
Aqaba, Gulf of, 43
Aquila and Priscilla, 205
Archelaus, 194
Artaxerxes, 93, 153-57
Asa, 70, 72-4, 137
Assur-dan III, 130
Assur-uballit II, 97, 149
Assyrian Eponym Canon, 67, 108-10, 116
Athaliah, 78-9
Augustus, 162, 189
Azariah, 80-83

Baasha, 70, 72-73
Babylonian Chronicles, 63, 94-97, 102, 111-12
Balfour Declaration, 214
Barak, 47, 51, 52
Bar Cochba, 211
Baruch, 59
Belshazzar, 143
Benhadad I, 137
Benhadad II, 33, 137-39
Benhadad III, 137
Berosus, 94

Cainan, second, 16
Caleb, 44-44
Captivity, 58, 94-96, 107
Carchemish, battle of, 60-62, 99-100, 102, 147, 149
Claudius, 203-4
Colossians, 213
Conquest of Canaan, 44
Corinthians, 1and 2, 212
Ctesias, 153-54
Cyaxares II, 143
Cyrus, 143-45, 157

Cyrus Cylinder, 151

Damascus, 113-14
Damascene region, 114
Daniel, 64, 93-4
Darius II, 63, 151
Darius the Mede, 143-45
David, 41-42, 54, 69
Day, the, 10
Deborah, 47
Desolation, Judgment of, 96, 146-47

Ebenezer, 48
Eber, 22, 38
Eleph, 32
Eli, 47-49
Elijah, 137
Elisha, 137
Enoch, 21
Ephesians, 213
Eutychus, 208
Evil Merodach, see Amel Marduk
Exile, see Captivity
Exodus, 42
Ezra, 153

Felix, 208
Festus, 208-9

Galatians, 211
Gallio, 205-6
Generations, 25-26
Gethsemane, 171
Gideon, 51-52

Haggai, 63
Hamul, 29-31
Heart of the earth, 170
Herod Agrippa, 203
Herod the Great, 165, 188, 193, 194-98
Hezekiah, 64, 67, 87-90, 91-2, 106-7, 123-7
Hezron, 29-31
Hilkiah, 59
Hoshea, 65, 86-88, 113-14, 119-20

Ignorance, 200
Isaac, 24
Ishbosheth, 53-54

Jabin King of Hazor, 51
Jacob, 29

Select Index of Bible Passages